Evaluating Human Services

A Practical Approach for the Human Service Professional

Reginald O. York

University of North Carolina Wilmington

PEARSON

Boston   New York   San Francisco
Mexico City   Montreal   Toronto   London   Madrid   Munich   Paris
Hong Kong   Singapore   Tokyo   Cape Town   Sydney

Senior Acquisitions Editor: *Patricia Quinlin*
Editorial Assistant: *Carly Czech*
Senior Marketing Manager: *Wendy Albert*
Production Supervisor: *Roberta Sherman*
Editorial-Production Service: *Pine Tree Composition*
Composition Buyer: *Linda Cox*
Electronic Composition: *Pine Tree Composition*
Manufacturing Buyer: *Debbie Rossi*
Cover Administrator: *Joel Gendron*

For related titles and support materials, visit our online catalog at www.pearsonhighered.com.

Between the time website information is gathered and then published, it is not unusual for some sites to have closed. Also, the transcription of URLs can result in typographical errors. The publisher would appreciate notification where these errors occur so that they may be corrected in subsequent editions.

ISBN-13: 978-0-205-50346-9

Library of Congress Cataloging-in-Publication Data

York, Reginald O.
    Evaluating human services : a practical approach for the human service professional / Reginal O. York.
        p.   cm.
    ISBN 0-205-50346-2
    1. Social service—United States—Evaluation.   I. Title.

    HV91.Y667   2008
    361.973—dc22

                                                                        2008000956

Printed in the United States of America

DEDICATION

To my wife, Susan,
whose love has inspired the best in me.
To my two sons, Will and Brian,
who have shown me what is really important in life.
And to my students,
who have taught me far more than I have taught them.

Contents

18   *An Exercise in Outcome Evaluation*   **365**

Preface

This is a book on the evaluation of human services. It is designed to equip the front-line human service practitioner (counselors, social workers, psychologists, educators, nurses, etc.) with the ability to evaluate services. It is designed to be practical, with emphasis on a step-by-step set of guidelines. Some of the assumptions that guide the content of this book are as follows:

- Competence in the evaluation of human services is built on a foundation of knowledge that includes understanding the nature of scientific inquiry.
- A review of the basic concepts of research that will be used to conduct the evaluation research is included.
- Human service practitioners and students learn best using a developmental approach that goes from general topics to specific ones, while at the same time, reinforcing each new concept as the complexity of the material grows.
- Students learn best by doing—i.e., doing practical exercises where they test their learning as they work their way through the course.
- Knowledge of both qualitative and quantitative research methods is essential to one's ability to pursue human service evaluation comprehensively.
- Students of human service evaluation need an understanding of broad concepts, but they also need very specific guidance on how to do certain things, especially data analysis.

In what follows, you will see an elaboration of these points, along with a note about accreditation guidelines for social work education.

While evaluation research is the focus, you will find information on all types of research

While this book is designed with the task of human service evaluation in mind, it can also serve as a general text on research methods because the vast majority of concepts included in a general methods text are included in this book. The difference is that the vast majority of examples that illustrate these concepts in the present book are taken from evaluation activities. An exception is the content of the first several chapters which focuses on the scientific method in general with examples of different kinds. In fact, one of these early chapters carries the reader through a research example that is not related to the evaluation of human services. In that particular chapter, readers examine whether a set of data support a given theory.

Essential competency in research is the chief goal

There are numerous competencies that will be acquired after careful reading of this book and completion of the exercises. This text focuses on competencies rather than broad abstractions, resulting in the acquisition of very practical skills for research and evaluation. Nowhere is this more evident than in the approach the author takes to the analysis of quantitative data. After reading this section, the reader will be able to determine the specific statistical test to use to study clients, both before and after treatment. He or she will then be able to insert collected data into a spreadsheet to determine whether the pretest scores are significantly better than the posttest scores. This is only one example of what the reader will learn about the analysis of data.

The developmental approach to learning is illustrated in the organization of this text

This text begins with an overview of research concepts and processes. Each concept that is defined and illustrated in early chapters is re-enforced through more complicated discussions and illustrations later. This means that the reader is not likely to become overwhelmed and lose the forest for the trees. Concepts and tools in research methods often seem to human service practitioners to be like learning a foreign language which must be repeated many times before it is committed to memory.

This feature is consistent with the developmental perspective upon learning, where concepts are first presented in simple terms with an emphasis on how the concepts connect to one another before a more detailed explanation is given. This should assure that students will see both the forest and the trees, not just one or the other.

This text employs both concept chapters and illustration chapters

The first few sections of this book alternate between chapters that discuss concepts and chapters that illustrate these concepts through exercises or examples. The first chapter, for example, provides an overview of scientific research, and this chapter is followed by one that takes the reader through a research experiment that tests a particular theory from the realm of discourse where scientific testing is not typically undertaken. It should encourage critical thinking about popular theories that would be better classified as pseudoscience rather than science. Another exercise chapter carries the reader through a content analysis of a set of qualitative data from open-ended questions while other exercise chapters carry the reader through the examination of research examples.

The themes of the major sections move from basics to more specifics

The **first section of this book** provides an introduction to the nature of research with special emphasis on evaluative research. Upon the completion of this section, the reader should be able to describe the scientific approach to knowledge development and recognize major deviations from the spirit of scientific inquiry when examples are encountered. In addition, the reader should be able to describe the nature of human service evaluation with regard to the systems concepts of input, process, output, and outcome. Furthermore, the most essential aspects of research ethics are covered. These competencies are addressed through a chapter that reviews the nature of scientific inquiry and a chapter that reviews the nature of human service evaluation. Both of these chapters are followed by chapters that provide exercises designed to illustrate the concepts.

In the **second section**, there is a review of the process type of evaluation with particular emphasis on qualitative research methods. At the completion of this section, the reader will be able to:

- Articulate the special connection between process evaluation and qualitative research methods.
- Describe how qualitative and quantitative research methods are similar and different, including the key issues that suggest which approach to knowledge development is more appropriate for a given evaluation situation.
- Conduct a content analysis using qualitative data.

The last item above is accomplished by a detailed exercise on the analysis of a set of qualitative data given to the reader. This exercise illustrates the practical nature of this text. Instead of being introduced to the various concepts related to content analysis as a qualitative research method, you will be carried through this method step by step.

The **third section** introduces you to the evaluation of human service outcome with more detail than presented in the earlier chapters. At the completion of this section, you will be able to:

- Describe the process of human service evaluation and recognize how various parts of the process are interdependent.
- Articulate essential concepts in each phase of the evaluation process.

These competencies are achieved through two concept chapters and two exercise chapters. The exercise chapters provide a review of examples of outcome evaluation.

In the **fourth section**, you will acquire special skills in how to conduct outcome evaluations. Each phase of outcome research is reviewed in a separate chapter and there is an exercise chapter that completes this section. The exercise chapter calls upon you to design an outcome evaluation study and carries you through this design step by step. At the completion of this section, you will be able to design an outcome evaluation study that will include:

- A definition of target behavior that is sufficiently clear to guide the selection of a means of measuring client progress.
- An analysis of target behavior sufficient to guide the selection, or critical appraisal, of an intervention or program.

- A description of a selected intervention that includes reference to goals, objectives, structure, model, and personnel.
- A description of the means used to measure client progress, including reference to the reliability and validity of the tools employed.
- A description of the study sample with reference to the implications of sample selection procedures for the generalizing of study results.
- Selection of the research design, with particular attention to the threats to internal validity of special concern in a particular situation.

In addition, you are given a set of practical guidelines for preparing the written report for an outcome evaluation study.

In the **fifth section**, you will learn how to select an appropriate statistical tool for assessing your outcome evaluation data and how to employ an Excel spreadsheet in the execution of the data analysis for your particular situation. **This is one of the most unique features of this text.** You are guided through a set of decision trees to determine which approach to statistical analysis is useful, and you are shown how to use an Excel file to determine whether statistical significance has been achieved. **A set of Excel files is provided on a website that accompanies this text (http://ablongman.com/york1e).** Your only task is entering your particular data and reviewing the cell in the spreadsheet that reviews statistical significance. At the completion of this section, you will be able to:

- Select an appropriate statistical method for analyzing data in regard to a variety of both single-subject evaluations and group evaluations.
- Employ Excel spreadsheet files in the computation of statistical significance with regard to:
  - The B single-subject design.
  - The limited AB single-subject design.
  - The AB single-subject design.
  - The one-group pretest-posttest group design.
  - The comparison group design.
  - The posttest-only group design.

A total of eleven Excel files are included on the website, each one being specific to the research design and the nature of measurement. The instructions about Excel in this book are <u>not</u> designed to teach you how to create formulas to cover your situation, a task that most human service students will find tedious. Instead, the reader merely loads a specific file, inserts data into cells in the file according to simple instructions, and finds the value of p and other relevant statistics.

No prior knowledge of research is assumed

From the above objectives, you can see that this book starts at the beginning level of knowledge regarding human service evaluation. The author made no assumptions about prior knowledge of research principles and methods in the design of this text. Also apparent should be the fact that this text goes much beyond the basics of research methods. It should equip you with the ability to engage in the practice of human service evaluation. For these reasons, this text may be useful in both an introductory research course and one designed for the intermediate level.

Practical guidance and experiential learning are the keys

Another special feature of this book is a set of **discussion boxes** interspersed throughout the primary content chapters. These boxes call upon the reader to reflect upon the recent content. If you feel unprepared to answer the question, this should signal to you that you need to re-read the prior content. The reader's comments in these boxes can serve as a guide for class discussion if this book is used as a research text. A third special feature is the presence of quizzes at the end of chapters, which the reader can use either as a pretest, to determine if he or she needs to read the chapter, or as a posttest, to determine how well it was read.

A very unique feature of this book is the data analysis section. In this section are chapters that provide practical guidance on the analysis of data using Excel spreadsheet software. This does not require any ability to compose Excel formulas. It only requires the ability to follow simple instructions. There is a file for the majority of outcome evaluation studies that the everyday practitioner is likely to use. The use of Excel spreadsheet software is considered to be of much more convenience than the traditional use of statistical software like SPSS. Most practitioners will have access to Excel but are not likely to have access to SPSS.

This book addresses accreditation standards related to research and critical thinking

Most professionals in the field of human services have degrees that are accredited by an appropriate body. One such accrediting body is the **Council on Social Work Education**. The accreditation standards offered by this body include reference to the following:

1. One of the purposes of social work is to prepare social workers to evaluate the processes and effectiveness of practice.
2. The student should learn how to evaluate research studies, apply research findings to practice, and evaluate their own practice.
3. Included in the research curriculum should be both qualitative and quantitative methods.
4. The student should learn how to apply critical thinking skills within the context of professional social work practice.

With the exception of the last item, you will note that each point is related to evaluation research, even though many research texts place as much emphasis on descriptive research, exploratory research, and explanatory research as they place on evaluative research. Each one of the four requirements noted above is addressed by this text on the evaluation of human services. The entire book is devoted to the first two points while parts of this text focus on the third and fourth requirements.

Both qualitative and quantitative research methods are examined

An understanding of both qualitative methods and quantitative methods are essential for a comprehensive understanding of how human services should be evaluated. Quantitative methods of analysis are employed when you have data that takes the form of scores, rank-ings, or categories. This would include scores on the Beck Depression Inventory, one's cat-egory for gender, or the ranking you gave to a given preference for service. Qualitative methods are employed when your data are words. This could include the client's comments on a client satisfaction survey. As you will see in this book, qualitative methods are more likely to be associated with the evaluation of service process while quantitative methods are more likely to be employed in the evaluation of service outcome. Each approach to research has a special role to play in our understanding of how well our services work, why they work well, and how they can be improved.

The question of whether quantitative or qualitative methods of measurement should be employed is addressed in a number of chapters that deal with measurement. In the very first chapter, you will encounter content that compares these two approaches while Chap-ter 2 addresses types of evaluation and models of evaluation that refer to both approaches. For example, the experiment normally employs quantitative methods whereas the case study approach and utilization-focused evaluations typically employ both approaches. In Chapter 4, you will review nominal group technique, an elementary approach to qualitative meth-ods. Chapters 5 and 6 are devoted entirely to qualitative research. On the other hand, there is a section of chapters that are devoted to quantitative data analysis. Many chapters, how-ever, cover content that is relevant to various research studies, whether the chosen method of measurement and analysis is qualitative or quantitative.

Cultural competence and research are addressed in various ways

There are several discussions of the concept of cultural competence in this book. This dis-cussion begins in the first chapter which addresses the nature of scientific research. The concept of cultural competence and research are introduced in this chapter with a summary of how this theme is relevant to many subjects of research. Included in other chapters are discussions of cultural competence with regard to problem formulation, grounded theory, sampling, and measurement.

A website has been developed for accessing special files that accompany this book

There is a set of files that accompany this book that can be obtained from the following website: http://ablongman.com/york1e.

This website contains three major items:

- A set of 11 Excel spreadsheet files that can be used for data analysis. Each file applies a certain statistical test to a specific situation, such as, for example, a set of data on pretest and posttest scores for a group of clients.
- The discussion boxes for each chapter presented in electronic form so that readers can provide their answers to the questions in printed form for review.
- A copy of each chapter quiz that appears at the end of content chapters. Readers may use these for re-testing themselves at a time after they have reviewed a given chapter

and given their answers in the book. These may also be used by instructors as a guide for constructing exam questions.

An Instructor's Manual can be a useful tool in accompanying this text

The Instructor's Manual to accompany *Evaluating Human Services* is designed to complete the portrait of a self-managed learning process offered in this text. Because the book itself provides the exercises and discussion questions necessary to guide the student, there is no need for formal lectures or instructor-designed materials. The instructor can choose to conduct class by facilitating the discussions that emanate from the discussion boxes in the text. The manual has the author's observations about each discussion question that can serve as a launching pad for healthy class dialogue. The instructor only needs to be prepared to lead these discussions and engage in further explanations of key concepts when certain students need more help. The manual also helps to explain the various student exercises, including the ones related to data analysis. The website, available to students, also can be useful because the instructor may choose to give students the assignment of completing answers to the discussion boxes and giving this document to the instructor. Also on this website is a copy of the quizzes contained in the text which instructors can use to construct exams.

Acknowledgments

I would like to offer special thanks to three persons who reviewed this book and offered helpful suggestions, most of which were incorporated into the materials presented here. These persons are Allan Barsky, Florida Atlantic University, Steve Marson, University of North Carolina Pembroke, and Brian Simmons, California State University Monterey Bay. It has been a pleasure to work with Patricia Quinlin, Carly Czech, and Nakeesha Warner of Allyn and Bacon who have worked diligently to assure that I have the best advice to make this book the best that I can under the normal demands of life. I must also acknowledge the critical assistance of Helene Harris and Brandi Farrell who helped to assemble, format, and bring the copy for this book to its final destination.

1

The Nature of Scientific Research

Science is a method of acquiring knowledge through the logical analysis of observations guided by theory. It is a special way of finding out. It means that you apply logic to your analysis and that you examine data in a systematic way. The scientific way of discovery contrasts with other ways we draw conclusions. We often believe things based on hunches, selective observations, or by what we have been told by those in a position of authority. Most of our beliefs are probably based on our own experiences in life guided by what we have been taught by those closest to us. These beliefs may serve us well. But they may also be subject to certain sources of human error. Those of us who wish to reduce the influence of common sources of human error will be very interested in learning about the scientific way of learning. This will help, but it will not eliminate error nor will it likely become the most important source of learning for us, even the most scientifically curious among us. It will simply guide us toward fewer errors in decisions than is made by those less influenced by science.

For the social scientist, there are several categories of research that are important. One is **descriptive** research. This is research that serves the purpose of describing social phenomena in specific ways. We may want to know the demographic characteristics of our clients. This would be an example of descriptive research.

Another form of research is **exploratory**. This is a type of research that is designed to discover new theories or new ways of looking at things in our world. Criminal profilers often intentionally isolate themselves from investigators and look at the facts in isolation in order to reduce the influence of each person's biases about what happened or who may be the murderer in this case. This might be characterized as an extreme example of exploratory research. These individuals are seeking a new way of looking at the crime scene. For this reason, criminal profilers are usually not brought into a criminal investigation until after the normal criminal investigation has led to a dead end and a new perspective is needed.

Explanatory research is a third category. In this research, you are seeking to explain one variable with reference to other variables. It may be that older clients are more satisfied with your agency's services because they are more likely to be retired. Thus, you may find that it is only the retired older clients who are the ones more satisfied and that older clients who remain on the job are no more satisfied than younger clients who are employed. Thus, you have explained the relationship between age and satisfaction with reference to employment.

Evaluation research is a special type of research that helps us to determine how well human service interventions are working and how we might improve them. It can be classified as a special type of explanatory research, but I prefer to distinguish it from other forms of explanatory research because of its special role in human service administration. A simple way to distinguish evaluative research from others is to ask if there is an intervention or program that is the focus of the study. If the answer is "yes," you can say you are doing evaluative research. If there is no specific human service program of intervention that is being studied in some way in a research study, it would not be classified as an evaluative research study.

At the completion of this chapter, you should be able to:

1. Describe the essential nature of scientific research.
2. Distinguish between practices that are and are not consistent with the scientific method.
3. Describe the four major purposes of research.
4. Explain the nature of scientific inquiry in a framework of selected common sense expressions.
5. Recognize the appropriate principle of scientific inquiry that is exemplified in research scenarios relevant to the common sense framework noted above.
6. Describe deductive and inductive processes of scientific inquiry.
7. Describe both qualitative and quantitative forms of information.
8. Describe the major methods whereby information is gathered in research.

There is a quiz at the end of this chapter. You may use it as a pretest, to determine if you need to read this chapter, or as a posttest, to determine how well you read it. If you wish to use it as a pretest, you should turn your attention to that quiz now.

The Nature of Scientific Inquiry

Science is a *method* of acquiring knowledge through the *logical* analysis of *observations* guided by *theory*. The **methodology** of science starts with a question that can be answered through observations in the natural world. The question "Is it God's will that my country wins this war?" is *not* a question of this nature. This question takes us into another world. On the other hand, if your question is whether older clients of your agency are more satisfied with your services than younger clients, you are in the natural world where science can make a contribution. The method of science leads one to select means of observation that can answer the question and to analyze those observations in an objective way, such that various possible answers to the question have equal chance of being confirmed by the data.

The **logic** of science says that you connect observations in such a way that makes sense. You may discover that cities with more persons born as twins also have more rapes. Is there a logical connection between these two variables (twins and rapes) such that one might be the cause of the other? Most people would say "no" to this question. They might recognize that there is a third variable that explains the correlation between these two variables—population. Larger cities have both more twins and more rapes. If you control for population in your analysis of the relationship between these two variables (twins and rapes), you will likely find there is not a relationship between these two things. For example, your data might reveal that large cities with more twins do not have more rapes than large cities with fewer twins.

Logic is about the rules for good argument. You might say something like "It just makes sense to me that you would be well advised to include the client's environment in your treatment plan because the client is subject to a complex array of influences from the environment." You could break down this argument as follows:

1. Clients exist in complex environments.
2. The client's behavior is influenced by various elements in the environment.
3. The client wants to change his or her life in some important way.
4. Therefore, you should include the environment in the client's treatment plan.

This is the way some logical arguments would be presented in a systematic way. It shows the assumptions upon which a conclusion about reality is drawn. In so doing, it provides a framework for debate or analysis. If it is untrue that clients live in complex environments, the above argument would fall apart. Likewise, if it is untrue that the environment influences the client's behavior, the above argument would fall apart.

On the other hand, let's look at the following list of arguments that might be problematic:

1. Politicians cannot be trusted.
2. John Smith is a politician.
3. Therefore, John Smith cannot be trusted.

You might have reason to question the first statement, which serves as a premise for the conclusion. While you may believe that many politicians cannot be trusted, would any reasonable person say that no politicians can be trusted? The above argument makes that assumption. The conclusion that John Smith cannot be trusted would only be logical if we can accept the fact that *no* politician can be trusted.

Sometimes the best way to illustrate the concept of logic is to examine some common logical fallacies. A logical fallacy is something that does not make sense, and does not stand up to the normal rules of logical argumentation. The example about politicians is an illustration. There is a large number of logical fallacies that we could discuss but that would take up too much of this text, so there will only be a few that will be listed. These are:

1. Attacking an idea by attacking the messenger rather than the idea. This assumes that someone without totally good human qualities cannot have a good idea. It should be the idea that is debated, not the human qualities of the messenger.

2. Presenting evidence on behalf of an argument by reference to authority—i.e., that because those in authority believe it, we should all believe it. This is especially problematic when someone's endorsement of something is out of the bounds of his or her area of expertise. This is exemplified when a famous actor endorses a candidate for office.

3. The false dichotomy refers to drawing improper conclusions about reality by limiting your analysis to two dramatically contrasting options while ignoring all other possibilities. For

example, someone may say that because you voted against the school bond that you do not love children. This line of reasoning suggests there are only two options about life that are included—loving children means voting for the bond and not loving children means voting against the bond. This simplistic reasoning fails to consider the vast array of reasons you might vote against the school bond.

4. Assuming that Event A caused Event B because Event A preceded Event B in time. This is known as the *post hoc, ergo propter hoc* fallacy in logic (Literally translated, "After this, therefore because of this."). The truth is that the time sequence between cause and effect is only one of the conditions required for the establishment of causality. For you to make the case that dialectical behavioral therapy was the cause of the improvement in the client's behavior, you must not only present information suggesting the client improved after treatment began, but you must also make the case that this change was due to the treatment rather than something else. This fallacy is one of the many that draw our attention to incomplete thinking.

Logic is about thinking patterns rather than scientific evidence. It is based on ways to organize our thinking. It is used in science to organize observations about reality. So, we might say that science is based on *both* logic and observations.

The idea of **observation** in research means that we collect data in a systematic way. We do not draw conclusions based on hunches, but, instead, based on the analysis of data. The scientist does not draw conclusions because she "feels" there is a connection between two variables, but because she has discovered the connection based on the systematic analysis of data. Her analysis of data is systematic, meaning that it is not highly selective. She does not base her conclusions on the examination of three or four examples of clients in her own caseload, but upon the collection and analysis of data from all clients of the agency.

Theory guides the scientific research that we do. It is theory that applies logic to observations. If someone discovered that cities with more twins had more rapes, the scientist would ask if this discovery is consistent with any recognized theory about the nature of the relationship between twins and rapes. A theory is an attempt to explain something. Cognitive theory, for example, explains certain problematic behavior, such as depression, as being caused by distorted thinking: Some people become chronically depressed because their thinking about life events is dysfunctional. The concept of theory is relevant to the scientist in two ways—discovery of theories and testing of theories. Some scientific processes are designed to lead to the development of new theories, while other scientific processes are geared to the testing of an existing theory.

So we can readily see that research is a means of discovery, or a way of knowing. Let's examine some ways to elaborate on the concepts defined above. Science is a method of finding out what you need to know. It contrasts with other ways we come to believe we know something. One such alternative way of knowing is through authority—often we believe things because our parents taught these things to us. Sometimes we believe in something because it is the way it has always been. This is an example of tradition as a way of knowing. A third avenue of discovery is through our personal experience. In other words, we acquire certain beliefs about reality because of our own experiences. These are only a few methods of discovery that are alternatives to science.

Science presents us with a method of discovery accompanied by a certain **spirit of inquiry** that attempts to build a level playing field for all possible ideas about reality. It does not promote a given view of reality. Instead, it helps us to develop a fair test of alternative ideas about reality. It suggests ways of collecting and analyzing data in the pursuit of a question or issue.

Thus, science is highly related to **critical thinking**, a concept that will be discussed later in this book. Critical thinking is a method of shining a light upon various aspects of our thinking, including the assumptions behind each part of an argument. This shining light helps us to avoid errors in thinking, such as fallacies in logic or failure to recognize the essential assumptions that must be correct statements if our argument is to be solid.

The process of scientific research begins with a question to be answered—the better the focus of the question, the better the scientific method will help us in our pursuit. It continues with a method of inquiry that provides a level playing field for contrasting views of reality. It ends with logical conclusions based on the data that were analyzed.

One part of the scientific process is the development of a method of collecting information. Perhaps this is really the key to scientific inquiry. If Paul says his agency has been proven to be effective in the reduction of depression for women experiencing post-partum depression, you would naturally want to know the method he used for backing up this assertion. How did his agency become one with a "proven" track record on treating this type of depression? Is it nothing but the opinions of the staff? Is it from a client satisfaction survey where 80 percent of the respondents indicated their depression had improved from treatment? Is it from a study in which a group of clients was measured on depression before and after treatment, with these data subjected to statistical analysis? The better the method, the more likely you would believe Paul's assertion.

Another part of the scientific process is the **analysis of data**. If you have administered a depression scale to a group of clients before and after treatment, you would analyze the data to determine if the scores after treatment were better than scores before treatment, and if the difference in scores before and after treatment was significant. In this book, you will encounter two types of significance—statistical significance and practical significance. The former addresses the degree to which your data could be explained by chance while the latter focuses on the extent to which the results were clinically noteworthy—i.e., of value in decisions about clinical practice.

The scientific method is orderly and strives for the achievement of **objectivity**. An inquiry that is designed to prove a point is not an example of research that fits the spirit of scientific inquiry. A study that is incomplete or illogical also fails to meet the standards of the scientific method. In the pursuit of objectivity, the scientist organizes a process of inquiry that does the best job of eliminating the biases of the scientist in the way that data are analyzed and the way that conclusions are drawn.

An important characteristic of scientific inquiry is the **falsifiability** of a claim. How can you scientifically test the idea of "God's will"? Most people who talk about God's will refer to whatever happened as being God's will, without there being any scientific way to directly observe this phenomenon. If your grandmother survived the car accident, it was God's will. If your grandmother did *not* survive the car accident, it was God's will. All forms of facts are believed to be explained by God's will. So this could never be tested scientifically. Thus, the idea of God's will is for the disciplines of philosophy or religion, not science.

For an assertion to be falsifiable, there must be a way to observe phenomena that would fail to support the assertion. In other words, you must be able to collect observations in such a way as to allow both for the support of the assertion about reality, or a refutation of the assertion. Suppose you observed people in a mental hospital only when the moon was full and drew conclusions about the effect of the full moon based on this limited collection of observations. This procedure would be inconsistent with the nature of scientific inquiry. Instead, you must also collect observations when the moon is not full. When you compare behavior during the full moon with behavior when the moon is not full, you have the prospect of either confirming or refuting the idea that the full moon makes people act differently.

Science is contrasted with *pseudoscience*, which refers to any body of knowledge or methods that are erroneously regarded as scientific. It is distinguished from revelations or theology in that these claims do not pretend to offer scientific explanation, whereas the claims of pseudoscience do. Pseudoscience is something that is parading as science. To parade as science does not necessarily mean the claim is false, only that it is not based on scientific processes. A famous example of pseudoscience, from a previous century, is phrenology, the theory that one's personality could be determined by examining the bumps on one's head. This theory was illustrated by complex graphs of the brain showing the parts of the personality that were illustrated by these bumps, but it was bogus.

An article from Wikipedia lists acupuncture, astrology, chakra theory, and many more ideas as examples of pseudoscience, but notes there is dispute regarding what qualifies as pseudoscience, especially given the fact there is no clear-cut formula for determining what is science and what is pseudoscience (en.wikipedia.org, retrieved 12-23-05). The key to resolving this issue is the extent to which each claim about the nature of reality has information that has followed all the elements of the scientific process. These elements include:

1. A system of thinking organized in such a way as to generate logical assertions about reality (propositions, hypotheses, theories) that can be tested through observations in the natural world.
2. The collection and analysis of observations (data) in the natural world that provide a level playing field for the claim of support for the assertion and the claim of denial of the assertion.
3. The drawing of conclusions from the data that are "fair" with regard to the opposing claims of support and falsification.

Assertions that can be classified as pseudoscience tend to provide a system of inquiry that is highly biased in favor of the assertion. For example, I might assert that the full moon makes people act weird. I might use as my evidence a number of examples of weird behavior that occurred in the mental hospital when the moon was full. In this presentation of "evidence" on behalf of my assertion, I would ignore the weird behaviors that occurred when the moon was not full.

The scientific method is designed to reduce human error in observation. How do we err? There are several prominent sources of human error in observation. First, we often overgeneralize from one example. This is typically based on our particular experience. If you have only three alcoholics in recent months and both were left-handed and intelligent, you might conclude that left-handed alcoholics were unusually intelligent. We assume that one or two examples are sufficient to construct a major conclusion about reality. The scientific method would normally take the form of systematic observation that is sufficient to overcome the limitations inherent in one person's experience.

Discussion Box 1.1

Think of a time when someone tried to present to you what was supposed to be an objective analysis, or scientific analysis, but you found that this person was selective in the kinds of information or data that were presented. All the information included in this analysis supported a specific opinion or policy, but you knew, or suspected, that there was information available to this person that was contrary to this particular opinion that was being advocated. How convinced were you after you suspected that information was being withheld? Provide a brief answer.

Another source of error is selective observation. Many people believe the full moon affects behavior. If you asked a group of nurses at a psychiatric hospital, you would likely find that many believed the full moon makes patients act out, and they can supply examples where they found this to be true. This means they have observed acting out behavior during the full moon. However, you might ask if they have made a concerted attempt to observe acting out behavior when the moon was not full. They may find the rate of acting out is essentially the same between these two periods but of course they have not done so, because they are only on alert to the moon when it is full. Their data are incomplete. A scientific approach would examine behavior both during the full moon and when the moon is not full. Selective observation is often tied to human need. What do you need to believe? Would a certain belief justify a pay raise for you or give you more power? If so, you have found a common source of bias in observation.

Selective observation and inappropriate generalization are only two of the many common errors in human measurement of reality. There are others that will be discussed in future chapters. The purpose here is to heighten your awareness.

There are many ways for you to achieve wisdom. The scientific method is only one. Your intuition is often a good way to achieve wisdom. You may intuitively understand a client's problem and you may be quite correct without employing the scientific method. You have, in fact, acquired a vast reservoir of wisdom through your life experiences. And most of your decisions are based on that wisdom rather than scientifically collected data. But it is argued in this text that your wisdom can be enhanced by the use of science.

An Examination of Some Common Sense Principles

There are many basic principles of scientific inquiry that should guide you in your efforts with research. In a previous text (York, 1997), I began with a description of some key principles, some of which are couched in familiar sayings. I will reiterate them here.

Discussion Box 1.2
_____

Think of an opinion you hold about how men and women are different. You might think that men are more boastful or that women are more sensitive to the feelings of others. Reflect on how you came to hold this observation about how men and women are different and see if you can identify any of the common errors in observation mentioned above. Make notes.

---

1. Evaluation Research Uses a Process of Discovery, Not Justification

We should not engage in research efforts for the purpose of justifying our preconceived ideas about reality. We do so because we want to find out whether certain ideas are supported by facts. If we are to take the scientific approach seriously, the discovery that certain explanations of reality are not supported by relevant facts will lead us either to change our minds about that reality or to seek other relevant facts, or both. As we seek more facts, we must do so in the spirit of scientific inquiry, which means that we will not select our facts according to our biases about the subject. We will consider all relevant facts and will try to place them into perspective so that our inquiry will be a carefully guided one.

The concept of bias is critical to this first principle. A bias is a mental leaning or inclination or a prejudice about a given subject. Sometimes we have made up our minds about a certain reality and are not prepared to accept contradictory information. Often this bias will be caused by our personal interests in a subject. If I am trying to sell you my used car, I will naturally have a bias about the value of it because I stand to gain by a perception that my car is worth top dollar. Thus, I am not in the best possible position to determine the true value of my car.

An important type of bias for the researcher is known as the social desirability bias. This is the bias we might have because of our desire to express ideas that are socially desirable rather than ideas that truly reflect our conceptions in their fullest representation. Are we always completely honest when we respond to the question "How do you like my new dress?" The desire to express ideas to others that will be agreeable to them is a very important bias that must be controlled in research if we are to make progress in our efforts to gain new insight into reality.

Sometimes our biases are the result of a limited experience with a given reality. We may only know one side of the story. To be scientific, we must gain information on all sides of the story.

2. Don't Reinvent the Wheel!

In the history of human inquiry, there has been an enormous amount of social research that has been undertaken. When we develop a research question, we usually find that there is a great deal of guidance that can come from an examination of the literature. Often, we

---

Discussion Box 1.3

What's wrong with this objective for an evaluation research study?

The purpose of this study is to demonstrate that cognitive-behavioral therapy is effective in the reduction of depression.

---

find a suitable answer to our question from this review and do not find it necessary to undertake a new study of the subject. Even when we do not find a suitable answer to our question, we find much guidance from the literature on what aspects of the question have been left more unanswered, and we can find assistance with the conceptualization of our study and the measurement of social phenomena required to answer our question.

It is not reasonable for us to expect a novice researcher to acquire an exhaustive review of the literature on a given subject. There is a wide range of knowledge that has been written in places that are not well known or easily accessed. However, we can expect a novice researcher to delve into the most available and best known literature on the subject of inquiry, so that he or she can avoid repeating the mistakes of early work on the subject, or failing to contribute anything of substance about the topic.

While there is normally a wide array of research that has been undertaken on any given subject, there is usually a good deal of research that needs to be added. Often what is needed is the use of a different type of person as the study subject or a different way of conceptualizing or measuring the phenomena under inquiry. Thus, we are not likely to encounter a situation in which the research we wish to undertake is substantially redundant. The greater reason for examining the previous literature is to help us to avoid the mistakes of the past. We might find that the way we wish to undertake our study was used many years ago and found wanting in its ability to provide a good means of addressing our research question. Later research will be found to have corrected for these mistakes in research methods.

3. Don't Put the Cart Before the Horse!

The research process follows the same basic path as good problem solving. Good problem solving starts with the identification of the problem and the objectives to be achieved by solving it. Methods of solving the problem are identified and implemented. Then, the results are evaluated in order to determine if the problem has been solved. One of the common pitfalls in basic human problem solving is for us to state the problem in terms of only one solution. In so doing, we are starting with a solution rather than with the identification of the human condition to be addressed.

Social research begins with the formulation of the problem, resulting in the articulation of the research question. After the research question has been clearly identified, we determine the methods to be used in the pursuit of the answer to our question. One of the mistakes commonly made by the novice researcher is to begin a process of inquiry that starts with a research instrument. It is not uncommon for a student of research to review a set of research instruments that measure certain psychological conditions and become especially interested in the use of a certain instrument in some kind of research.

The process of research conceptualized in this book starts with problem formulation and moves logically to research methodology, then to data collection and analysis, and ends with conclusions. Obviously, we should not start with conclusions about the research question. We have covered this mistake in our examination of the purposes of scientific inquiry (discovery rather than justification). Likewise, it is not logical to start with data and formulate a research question that fits the data. (However, it is legitimate to use an exploration of data as a springboard for focusing a set of questions which guide the investigation of the literature.) Further, as mentioned above, we would not start the process with the selection of study methods.

Discussion Box 1.4

As the instructor for a research course, what would you say to a student who said he wanted to conduct a telephone survey for his research project for your course? He does not yet have a research topic.

---

4. Two Heads Are Better than One!

Because objective reality is so difficult to discover in the field of human behavior, we must rely upon a method of inquiry that reduces human error in observation. One such method is to ask for more than one observation of a given phenomenon in order to become confident that we have a true picture of it. In research, we make the assumption that reality is more likely to be discovered the more that we find different people perceiving things in the same light. We know, of course, that it is possible that one person who is in the minority has the true picture while those in the majority are incorrect. But, in view of the fact that we have so little truly "hard" evidence of reality about human behavior, we make the assumption that our best bet is to go with the consensus rather than the unsupported opinion of one person. And we have many methods which have been developed to test the dependability of a given method of measuring our subjects of study. Thus, we could say that this principle serves as one of the assumptions of scientific inquiry.

5. Some Things Happen Just by Chance!

The fact that I had eggs for breakfast this morning does not necessarily mean that I prefer eggs to cereal for breakfast in general. It could be that I have eggs half the time and cereal half the

---

Discussion Box 1.5

Let's suppose you developed a research anxiety scale to measure the degree to which students in research courses are anxious about the subject of research. Suppose further that you administered this scale to a group of students and gave them another scale designed to measure research anxiety. You found a really low correlation between these two scales. For instance, you found that John had a higher score on your instrument than Mary, but Mary had a higher score than John on the other scale. You found this pattern repeated many times with students in your study, so that you had to conclude there was no meaningful relationship between scores of these two scales. Is this finding related to the idea that two heads are better than one? If so, how?

---

time and I just happened to have had eggs this morning. If you observed me at breakfast several times and noted that I had eggs each and every time, you would have more reliable evidence that I prefer eggs for breakfast. The more observations, the more confident you would be in your conclusion that I prefer eggs for breakfast.

We are referring to a thing called "probability." We will deal with some of the technicalities of this concept in future chapters of this book, but for now, we will only address the concept in a very general way. Logic would suggest that there is a 50 percent chance of getting a heads on a given flip of a coin because there are only two possibilities—heads and tails. When we roll a die with six sides, we have one chance in six of rolling any one of the numbers from one to six. But let's suppose that someone said that there was one coin in a set of coins that was rigged to land on heads more often than tails because of the distribution of the weight of the coin. You pick out one coin and you want to know if this is the one that is rigged. Let's suppose that you had the following results when you flipped this coin 18 times (Table 1.1).

After three flips of the coin, you might wonder if this coin was rigged to land on heads more often than tails. But you would more likely realize that three flips of the coin are not very many flips. So, you continue to flip the coin in the pursuit of your question. After the sixth flip, your coin has landed on heads 67 percent of the time, so it is going in the direction of 50 percent. But it is not there yet. Is it rigged to land on heads two-thirds of the time? Most likely you would say you do not yet have enough information and you would continue to investigate this question with more flips of the coin.

After 12 flips of the coin, you have 58 percent of heads. Starting with the fifteenth flip of the coin, you notice a pattern that the percent of heads hovers around 50 percent, with a few times being over 50 and a few times being under 50. This suggests a pattern that would suggest that the best estimate of 50 flips of the coin or 100 flips of the coin would be a 50–50 split between heads and tails. You realize, of course, that the percent of heads may vary slightly from 50 percent for any given number of flips, but it seems that the safest bet is 50 percent.

Now, let's put this same lesson to use with a more practical example. Let's suppose that you wanted to know whether males and females differ in their satisfaction with instruction in research

TABLE 1.1 *An Experience with Probability in Coin Tosses*

Flip Number	Heads or Tails	Percent of Heads
1	Heads	100
2	Heads	100
3	Heads	100
4	Tails	75
5	Heads	80
6	Tails	67
7	Heads	71
8	Heads	75
9	Tails	67
10	Tails	60
11	Heads	64
12	Tails	58
13	Tails	54
14	Heads	62
15	Tails	53
16	Tails	50
17	Heads	53
18	Tails	50
19	Tails	47
20	Tails	45
21	Heads	48
22	Heads	50
23	Tails	48
24	Heads	50
25	Tails	48
26	Tails	46
27	Heads	48
28	Tails	46
29	Heads	48
30	Heads	50

courses. Are females higher or lower than males in their level of satisfaction? You could ask a given group of students if they are generally satisfied with their research instruction, with the options of YES or NO. You could then compare the proportion of these females who answered YES with the proportion of these males who answered YES. What if you found that 63 percent of females were satisfied and that 65 percent of males were satisfied? Does that mean that you can conclude that there is truly a difference between males and females? If so, would you be prepared to bet a large sum of money that a new study of this subject would result in males having a higher level of satisfaction? I doubt that you would, because you would realize that this small a difference between males and females could be easily explained by chance. If you had found 60 percent of females were satisfied as compared to only 40 percent of males, you would be more likely to see this difference as noteworthy. However, such a difference with a sample of only 10 total students would likely make you wonder if you should take these results seriously. A sample of 100 would be much more impressive.

Those of you with previous training in research and statistics will recognize this discussion as being related to the concept of statistical significance, which will be examined later in this book. As we will see later, methods have been developed for estimating the likelihood that a given set of data results could be explained by chance.

Discussion Box 1.6

Suppose a colleague at work said to you and group of your peers, "I can tell whether you are left-handed or right-handed just by looking intensely into your eyes." A colleague challenged him. He looked intensely into this person's eyes for a few seconds and then said, "You are right-handed." The colleague said "Yes." He then said "See, I told you I could do this." What's wrong with this picture?

---

6. When We Wear the Research Hat, We Must be Very Cautious in Our Conclusions.

Due to the limitations inherent in social research methods, we normally are cautious in the conclusions that we draw from our data. Our methods of measurement may not be optimal. Our study subjects may not be representative of others. Thus, a repeat of our study may provide different results.

Human service professionals are called upon to wear many hats. We might wear the hat of client advocate, in which case we are committed to the organization of information that advances the causes of our client. When we wear the research hat, we accept the norms of the scientific community and the spirit of scientific inquiry. This obligates us to pursue our interests with as much objectivity as we can muster, with the goal of advancing knowledge.

When we conduct a research study, we pursue a given research question. After data is collected and analyzed, we draw conclusions about our research question. Our data might provide strong support, or weak support, or no support for a given explanation of our study subject. Often our results are not entirely conclusive, and we might conceptualize new avenues of inquiry which might better illuminate this subject. The critical point here, however, is that we must avoid the temptation of drawing conclusions based upon prior understandings about our study subject which are not supported by the data we collected. We are, of course, at liberty to maintain any kind of personal opinion about our study subject which we believe to be true. But we must not pretend that this view is supported by our study if this is not true.

When we wear the research hat, we view study results as tentative. We seldom are in a position, after a single research study, to draw definitive conclusions about our research questions.

We do not speak of proof or disproof, but, instead, we speak of how our data either supports or fails to support a particular theory or conclusion.

Applying the Basic Principles—Does the Full Moon Make People Act Different?

Let's employ our learning about these principles with regard to a research question. This is an example I presented in a previous text (York, 1997). We will use one that is simple, and may even be fun. Have you ever heard someone say "It must be the full moon" when they witness strange behavior? When this author has asked the question of whether the full moon affects the behavior of mental health clients, he has often received an affirmative response from social workers. Some social workers seem convinced that the full moon has such an effect.

What is the purpose of our study? Is it to prove that the full moon does cause strange behavior? Is it to prove that it does not cause strange behavior? Or, is our purpose better stated as an attempt to find out whether or not there is a relationship between the existence of the full moon and the existence of strange behavior? You should have no difficulty recognizing the last statement as the best statement of the purpose of our study. If we seek to prove a point, we will naturally fall into various traps which will hamper our pursuit of knowledge about this subject. Remember that research is a process of discovery, not justification. We should engage in a process of inquiry that is designed to provide an objective appraisal of our research subject. The reduction of the potential of human bias is a key to this accomplishment.

With these thoughts in mind, let's consider several ways to collect information regarding our research question. The following are several such methods:

1. Ask a group of mental health clinicians to record the strange things they observe during the full moon. In other words, ask them to stop at the end of the day when there is a full moon and record the strange things they have observed from their clients that day. Explain that you are asking them to record these behaviors on this day because it is the full moon and you are seeking information on whether the full moon makes people act strange.

2. Ask a group of mental health clinicians to record the number of things that meet certain qualifications for being out of the ordinary for each client for a given day, but do not tell them that you are asking for this information because there is a full moon on this particular day. You might find, for example, that 60 percent of these clients evaluated had at least one incidence of strange behavior on this particular day, and that 20 percent had more than one incidence of strange behavior. Use these data about the incidence of strange behavior during the full moon as the basis for your conclusions.

3. Ask a group of mental health clinicians to give their opinions about whether the full moon makes people act strange. You might find, for example, that 70 percent of these individuals could be classified as believing the full moon makes people act strange. Use this as the basis for drawing your conclusions.

4. Ask a group of mental health clinicians to record, for each client, whether the client was acting in a manner considered to be somewhat strange, given their normal behavior. The clinicians would record either Yes or No for each client for one day of the month when the moon was full and also one day of the month when the moon was not full. You do not tell them that you are comparing behavior during the full moon with behavior when there is not a full moon. In other words, you do not let them know that day one is a full moon day and that day two is not. Compare these data for these two days as the basis for your conclusions. In other words, you would compare the percentage of clients with strange behavior during the full moon day with the same for the day when the moon is not full. If 70 percent of clients had strange behavior during the full moon day and only 30 percent had strange behavior on the day without a full moon, you would conclude that your data supported the conclusion that more strange behaviors occur during the full moon than other times.

Discussion Box 1.7

Can you comment on the extent to which each of the above options fit within the spirit of scientific inquiry? Is one approach better? If so, what makes it fit better within the spirit of scientific inquiry?

Let's examine each of the above options. Option 3 has great potential for bias and does not ask for the systematic collection of data at all. If these clinicians are in error because of selective observation, this will unduly influence the outcome of the study. Option 1 calls for the collection of data but provides the basis for a bias, because those making the observations know that the study is about the full moon. This may tempt them to interpret many behaviors as strange simply because their attention has been drawn to this issue. In other words, they are likely to be vulnerable to the error of selective observation.

Option 2 has the advantage that the observers have not been informed that the subject of study is the full moon, so they may not be tempted in the same way as those in option 1. It also has the advantage of data collection. The following is a display of what these data may look like if you actually conducted this study.

From Table 1.2, you can see that a majority of clients exhibited strange behavior during the full moon. Would this lead to your conclusion that the full moon leads to strange behavior? If so, what about the data that might be collected when the moon is not full? Shouldn't you use this for comparison?

Option 4 provides you with this information. With this option, you compare the rate of strange behaviors during the full moon with the same when there is not a full moon. For example, you might find the following from your hypothetical study (Table 1.3).

TABLE 1.2 *An Illustration of Incomplete Data*

Did client exhibit strange behavior?	Moon is full.
Yes	14 (58%)
No	10 (42%)
Total	24 (100%)

TABLE 1.3 *An Illustration of Complete Data*

Did client exhibit strange behavior?	Moon is full.	Moon is not full.
Yes	14 (58%)	14 (58%)
No	10 (42%)	10 (42%)
Total	24 (100%)	24 (100%)

From these data, you can see that 58 percent of clients exhibited strange behavior when the moon is full and that *the same percent of clients exhibited strange behavior when the moon was not full.* Thus, there is no relationship between the moon being full and the exhibition of strange behavior, according to these data. Now, you have a real scientific study.

The second principle tells us to avoid reinventing the wheel. We can best apply this principle by examining the literature. We will return to this principle later, but for now, let's examine some of the other principles.

According to the third principle, we should not get the cart before the horse. Thus, we should not start our study process with the discovery of an instrument for measuring strange behavior. We will start with the question which has to do with the relationship between the full moon and strange behavior. However, as we will see in later chapters, the research process can start with observations which arouse our curiosity. Our perception of the nature of a research problem or question normally starts with some form of observation.

The fourth principle suggests that two heads are better than one. If we believe this statement, we will want to assess the dependability of our method of measuring strange behavior. Do our clinicians know what strange behavior is? Are they likely to be consistent in recording this behavior from one situation to another? Is one clinician likely to be consistent with another in their observations? We can assess these questions by such methods as having two clinicians working together to record their observations independently. We could compare these observations to see if they are consistent. If not, we will have less confidence in our use of their observations as a means of measuring strange behavior. The more that we see different people agreeing on their observations, the more confidence we can have that we have accurately measured the thing we are trying to measure. If we cannot have confidence in our means of measuring strange behavior, we will have a weak method of testing our research question.

The fifth principle is that things sometimes happen just by chance. In the example where clinicians were asked to record whether their clients acted in a strange manner, we found that the percent who did so during the full moon (58%) was exactly the same as when the moon was not full (58%). This finding was simple to interpret. But what if we found the percent favored the full moon, but only by a little? For example, instead of exactly 58 percent of behaviors during the full moon being in the strange category, suppose that this figure was 62 percent? Would we feel safe in concluding the data supported the conclusion that more strange behaviors occur during the full moon than other times? After all, you are now comparing 62 percent of full moon behaviors being strange as compared to 58 percent of behaviors when the moon was not full. If you applied the principle that some things happen just by chance, you would not draw this conclusion. In your deliberations as a scientist, you would be assisted by methods of statistical analysis, a topic covered in various parts of this book. When you applied these methods, you would find that the likelihood of data like the above being explained by chance is rather high. So, you merely have chance rather than data that could be credible in supporting the conclusion that more strange behaviors occur during the full moon. And you would be well informed not to bet your money that a repeat of this study with other clients would have similar results that favored the full moon theory. The next time this study was conducted, your chances of winning your bet would be far from a sure thing because there is a reasonable chance the data would slightly favor the day the moon was not full rather than when it was full. In other words, it is best not to bet on something that seems very close to 50–50 unless you just really like betting.

The final principle related to the nature of scientific inquiry is that we should be cautious in drawing conclusions when we are wearing the research hat. For example, we should be very careful to ensure that study conclusions should be consistent with the data that we analyzed. If we had applied a statistical measure to our data and found that the likelihood that our results would occur by chance to be high, we would be reluctant to conclude that we have found a legitimate relationship between the full moon and strange behavior. This principle is rather easily applied to our example because it is a simple one; more complex examples would provide a better challenge. However, before you complete all the material and exercises in this text, you will confront published research in which there appear to be study conclusions taken seriously by study authors in situations in which the results can be easily explained by chance. And you might even find that study authors have strayed into the arena of conclusions that are not related specifically to the data that were analyzed.

When we examine the literature, we will find that different researchers have found many methods for studying our research question. The results are not always consistent. Thus, the results of any one study must be treated cautiously.

We have examined a few questions about how we might go about the examination of whether the full moon makes people act strange or different. Before we venture into our own research on this question, we should examine the literature to see what others have found. Perhaps the answer to our question already exists in the work of others.

7. Studies on the Effect of the Full Moon

There have been numerous studies of this question. One such study was conducted of attempted suicides (Matthew, et al., 1991). The records of the Accident and Emergency Department of a large urban hospital were examined to determine if the rate of suicide attempts which came to the attention of this hospital were different during the full moon than other times. The number of suicides attempted for each day of one month were recorded. The full moon fell on day 15. On that day, a total of 19 suicide attempts were recorded. The largest number of suicide attempts (23) were recorded on days 3 and 17, one of which was close to the full moon, the other was at a great distance from it. The number of attempts on the day of the full moon was slightly higher than the average for the entire month, but the difference was determined to be nonsignificant. When we examine this question, we might also want to compare the three days when the moon is fullest with the three days in which it is least full. If the full moon causes suicide, we would expect the three days of the full moon to be significantly higher. For the data from this study, the average number of suicide attempts during the full moon period was 18 as compared to 17 for the new moon period (the three days in which the moon is least full). This would clearly not be considered to be very significant.

Well, you might say, this is only one study. And you would be wise if you exhibited such caution in your conclusions about our research question. But there have been many other studies.

Discussion Box 1.8
_____

What do you think about this evidence? Is it convincing enough just by itself?

In one such study, a set of researchers examined the records of a psychiatric hospital to determine if dangerous behavior of patients was more prevalent during the full moon than at other times. Dangerous behavior was defined as "erratic behavior which was assessed by qualified mental health professionals as dangerous to self or others to the extent that isolation (seclusion) or restraints were necessary to prevent harm to self or others." (Durm, Terry, and Hammonds, 1986, p. 988). Data for three years (1982, 1983, and 1984) were collected. The average number of such incidents of dangerous behavior was actually higher (13.17 per day) during the period that the moon was not full than it was during the period of the full moon (11.61 per day).

Discussion Box 1.9
_____

Are you convinced yet that the full moon has no effect?

If you are not yet convinced perhaps a certain degree of caution is still warranted because we have only examined two studies. But, we can go further. Our best bet in our investigation now is to examine an article where numerous published studies were reviewed and summarized. Such was the case in an article by Byrnes and Kelly (1992). They reviewed 12 studies which examined the relationship between the lunar cycle and such things as crisis calls to police stations, poison centers, and crisis intervention centers. Their conclusion from this review was that "there is no evidence whatsoever for the contention that calls of a more emotional or 'out-of-control' nature occur more often at the full moon." (Byrnes & Kelly, 1992, p. 779).

Another review of many studies was undertaken by Rotten and Kelly (1985). A total of 37 published studies were included in their review. They also concluded that there was little evidence to support the theory that the full moon affects people's behavior. This pattern of findings of nonsignificant differences between behaviors during the full moon and other periods is found in a review of other sources. But one study was found that claimed to have found a relationship between the full moon and behavior. That study was conducted by Hicks-Casey and Potter (1991). They found that there was more aggressive acting-out misbehaviors in a sample of 20 developmentally delayed women during the full moon than at other times. However, the analysis of their data was challenged by Flynn (1991) as having major flaws. Additionally, it is only one of many studies that have been conducted on this subject. If we were to find this study's methods adequate in its methods to be included in our analysis, we should be careful to put this study's results into the perspective that it is perhaps the only study of many that found support for the full moon theory.

Discussion Box 1.10

Well, where do you stand now on our question about the full moon? Does it have an effect?

Do we still want to conduct a study of the effect of the full moon on behavior? Our review of the existing literature would suggest that this question has already been substantially answered. Do we want to spend our time reinventing the wheel? We would not, however, be reinventing the wheel if we found a new angle on this topic, such as a type of behavior not yet examined. But, generally speaking, it seems the evidence clearly fails to support the conclusion that the full moon affects behavior.

Ethics in Social Research

When you use human subjects for research, you must abide by certain ethical principles. In the next section of this chapter, you will be asked to participate in a study whereby you will respond to an instrument and report your data which will be combined with the data of others to test a theory. Universities and major institutions normally have a committee that reviews proposals for using human subjects in research in order to protect study subjects. These bodies are guided by ethical principles. One list of such principles can be obtained from the Code of Ethics of the National Association of Social Workers. This code spells out several guiding principles:

1. The social worker engaged in research should consider carefully its possible consequences for human beings.
2. The social worker engaged in research should ascertain that the consent of participants is voluntary and informed, without any implied deprivation or penalty for refusal to participate, and with due regard for participants' privacy and dignity.
3. The social worker engaged in research should protect participants from unwarranted physical or mental discomfort, distress, harm, danger, or deprivation.
4. The social worker who engages in the evaluation of services or cases should discuss them only for professional purposes and only with persons directly and professionally concerned with them.
5. Information obtained about participants in research should be treated as confidential.
6. The social worker should take credit only for work actually done in connection with scholarly and research endeavors and credit contributions made by others. (National Association of Social Workers, 1980, *Code of Ethics*, Silver Spring, MD).

The most profound requirement of the above is that research participants must be protected from any harm that might come from the research experience. This is seldom an issue in human service evaluations because the participants are typically asked only to supply information. Medical experiments that put people into hypnosis or administer drugs or electric shocks are in an entirely different arena as far as this issue is concerned.

In evaluation research, confidentiality of responses is an important consideration. Persons who are called upon to answer research questions are normally informed that their responses will be treated confidentially, meaning that their identities will not be revealed in the report that emanates from the research. It is even better if their responses can be anonymous, because privacy is assured in this way and research subjects do not have to worry about whether confidentiality will be violated.

Another issue is voluntary participation. It is important that each study subject's participation be voluntary. This issue may not be as simple as it seems at first. An agency supervisor may ask supervisees to volunteer for a study. A college professor may ask students to volunteer to respond to a survey. Normally, this is not controversial. However, it is important that persons in positions of power provide methods for reducing the potential of retribution for nonparticipation. A good way to do this is for participation to be unknown if this is possible. In the case of a survey, this is easy to do. In other types of studies, it may not be.

Four Purposes of Research

Scientific research can be grouped into four major categories for the human service practitioner. In a previous section, *evaluative research* was distinguished from other types of research by the fact that the evaluative study has an intervention that is a major part of the research question. You may want to know whether the new approach to child protective service has had the effect of reducing repeat offenses. You may want to know if the introduction of school social work for all middle schools in Hampton County has had the effect of reducing school problem behaviors or increasing grades for at-risk youth. You may want to know if the new discharge service for Memorial Hospital has had the effect of improving the extent to which discharged patients comply with follow-up medical treatment. You may want to know if your psychotherapy service for Janet Johnson has had the effect of reducing her depression. In each of these examples, there was an intervention.

But what if you wanted to know about the demographics of the students at Harper High School? What is the percent of males or minority students or minority males? What percent are living without at least one parent? These questions would be pursued by descriptive studies, which are designed to describe things. With *descriptive research*, you are normally studying only one variable at a time, even if you have long list of such variables. You may want to know the frequencies or percentages of people who are patients of your hospital by gender, race, income, category of financial payment, age, or any number of variables. You are studying one variable at a time because you are calculating each one separately.

If, however, you were examining the relationship between variables you would be in the category of *explanatory research*. The reason you would be examining the relationship between two variables is to examine whether one explains the other. Does gender explain grades in school? Does poverty explain disciplinary problems in school? For the former question, you would examine the relationship between gender and grades by comparing the grades of males and females. For the latter question you would compare the rate of disciplinary problems between those in poverty with those who are not.

The evaluative study could be considered a type of explanatory study because these studies examine whether treatment explains recovery. Do clients display better target behavior after treatment than before? Are treated clients better off than nontreated persons? But for our purposes, we will treat evaluative research as a separate category.

There is one more type of research that is relevant to human services even though it is not evaluative in nature. That is the type categorized as *exploratory research*. The exploratory study has the purpose of either developing a theory or new perspectives on things. If you didn't have an adequate theory to explain moral development in youth, you could use an exploratory study to help develop one.

Discussion Box 1.11

Think of a research study you would like to undertake. Determine the category this study falls into. Briefly describe the study and label its type (descriptive, exploratory, evaluative, or explanatory).

How are Different Types of Research Similar?

This book focuses on evaluation research. Through these pages you will see various examples of evaluation with particular attention to the information needs that evaluative research meets. But *evaluative research has much more in common with the other types of research than it has in contrast to them*. In fact, you would have a great deal of difficulty identifying any major concept in research methods for any of these types of research that would not be covered in this text on evaluation. All types of research, for example, require attention to the issue of how the research question is articulated, the knowledge base on which your study relies, the nature of the study sample, the means of measurement, the nature of data analysis, and the conclusions that are consistent with the data that were analyzed.

Whether your research study is explanatory, descriptive, exploratory, or evaluative, your research question must be researchable in the natural world and must be consistent with the spirit of scientific inquiry. Regardless of the type of study you are conducting, you must have research methods that identify whether the tools used in measuring variables provide an accurate method of doing so, whether your sample provides the basis for a certain type of generalization of study results, and whether your research design adequately addresses the issue of causation, where appropriate. Furthermore, you will be required to collect and analyze data in a systematic method, regardless of the type of study being conducted. Finally, the conclusions must always be consistent with the data, demonstrating that you have not gone beyond this information in your presentation. Issues of reliability, validity, generalization of results, causation, and significance are among the topics germane to all types of scientific research.

The relative importance of certain issues will vary from one type of research to another, but what is included in each is rather similar. Among the differences is that sampling and generalization are critical to descriptive research because the goal is to describe something with precision. Causation, on the other hand, is more critical to explanatory and evaluative research. In the latter cases, you are trying to explain one thing by reference to its relationships with other things. If clients have experienced a measured gain in functioning, you will want your research study to adequately address the question of whether this change was caused by the intervention. The critical point here, of course, is that differences exist, but are overwhelmed by the similarities among basic concepts.

Two Processes of Scientific Inquiry—Deductive and Inductive

There are two approaches to knowledge inquiry that are discussed in most research texts—deductive and inductive models. These models offer differences in the processes employed for inquiry. The **deductive** model is employed when you start with a theory and make observations to test it. It begins with an examination of the logical relations among things. From this analysis is derived a theory or hypothesis. The theory or hypothesis is subjected to scientific testing.

For example, cognitive theory asserts that problems derive from dysfunctional thinking patterns in response to life events. From this theory arose a model of psychotherapy known as cognitive-behavioral therapy, which addresses thinking patterns so as to change the client's ways of thinking about life events and thereby reducing their problems. A key problem addressed by this model is depression. Some people become chronically depressed after divorce or the death of a **spouse** or the loss of a job, while others do not. A reason for the difference could be that the chronically depressed person reacted to the divorce with dysfunctional thinking, whereas the healthy person did not. It seems logical to assume that a model of therapy that intervenes in thinking patterns would be effective in reducing depression. The hypothesis that would emanate from this thinking could be "Depressed persons will have lower levels of depression after receiving cognitive-behavioral therapy than before." This hypothesis would be tested by the measurement of depression before and after therapy for a group of depressed persons.

The **inductive** model starts with observations from which general principles or theories or hypotheses are derived. Before you have a theory to test, someone must have made observations that were subjected to logical analysis from which the theory was articulated. So, knowledge in general typically starts with observations from which general principles or theories are derived which, in turn, are subjected to testing and refinement.

Figure 1.1 shows how the process of discovery can move from a period of initial exploration of a topic to the development of an initial theory, to the testing of the theory, to the revision of the theory.

In evaluative research, you could use an inductive process to explore the reasons why some people recover from a problem (e.g., depression, anxiety, substance abuse, child neglect) without treatment. This is based on the assumption there is not a sufficient theory in existence to explain this phenomenon. If there was such a theory, you might use a deductive process to test

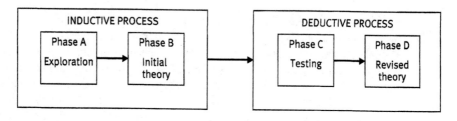

FIGURE 1.1 *The Inductive and Deductive Processes*

it. In the absence of such, you could use an inductive process to develop a theory or a set of principles about the topic under investigation. That theory could then be tested using the deductive process.

Discussion Box 1.12

Let's suppose that Mary has developed a theory about the effect of the full moon on behavior by considering the effect of the moon's cycles on the tides and examining how changes in tides are accompanied by changes in barometric pressure, and has speculated that barometric pressure affects brain chemistry. No data has yet been collected by Mary on human behaviors and the moon's cycles. Suppose further than Barbara has made a number of observations from the nurses' station in the hospital about how crazy things seem to be during the full moon. Which of these persons is operating more from a deductive process of inquiry and which is operating more from an inductive process of inquiry?

Two Forms of Information—Quantitative and Qualitative

Scientific research relies upon two major forms of information—qualitative and quantitative. When you have completed the **quantitative** measurement of a study variable with your study subjects, you will have either a category or number to assign to each study participant for each variable. For example, each study subject may be classified as male or female for the variable of gender. The age for each person may be recorded in its basic form or by reference to a category of age (e.g., 0–19; 20–29; etc.). You may have each person in a category according to whether they checked "agree" or "undecided" or "disagree" in response to a particular statement about political ideology.

When you have completed the **qualitative** measurement of social phenomena, you will have *words* rather than numbers or uniform categories. These words may come from your observations of people in action or from the direct quotes from your study participants. These words will be examined for themes and will be coded accordingly. Thus, qualitative measurement is more flexible, and characterizes each study subject in a more unique format. Persons are not placed into preconceived categories but are given the opportunity to express themselves in their own words or actions.

Quantitative research has a more natural fit with deductive inquiry, while qualitative research has a more natural fit with inductive inquiry. When you are testing the hypothesis that clients will exhibit less depression after cognitive-behavioral treatment than before, you are employing a deductive process in which you will likely measure client progress quantitatively. If you want to know why Hispanic teenagers often fail to show up for therapy appointments, you will normally employ an inductive process with qualitative means of observation (e.g., interviews).

An evaluation of service outcome typically takes the form of measuring the client's target behavior before and after treatment using quantitative means of measurement (e.g., the Beck Depression Inventory). Some evaluative research, however, focuses upon processes. A question may be raised about why certain types of clients improved more than others, or whether certain standards of service were implemented. A researcher might want better to understand the processes of recovery for a typical client with a given problem. When the focus of evaluative research is upon process, qualitative means of measurement is usually more appropriate. Because quantitative means of measurement are typically associated with outcome evaluation and qualitative means, with process evaluation, there is certainly no rule that negates the use of either method for either type of evaluation.

The choice of a qualitative or quantitative means of observation (measurement) should be guided by the nature of the research question and the existing knowledge about it. Thus, one should not begin the research experience with the idea of conducting a quantitative study or a qualitative study. This would be "putting the cart before the horse." Methods of observation spring from the nature of the study subject, not the other way around.

While either qualitative or quantitative methods can be applied to a wide variety of purposes and circumstances, there are a few guides which can assist the beginning research student in the choice of an observation mode. For example, a qualitative method is typically more appropriate to the extent that each of the following conditions exist:

1. You are seeking to develop theories or hypotheses rather than testing existing ones.
2. You are seeking an understanding of the subjective meaning of behaviors or social processes rather than the precise description of social phenomena.
3. The concepts of interest are not easily reduced to categories or numbers.
4. There is relatively little that is known about the subject of study from the existing literature, or this knowledge base has important missing links.

You could say that the opposite of the above suggest a quantitative method of observation. For example, you would normally use a quantitative method when you are testing a theory, when you wish to measure something precisely, when study concepts are easily reduced to categories or numbers, and when there is a good deal that is already known about the phenomenon under study. Unfortunately, there is no clear-cut means of employing the listed criteria. We cannot say, for example, that if any two of the conditions exist, you must use a specific means of observation. These are meant only as a general guide.

Discussion Box 1.13

Consider these two questions on a client satisfaction survey:

What is your age? _____
What is your most important unmet need?

Which of the above is an example of a quantitative question? A qualitative question?

Four Methods of Gathering Information: Surveys, Interviews, Direct Observation, and Documents

There are a number of methods of gathering information for scientific research. These include social surveys, interviews, direct observation, and documents. The social survey is a form of gathering information in which the study subject is given an instrument for response. We are all familiar with the mailed survey whereby someone wants our opinions or ideas in regard to a set of questions. When a therapist asks a client to respond to a depression scale, this is also a form of survey.

The interview is a personal encounter between persons in which one person (or persons) is seeking information from another person (or persons). It can take place face to face or through another mode of personal interaction, such as the telephone. It is distinguished from the social survey in which researchers are asking for written responses to questions from the study subject.

Direct observation refers to the situation where the researcher observes behavior directly and makes notes and analyzes these notes. Conclusions are drawn from this analysis of notes. Direct observation is normally associated with exploratory research because it is a good vehicle for developing new theories or perspectives on a given phenomenon.

A fourth method of gathering information is through documents. Agencies normally collect a variety of information for reporting to funding sources. This information can be used for research. Client files may be a good source of information.

Scientific Research and Cultural Competence

Cultural competence refers to one's ability to understand and feel comfortable with people of different cultures. The term is rather recent in our language and is very important to the evaluation and administration of human services. A key aspect of cultural competence is the ability to understand and communicate with people of different cultures. Without this ability, it will be next to impossible to design an evaluation study that makes sense, or to collect data using instruments that accurately measure the critical study concepts. Measurement tools, for example, are designed by people of a given culture who may not be conversant with how people of different cultures attach certain meanings to certain words. The implication is that tools should be scrutinized for culturally specific language and should be tested for validity using people of the cultures that are relevant to the specific study population being employed. In another example, you may find that the variables you choose to employ in your study may be more meaningful to people of one culture than another. The implications are that you should identify this in your conclusions or you should redesign your study to be more meaningful to its relevant cultures.

One set of topics for research and cultural competence can be found in a text by Rubin and Babbie (2001, pp. 92–94). These authors summarize critical issues with the following suggestions:

- Understand the culture of your study population before completing the design of the study.
- Engage minority scholars and community representatives in the formulation of the research problem and in all stages of research.
- Do not assume that instruments successfully used in prior studies of whites can yield valid information when applied to minorities.
- Use culturally sensitive language in your measures, perhaps using non-English translation.
- Use in-depth pretesting of measurement tools to correct for problems with culture or language.
- Use interviewers who will be appropriate to the study population.
- Examine data regarding cultural differences in response to questions.
- Avoid an unwarranted focus exclusively on the deficits of minorities.
- Assess your own cross-cultural competence.
- Use special sampling strategies that will solicit appropriate representation of those in minority groups.
- Look for cross-cultural studies in your literature review.

In various places in this text, you will review information about cultural competence. This theme begins with potentially involving people of given cultures in framing your study. It continues with the necessity to define variables grounded in cultural competence with regard to the relevant cultures. It moves to more technical topics such as the validation of study instruments in the relevant cultures, the inclusion of sampling strategies that are culturally relevant, and the choice of a general measurement method based on cultural understandings.

Summary

In this chapter, you have examined the nature of scientific research as a unique way to seek knowledge. You reviewed the spirit of scientific inquiry through several common sense principles and saw their illustration in the examination of the question of whether the full moon changes behavior. You saw that scientific research can be classified into four categories by using the idea of the purpose of the study as the vehicle for classification. By now, you should be able to label a study as either qualitative or quantitative in nature by reference to the form of the information gathered and you should be able to determine whether a given study employed more of a deductive or inductive process of inquiry. Finally, you should be able to describe a given method of gathering information as being in the form of a survey, an interview, direct observation, or an examination of documents.

Quiz

The following is a brief quiz regarding the content of this chapter. You can use it either as a pretest, to see if you need to read this chapter carefully, or as a posttest, to see how much you understand at the end of this experience of reading the chapter.

1. The scientific method:
   a. Assumes that humans are not likely to err in observation.
   b. Attempts to control for human error in observation as much as possible.
   c. Assumes that humans are likely to err in observation but simply accepts this as a limitation of the scientific method and not something to do anything about, because it is impossible to control for all possible sources of error.
   d. Attempts to insert human error into observation in order to create a realistic situation.

2. Suppose you have decided to conduct a client satisfaction survey. Which of the following would logically come first in the research process?
   a. Selecting the questions to put on the questionnaire
   b. Selecting the sample of persons to receive the questionnaire
   c. Determining the purpose of the study and the research questions to be answered
   d. Selecting the statistical measures to employ in the analysis of the data

3. Which of the following statements of the purpose of a research study is consistent with the spirit of scientific inquiry?
   a. To demonstrate that dialectical behavioral therapy is effective in the treatment of persons with borderline personality disorder
   b. To challenge the criticism that human services are not worth the cost
   c. Both of the above
   d. None of the above

4. Suppose that you were given an instrument (questionnaire) that was designed to measure the extent to which you had a tendency to be emotionally supportive of others. Suppose further that you gave this instrument to another person who knew you very well and you asked this person to answer these questions as he/she thought you should have answered them about yourself, and you found that your answers about yourself were substantially different from the answers that the other person gave about you. Which of the following is *not* a plausible explanation of this result?
   a. You know yourself well, but this other person does not.
   b. The other person knows you well, but you do not.
   c. Both you and the other person are incorrect in their perceptions of you.
   d. Both you and the other person are correct in their perceptions of you.
   e. None of the above—i.e., all are plausible explanations for this result.

5. Suppose you were given an instrument to measure your "soul urge," a concept from the theory of numerology. The instrument determines which of 10 personality types (soul urges) is the correct one for you. This instrument is given to 10 persons in your class, along with an instrument that asks each person to identify what they believe to be the best fitting statement for themselves, from among these 10 descriptions of soul urges. The class decides to compare their own self-perceptions to the soul urge designated from the instrument derived from the theory of numerology as a test of the validity of that theory. Only one person in your class of 10 finds that the number they found best described themselves was the one selected by the instrument from the theory of numerology. This one student says "There must be something to this theory because it correctly described me." How should this statement be treated with respect to the common sense principles related to the scientific method?
   a. This statement is consistent with the principles of the scientific method because any single piece of data has validity in and of itself.
   b. This statement is consistent with the principles of the scientific method because this method recognizes multiple realities.
   c. This statement is not consistent with the principles of the scientific method because some things happen just by chance.

d. This statement is not consistent with the principles of the scientific method because two heads are better than one.

6. Given the above results where 9 students out of 10 were found to have a self-description that was not consistent with the description given by the theory of numerology, how should the conclusions from this study be presented?
   a. This study proved that the theory of numerology is correct (valid).
   b. This study proved that the theory of numerology is not correct (not valid).
   c. This study produced evidence in support of the theory of numerology.
   d. This study failed to produce evidence in support of the theory of numerology.

7. Suppose you had decided to conduct a study of whether the full moon makes people act strange. Many people have asserted that the full moon makes people "crazy" or "strange" or "weird" and so forth because they have witnessed such behavior during the full moon. Is this information sufficient to draw a conclusion about the effect of the full moon?
   a. Yes, because the perceptions of people of the behavior of others should be considered trustworthy; otherwise, there would be no way to do scientific studies of social behavior.
   b. Yes, because this information provides a clear connection between this kind of behavior and the presence of the full moon. If people act this way during the full moon, it is logical to assert that the full moon has an effect.
   c. No, because you would need to employ only instruments published in books to measure your variables.
   d. No, because you need also to analyze information about the presence of this behavior when the moon is full and when it is not full as well as the absence of this behavior when the moon is full and when it is not full.

8. Which one of the following are *not* among the ethical guidelines for the use of human subjects in research?
   a. Information collected from human subjects for research must always be collected in a way that allows the subject to remain completely anonymous.
   b. Research studies must respect the study subject's right to privacy.
   c. Research studies should protect the study subject from undue harm, and notify the subject of any possible risks to harm that could be present.
   d. None of the above. In other words, all of the above are clearly included in the ethical guidelines for the use of human subjects in research.

9. Which of the following statements is/are true?
   a. A deductive process of inquiry, where the researcher starts with general ideas that are tested through observation, has a more natural fit with quantitative means of measurement than quantitative means.
   b. When you have completed the qualitative means of observation, you typically have placed study subjects into categories or given them a number that represents their value on the variable being measured.
   c. Both of the above.
   d. None of the above.

10. Under which of the following conditions would you normally be better advised to employ a quantitative means of observation rather than a qualitative means?
    a. When you are testing an existing theory rather than developing a new one
    b. When you are seeking an understanding of the subjective meaning of behaviors or social processes rather than the precise description of social phenomena
    c. Both of the above
    d. None of the above

Following the list of references is a key to the answers to the above quiz.

References

Byrnes, G., & Kelly, I. W. (1992). Crisis calls and lunar cycles: A twenty-year review. *Psychological Reports, 71,* 779–785.

Durm, M. W., Terry, C. L., & Hammonds, C. R. (1986). Lunar phase and acting-out behavior. *Psychological Reports, 59,* 987–990.

Flynn, M. (1991). Critical comment on Hicks-Casey and Potter, "Effect of the full moon on a sample of developmentally delayed, institutional women." *Perceptual and Motor Skills, 73,* 963–968.

Hicks-Casey, W. E., & Potter, D. R. (1991). Effect of the full moon on a sample of developmentally delayed, institutionalized women. *Perceptual and Motor Skills*, 72, 1375–1380.

Matthew, V. M., Lindesay, J., Shanmuganathat, N., & Eapen, V. (1991). Attempted suicide and the lunar cycle. *Psychological Reports, 68,* 927–930.

National Association of Social Workers (1980). *Code of Ethics.* National Association of Social Workers: Silver Springs, MD.

Pseudoscience. (2007). *Wikipedia, The Free Encyclopedia.* Retrieved 12-23-05 from http:en.wikipedia.org/wiki/Pseudoscience.

Rotten, J., & Kelly, I. W. (1985). Much ado about the full moon: A meta-analysis of lunar-lunacy research. *Psychological Bulletin, 97* (2), 286–306.

Rubin, A., and Babbie, E. (2001). *Research methods for social work* (4th Ed.). Belmont, CA: Wadsworth.

York, R. O. (1997). *Building basic competencies in social work research.* Boston: Allyn & Bacon.

Answers to the Quiz

1. b	**6.** d
2. c	**7.** d
3. d	**8.** a
4. d	**9.** a
5. c	**10.** a

2

Conducting a Study to Illustrate Common Sense Principles of Science

In this chapter, you will be offered the opportunity to apply the basic principles enumerated in the last chapter through a study in which you will be both study subject and researcher. You will respond to an instrument as a test of a theory. You will be asked to combine your data with others who are in your class. If you are not reading this book in a class, you will need to obtain other people to participate in this study in order to complete it. There is a quiz at the end which should be used as a posttest rather than a pretest, because it depends on the unique exercise of this chapter which can only be understood with the experience you will have with it.

This is not an example of an evaluative study. It falls more into the category of an explanatory study, where you are testing a theory, rather than the category of evaluative research, where you are evaluating a human service intervention. The remainder of this book is devoted to the latter, but it should be noted that evaluation research is built on a foundation of basic research principles, and that foundation is being illustrated in this chapter.

At the completion of this chapter, you will be able to explain how a particular study in which you participated was able to:

1. Implement the spirit of scientific inquiry.

2. Follow a set of logical steps in systematic inquiry.

3. Abide by research ethics.

4. Demonstrate common sense principles related to scientific inquiry.

A Brief Review of Research Ethics

Before we take the first step in our study, let's review the basic principles of research ethics to assure our study is consistent with these principles. First, our study should not place subjects at risk of emotional or physical harm, unless we have undergone severe procedures for obtaining informed consent. Our study merely asks that you answer a set of questions about yourself in regard to your personality. These questions do not probe deeply into your emotions or ask you to recall emotionally disturbing events in your life. Consequently, there is no expectation that this experience would put you at risk of harm.

Secondly, participation in our study should be voluntary, unless involuntary participation is a requirement of the methodology and the benefits can be justified when compared to the costs of involuntary participation. Justification for involuntary participation is not often viewed by research review boards as warranted, so it is highly discouraged. In our case, participation is voluntary. If you do not wish to participate, you can simply decline to do so. In view of the fact that you may be undertaking this study with a college course and the instructor is collecting the data for review, it is important that a procedure be employed that protects your anonymity with regard to participation by doing something like allowing you to turn in a blank form without it being noticed. You may not view your participation as completely voluntary if your professor is collecting your form and can see that you have declined to participate.

Third, your privacy should be protected. The ideal way to protect your privacy is to collect information anonymously. It is not the only way, but it is the ideal way. If your name is not displayed with your answers to the questions on the instrument, no one has the opportunity to know what you said. In some cases, it is appropriate to collect information that identifies you, but your information should be treated confidentially, unless you have agreed otherwise. If the researcher treats your information confidentially, your name will not be revealed with your information in a report. In our study, data will be collected anonymously.

Discussion Box 2.1

In your opinion, have the key issues in research ethics been adequately addressed in this study?

Our Initial Steps in the Study

This study will call upon you to respond to a questionnaire about your personality. The data from this questionnaire will be used to test a theory. Data from all persons in your class will be combined in this study.

Responding to the Personality Profile Questionnaire

Your first step is to respond to the instrument in Exhibit 2.1. Be sure to follow the instructions carefully and give a rank to each of the 10 statements. Do not read ahead to determine what the study is all about. *So turn the page and respond to this instrument. It should take only about 10 minutes to complete. You must respond to each item on the questionnaire; Failure to do so will disqualify your data from our study.*

EXHIBIT 2.1 • *Choosing Your Self Description*

Directions: Examine the list of 10 descriptions given below and rank order them from 1 to 10 by assigning a rank of 1 to the statement that is most like yourself, a rank of 2 to the next best description of yourself, a rank of 3 to the next, and so on until you have assigned a rank to each of the 10 statements, with the rank of 10 being given to the statement that is the least like yourself. Be sure to place a different number by each item. Ties are not allowed. (Note: There is no statement numbered 10).

____1. Wants to lead and direct. Prefers to work alone or to be the boss. Is proud of abilities and desires praise. Wants to create and originate. Is not very emotional. Is capable of great accomplishment, a loyal friend. May be boastful, critical, impatient.

____2. Wants and needs love, companionship. Prefers to work with or for others. Wants harmony and peace. Wants ease and comfort (not necessarily wealth and luxury). Is kind and thoughtful. Attracts friends. Is sensitive and emotional. Falls in love easily. Devoted, easygoing.

____3. Wants to give out joy and happiness. Wants popularity and friends. Wants beauty. Never mopes over mistakes—tries again. Artistic, expressive, entertaining, playful. Doesn't worry or get depressed. Wants to scatter love, energies, talents.

____4. Wants respectability and solidity. Wants to be a rock of dependability. A great disciplinarian. Loves home and family. Is not fond of innovation. Loves order and regularity. Is thorough and methodical. Needs and wants love, but often repels it.

____5. Wants personal freedom in every direction. Wants change, variety, and constant new opportunity. Wide open to life's experiences. Loves pleasure, travel, strange and new people. Injects new life into all that s/he touches. Will not be hampered by convention. Is progressive, intellectual, emotional, spiritual.

____6. Wants roots, responsibility, home, steadfast love. Loyal friend, good counselor. Inclined toward conventionality, but broad-minded. A "cosmic" parent. Centers life on home. Loves to work with others, never alone.

____7. Wants silence, peace, meditation, analysis. Hates noise and confusion of business world. Is conservative, refined, reserved, spiritual. Is deeply emotional, but has horror of showing it. Shy, withdrawn. Must be known to be loved.

____8. Wants big affairs and the power to handle them. Wants success in all material matters. Loves organization, finances. Loves to manage and direct. Is generous, enthusiastic, courageous, determined. Has vision and imagination. Is cornerstone of community. Is power for good. May be dominant.

____9. Wants to serve the world. Boundless faith in own source of supply. Has wisdom, intuition, understanding. Is attractive to all and loved by all. Is ready to give his/her life for humanity. Wants personal love, but belongs to the Universe. An interpreter of the greatness of life.

____11. Wants to reveal beauties s/he has seen. Is always the universalist, never concerned with individuals. Is a dreamer, visionary with a passion for salvation and uplift. Wants to indulge in impracticality, but seems practical. Has "electrical" mind. Can be a martyr.

Your responses to the questions in Exhibit 2.1 will be used in a study of the theory of numerology. Please remember that you cannot have any ties in your assignment of ranks to the statements in Exhibit 2.1. If you did this, please return to this exhibit and correct this problem.

The theory of numerology is explained in Exhibit 2.2. It is one with which you are probably not familiar, and that is a key to the choice of this theory for this initial exercise in the applications of the spirit of scientific inquiry. This is a theory that is believed by many people.

I once saw a full page advertisement in a magazine that offered people the opportunity to learn more about themselves by sending their birthdates, after which they could expect to receive a profile that would help them understand themselves better.

The study we will be conducting will compare your self-description to a description provided by the theory of numerology. To the extent that self-descriptions are congruent with the theory, we will produce evidence in its support. To the extent they are not congruent; we will provide evidence that challenges the theory.

Let's Make Sure We are not Reinventing the Wheel

You can review the information in Exhibit 2.2 to ascertain whether our study comparing self-descriptions to the description given by the theory is tantamount to reinventing the wheel. If we had found this theory had been thoroughly tested with consistent results, we could be so accused. However, keep in mind that a study with a new type of study sample is almost always warranted. Review the following section to add further evidence to address the question of whether we are reinventing the wheel.

EXHIBIT 2.2 • *A Brief Literature Review on the Theory of Numerology*

(Taken from York, 1997)

Numerology presents a theory about life. It proposes that the vibrations from our birth names and the constellation of the universe in relation to our birth dates will explain life. It will explain much about us, what we are like, how we can be in a better state of harmony with nature, and what is our destiny. But how did this knowledge come about?

Among the published books on numerology are ones by Vincent Lopez entitled *Numerology* (New York: The Citadel Press, 1961) and by Florence Campbell entitled *Your Days are Numbered* (Ferndale, PA.: The Gateway, 1931). The latter is generally recognized as one of the most important works on the subject. According to both books, the origins of numerology go back to an ancient philosopher and mathematician, Pythagoras, who developed the theory in the sixth century.

Neither book provides evidence that the knowledge base upon which this theory is built was derived from anything other that the shared thoughts of people throughout the centuries. It was conceived by one person who was influenced by earlier works on the so-called "science of numbers." Over the centuries people have interpreted this theory in their own ways and have handed it down to others. For advocates of this theory, the wisdom of it seems to

be self-evident and requires no systematic investigation of a scientific nature.

To understand how such theories originate, we should examine the impressions of Vincent Lopez (1961) who notes:

> Numbers are truly awe-inspiring. There is something sublime about their sequence as it continues on and on into Infinity. Suddenly, when you study them arduously, there is revealed to your mortal mind the humming rhythm of the galaxies, the ebb and flow of Time, and the Law of Periodicity which operates throughout the Universe (p.125).

Numerology is founded upon the metaphysical plane of thinking. Lopez (1961) explains:

> All schools of metaphysical thought have made this point clear: there is an "outer" vibration or esoteric side and an "inner" vibration or esoteric angle to all forms of occult learning, and numerology is no exception. You may use the practical numerical values for your daily living and material problems. But there is also a spiritual expression to each number . . . Through meditation and a constant research into the esoteric

(continued)

EXHIBIT 2.2 • *continued*

philosophy of numbers you will soon recognize your own pattern of transmutation (p. 150).

While the word "research" is used here, there is no suggestion that one employ the scientific method in testing the validity of numerology. The scientific method requires objective methods of measuring phenomena and attempts to control for biases and other sources of human error in the pursuit of knowledge about reality.

We are expected to believe numerology because it makes sense to us. According to Campbell (1931):

> In trying to relate ourselves to life as we find it, we must discover how to play harmonies instead of discords. The piano, for example, stands in the living room, capable of many varieties of sounds and noises. If we do not understand how to play it, perhaps it will remain silent until some one comes alone who does; if we make the attempt without any understanding, the attempt is likely to be disastrous to ears and nerves.
>
> Why not learn what will produce the harmonies?
>
> We are all equally capable of harmonies and discords but, unlike other manufactured instruments, we may not remain mute and inexpressive. We must take our place in the Cosmic Orchestra . . .
>
> The clue to this we find in the world around us, for if we pause long enough to sense and feel it we discover: Vibration (p. 1).

Campbell further explains:

> We are all affected by the vibrations that govern the Universe for we are all part of it. As a part of the whole we are affected by every change in the Universal rate of vibration—and the rate changes every time there appears a different number in year, month, or day . . . Finding your own number gives you the chance to take your place in the world and keep it (p. 2).

One of the critical elements in the theory of numerology is that of the *soul urge.* Each person has a soul urge which is determined by the numbers associated with the vowels in their name given at birth. Campbell (1931) explains the soul urge as follows:

The *Soul Urge,* or Identity, is the number of your heart's desire—that which you would like best to do (or that your best self would like to have you do). It is the *motive* that lies behind your acts; the feeling and inclination you put into the day's work; your attitude toward things and people; your judgment, your principles and point of view. This is the great HOW that answers every move you make and every thought you have (p. 3).

Lopez offers the following keywords to help us to understand the nature of each personality type. The number by each statement corresponds with the number which is derived from the formula offered by numerology.

Keywords for each Soul Urge
(from Lopez, pp. 98–105)

1. Initiative, leadership, originality, creativity, self-started drive, inspirational, spontaneity, organization and self-sufficiency
2. Tact, diplomacy, coordination, negotiation, collector, and appraiser
3. Charm, culture, form-perfection, attraction powers, affability, artistic leaning, literary talents
4. Facts, logic, practicability, sobriety, partial harvests, perfection of form
5. Magnetism, nervous tension, inspirational ideas, restlessness, curiosity, inventiveness, salesmanship
6. Association, partnership, domesticity, personal adjustments, marriage and divorce, a permanent home
7. Receptivity, passiveness, secretiveness, diplomacy, and silence
8. Honor, prestige, conservatism, wealth, business, acumen, financial genius
9. Universalism, fame, artistic achievement, idealism, global consciousness
10. Analysis, inspiration, moral courage, discrimination, inventiveness, revelation

Theories such as numerology are taken seriously by many people today who are attracted to metaphysical explanations of reality. One such group are persons who publish a newsletter called *In Harmony* from Charlotte, NC. The January

1988 issue contains an article on numerology from which the instrument for the present test was derived.

Little, if any, research has been published in the social sciences literature on this theory. A search of the electronic database PsycINFO on 6-15-04 using the key word "numerology" yielded only 15 articles, none of which reported a scientific study of the validity of this theory. Most articles were reflections on science and its alternatives as a way of knowing. Wikipedia refers to numerology as a pseudoscience (http://en.wikipedia.org; retrieved 5-25-06), meaning that it is not based on science but parades as a theory that seems to be scientific. The Skeptic's Dictionary (http://skepdic.com, retrieved 5-25-06) refers to it as the study of occult meanings of numbers and their influence on human life. Neither of these sources referred to any scientific studies that had been conducted. You can receive guidance on numerology through the website http://members.aol.com/AspireA1/index2.html. This source also fails to provide any scientific evidence to support the theory, but offers testimonials.

The latter source listed the following traits that go with each of the numbers that are derived from your birth name:

1. Is ambitious, independent, and self-sufficient
2. Is supportive, diplomatic, and analytical
3. Is enthusiastic, optimistic, and fun-loving
4. Is practical, traditional, and serious
5. Is adventurous, mercurial, and sensual
6. Is responsible, careful, and domestic
7. Is spiritual, eccentric, and a bit of a loner
8. Is money-oriented, decisive, and stern
9. Is multi-talented, compassionate, and global
10. Is enlightened, intense, and high-strung

There could be a little of most of us in each statement. So finding yourself may not be easy. This serves as a source of difficulty in the use of an instrument to test the theory, but we will do our best to engage in such a study.

The Author's Testing of the Theory.   Because there seemed to be a serious absence of research on this theory, I have conducted several studies using students in a graduate social work program. These students were asked to describe themselves on the instrument found in the literature and to compare their perceptions with the number assigned to them from the theory. In other words, they were given the instrument presented in Exhibit 2.1 whereby they ranked these 10 statements. They were also give the formula from numerology that determines which number is their number based on their name given at birth. They compared to see if their first choice was the same as the number derived from the formula. The proportion of students with a match between their first choice of a profile and the number derived from the numerology formula was the basis for the test.

One such study asked 25 students (in a research course at East Carolina University in the summer of 2004) to participate in this study. If the theory of numerology is truly a profound statement of reality and if we can assume that social work students know themselves perfectly well, we could expect that all 25 students would have a match between their first choice of a personality profile (soul urge) and the numerology formula. Because there were 10 statements on the instrument, the theory can predict your number strictly by chance one time in 10. In other words, if there were only 10 percent of students with a match, this would suggest that numerology is not valid, because the data can easily be explained by chance. A percentage somewhat higher than that would also be considered too close to chance to be taken seriously. For 25 students, the "strictly chance" number of matches would be 2.5 (10 percent of 25). In this situation, numbers such as 3, 4, or 5 would also likely be considered too close to chance to be taken seriously. The study in the summer of 2004 revealed that 3 out of 25 students had a match of self-perception with the number assigned from the theory, while the others did not. When the figures of 3 out of 25 were subjected to the binomial statistical test, the results suggested, as you might already have expected, that this level of match was best explained as chance. Thus, the data did not support the theory.

In a second study, I examined three different things—the number of students who had a match between their first choice of a personality profile (soul urge) with the numerology formula, the number of students who had a match between either their first or second choice of a soul urge with the numerology formula, and the number of students who had a match between their *last* choice of a soul urge and the numerology formula. This study was conducted with a class of research students at East Carolina University on January 25, 2005. With this study, I conducted three separate analyzes of the data that were collected.

With the first analysis, I found that 3 out of 24 students had a match between their first choice and the numerology formula. This means that three students found their first choice of a personality profile was the same as the number given by the formula. These data were not found to be statistically significant. Thus, this analysis did not support the theory.

In the second analysis, I found that 9 students had a match between either their first or second choices and the numerology formula. In this case, I would expect there to be 4.8 students to have a match strictly by chance because I was comparing these students' first two choices out of 10, or the equivalent of 1 in 5, or 20 percent. Twenty percent of 24 is 4.8. In fact, I found 9 matches out of 24 students, which moves in the direction of statistical significance, but does not achieve significance at the normal standard in the social sciences of 5 times in 100 (i.e., $p < .05$).

In the third analysis, I computed the number of students who had a match between their *last* choice of a soul urge and the number derived from the theory of numerology. I was curious to know if the theory was just as likely to identify the student's last choice as their first. In fact, I found no matches between these students' last choices and the number derived from the numerology formula. So, the theory did slightly better at predicting the student's first or second choices than their last choice, which would support the theory, but statistical analysis suggests these differences can too easily be explained by chance.

In August of 2005, I conducted the same study with a group of undergraduate social work students at the University of North Carolina Wilmington. Data were collected on all 25 students who attended class on the appropriate day. Only 2 of these 25 students had a match between their first choice of a profile and the number given by the numerology formula. Only 3 out of these 25 students had a match between either their first or second profile and the number from numerology. Needless to say, neither of these analyses achieved statistical significance. So, once again, we have a failure of the data to support the theory.

I have conducted this same exercise with other classes of students, always with the same results—i.e., the data fail to support the theory.

Would Another Study Fall Into the Category of Reinventing the Wheel?   One of the common sense principles associated with scientific inquiry is "Don't reinvent the wheel," one of several principles examined in Chapter 1. This principle is secondary to others because the only consequence of this failure is the wasting of resources. It is better that we waste resources by doing a study that does not need to be done than for us to do a study that misleads us in our search for knowledge.

Discussion Box 2.2

If we replicate the study that has been conducted several times are we in danger of reinventing the wheel?

Let's Make Sure We are Using a Process of Discovery, Not Justification

The purpose of scientific inquiry is to find out; it is not to justify. It is not at all unusual for us to engage in a particular line of inquiry that is designed to prove a point. If you have any doubts about the wisdom of this assertion, ask yourself why the overwhelming majority of Democrats thought President Clinton should not be impeached, while the overwhelming majority of Republicans thought he should. Many such people presented many facts in support of their position and presented their arguments under a veil of "objectivity." To some, the facts and the constitution proved that he should be impeached. To others, the facts and the constitution proved that he should not be impeached. Why? Is it because of people's biases and their selective treatment of the facts? I think the answer is clear.

How do we avoid falling into this trap? We start with the statement of the purpose of our study. How should it be stated? Consider the following options:

1. To prove that the theory of numerology is valid
2. To prove that the theory of numerology is not valid
3. To challenge the metaphysical basis for explanation
4. None of the above

Discussion Box 2.3

What is your answer to this question? If your answer is 4, provide another statement of the purpose of this study we are about to conduct.

You should recognize quickly that the first two statements are inconsistent with the spirit of scientific inquiry. You do not conduct scientific research for the purpose of proving a point, regardless of how noble that point may be. What about number 3? Is it okay to say your purpose is to challenge a particular basis for explanation? Don't you believe that science is a better way of explaining things than metaphysical thought, with its avoidance of evidence as a test of a particular point of view?

I once read a statement in the introduction to a published study in which the author asserted an intent to challenge a certain criticism of social work as a profession. This was a report of a research study, not an essay. I was uneasy with that statement because it seems inconsistent with the spirit of scientific inquiry. It seemed to me to be a veiled assertion that the author's intent was to prove a point.

You should not state your purpose in such a way that only one of two possible outcomes would be considered successful. Suppose we like the theory of numerology. If we fail to find evidence in support of numerology, has our study failed? If we don't like the theory, would a finding in support of the theory mean we have failed? The answer to each should be *no*. If our data support the theory of numerology, we have contributed to the knowledge base about them. The same is true if our data fail to support it.

A second way we avoid the trap of justification rather than discovery is through the methods we use to test the theory. If our methods are consistent with the stated purpose of testing the theory rather than proving it is valid or not, we will develop a methodology for our study that provides a fair test of the theory. The methods should not make it more or less likely that a certain outcome will be achieved. Further, we should develop methods that reduce the potential of human error in observation.

We could ask you to give your opinion about this theory. We could report the results as our test of this theory. We might discover that three-fourths of those in our sample of human service professionals do not believe the theory to be valid; thus, we conclude that it is not valid. This would be a method that did little to reduce human error in observation.

Another study procedure would be to give you the statement from the list in Exhibit 2.1 that the theory of numerology says best describes you, and then ask you to agree or disagree with it. This procedure would have the flaw of giving you information about what you are supposed to be like and then asking you if it is true. This would solicit a social desirability bias because some people want to offer answers that are socially desirable. Any list like that in Exhibit 2.1 will have several statements that describe us to some extent. If we have already been told what the theory says we are, we just might lean in that direction without recognizing anything about social desirability. Our attention might be pulled in a certain direction. Instead, we are using a procedure that solicits an observation that is considered "independent." Instead of the above options, we are using a method that asks you to respond to the instrument about your traits before you know what the theory says about you and before you are told about the theory.

Are We Putting the Cart Before the Horse?

Our process of study began with a curiosity about the theory of numerology. It appears that a good number of people believe it is valid. I have known a few graduate social work students who believed in this theory. A spouse of a close friend was an adherent to this theory. But this theory is not based on scientific studies. So, we decided to conduct this study. Its purpose is to test the validity of the theory of numerology. The sample will be students in the course using this text. Because this theory is posed as universal, there is no reason to believe the test of it should be conducted with special attention to the nature of the sample. However, this sample will not be a random one, so we will be able to generalize our findings only with caution. The methods for testing this theory were developed after the purpose of the study was articulated. Individuals will respond to an instrument taken from a writer on the theory of numerology that supposedly depicts one's "soul urge," or general personality. They will also respond to an instrument that determines their own soul urge as determined by the theory. These will be compared to see if they are consistent. Inconsistency between the study sample's self-descriptions and the theory's descriptions will be viewed as failure to support the theory, while consistency would be viewed as the opposite.

Are we putting the cart before the horse? We did not decide to use a particular instrument and then decide what purpose we should have for the study. We did not draw conclusions about this theory before testing it, even though we may have an initial opinion about it. The important thing is not whether we had an opinion but what we did with it. We are not entering this process (I hope you are with me here!) with the idea that we will prove (or disprove) it and will interpret our data in this light without giving the theory a fair test.

I once told a fellow professor, who I knew had an affinity to metaphysical thought, about a similar study when I experimented with another group of students. I wanted his advice on whether my methodology constituted a fair test of the theory. I had already collected my data but I did not tell him the results. He asked for the results before responding to my question about fairness of method. I refused to tell him the results because I wanted his independent appraisal of the methodology. He replied that he thought it was a fair test. However, I am convinced that if I had told him the results, which did not support the theory, he would have become biased in his appraisal of my methods. This is the classic response of those who are prejudiced—if you don't like the message, attack the messenger. In this case, if you don't like the results of a study, attack the methods used in the study.

Discussion Box 2.4

Consider the study procedures noted. Does this constitute a fair test of the theory? Are we in danger of putting the cart before the horse?

The Next Steps in Our Study Process

There are several steps in our study of the theory of numerology. First, we examined the nature of the theory and found scientific research to be insufficient. Next, we designed a study that called for a group of persons to respond to an instrument about personality profiles relevant to the theory. They were asked to rank order 10 statements.

Our next steps call upon you and your classmates to determine the number from the theory of numerology that is derived from the formula based on your name given a birth. Following that procedure, we will combine the data of all students in class and subject these data to statistical analysis.

We have examined several basic principles that guide the spirit of scientific inquiry. We have reason to believe we are following a process of discovery rather than justification because we are attempting to test a theory rather than prove it or disprove it. We are not reinventing the wheel because we believe there is a need for further investigation of this theory, even though we are familiar with a few such attempts to test it. We are not putting the cart before the horse because we have determined the study purpose before we have designed the study (which will be addressed in this section), and because we have decided that we will only draw conclusions after we have analyzed the data.

There are two basic principles left for consideration: "Some things happen just by chance," and "When we engage in scientific research, we should be rather cautious in our conclusions." Before we apply these principles, we must collect data.

The first step in the testing of the theory was completed when you responded to the instrument at the beginning of this chapter. You should have ranked the 10 statements in Exhibit 2.1, with the number 1 assigned to the statement most like yourself, the number 2 to the next best description, and so forth.

Your next step is to determine the soul urge derived from the theory of numerology. You will do this by responding to the instructions in Exhibit 2.3 and inserting your information in the tables that follow this exhibit.

EXHIBIT 2.3 • *Determining Your Personality (Soul Urge) as Determined by the Theory*

To determine your soul urge as determined by the theory of numerology:

1. Print out your full name as given at birth.
   Example: AMELIA CLARE BRONN
2. Circle each vowel in your full name: *a, e, i, o, u,* and sometimes *y* (when pronounced like a letter that is a vowel, such as when it is pronounced as the letter *e*).

3. Using the numbering scheme below, place the appropriate number above each vowel in your name. For example, the letter A has the number 1, the letter M has the number 4, and so forth.

Letter	Number	Letter	Number	Letter	Number	Letter	Number	Letter	Number
A	1	G	7	M	4	S	1	Y	7
B	2	H	8	N	5	T	2	Z	8
C	3	I	9	O	6	U	3		
D	4	J	1	P	7	V	4		
E	5	K	2	Q	8	W	5		
F	6	L	3	R	9	X	6		

The chart below uses the name AMELIA CLARE BRONN and illustrates the numbers to be assigned to the letters.

#	1		5		9	1		1		5		6	
Ltr	A	M	E	L	I	A	C	L	A	R	E	B	R	O	N	N

4. Add up these numbers for each name and reduce this number to its final number by adding the two figures together if they number more than 9. For example, the name AMELIA has the numbers 1, 5, 9, and 1. When you add these together, the result is 16. But 16 is greater than 9. Therefore, you add these two numbers to determine the value given by the name AMELIA; you add 1 and 6 and get the number 7.

Example

AMELIA = 7	(1 + 5 + 9 + 1 = 16)
	(1 + 6 = 7)
CLARE = 6	(1 + 5 = 6)
BRONN = 6	

5. Add these numbers together: 7 + 6 + 6 = 19.
6. Reduce this number to its final number by adding the two numbers together if the figure is greater than 9, as done in step 4.

Example

1 + 9 = 10

1 + 0 = 1   This person's soul urge is 1.

An exception is the case of the numbers 11 and 22, which are not to be reduced to their final numbers, but which remain as they are. Unfortunately, if your final number is 22, you cannot be included in the present study. This is due to the need to simplify the methodology for the purpose of this exercise.

Calculating the Number of Your Soul Urge

To determine your soul urge from the numerology formula, present your name, given at birth, in Table 2.1, beginning with your first name. Place your first name in the first table, your second name in the second table, and your third name in the third. If you have more names, construct another table. You should use your name given at birth, not a name you took later in life. After you have placed your first name in the first table, find each letter that is a vowel (*a, e, i, o, u*, and sometimes *y*) and find its number from the chart of numbers given in Exhibit 2.3. If there is the letter *e* in your name, the number for this letter would be 5. The letter *p* is not a vowel, so it would get no points. Repeat this procedure for each of your names.

Reduce these numbers to their final number if any one is higher than 9. Place your initial number from Table 2.1 for your first name in the row labeled First name and the column labeled initial number assigned in Table 2.2. If this number is greater than 9, it should be

TABLE 2.1

First Name															
Letter in your name →															
Number for this letter →															
Second Name															
Letter in your name →															
Number for this letter →															
Third Name															
Letter in your name →															
Number for this letter →															

reduced by adding the two numbers together. The reduced number is placed in the third column or the initial number is placed here if it was not reduced. Add these reduced numbers and enter this number in the cell in the bottom right.

If the number from the procedure is greater than 9, it will need to be reduced to your final number by the same procedure, adding the two numbers together.

Taking into Consideration that Some Things Happen Just by Chance

The next step in Study 1 is to subject the data of yourself and your classmates to statistical analysis. The numbers assigned to the self-descriptions in Exhibit 2.2 correspond to the soul urge. In other words, if your soul urge is 4, then the theory of numerology tells us that you are supposed to be like the description given for the number four. The person with a soul urge of 4, according to Numerology, "wants respectability and solidity; wants to be a rock of dependability . . ." and so forth. Our research question is whether your choice of a personality profile (soul urge) matches with the number derived from the numerology formula presented.

TABLE 2.2

	Initial Number Assigned	Number After Reduction
First name		
Second name		
Third name		
TOTAL	xxxxxxxxxxxxxxxxxxxxxxxxxxxxxxxxx	

Enter your soul urge derived from the numerology formula here → _____

Return to Exhibit 2.1 and find the statements that were among your first five choices. You will be dividing these statements into two groups, one for those in the high category (first five selections) and one in the low category. Was the number derived from the numerology formula in the top group? If not, you did not have a match. If so, you would be considered to be one of those study subjects with a match.

Did you find a match between the number given from the numerology formula and your top five choices of a personality profile (soul urge)? If the formula indicated that your number was 3, you should look to see if the statement numbered 3 (Exhibit 2.1) was in your top five choices. If you had ranked statement number 3 as your first choice, your second, your third, your fourth, or your fifth, you would be among those students with a match with the theory. If you are a match, you have little reason to make a big deal about it because the numerology formula had a 50–50 likelihood of matching just by chance. You have to combine your data with others in order to test the theory.

When you combine your data with those of your fellow study subjects, you will review the number with a match and the number without a match. If the proportion of matched study subjects is less than 50 percent of the total number of study subjects, we will conclude that our data failed to support the theory because the theory had a 50–50 likelihood of matching just by chance, in view of the fact that have reduced our data to only two categories.

What if the proportion of students with a match is greater than 50 percent? This would suggest the data are in the direction of supporting the theory. But it must be significantly better than this 50 percent rate in order for us to declare statistical significance and conclude that our data supported the theory.

For this task we will turn to the binomial test, a statistical test that determines the likelihood that the number of persons in each of two groups is significantly different from a 50–50 split (50 percent). If we have 20 students in our class, we would expect 10 matches strictly by chance. But 11 matches would still not be good enough to meet the .05 standard in the social sciences. In other words, 11 matches is too close to 10 in order for us to declare statistical significance.

In Table 2.3 you can find the information on statistical significance using the binomial test when the known probability is .50 (50 percent). The first column shows the total number of persons in the study. In column 2 is the number of matched students needed to achieve statistical significance at the .05 level. The third column indicates the number of matched students needed to achieve statistical significance at the .10 level, just in case you are feeling generous with the theory. You should start with the number of persons in your class and read across

TABLE 2.3   *Statistical Table of Binomial Test When Known Probability is .50.**

Number of persons in the study	Number of matches needed to achieve significance at .05	Number of matches needed to achieve significance at .10
10	8	8
11	9	9
12	10	9
13	10	10
14	10	10
15	11	11
16	12	11
17	13	12
18	13	13
19	14	13
20	14	14
21	15	14
22	16	15
23	16	15
24	17	16
25	17	17

*The above data are derived from Table D of Sidney Siegel (1960), *Nonparametric statistics for the behavioral sciences.* New York: McGraw-Hill.

to determine the number of matched students needed for significance at the two levels (i.e., .05 and .10). The number of matches enumerated reveals the minimum number needed. If you have a number of matches that is greater, you have achieved statistical significance. In fact, a greater number of matches would suggest a greater level of statistical significance.

From Table 2.3 you can see that a class of 10 students would have data that supported the theory if 8 or more of these students had a match between the number from the numerology formula and one of their top five choices of a soul urge. For a class of 22 students, support for the theory would result from our having 16 (or more) students with a match. This statement is predicated on the assumption that we are employing the normal standard for statistical significance ($p < .05$). If, however, we are employing a more generous standard of .10, we would have support for the theory if 15 students had a match.

Be sure to keep in mind that you have achieved statistical significance if your number of matches is at the level suggested above or better (i.e., more matches than the minimum needed).

Discussion Box 2.5

After you have had the opportunity to collect data from your group, answer the following question: What were the results of your study? Did your data support the theory? Explain.

We're Wearing the Research Hat, So Let's Be Sure We are Cautious in Our Conclusions

Well, what did you find? Did the data support the theory of numerology? How would you interpret the data? What conclusions would you draw? Don't forget that the principle "When we wear the research hat, we should be cautious in our conclusions." One set of data does not support definitive conclusions. Instead, it provides support for a given proposition or it fails to support this proposition. In our case, we are asking if our data supported the theory of numerology.

First, did our data support the theory? If it did, can we say we *proved* that numerology was valid? Can we draw a definitive conclusion like that? If we are cautious we will not say something like that. We should be equally cautious if our data fail to support the theory. We should not say we have *proved* that numerology was not valid. Instead, we should say that our data failed to support this theory.

Please note the limitations of this study's methodology. We only tested one aspect of the theory of numerology. We only tested this aspect of the theory with one method. We could have thought of any number of other ways to submit this theory to testing.

Discussion Box 2.6

In the box, fill in the blanks for one approach to the summary of this study. If you prefer, you can prepare the entire summary yourself without reference to the content given.

In the study reported in this paper, the theory of _____ was tested. This theory suggests that one's personality, known as the _____urge, is determined by the _____ associated with the letters from the vowels in one's name given at _____. The study sample included persons from _____. These individuals determined which of a set of _____ statements were most like themselves, and then determined the appropriate number for themselves by reference to a formula derived from the theory of _____. The preferences for self-descriptions from these individuals were compared to the number from the theory to determine if the number from the theory matched with any of their first _____ choices of a personality profile, or soul urge in the language of the theory.

In this study, there were _____ study subjects, _____ of whom had a match between the number from the theory's formula and one of their top five choices. Because there were _____ total items to choose from and the comparison was between the study subject's top five choices and the selection from the theory, there would be an expected match for _____ percent of the study subjects, strictly by chance. Matches for proportions of students slightly higher than this percent would also be too close to chance for these data to support the theory. The results revealed that the data _____ (did/did not) support the theory because the proportion of matches _____ (was/was not) significantly higher than chance at the normal level for determining statistical significance in the social sciences (i.e., $p < .05$).

One of the limitations of this study is _____.

I suggest that you reflect on this experience by responding to the quiz below.

Quiz

The following questions cover the exercise from this chapter. It can serve as your review of the nature of the study contained in the exercise. Answers are given at the end.

1. Which of the following would be statements of the purpose of our study of numerology that would be consistent with the spirit of scientific inquiry?
   a. The purpose of this study is to find support for the theory of numerology.
   b. The purpose of this study is to challenge the metaphysical way of thinking.
   c. Both of the above.
   d. Neither of the above.
2. Suppose that the first step in our study had been to determine that we wanted to conduct a study of the theory of numerology that entailed interviews of students in our class. What common sense principle would we have violated?
   a. The principle that research is a process of discovery rather than justification
   b. The principle that two heads are better than one
   c. The principle that you should not put the cart before the horse
   d. The principle that some things happen just by chance
3. Which of the following ethical principles in research was violated in our study?
   a. The principle related to voluntary participation
   b. The principle related to avoidance of harm
   c. The principle related to privacy
   d. None of the above
4. Which of the following statements is/are true?
   a. It would have improved the study methodology if participants had been told their number from the numerology formula before they responded to the instrument that called upon them to rank the 10 statements based on their self-perceptions.
   b. It would have improved the study methodology if the study participants had

compared their self-perceptions to the perceptions of themselves held by close friends, because two heads are better than one.
   c. Both of the above.
   d. None of the above.
5. Suppose that you had 20 students in your class and found that 11 students had a match between one of their first five choices of a soul urge and the number from the numerology formula. Suppose further that these data had been subjected to statistical analysis and you found that 11 out of 20 is not significantly different from 10 out of 20. Would you have support for the theory?
   a. Yes, because 11 out of 20 is better than 10 out of 20, which is the number that would be strictly chance.
   b. Yes, because you have support for the theory if anyone has a match between their first five choices and the numerology formula.
   c. No, because there must be 20 out of 20 in order for our data to support the theory.
   d. No, because our data is too easily explained by chance.
6. Given the fact that the author presented data on three studies of this theory, each of which had failed to support the theory of numerology, which common sense principle is the one most likely violated in this study?
   a. The principle that research is a process of discovery rather than justification
   b. The principle that two heads are better than one
   c. The principle that you should not reinvent the wheel
   d. The principle that some things happen just by chance
7. Suppose that you found a match between your first choice of a soul urge with the number from the numerology formula. Should you conclude that this theory must have something

of value to offer because it knew who you were, even if the data for the entire class failed to support the theory?

a. Yes, because any one piece of data should be respected according to the principles of science.

b. Yes, because we don't want to reinvent the wheel.

c. No, because two heads are better than one.

d. No, because some things happen just by chance.

8. Let's assume that someone conducted a study using the methodology employed in our study and found a statistically significant number of persons with a match between their personality profile choices (soul urges) and the number assigned by the numerology formula. Suppose, further, that this researcher had concluded that "the theory of numerology has been proven to be valid and there is no doubt it will clearly be a helpful guide for understanding ourselves." Which common sense principle would have been violated by this statement?

a. When you wear the research hat, you should be cautious in your conclusions.

b. Two heads are better than one.

c. You should not put the cart before the horse.

d. None of the above.

References

Campbell, F. (1931). *Your days are numbered.* Frendale, PA: Gateway.

Lopez, V. (1961). *Numerology.* New York: Citadel Press.

York, R. O. (1997). *Building basic competencies in social work research.* Boston: Allyn & Bacon.

Answers to the Quiz

1. d

2. c

3. d

4. b

5. d

6. c

7. d

8. a

3

An Overview of Evaluation Research

In this chapter, you will be given an overview of evaluation research. You will see that evaluation is an assessment of value. You will note that the scope of an evaluation can focus on broad programs (e.g., child protective services) or clinical assessments (e.g., How well is multi-systemic therapy working for my group of eight clients?). You will examine four types of evaluation—input, process, output, and outcome. And you will consider three selected models for evaluation. There is a quiz at the end of this chapter which you can use either as a pretest or a posttest. If you use it as a pretest, you may do so well that you realize you already know the content of this chapter. If you use it as a posttest, you can see how well you have acquired the knowledge presented.

At the completion of this chapter, you will be able to:

1. Define the concept of evaluation and describe its essential nature.

2. Identify the four key questions that are answered by typical evaluations.

3. Distinguish among input, process, output, and outcome evaluations.

4. Distinguish between program evaluation and clinical evaluation.

5. Identify the essential steps in the evaluation of outcome.

6. Articulate the essential connections among the critical phases in the evaluation process.

7. Identify the strengths and weaknesses regarding the evaluation of client satisfaction.

8. Distinguish among case studies, experiments, and utilization-focused evaluation as selected models for evaluation of human services, and identify how each is conducted.

What Is Evaluation?

In previous chapters, you have seen that evaluation research is a special type of research that involves some efforts to improve social behavior. Evaluation research focuses on an intervention. It goes beyond the description of things and is not concerned with the testing of general theories of social behavior or their development. Instead, it is used to help us learn how well interventions are working and how we can improve them. All evaluation studies have relevance to an identified intervention or program.

Evaluation is essentially a judgment—we use it to determine worth or value. We cannot evaluate without applying some standard of propriety or efficacy. The statement "Twenty percent of our clients have preschool age children" is not an evaluative statement. It is merely a statement of a fact. The statement "Twenty percent of our clients indicate they would recommend our agency to their friends" is a statement that moves in the direction of evaluation, but it is not complete because there is no standard included in this statement that can be used to judge whether this is good news or bad. Now, let's examine this statement: "Surveys have found that our clients are twice as likely to recommend our agency to others than similar agencies in neighboring counties." This statement has a standard for comparison—a basis for judgment. Comparisons can be made to other agencies, to the nature of things in our agency a year ago, to established expectations as dictated by goals or objectives, or to a certain national standard. But you cannot say you have a fully competent evaluative statement without some basis for judgment.

The two major purposes of evaluation are to determine the extent to which objectives have been achieved and to discover ideas for improvement. Evaluation, as discussed in this book, is founded upon the principles of science. The purpose of scientific inquiry is to control, as much as is feasible, the subjectivity that is inherent in the judgment of worth. It is not reasonable to expect that the scientific method will eliminate subjectivity from evaluation. Instead, this method should reduce the subjectivity inherent in the assessment of worth by offering a systematic method of inquiry that enhances the transparency of our means for coming to our conclusions. Thus, we will distinguish evaluation *research* from other uses of evaluation with reference to the systematic collection and analysis of data in a manner that is consistent with the spirit of scientific inquiry. This text focuses on evaluation research rather than clinical case evaluation as it may be practiced by clinical staff on a regular basis through various forms of discussion.

Discussion Box 3.1

Indicate whether a study of the relationship between gender and salary is an example of an evaluation study.

Discussion Box 3.2
_____

Indicate what is missing from the statement "54 percent of our clients indicate they would recommend our agency to their friends."

Key Questions in Evaluation

Evaluation entails the assessment of how things are going. One way to put it is that evaluation is an assessment of worth. We need to know how we are doing. We can examine this topic from a systems perspective. A client comes to the agency for help. In systems terminology, this refers to **input**. We offer services, which can be classified as **process**. These services can be quantified in a certain way, such as an hour of counseling or a child abuse investigation completed. In systems terminology, we would label this quantification as **output**. These outputs are supposed to achieve certain **outcomes**, such as the improvement of the client's self-esteem, the reduction of high-school dropouts, the improvement of medical compliance for discharged patients, or the improvement of social support for victims of violence.

There are a number of prominent questions that we are called upon to answer in the assessment of human services. They are as follows:

1. Are persons in our target groups making use of our services? In other words, are we reaching those most in need?
2. Are clients satisfied?
3. Have our clients experienced a gain?
4. Were the client gains caused by our services?

There are a several types of information that are used for each of the above questions. For question 1, it is expected that agencies collect information on the number, and characteristics, of the clients served. These data are descriptive in nature. For the client satisfaction question, the survey is often used. This is also descriptive in nature because we are typically describing the clients' level of satisfaction rather than measuring client growth. We get into a different type of data when we pursue questions 3 and 4, because we begin to include the idea of statistical significance (chance) in our analysis.

How Well are Our Services Reaching the Target Population?

Most funding sources require data on client characteristics and the service that has been delivered. This typically refers to such client characteristics as gender, race or ethnicity, income level, and family structure (e.g., proportion of one-parent families served). Also included in service statistics would be the nature of the services that have been used by clients. You might need to report the number of clients receiving counseling services or employment support services or discharge planning services. You also might need to quantify these services by reference to a unit of service. This might include such data as the number of clients served, the number of hours of counseling service delivered, the number of referrals made to other services, or the number of child abuse investigations completed.

Service statistics often are compared to some norm, such as the data from previous years or the data from similar agencies. The main issue is the extent to which the services of the agency are being used by the intended target audience. If few low-income clients are using your counseling services, questions may be raised by your funding source. If intake has gone down gradually over the past three years, you may have trouble maintaining the same amount of funding support you have received in the past.

Are Clients Satisfied?

Funding sources also want to know if clients are satisfied. This will vary with the type of funding source and the nature of the service. Client satisfaction is typically measured by surveys, sometimes mailed and sometimes given to the client in the office. Client opinions about the acceptability of the services delivered provide an important source of information, but are somewhat limited as a measure of program outcome, because they are vulnerable to the social desirability bias. Satisfaction surveys can be improved, as a measure of outcome, by specific questions that address behaviors in a somewhat concrete way, especially if they ask the client to reflect upon their condition prior to service. This topic will receive elaboration under the topic of measuring client growth.

Have Our Clients Experienced Growth?

The outcome objectives for a program or intervention specify the client growth that is expected from the service that will be delivered. In a fundamental way, we can assess client gain either retrospectively or prospectively. For the former, after service has been completed, we simply ask clients to reflect on their condition prior to service and again after service has been delivered. We treat the first as the client's condition prior to treatment (pretest score) and their second assessment as the condition after treatment (posttest score).

Another way to measure client growth, considered more legitimate by evaluation professionals, is to measure these gains prospectively. This means asking the clients to assess themselves at the beginning of service, and again at the end of service. The difference is that you are asking clients to report at two points in time rather than only at the end of service. Most evaluation professionals would consider this approach to be better because it would be viewed as less vulnerable to the social desirability bias—the tendency to respond according to that which is considered more socially acceptable than the truth. However, more research should be conducted to put this assumption to the test of scientific inquiry. I am not as concerned as most professional about this issue; I am not sure this is a safe assumption.

Did the Service Cause the Client Growth?

The final and key question focuses on whether the clients' measured growth was caused by the services that we offered. The question of causality requires that we take into consideration the fact that clients sometimes get better without service. My depression may go down without your psychotherapy service; I may get a job without your employment support service; I may comply with the suggested medical treatment without your medical social work service.

A way we address this issue is by using a comparison group. A comparison group is a group of people who did not receive the service. If this group achieved a 10 percent gain, we should compare the level of gain of our clients to a 10 percent gain, rather than a 0 gain, as would be the case if we merely measured our clients before and after treatment. In this way, we are controlling for some of the things that cause client change other than service.

The Scope of Evaluation Research

An evaluation can focus on a program or a clinical experience. The evaluation of the extent to which your therapy with Paul Jones had the intended effect of reducing his performance anxiety would be an example of a clinical evaluation study. The evaluation of your group therapy with a group of women suffering from post-partum depression would be another example of a clinical evaluation. But the assessment of the extent to which the Dropout Prevention Program for the Brown County School System had improved self-esteem, study habits, grades, and general behavior for youth at risk of dropping out of school would be an example of a program evaluation. The latter is broader in scope.

The Nature of Program Evaluation Research

What is a program? A **program** is an *organized set of activities designed to achieve a particular goal or a set of objectives.* The activities are interdependent in that they depend upon one another for the achievement of the objectives. A program has an identity and specified resources. Programs within an agency or system can be conceptualized at various levels. You may be working with a support group for abused women. You could employ the methods of clinical evaluation described in the previous chapters to this intervention. However, this intervention most likely is a part of an overall program of services for addressing the needs of victims of violence. While you could call this support group a program, this term is normally used to describe something bigger, with various parts.

A **program evaluation** is *an effort to apply the principles of scientific inquiry to program decision making.* For example, program managers need to know the character and incidence of the needs associated with target problems. They need to identify the characteristics of effective service so that programs can be well designed. And they need to be able to justify their programs by demonstrating that they have been effective in meeting human needs.

In this chapter, program evaluation will be discussed with regard to the evaluation of need, the evaluation of service process, and the evaluation of client outcome. Project PARENTING is a program designed to alleviate the negative social consequences of adolescent parenthood.

These consequences include child neglect and public dependency. This program offers classroom instruction on parenting, supervised training in a day care center, and in-home modeling of good parenting practices. How could Project PARENTING have been evaluated with regard to input or process? A need assessment could have been undertaken in which the extent of need for parent training for adolescent mothers would have been measured. How many adolescent mothers does this community have? What is the extent of parenting skills of these mothers? What proportion has a serious deficit in skills? What obstacles to improvement do they tend to face?

Service process could have been evaluated through the monitoring of service activities to obtain information on the extent to which the components of the program were implemented according to design. The characteristics of clients who achieved the most gain or participated most fully could have been identified. Client interactions with others could have been observed so that a portrait of the service process for the typical client could have been painted for the purpose of adding insight into how this process might be improved. The cost per client served could be compared to the same costs of other alternatives for achieving the same objectives. Perhaps short-term participation could be compared to long-term participation to see if long-term intervention, which costs more, achieved significantly more gain than short-term.

The evaluation of outcome entails the measurement of client gain, or the achievement of the program's objectives in some other way. For Project PARENTING, it could involve the comparison of clients' scores on parenting skills after treatment with the same scores before treatment. It could include the comparison of parenting skills of clients with nonclients.

An illustration of the various points for collecting evaluative data can be found in York (1998, p. 145) regarding the evaluation of a health education program:

1. A substantial number of persons has to be exposed to the program's message. Use survey research to determine how many people were exposed.
2. A substantial proportion of these people has to pay attention to the message. Use survey research to determine how many people paid attention to the message.
3. They have to understand the message. Use survey research to see how many people understand the message (e.g., by asking persons questions about the program).
4. They have to attend the clinic which the message encouraged them to do. Survey the persons attending the clinic. How many did so as a result of the health education program?
5. If they have a disease, it must be detected. Use program data. How many diseases have been detected in those persons attending as a result of the health program?
6. They must follow the medical advice obtained at the clinic. Use follow-up data on persons attending the clinic to discover if they followed the advice.
7. The disease must be favorably altered as a consequence of the program. Use long-term follow-up data by medical personnel to learn if the disease was successfully altered among the group attending as a result of the health education program.

These steps do not directly address the evaluation of need. However, there probably was an assessment of need prior to the development of the health education program that was the focus of this list. Furthermore, information from each step in this evaluation could generate need information to be used in the future.

This list covers a wide range of information, some of which goes beyond normal accountability for evaluating an educational program. Let's assume we have a Health Education Program that is a part of our Health Program. All seven of the listed types of information would be relevant to the evaluation of the Health Program, which has a broad goal related to the improvement of health. The first four items are directly related to the Health Education Program. It is possible that health education is effective in getting the message out that draws people to the clinic, but it is also possible that the clinic does a poor job of treating people's health. If you were the director of the Health Education Program, you would probably only want to be held accountable for the first four items in the list. If people attend the clinic because of the message, your program has done its job. However, if the clinic is not effective, your efforts are in vain.

This discussion is relevant to the question of goals and objectives for programs. The goal of a program is the long-range statement of major outcome, whereas the objective is a measured amount of progress toward the achievement of that goal. The Health Education Program might have a goal to improve the health of the community, and the major outcome objective of increasing the knowledge of people about prevention strategies. The program manager for the Health Education Program should be sure to measure the achievement of the outcome objective, and should pay attention to information related to the ultimate health outcomes documented by the health information system. Information that indicates how the service process was carried out could be the focus of a set of process objectives.

The Nature of Clinical Evaluation Research

A clinical evaluation is one that is done to determine how well a specific intervention is working and to get ideas on how it could be improved. It is less broad in scope than a program evaluation. It could be used with a single client for the purpose of improving treatment. For example, a single-system evaluation can take the form of collecting baseline data (before treatment begins) for a single client, then collecting data during the treatment period, then changing treatment, then collecting more data to see if the change in treatment is working better for the client.

Clinical evaluations can focus on a single client or a group of clients. When it focuses on a group of clients, the distinctions between clinical evaluation and program evaluation can become a little blurred. As mentioned in the previous section, a program can be conceptualized at various levels. Whether you wish to conceptualize your treatment of eight patients in a nursing home with reality orientation as a clinical encounter or a program is your choice. The purpose here is to point out the various scopes of evaluation studies.

A major consideration that often distinguishes the clinical evaluation from the program evaluation is that you will often find it useful in the clinical evaluation study to begin with the task of identifying the sample. Following this identification, you might find it most useful to move to the examination of the target behavior, the selection of the intervention, and so forth. We often find it most useful, however, to begin our evaluation study of a program with the examination of the target behavior and the intervention, which is followed by a selection of a study sample to employ in the assessment of the extent to which the program has been effective.

Discussion Box 3.3

Indicate whether an evaluation of the services of the County Department Services in the investigation of child abuse and neglect and the offering of treatment to relevant families is an example of a program evaluation or a clinical evaluation. Outcomes assessed will include child abuse recidivism for this county.

Distinguishing Clinical Evaluation Research from Ongoing Case Evaluation. Clinical supervision in human services usually includes some type of case evaluation. This supervision normally takes the form of a clinician offering a case study for discussion to a supervisor or the treatment team of the agency. The clinician offers information about the client's progress for discussions. This information may lead to a recommendation for service referral, service termination, or a change in the nature of the service. You can say that this dialogue is evaluative in nature because you are speaking of the client's progress in regard to the target behavior. *But this is not an example of a clinical evaluation research study.*

A clinical evaluation research study entails the systematic collection and analysis of data. If we are speaking of a single case, the data on target behavior would be collected repeatedly on this single case and these data would be subjected to some form of analysis. This would normally include the analysis of statistical significance. While it would not be typical of clinical research, you could engage in a qualitative analysis of client data in conducting a clinical evaluation research study. But to qualify as clinical research, you would need to have a systematic analysis of your qualitative data, employing a recognized qualitative data analysis protocol. Clinical evaluation discussions among professionals do not qualify.

Types of Evaluation

There are numerous types of evaluations you could undertake. You may be called upon to evaluate need. An essential connection between need assessment and the evaluation of outcome is the issue of how society's mechanisms of helping have had an impact upon a given need. You may be interested in evaluating service process to determine how well staff are implementing what they are supposed to implement and to gain knowledge of how to make services better. Or, you may want to evaluate outcome. Increasingly, human service practitioners and human service programs are being called upon to demonstrate their achievement of client outcomes.

We can use the systems model to illustrate the variety of types of evaluations one might undertake in human services. This includes reference to input, process, output, and outcome as depicted below.

Input → Process → Output → Outcome

The client comes to the human service practitioner with a need (input) and receives a service (process) which can be quantified in regard to product (output), which hopefully is effective in meeting client need (outcome).

The human service evaluator could evaluate client need to determine how services should be designed or how well present services are meeting this need. What is the incidence of child abuse or alcoholism in your community? Has this changed over the previous years as different programs were implemented? What are the special needs of persons confirmed as child abusers, or children who have been abused? These are among the questions that could be pursued in an input evaluation. Keep in mind, however, that need assessment is only considered to be an evaluation study to the extent that it focuses information on social programs or interventions—i.e., it analyzes data relevant to a social remedy for a given problem.

The service system provides a service to meet that need. It designs and delivers a process that is supposed to respond to client need. You could evaluate the extent to which certain services are delivered according to acceptable standards. Do practitioners have certain credentials, such as licensure, or certain educational degrees? Are services delivered according to a recognized protocol? These are process-oriented evaluation questions.

The service is delivered in regard to outputs, or products, such as an hour of counseling, or a child abuse investigation completed, or a child placed for adoption. You could evaluate the amount of the outputs delivered, or the extent of the efficiency of service delivery by computing the cost per output. These would be output-oriented evaluation questions. Some who write about the systems model would suggest that products and outcomes are both examples of output, but I prefer to distinguish between these two measures of success.

The service is supposed to achieve an outcome, such as enhanced marital harmony, improved school grades, enhanced self-esteem, reduced depression, and so forth. It is the evaluation of outcome that receives the greater share of the attention in this text. In the next sections, you will explore each of these types of evaluation in more detail.

Discussion Box 3.4

Give an example of an evaluation that would be classified as either a process evaluation or an outcome evaluation, and indicate the label for this example (either process or outcome).

The Evaluation of Need

A need is a gap between what is and what should be. A need assessment is an attempt to identify the community's perceptions of gaps and to measure them. What one identifies as a need, another may not. What is generally recognized as a need in a given community may not be recognized in another community. What is recognized today as a need (or a social problem) may not have been recognized as such 50 years ago.

Needs arise from social problems, the latter being defined as an undesirable condition of the individual or the environment. We normally recognize unemployment as a problem. Society's goal regarding this problem is to reduce it as much as possible. The needs of the unemployed could entail skill development, enhanced motivation, increased self-confidence, improved knowledge about job openings, transportation, and so forth.

Social problems and social needs serve as guides for program goals and objectives. The goal of an employment training program might be to reduce unemployment or to place certain persons into jobs while the objectives might be to improve job interviewing skills, or job motivation, or knowledge of job openings, and so forth.

You can assess need through both quantitative and qualitative approaches to measurement. When you measure something quantitatively, you are placing people or things into various predetermined categories (e.g., male or female) or giving a score of some kind (e.g., score on the Beck Depression Inventory). When you measure something qualitatively, you are reviewing words or images that characterize something about the people being observed.

Quantitative measurements of need utilize such data sources as the number of people on the waiting list for a service, agency records on the types of services requested and utilized, demographic reports such as the census, and the social survey. Some of these sources of information could employ qualitative methods. For example, a social survey could use open-ended questions and narrative text in agency records could be subjected to content analysis. But these sources normally are used to collect quantitative data.

Among the qualitative approaches to needs assessment are public hearings, interviews of key informants or clients, focus groups, and the nominal group technique. These approaches are better suited for the identification of the nature of need and to unearth new needs than for the precise measurement of it, the latter being better served by quantitative methods.

Service statistics probably serve as the most prevalent means of needs assessment for the human services. There is no more powerful indicator of need than the extent to which a given service has been requested by people in the community. If people view something as a need, they are likely to express this view through a request. Furthermore, if they make a request, they are more likely to make use of the service. A waiting list is the foremost measure of unmet need for most human services.

This source of information on need has the limitation of missing need that is perceived but not turned into action through a request. One of the reasons that a perceived need is not turned into action is that people may not know that the service exists, or, in fact, a service for this need may not exist. In this case, people do not have the opportunity to make their need known.

Needs that are not yet served can be assessed through social surveys. The citizens of a given community can be asked to respond to a questionnaire related to a given type of need. The social survey is especially useful in this regard. It is also useful in the collection of information on the extent to which a problem (or need) exists in a community. Some people who have a need and know about a service that addresses it do not request that service. How many such people are there in a given community? What are the reasons they have not requested the service? These are among the questions that can be answered through a social survey.

Another quantitative approach to needs assessment is the demographic report, best exemplified by the census. From such sources, you can obtain information on the characteristics of the community that are most relevant to a given need. For example, knowing how many children under school age are living in a household under a certain income level in a given county can assist in the assessment of need for day care among low income households in that county. The major limitation of that source of information is that data are not very specific to the agency's need for information.

Qualitative approaches to needs assessment include all those means of measurement of need where categories of things are not specified ahead of time. As previously mentioned, a social survey could have open-ended questions, and this would be an example of qualitative measurement. A more common use of qualitative methods is the public hearing in which people are invited to say what they wish rather than respond to categories. Interviews with open-ended questions would constitute another example of qualitative measurement. The focus group is another example. These are small groups of people, usually six to eight individuals, who participate in a structured discussion of a selected theme (for more information, see Krueger, 1994). That theme could be the unmet needs of senior citizens of Hinshaw County, or the needs of the homeless in Cedar City, or the relative need for support, enhanced self-esteem, or legal assistance for abused wives.

The **nominal group technique** is a qualitative approach to collecting information that combines qualitative and quantitative methods. It entails the engagement of a small group of key informants in the identification and prioritizing of ideas. It is well suited to questions related to need and will be illustrated in the next chapter.

Discussion Box 3.5

Think of a familiar program and indicate whether you believe it would be better served through a qualitative need assessment method or a quantitative one.

The Evaluation of Service Process

Service process refers to the things that are done in behalf of the program in order to achieve the desired results. In order to achieve the goals of the program, staff with certain credentials are hired. These credentials are believed to be necessary for effective service. These persons are instructed to administer services as designed. This might include restricting services to clients who are eligible for the service according to established policies. It might include assuring that each client is informed of his or her rights. It might include referrals of certain clients to certain other services. It might include assuring that each client is served through an established protocol of services so that important considerations are not overlooked, as, for example, a protocol for how the emergency room of the hospital will treat each victim of rape.

The monitoring of such variables as those mentioned above serve as the focus of quality assurance efforts. The word quality is used in many ways by human service professionals.

It can mean anything from whether the credentials of staff are appropriate (Are the staff *qualified*?) to whether the clients gained in their social functioning. According to Coulton:

> Quality is an elusive concept that implies value. A service that is of high quality has features that are valued by relevant individuals or groups. Quality assurance programs seek ways to objectify what are essentially subjective phenomena so they can be examined (Coulton, 1991, p. 253).

Coulton divides quality into three categories: structure (or inputs), process, and outcome. Staff qualifications would fit into the first category, service process into the second, and client outcome into the third.

Quality assurance is highly focused upon process variables rather than outcome. We often refer to these variables as standards. Standards are developed because they are believed to lead to effective outcomes, but we should not lose sight of the fact that standards are not outcomes. The primary reason for the high degree of focus upon standards is the lack of good information on client outcome and the difficulties in gathering such information.

Service process can be examined through qualitative as well as quantitative approaches to measurement. A key question that can be best answered through qualitative methods is "What is it like being a client of this program?" What if you were to follow a client through the entire process from calling the agency, to being greeted by the receptionist, to being given the intake interview, to being given the central service, to being discharged? What kinds of insights would you gain from this experience?

Discussion Box 3.6

Identify one standard for good practice for a familiar program.

The Evaluation of Efficiency

When we say that a service is delivered more efficiently, we normally are saying that we are getting more for the money. If the Hampton Family Counseling Center delivers family therapy at a cost of $55 per hour, we might say that it is operating more efficiently than the Hampton Psychiatric Center, which is delivering family therapy at a cost of $93 per hour. If the child abuse investigation program for the Parker County Department of Social Services spent $200,000 this year and completed 200 child abuse investigations, you could say that the cost per child abuse investigation was $1,000 $($200,000 / 200 = $1,000). If the Walker County Department of Social Services was spending $1,400 per child abuse investigation, you could say that the Parker County DSS was operating its program more efficiently than the Walker County DSS.

Efficiency is defined as *the ratio of input to output or outcome.* In the earlier examples, costs constituted the input, and units of service delivered were measured as the output. You could use outcome rather than output as a measure of efficiency, but we seldom have good information on client outcome. The ultimate study of efficiency would be the computation of costs per client achievement or the benefits to the community. If we could compute the cost per child abuse incident prevented or the cost per client rehabilitated, we would be in the best place to examine efficiency. However, this is not often feasible in human services; therefore, efficiency will be examined in this chapter in regard to units of service delivered.

The first step in the examination of service unit cost is the definition of the unit of service for a given program. A simple way to define the unit of service is per client served. If your program spent $123,443 and served 890 persons, the cost per client served would be $138.70 ($123,443 / 890 = $138.70). Measuring service by nothing more than clients served is less meaningful than measuring service time or episodes of service. An hour of counseling or a day of residential care or a child abuse investigation completed are examples of the breaking down of services into time or episodes of service.

The next step is the computation of the total costs of delivering the program's service units. This may be problematic because agencies often do not break down their costs in ways that the cost per unit of service can easily be computed. When you compute total program costs, you will need to consider indirect as well as direct costs. Direct costs are those that can be easily identified with the program, such as the costs of salaries for the staff who deliver the service and the supplies they use, the cost of their transportation, and so forth. Indirect costs are those costs that the agency incurs in support of the programs; for example, the agency has an executive with a salary and an office. These costs have to be assigned to the agency's programs so that the total agency budget is assigned to one or more programs. You might need to compute the indirect costs and arbitrarily assign a portion to your program in the computation of the total cost of delivering the units of service that you are analyzing.

Your next step is to compute the cost per unit of service. This entails dividing the total program costs by the number of units of service delivered. The final step is to place that figure into perspective by comparing it to something. You could compare it to your unit costs of last year or the unit costs of another agency that delivers the same service. You might compare it to some idea of what a reasonable cost per unit of service would be.

Discussion Box 3.7

Which of the following is an example of the better statement from an evaluation of efficiency?

My agency is not administratively top-heavy like some other agencies I know.
It costs my agency $78 to deliver each hourly therapy session, which is less than the average of $88 per session for other agencies in my county.

The Evaluation of Outcome

In an earlier section of this chapter, you reviewed a number of key questions about evaluation, a few of which are related to outcome evaluation, which focuses on the clients' target behavior. Treatment goals and objectives also focus on the clients' target behavior. The target behavior may be depression, grades in school, marital conflict, compliance with medical treatment, and so forth. Your outcome evaluation should help you to determine the extent to which the target behavior was improved, and the extent to which you can claim that the improvement was due to the service.

You could ask for the opinions of clients about service effectiveness through a client satisfaction survey. This would help you to answer the question of whether clients are satisfied. But this normally does not measure client growth directly. A better alternative is to engage in a direct measure of target behavior. In this regard, you should address two key questions:

1. Did clients achieve a gain on the target behavior?
2. Was the client growth due to the intervention?

Did clients achieve a gain on the target behavior?   With regard to this first question, you may want to examine whether the client achieved a reduction in depression, or whether the high school dropout rate went down, or whether the client improved on her compliance with the medical treatment plan. You should notice that none of these statements ask about how much service was delivered or whether services were delivered according to a certain treatment protocol. The latter would be issues related to process evaluation.

These are examples of outcomes your intervention may be designed to achieve. You can examine client gain by measuring target behavior before and after intervention. You could, for example, evaluate your new school social work initiative by comparing school grades for a group of at-risk youth at two points in time. These two time periods could be the first grading period of the school year and the third grading period of the year. In the interim, the treatment period, these at-risk youth would receive the services of the new school social work initiative.

You can measure client growth either prospectively or retrospectively; the usual way is to do this prospectively—You measure target behavior before treatment and again after treatment. The way to do this retrospectively is at the end of the treatment period to ask clients to respond to a scale that calls upon them to reflect on their pretreatment condition and answer the questions according to how they perceive they were at the beginning of the treatment period. They are also asked to respond to the same scale as they view themselves now. These two perceptions of the target behavior are compared for gain, in the same way you would undertake a normal pretest–posttest analysis for a group when the data are collected prospectively.

For example, let's develop an instrument for measuring the research student's self-efficacy in the performance of selected tasks that are covered in this book. Exhibit 3.1 gives a small portion of a scale that might be used this way.

The example in Exhibit 3.1 would be the one given at the end of the course (service) where the student (client) is asked to reflect on the prior condition. Another scale would be given at the same time that asked the student (client) to reflect on how things are at present. In this above example, the questions would be the same except that the wording would ask for how confident the student is at the present time, rather than at the beginning of the course. The score

EXHIBIT 3.1 • *Illustration of a Retrospective Pretest Survey Instrument*

Directions: We want to know how confident you were in your ability to perform specific research tasks before you took this course in research. After you consider each task, please rate your confidence in your ability to perform this task at a level that would be considered excellent by an expert on research. Give yourself a rating of 10 if you were certain you could have performed this task before the beginning of this course experience. Give yourself a rating of 0 if you believe you could not have done this task at all at the beginning of this experience. If you are moderately certain you could have done this task, give yourself a rating of 5. Give yourself a rating from 0 to 10 using these guidelines.

How confident are you that you can ...	*Cannot do at all* *Certain I can do*
	0 1 2 3 4 5 6 7 8 9 10
Define client target behavior sufficient to guide the selection of a means of measuring progress.	0 1 2 3 4 5 6 7 8 9 10
Analyze target behavior sufficient to determine a good intervention for the client(s).	0 1 2 3 4 5 6 7 8 9 10
Articulate treatment goals and objectives sufficient to guide the evaluation of treatment effectiveness.	0 1 2 3 4 5 6 7 8 9 10
Describe a human service program or intervention sufficient to facilitate replication by others.	0 1 2 3 4 5 6 7 8 9 10
Select a research design sufficient to address those things that should be controlled in the examination of causation.	0 1 2 3 4 5 6 7 8 9 10
Determine how the study results can be generalized to persons not included in the present study.	0 1 2 3 4 5 6 7 8 9 10
Apply statistical analysis to evaluative data sufficient to determine if the hypothesis was supported and whether practical significance was achieved.	0 1 2 3 4 5 6 7 8 9 10
Draw study conclusions that are relevant to the data and avoid common pitfalls in this endeavor.	0 1 2 3 4 5 6 7 8 9 10

for Exhibit 3.1 would be the pretest; the other scale score would be the posttest. These two scores would be compared to measure the level of gain.

Another means of evaluation that is slightly different, but tends to fit better into the category of retrospective evaluation than prospective evaluation, is the use of the threshold score

EXHIBIT 3.2

Threshold Score (Mean of past clients)	Posttest Scores for Present Clients (at end of service)	
	Client ID Number	Depression Score
32	HD-14	23
	SKI-12	21
	SKI-7	19
	HD-22	28
	SK-16	33
	SKI-11	16
	SK-4	19
	HD-3	21
	HD-1	23
	Mean Score →	22.55

as the basis for determining client condition at the beginning of service. If the average level of depression for your clients at intake has rather consistently ranged from 31 to 33 over many years, you might use the average of these figures as the threshold score to which you will compare the posttest scores. You might measure 9 clients at the termination of service and compare the average for this group to a threshold score of 32 and examine whether the average posttest score (after service) was significantly better than this threshold score. Exhibit 3.2 is an illustration.

The statistical question is whether the mean score of 22.55, given the array of depression scores in Exhibit 3.2, is significantly different from a threshold score of 32.

Did the service cause the client gain? The second question addresses the issue of whether the treatment caused the outcome. Clients can improve for reasons other than the intervention. Sometimes other things cause a client to achieve a gain in self-esteem or a reduction in depression. School dropout rates might go down independent of the program you are administering. Some clients improve on medical compliance without a specific service designed to improve this behavior.

How do we address this issue? The answer lies in the research design that is employed. If you compare your clients' growth to that of a group of persons who did not get the intervention, you have a basis for controlling for some of these influences. For example, the level of growth of the comparison group should reflect normal growth and development over time. If you compare your treatment group's level of growth with that of a comparison group, you

EXHIBIT 3.3

Comparison Group Scores for Anxiety			Treatment Group Scores for Anxiety		
Pretest	*Posttest*	*Gain*	*Pretest*	*Posttest*	*Gain*
18	19	1	15	21	6
15	18	3	14	26	12
12	18	6	19	24	5
18	15	−3	14	15	1
17	17	0	23	21	−2
15	18	3	12	28	16
12	12	0	17	23	5
17	19	2	13	28	15
15	15	0	15	25	10
12	18	6	14	25	11
Mean Gain Score →		1.8	**Mean Gain Score →**		7.9

can say that differences between the two groups cannot be explained by this phenomenon, so you are in a better position to say that the clients' growth was caused by the intervention. You would be in a weaker position to make this assertion if you only measured your clients before and after treatment and had no comparison group. In the latter case, you have not controlled for normal growth over time, which may be the best explanation of why your clients achieved a gain.

Exhibit 3.3 is an illustration of the comparison of self-esteem scores of those in the comparison group who did not receive the service and those in the treatment group who did have the service, where higher scores represent better functioning.

The statistical question is whether the mean gain score of 7.9 for the treatment group is significantly different from the mean gain score of 1.8. Some people gain for reasons other than treatment. The mean gain of the comparison group of 1.8 is used as the estimate of how people might change through normal growth and development over time. Consequently, we could assert that the difference between 7.9 and 1.8 can be attributed to the treatment rather than normal growth over time: This is the amount of difference that treatment made in the client's self-esteem, when normal growth is taken into consideration.

In this example, the comparison group was used to control for one of the other things that can cause client improvement. Normally, a comparison group is composed of those who have not had treatment and may be similar in many ways to the group that did get treatment. This is one way to address causation. A better way would be to employ the experimental design. The experimental design is one where you select a group of people and randomly assign these individuals to a treatment group (receiving service) and a control group (not receiving service) and you compare the gain of these two groups. If you have the luxury of using this design, you will be controlling for a number of things that cause client gain other than service.

Steps in the Process of Outcome Evaluation.   Outcome evaluation starts at different places in the research process based on the kind of outcome evaluation being undertaken. Often, the clinical evaluation study begins with the selection of the study sample, because you have a client and want to evaluate your treatment with this client. The outcome evaluation for a program would likely start with an assessment of the target behavior. But all outcome evaluations should have information on the following:

- The target behavior
- The intervention or program
- The goals and objectives of the intervention or program
- The study methodology, including:
  - The study sample
  - The means of measuring outcomes
  - The research design employed
- The analysis of the outcome data
- The conclusions drawn from the outcome data

These parts of the outcome evaluation process are interconnected. For example, your treatment goals and objectives should focus on the target behavior. You need a good definition of target behavior in order to do a good job of selecting a means of measuring client progress. You need a good target behavior analysis in order to select an appropriate intervention. This analysis can also be helpful in selecting the research design, because it might identify things other than treatment that may cause the behavior to change. Your data analysis is guided by your measurement tools and your research design. Your conclusions should be congruent with your data analysis and should reflect on the extent to which the intervention achieved the treatment objectives. The depiction of these interconnections is provided in Figure 3.1.

The Evaluation of Client Satisfaction

A common method of evaluating human service programs is through the client satisfaction survey in which former clients are asked to indicate their level of satisfaction with the services they received. Being able to quote figures on the percentage of former clients who were satisfied is useful to the program administrator in the achievement of accountability for the program. Furthermore, if clients are satisfied, staff will feel better about their efforts. If clients are not satisfied, the evidence is available to promote change.

The central assumption of the client satisfaction survey is that satisfied clients had their needs met. If a client is satisfied, it is assumed that he or she actually improved in functioning. Thus, the higher the level of satisfaction, the more effective the services.

But satisfaction is an opinion, not a measure of functioning. A direct measurement of functioning is required to overcome the limitations inherent in this assumption. In the absence of such a direct measure of client conditions, satisfaction is often used as a surrogate for treatment effectiveness.

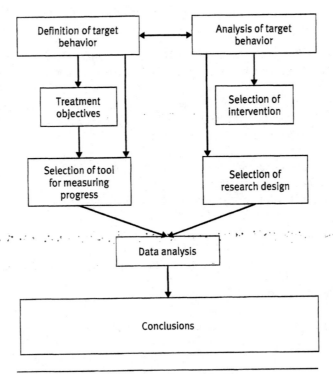

FIGURE 3.1   *The Interconnections of the Parts of the Evaluation Process*

An excellent discussion of client satisfaction surveys can be found in Royse, Thyer, Padgett, and Logan (2001). They note the popularity of client satisfaction surveys for human services and the major advantages:

> There is much to commend the use of client satisfaction as a form of evaluation. Such approaches tend to be relatively inexpensive and easy to interpret, and they can be implemented on short notice without a great deal of planning. Furthermore, they indicate to clients that their experiences and observations are important. Whether we inquire about the accessibility or the acceptability of our services, these approaches are a "client-oriented," democratic form of evaluation (e.g., everyone gets a vote). They stem from the assumption and belief that clients are the best source of information on the quality and delivery of our services, if not also the best judges of impact and effectiveness. High client satisfaction levels are, understandably, desired and useful for public relations and marketing efforts. (Royse, Thyer, Padgett, and Logan, 2001, p. 193)

If client satisfaction is a good measure of outcome, we would find a positive correlation between satisfaction and behavior improvement. In at least one study (Ankuta & Abeles, 1993), it was found that client satisfaction was positively related to client improvement. In other words, the more satisfied clients were found to be more likely to have improved in functioning. This provides a little evidence for client satisfaction as a measure of improvement.

But Royse et al. (2001) note several problems with client satisfaction being used as a measure of program success. One of these problems is the uniformly high level of satisfaction typically expressed by clients in these surveys. In practically every study, the vast majority of respondents indicate satisfaction with services received. Why is this a problem? Information on client outcome is not so uniformly positive. If satisfaction is uniformly positive, it must not be an especially accurate measure of outcome. In one study cited by Royse, et al. (Sanders et al., 1998), clients in an ineffective program were found to be satisfied. This discussion by Royse and others pointed out that reviews of various satisfaction studies revealed that about three out of four clients typically indicate satisfaction with services, as exemplified by ratings of 3 or more on a 4-point scale. It is not uncommon to find 90 percent of clients indicating satisfaction.

Another problem is that client satisfaction surveys may not be representative of all clients. People who drop out of service often are less satisfied, yet they are normally excluded from the sample of persons sent a survey. Furthermore, the response rate for these surveys typically is a little more than one-third, and it has been found to be as low as 15 to 20 percent in some studies (Royse et al., 2001, p. 197). It is believed that less satisfied clients are less likely to respond to the survey.

A few of the observations about client satisfaction surveys by Royse et al. (2001) are the following:

- Clients may be satisfied with one aspect of the experience but not satisfied with others; thus, surveys should include several dimensions of the experience.
- Qualitative survey items (open-ended questions) usually yield more negative information, but also yield more meaningful information for program improvement; thus, you should include some items like this on your survey.
- Older persons are more satisfied than younger ones. Perhaps this variable should be controlled in any analysis you might undertake that compares agency units with each other.
- Less satisfied clients drop out of service. A good idea is to use a "ballot box" approach where days are selected at random for asking all clients to drop off a survey in the box in the waiting room. This will include some clients who will drop out later.
- Telephone surveys yield higher participation rates than mailed questionnaires.

A major difficulty with the use of client satisfaction surveys, given this information, is that it is not easy to interpret a given level of satisfaction. If clients normally are satisfied at the rate of about 75 percent, what do you make of your survey if it falls in this range? Is this good news? Maybe it is only average for human service agencies and not a good basis for boasting. Perhaps you should collect this data periodically so you can develop a baseline by which each survey can be compared. This will let you know if client satisfaction is changing. You could also solicit client satisfaction data from other agencies with similar services and use these data as a basis of comparison.

Using Client Surveys to Assess Outcome Retrospectively

One method of advancing the clients satisfaction survey to a higher level with regard to outcome evaluation is to employ questions that ask the client to engage in a retrospective outcome assessment. This method was discussed in a previous section where the retrospective approach to outcome assessment was described, using the example of a research course experience. The idea is to get clients to rate themselves on their target behavior both before and after services were received. Both assessments are done at the completion of service through a survey. If you are administering a program with a set of outcomes for all clients that have been clearly artic- ulated, you could employ a standard scale for all clients. Suppose, for example, that you are administering the Adolescent Parenting Program that has the improvement of social support as an objective. You might include the following questions on the post-treatment survey:

> Think of the way things were for you before you entered the Adolescent Parenting Program. As you reflect on your life at that time, how much did you feel that you were very close to some of your friends? Select an answer below that best describes you at that time.
>
> 1 = I did not feel at all like this before I entered the APP.
> 2 = I felt a little like this before I entered the APP.
> 3 = I felt somewhat like this before I entered the APP.
> 4 = I felt very much like this before I entered the APP.
>
> Now reflect on how you feel right now. How much do you feel that you are very close to some of your friends?
>
> 1 = I do not feel at all like this now.
> 2 = I feel a little like this now.
> 3 = I feel somewhat like this now.
> 4 = I feel very much like this now.

The above provides data that can be evaluated statistically like you would assess data from a pretest–posttest administration of a scale. In other words, you would compute a pretreatment score and a posttreatment score and take the difference as the level of client gain.

A key advantage to this approach, when compared to the typical client satisfaction sur- vey, is that the client is called upon to answer specific questions that are less vulnerable to the social desirability bias (the tendency to answer questions the way you think other people want you to answer them). Global questions about satisfaction often tempt clients to be nice and say they are generally satisfied with services. But if asked to rate themselves on specific condi- tions, they may be less tempted to do this. Furthermore, these types of questions focus on their conditions rather than their opinions about how well they were treated by agency personnel.

Compare this example with the question you may find on a typical satisfaction survey: "To what extent did the service you receive help you to achieve the goals that brought you to our agency for help?" Now, the focus is on how well you rate the agency rather than how you assess your own behavior. The question may be raised about whether clients can accurately reflect on their behavior at a former time, rather than the present. It is normally better to mea- sure clients before treatment than ask them to recall their conditions, but a retrospective pretest measure is probably better than the common client satisfaction questions. And there may be sit- uations where the retrospective pretest measurement is superior. For example, at the end of a research course, are you in a better position to reflect on your level of knowledge at pretest time than the actual pretest time? Maybe you now know better about your level of beginning knowl- edge about the content.

Discussion Box 3.8

How would you interpret a study finding that the Senior Citizens Support Program has received a higher level of client satisfaction than the Adolescent Support Program?

Discussion Box 3.9

How would you interpret the finding that the clients of the Hampton County Senior Citizens Support Program has a higher level of client satisfaction than the Johnson County Senior Citizens Support Program?

Selected Models of Evaluation

There are several models you can use for evaluation, only three of which will be highlighted in this chapter. Your selected evaluation model will provide general conceptual guidance on your approach to evaluation and will suggest procedures you should use. For example, an experiment calls upon you to measure client progress in such a way as to put you in a position to make assertions about whether the treatment caused the behavior to change. A highly sophisticated experiment might call upon you to randomly assign your clients to a group that receives treatment and a group that does not receive treatment (or receives it later) and to measure target behavior for both groups. In this situation, you would be in a good position to assert that the differences in client functioning at the end of treatment between the two groups were caused by the treatment rather than something else, like normal growth and development over time.

A case study is quite different in its focus and procedures. It calls upon you to select a single case, which can be a person or an organization or a community or something else. You collect a wide variety of information about that single case and draw conclusions from this information.

The utilization-focused evaluation model suggests a different approach from the experiment or case study. With this model, you select a group of people who have a research need and help carry them through a research process, with yourself as the facilitator rather than leader.

Discussion Box 3.10

At first glance, which of these three approaches seems best suited to the study purpose of identifying the variation in ways that different programs are implemented in the Oak Hill Mental Health Center? It is believed this study will identify best and worst practices and help find ways to improve the overall effectiveness of this agency.

The Experiment

A social experiment is a mechanism for assessing causation using the best principles of the scientific method. In the social experiment, you introduce an intervention and measure its effects upon a behavior. The outcome evaluation protocol is an example. You are testing to see if the intervention had the intended effect upon target behavior. You do this by measuring client behavior in such a way as to determine the extent to which we can assert that the treatment was effective.

In simple terms the experiment entails trying something and observing its effects. Viewed this way, we can say we experiment in our daily lives. We might taste the stew we are preparing on the stove, add salt to the stew, and taste it again to see if it is better. You might change your study habits to see if it improves your grades.

The classical experimental design calls upon you to measure behavior prior to the intervention, and after the intervention, and to compare this gain to the same for a group of persons who did not have the treatment. The persons in the two groups are assigned to their group status on a random basis. When you have the luxury of doing this, you are placing yourself in an ideal position to assert that any differences in gain between the two groups were due to the intervention rather than something else.

When you evaluate an intervention you are normally aware that various things influence the client's target behavior other than the intervention. Some clients are more motivated to change. Some clients have a better support system. Some clients will have things to change in their environments, independent of the intervention, that affect the target behavior.

So how can you assert that the measured change in target behavior is due to the intervention rather than something else? With the classic experimental design, the random assignment of people to the two groups takes care of this issue. Because people are in their groups strictly on a random basis, it is likely that the proportion of persons with high motivation is similar in the two groups. The proportion of persons with good support systems in the two groups is probably similar. And the proportion of persons with positive changes in their environments between the two groups is probably similar. Thus differences in behavioral gain between the two groups cannot be explained by motivation, support, or the environment. More likely, these differences are due to the intervention.

Random assignment typically has the effect of reducing, or eliminating, meaningful differences between groups. These assumptions, however, are easier to make the larger the number of persons in the two groups. Random assignment may not do a good job of taking care of this business if there are only six people in each of the two groups, because chance is highly related to sample size. The larger the sample size, the more likely that differences between people will be offset through random assignment.

Discussion Box 3.11

Suppose you wished to evaluate the effectiveness of the Dropout Prevention Program in the reduction of risk factors for middle school students in regard to dropping out of school. There have been 40 persons referred to this program and you have decided to serve those most at risk at present. Someone has suggested that you compare the target behaviors of your clients to those on the waiting list. Explain why using a random assignment of persons to the treatment group and the control group would be better than this approach.

The Case Study Method

The case study method is appropriate when you wish to investigate a single individual, event, or social setting (e.g., a single organization) in sufficient intensity to obtain an in-depth understanding of how it operates or functions.

> The approach of case studies ranges significantly from general field studies to the interview of a single individual or group. Case studies may focus on an individual, a group, or an entire community and may utilize a number of data technologies such as life history, documents, oral histories, in-depth interviews, and participant observation (Bern, 2001, p. 225).

According to Yin (1989), the case study is a way of investigating an empirical topic by following a set of prespecified procedures. It is recommended for use when the research question is about How or Why and the researcher has little control over events. It is also appropriate when the focus is on a contemporary phenomenon within some real-life context. The case study method normally uses multiple sources of data, both quantitative and qualitative. (Yin, 1989).

Yin (1989, p. 25) has noted several applications of the case study approach to the program evaluation. One application would entail the examination of the causal links in situations too complex for survey methods or experimental strategies. A second application is to use this approach to describe clearly the experiences of clients as they move from contemplation of service, to access to service, to receipt of service, and discharge, in order to gain insight into how this process could be improved. Another application is the assessment of the program that has unclear goals and objectives and you need a comprehensive examination of a wide array of outcomes, both intended and unintended.

There are five major components of the case study design:

1. The development of the study's questions
2. The development of study propositions
3. The determination of the unit of analysis
4. The development of the logic that links selected data to the propositions
5. The development of the criteria for interpreting the findings

The first consideration is that your study question be a good fit with the case study method. According to Yin (1989), the case study approach is better suited to questions of How and Why rather than questions of Who, What, or Where. The case study is best when you have a complicated question that could be best addressed by multiple sources of data, including both qualitative and quantitative. If you wish to know whether your group therapy intervention is improving depression for eight clients, you would be better advised to use an experiment rather than a case study. But if you wanted to study the overall effects of the privatization of the mental health system for your county, you might be well advised to conduct a case study.

You might want to know how your program's services achieve their outcomes. This would require information on the components of the service that are most emphasized, the relationship between service emphasis and service outcome, and so forth. You may want to know why certain clients achieve better outcomes than others. This might require information on the characteristics of clients, the relationship between client characteristics and client outcome, the opinions of practitioners about clients that do best in treatment, and so forth.

The second consideration in the use of the case study is the study's propositions. A study proposition is a little like a hypothesis, but is more general and likely to be lacking in empirical support. The type of proposition appropriate for the case study is one born of a logical observation of the phenomenon under study by the research stakeholders or users. In case study terminology, a study proposition is a theoretical guess about the phenomenon under study. It is your preliminary attempt to explain. It provides guidance on the places you need to go to find relevant information. For example, you may have little reason to measure whether your clients are left handed or right handed because it does not make sense that this variable influences client response to treatment. So you would not have a study proposition about being left handed. But you might have one about the environmental stresses faced by clients.

The unit of analysis is the third consideration in the implementation of a case study. This is the entity on which you will collect your data. In case study terminology, it refers to how you are defining your case. A case could be a single individual. If it is a single case, you would collect all your data on this individual case. You could define your unit of analysis as an event, such as an election. In this situation, you would collect data on that election. The unit of analysis could be a program. If so, you can collect any amount of information that seems relevant to this program with regard to your study question.

Another consideration of the case study design is the logic that links data to propositions. In this endeavor, you need to think of the kinds of data that would support your propositions, and, conversely, the nature of the data that would refute these propositions. You should derive these ideas before you collect your data.

There is one additional consideration in the use of the case study—the criteria for interpreting your findings. On what basis will you believe you have sufficient evidence to reach noteworthy conclusions? Like the logic consideration noted above, the criteria for interpreting findings should be addressed before you collect your data to the extent this is feasible. This is a matter of judgment, so there are not formulas or concrete guides for making this decision. One suggestion is to obtain ideas about this issue from key informants who are not among the study researchers.

Discussion Box 3.12

Think of a research question that might be pursued through a case study and one proposition that might guide this study.

Utilization-Focused Evaluation

Utilization-focused evaluation is a model of evaluation that focuses on "intended use by intended-users" (Patton, 1997, p. 20). Developed by Patton (1997) in the 1970s, it is designed to suggest ways that program evaluation can make a difference. Too often, evaluation reports have been ignored. The idea is that evaluations will be put to use if they focus on the information needs of the key stakeholders. In this model, the evaluator acts as facilitator of decisions rather than a distant expert.

> Since no evaluation can be value-free, utilization-focused evaluation answers the question of whose values will frame the evaluation by working with clearly identified, primary intended users who have responsibility to apply evaluation findings and implement recommendations. (Patton, 1997, p. 21)

A key to this model is the relationship between those who serve as evaluation facilitators and the intended users. The first step is to help the intended users to identify what they need. The role of the evaluation facilitator is to offer possibilities and serve as a technical consultant. This is done within a framework of established standards that adhere to the spirit of critical thinking and scientific inquiry. The evaluation facilitator would not participate in a process designed to fool the public with misinformation.

The utilization-focused evaluation model does not advocate any particular approach to evaluation. For example, it does not favor quantitative data over qualitative data. It does not advocate for the use of the experimental design or place a higher priority on outcome evaluations than process evaluations. Instead, it is a model for helping intended users to select the most appropriate approach to meet their information needs. It can be helpful for evaluation studies but can be just as useful for other types of studies.

Patton has proposed the following criteria for a utilization-focused evaluation:

1. Data can be brought to bear on the question; that is, it is an empirical question.
2. There is more than one possible answer to the question; that is, the answer is not predetermined by the phrasing of the question.
3. The primary intended users want information to help answer the question. They care about the answer to the question.
4. The primary users want to answer the question for themselves, not just for someone else.
5. The intended users can indicate how they would use the answer to the question; that is, they can specify the relevance of an answer to the question for future action. (Patton, 1997, p. 32)

Questions such as "What should we do about the new state regulations?" may be relevant to a utilization-focused evaluation effort, but it probably needs more focus in order to adhere to criterion 1 above, because it does nothing to guide the collection of data. The second criterion is quite relevant to the spirit of scientific inquiry because you do not do an evaluation study to prove a point; you do it to discover information which may or may not encourage certain individuals to say it proves something. The second and third criteria illustrate the primary focus of this model—the user. It should truly be meaningful to the user. Patton has suggested that evaluation facilitators ask intended users to identify things they would like to know that would make a difference in what they do. You should recognize that this did not ask people to identify information that would make a difference for others, but for themselves.

I have found the last item on the list to be quite useful for my own evaluation consultation. I often have found myself making up a hypothetical result of the intended study and asking intended users to talk about what difference this would make to them. If intended users cannot imagine a difference the study would make, I suggest a different direction for analysis.

In the following paragraphs you will review the steps in the use of the utilization-focused evaluation model. You will see from these steps the difference in the approach of this model from the experiment and case study. Especially note the role of the research person as being facilitator rather than leader or expert.

Step One: Selecting Intended Users from Identified Stakeholders.   Stakeholders are people who can benefit from an evaluation. Intended users are persons from the stakeholder group who will determine the focus of the particular evaluation—they will be the researchers. We could start by identifying a social program and listing the stakeholders. This could include staff, administrators, clients, agency board members, representatives of funding sources, and so forth. We would then identify a specific group from among these stakeholders as the intended users. The questions that interest board members might be different from those that interest staff or clients or administrators.

One of our options would be to identify one of these groups for the exploration of an evaluation. An alternative would be to investigate the evaluation information needs of all groups in some kind of survey and select a focus based on common interests and develop a group of intended users with representatives from each of several groups.

Because utilization-focused evaluation seeks to meet the information needs of intended users, you should have a clear basis for selecting a group of intended users. You could, of course, just randomly select a group. But I would advise you to stop and listen to what various stakeholders have been saying and use this information to identify a basis for expecting that a given group would have a serious interest in participating in an evaluation process—that they have serious needs for information to help in their work. This does not mean that you have identified the specific information they need—indeed, this would be contrary to the spirit of utilization-focused evaluation. It means that you have reason to believe that a given group would put energy into a utilization-focused evaluation.

When you have completed this part of the process, you will have identified both the stakeholders and the intended users. The intended users will lead the research process with your help. They will be the people in authority.

Step Two: Identifying Intended Uses of Evaluation.   Patton (1997) has identified at least three types of uses for evaluation—to judge the worth of a program, to improve a program, or to produce general knowledge. The first of these options—the judgment-oriented evaluation—is one that is familiar to most of us because it focuses on the worth of a program (or whatever is being evaluated). But different actors will use different criteria to determine worth. One actor may be especially conscious of efficiency and focus on the cost per unit of service. Another may be interested in professional standards, while still another may focus on client outcomes. The second of these types of evaluation is devoted to the discovery of how a program can be improved. Those most interested in this type of use of an evaluation may be prepared to operate on the assumption that the program is worthwhile but can be improved. The third type of evaluation is most familiar to those in academia, but can be just as important to those in practice. The question here is what have we learned about the operation of this program that can be generalized to others. There may be certain things that successful programs have in common or successful clients within a given program. This information can be useful to others outside of your own program.

In the judgment-oriented evaluation, according to Patton (1997), it is critical that the criteria for judgment be made explicit. Is the program to be judged on the basis of the extent to which it adheres to acceptable standards, or operates efficiently, best achieves certain client outcomes, or best includes public input in policy decisions? Are there specific guidelines for implementing these criteria?

The second type of use—the improvement-oriented evaluation—addresses such questions as the following:

1. What are the program's strengths and weaknesses?
2. To what extent are participants progressing toward the desired outcomes?
3. Which types of participants are making good progress and which types aren't doing so well?
4. What kinds of implementation problems have emerged and how are they being addressed?
5. What's happening that wasn't expected?
6. How are staff and clients interacting?
7. What are staff and participants perceptions of the program? What do they like ... dislike?
8. How are funds being used compared to initial expectations?
9. Where can efficiencies be realized?
10. What new ideas are emerging that can be tried out and tested? (Patton, 1997, p. 68)

The third use of this model of evaluation—the knowledge-oriented evaluation—seeks generalizations from information that has been collected, such as the information that might be derived from the second type of evaluation. The generation of knowledge is the primary purpose of major research projects that are funded by the government. On a smaller basis, the agency may find certain generalizations about the delivery of a certain service from their evaluations of it.

As a part of the process of identifying intended uses of an evaluation, it is useful to explore how certain types of discoveries might be put to use. I have previously mentioned how I have asked intended users to react to a hypothetical result of data collection. Patton (1997) has identified several questions that can further facilitate this task:

- What decisions are the evaluation findings likely to influence?
- When will decisions be made, and by whom?
- What is at stake? For whom is this at stake?
- Realistically, how much influence will this evaluation have upon the decision?

The evaluation facilitator may find that decisions have already been made, or that only a small consideration is left undecided. Perhaps these questions will inspire your exploration of this theme.

Step Three: Identifying Evaluation Questions.   In the third major step, the evaluation questions are identified. These are identified by the intended users. The process for discovering these questions is coordinated by the evaluation facilitator. This process should start with a relatively general question, but you might want to narrow the turf a little, depending on the context. You could start with a very general question such as "What would you like to know in order to do your job better?" You could narrow the scope to a certain theme such as client service, or you could keep it general.

There are two major tools for qualitative inquiry that could help with this task—nominal group technique and the Delphi method. Each of these tools asks a group of persons to list answers to an open-ended question. This step in the process is followed by a dialogue among participants regarding the various answers given by each participant. A major list is generated that reveals the priorities of the group members in regard to the answers to the general question. These techniques will be examined in more detail in the next chapter.

Step Four: Designing the Means for Collecting Data.   After the questions have been determined, it is time to decide what data will be collected and how. This is a stage in which evaluation facilitator and intended users interact and discuss and decide. It is not strictly in the hands of the evaluation facilitator. It is important that the intended users reveal the kind of data that will be credible and cost-effective. There are limits on what people will find credible and there are limits on how much a study can cost, both in terms of actual expenditures of funds and in terms of the volunteer time required by the intended users and stakeholders.

Step Five: Collecting and Analyzing Data.   The collection and analysis of data is another step in which evaluation facilitator and intended users must interact. While the evaluation facilitator may be called upon to put certain data in a database and generate charts or graphs for its display, it is important that intended users be involved in the interpretation of the data.

Step Six: Facilitating Intended Use.   After data have been collected and analyzed, it is time to determine how the results can be put to use. How should these results be disseminated beyond the intended user group? If the intended users have full control over implementation this may not be necessary, but I suspect this will be unusual. In human services, most changes require multiple levels of approval.

When the utilization-focused evaluation study is complete, you should have a study with a high degree of likelihood of making a difference. You will have overcome the limitations inherent in the more common expert-oriented evaluation study that may not make any difference in the way things are done.

Discussion Box 3.13

Suppose someone wished to conduct a utilization-focused evaluation of the services of a county social services agency. She asked the five intake social workers of this agency to identify the questions that should be asked of clients with regard to how services could be improved. She mailed a questionnaire to clients with open-ended questions and has analyzed these responses and written a report. What key ingredient is missing from this process?

Summary

By now, you should know about the essential nature of evaluation and how the evaluation study is different from other types of research. You should know that evaluations vary in scope from the simple study of a single client to the evaluation of a large program. You should be able to classify evaluation examples according to the components of the systems model (input, process, output, and outcome). And you should be able to identify several models of evaluation.

You should now be equipped, for example, to point out that a study testing the proposition that left-handed people are more creative than right-handed people is not an example of an evaluation study because there is no intervention that can be aided by this information. You will be able to notice that a program evaluation is more likely than a clinical evaluation to contain a broad range of types of information according to those things that constitute the systems perspective. You will be able to distinguish an evaluation of efficiency from an evaluation of need. And you will recognize that the case study is best used for broad questions related to how and why rather than what.

The following questions test your knowledge of the content of this chapter. You may use it as a pretest in order to determine if you already know this content before you read the chapter, or as a posttest which should help you determine how well you know this content after reading the chapter. The answers are given at the end of the reference list.

Quiz

1. Evaluation research refers to:
   a. Clinical case discussions between professionals when the client's progress on target behavior is the focus of the dialogue.
   b. A systematic collection and analysis of data regarding a specific program or intervention.
   c. Both of the above.
   d. None of the above.

2. Which of the following statements is/are true?
   a. It is a reasonable expectation that the scientific method will eliminate all subjectivity that is inherent in the judgment of worth.
   b. In evaluation research, comparison is essential. You must have a basis for comparing the present state of affairs, as reflected in data, with something else, such as past data, recognized standards, and so forth
   c. Both of the above.
   d. None of the above.

3. Which of the following statements is/are true?
   a. A program evaluation is broader in scope than a clinical evaluation.
   b. A program evaluation is more likely than a clinical evaluation to focus on input or process.
   c. Both of the above.
   d. None of the above.

4. The evaluation of the extent to which an agency is adhering to good standards (e.g., employing only licensed practitioners) would be an example of what kind of evaluation?
   a. An evaluation of service process
   b. An evaluation of service output
   c. An evaluation of service outcome
   d. All of the above

5. The evaluation of the extent to which the High School Dropout Prevention Program is reducing the incidence of high school dropouts would be an example of what kind of evaluation?
   a. An evaluation of service process
   b. An evaluation of service output
   c. An evaluation of service outcome
   d. All of the above

6. Which of the following are examples of qualitative approaches to need assessment?
   a. Public hearings
   b. Interviews of key informants
   c. Both of the above
   d. None of the above

7. Clear evidence for efficiency is provided in which of the following examples?
   a. Agency A has fewer bureaucratic procedures than Agency B.
   b. Agency A employs only persons who have been certified in their field of work, whereas Agency B does not.
   c. The cost per therapy session for Agency A is $73, compared to $88 for Agency B.
   d. All of the above.

8. Which of the following statements is/are true about client satisfaction surveys?
   a. A key assumption of the client satisfaction survey is that satisfied clients are more likely than unsatisfied clients to have improved in their functioning as a result of the service.
   b. There is absolutely no evidence to suggest there is a positive relationship between client satisfaction and client improvement.
   c. Both of the above.
   d. None of the above.
9. Which of the following statements is/are true about the client satisfaction survey?
   a. Qualitative survey items (open-ended) provide more negative information, but also more useful information.
   b. Telephone surveys yield a higher participation rate than the mailed questionnaire.
   c. Both of the above.
   d. None of the above.
10. Which of the following models of evaluation has the greatest clarity of method for collecting and analyzing data?

    a. The experiment
    b. The case study
    c. The utilization-focused evaluation
    d. The primary evaluation
11. A good definition of target behavior is most helpful in ...
    a. Selecting the research design.
    b. Choosing the model of the intervention.
    c. Selecting a tool for measuring client progress.
    d. Determining the statistic to employ in the analysis of data
12. A good analysis of target behavior is most helpful in ...
    a. Selecting the research design.
    b. Choosing the model of the intervention.
    c. Selecting a tool for measuring client progress.
    d. Determining the statistic to employ in the analysis of data.

References

Ankuta, G. Y., & Abeles, N. (1993). Client satisfaction, clinical significance, and meaningful change in psychotherapy. *Professional Psychology: Research and practice.* 24 (1), 70–74.

Berg, B. L. (2001). *Qualitative research methods for the social sciences* (3rd ed.) Boston: Allyn & Bacon.

Coulton, C. J. (1991). Developing and implementing quality assurance programs. In R. L. Edwards, & J. A. Yankey (Eds.), *Skills for effective human services management* (pp. 251–266). Washington, DC: NASW Press

Krueger, R. A. (1994). *Focus groups: A practical guide for applied research* (2nd ed.). Thousand Oaks, CA: Sage Publications.

Patton, M. Q. (1997). *Utilization-focused evaluation.* Thousand Oaks, CA: Sage Publications.

Royse, D., Thyer, B. A., Padgett, D. K., & Logan, T. K. (2001). *Program evaluation* (3rd ed.) Belmont, CA: Brooks/Cole.

Sanders, L. M., Trinh, C., Sherman, B. R., & Banks, S. M. (1998). Assessment of client satisfaction in a peer counseling substance abuse treatment program for pregnant and postpartum women. *Evaluation and Program Planning*, 21, 287–296.

Yin, R. K. (1984), *Case study research.* Beverly Hills, CA: Sage Publications.

York, R. O. (1998). *Conducting social work research.* Boston: Allyn & Bacon.

Answers to the Quiz

1. b		**7.** c	
2. b		**8.** a	
3. c		**9.** c	
4. a		**10.** a	
5. c		**11.** c	
6. c		**12.** b	

4

Preliminary Exercises in the Evaluation of Human Services

In this chapter, you are given three exercises that introduce you to human service evaluation. The first is related to the evaluation of input (or need). In this exercise, you will employ a group decision making technique (NGT) in the evaluation of client need. The second exercise calls upon you to engage in a process evaluation of a familiar human service program. The third exercise asks you to answer several key questions in the preliminary design of an outcome evaluation study. When you complete these exercises you will have delved into input, process, and outcome evaluations, the three major categories you might encounter in the practice of human services. Later chapters will provide you with the opportunity to dig deeper into these types of evaluation.

Exercise A: Using NGT to Evaluate Client Need

In this exercise, you will be carried through the use of Nominal group technique (NGT) as a mechanism for input (need) evaluation. This is a method for group decision making that is useful for obtaining group advice on a wide range of decisions, but it seems especially suited for need assessment.

Nominal group technique (NGT) is a means for group decision making designed to generate ideas democratically. It entails the independent generation of ideas by group members, the sharing of these ideas, and the voting on priorities among these ideas. This technique was developed by Delbecq and Van de Ven in the late 1960s as a tool for planning (Delbecq, Van de Ven, & Gustafson, 1975). I have used it many times in situations where human service staff needed to identify problems or issues of concern. I have found it to be quite useful for generating a lot of ideas and equalizing participation.

In keeping with the intent of this book to offer practical guidelines for the human service professional, you will find step-by-step instructions on the use of NGT along with charts and forms that you may find useful as tools when you employ it. This chapter may be useful in research instruction as an option for a student exercise or paper.

The NGT Process

There are six steps in the NGT procedure:

1. The silent generation of ideas in writing by each participant
2. A round-robin recording of all of each participant's ideas on a flip chart
3. The serial discussion of each idea for purposes of clarification
4. A preliminary vote on item importance
5. A discussion of the preliminary vote
6. A final vote

When you complete this process, you will have a list of ideas in priority order that will represent the will of the group.

A review of the six steps in the NGT process will illustrate the spirit of the technique. In step 1, the group facilitator presents the question to be addressed and the time limit for thought (usually 5 minutes). It is presented both verbally and in writing to ensure clarity. The level of abstraction is defined by the facilitator, who avoids offering examples that may tend to lead group members in a narrow direction. In the example of the question "What are the chief problems encountered by children in one-parent, low-income households?" the facilitator may go on to define "problem" as a condition, not a lack of a certain service. But she would want to avoid offering examples or responding to such examples offered by group members. In this step, it is important that one group member not be allowed to disturb another or attempt to influence their ideas. The leader should model such behavior by working quietly rather than engaging in hushed dialogue with individuals in the room.

In the second step, the facilitator asks for one item from each member's list and records it on a flip chart, after which he or she asks for a second item from each member, and so on until each member's list has been exhausted. Group members are encouraged to add additional items to their lists as this step progresses. It is important that the facilitator not allow group members to debate their ideas during this step. All members should be given equal opportunity to offer their ideas in their own words but they should be encouraged to express them in brief phrases that can be placed on a flip chart. Neither the group facilitator nor other members should suggest the wording for a member's idea unless it is necessary.

In the next step, each idea is discussed in turn for purposes of clarification and to eliminate duplication. Items are not, however, debated or grouped into broad categories. Items that are fundamentally duplicates of others are eliminated, but all group members have the option of having their ideas stand if they so desire.

In step 4, group members select five to nine items of most importance and rank order them. (Everyone should select the same number of items.) The votes are tallied by assigning the highest value for a rank of one, the second highest value for a rank of two, and so forth. If the decision is to select five items, the highest ranked item would receive five points while the second would receive four points, and so on. No points are given for items not included in the priority category (e.g., the top five). These points are totaled for each item and the results are presented to the group. (It is important *not* to tally the score by assigning one point for the top item, two to the next, and so on, with the idea you will view the lowest scored item as the winner. This procedure will give top rating to items left off the list altogether.)

A certain degree of anonymity is important in this step. The facilitator could ask the group members to write their votes and pass them in. The range of votes should be displayed for each item to illuminate the group's variability and to facilitate a discussion of the preliminary vote.

The discussion takes place in step 5 of the NGT procedure. Participants are encouraged to reflect upon the vote and share their observations. If, for example, item 14 on the list received ranks of 1,1,2,6,7,7 from six members and was not ranked at all by three participants, it may be revealed that certain members had information not available to others. The sharing of this information could influence the final vote on item importance, which constitutes the final step in the process.

In step 6, participants are asked to rank order the items once again. The votes are tallied and the results are reported to group members.

Advantages and Limitations of NGT

The benefits of NGT are numerous. Its greatest contribution to problem solving is that it promotes equality of participation, greater tolerance of nonconformity, and a high level of task motivation. Persons who become engaged in an NGT meeting tend to come away with a heightened feeling of involvement and contribution to the outcome of the meeting. They tend to be more committed to follow-up efforts. The practice of requiring participation leads not only to higher motivation but tends to result in a larger quantity and range of ideas for consideration. It is rather different from the free-for-all approach to group decision making that is more typical. The latter tends to be dominated by selected individuals.

The limits of this tool, however, should be assessed. It is, after all, a special purpose technique useful for generating ideas and equalizing participation but not for routine meetings, coordination, bargaining or negotiation. It is not very useful for resolving conflict since the procedures limit debate rather severely.

The NGT approach is also of limited utility in situations where power or knowledge among participants is significantly disproportionate, unless there is a particular need to employ a strategy to equalize influence. The product of the NGT meeting may be practically useless if one or two powerful individuals are the real decision makers and plan to decide in accordance with their own preference. In this situation, NGT may do more harm than good because it will enhance expectations that will lead to disappointment.

A final caution is concerned with the NGT procedure that discourages the grouping of ideas into categories for voting purposes. This procedure is designed to prevent ideas from getting lost in the shuffle, but it poses a potential problem. Very similar ideas are often stated in different terms with varying shades of meaning that can be distinguished one from another. While the retention of all shades of meaning may serve an important purpose, it is often the case that a voting of priorities among items is most useful in distinguishing the relative value of general categories. If items are left ungrouped, those participants who value a particular category may scatter their votes among a number of individual items related to it and the underlying factor may not be identified in the vote as a priority. A less important category stated in only one form may achieve a higher score simply because it is not divided into several items. Thus, I would suggest another step in which this question is examined so that items can be grouped if they seem rather similar. Another option would be to employ the procedures strictly and engage in a dialogue whereby items on the list may be grouped later, with arguments being made to combine the points of all items in this list in determining priority.

Discussion Box 4.1

Which one or ones of the following objectives would be appropriate for the use of NGT?

1. Identifying how your degree program can be improved, using present students in the program as participants in the NGT exercise.
2. Determining whether all categories of staff should receive the same percentage pay raise, by using groups of staff from each category.
3. Resolving the conflict between the nursing staff and the hospital social workers, using a group consisting of representatives of nurses and social workers.
4. Identifying the most important needs of families with children who have learning disabilities, using the parents of such families.

Provide your answer in the box below.

Step-by-Step Procedures for Using Nominal Group Technique (NGT)

The following procedures are designed for instruction on the use of NGT in general. These procedures should carry you through the process. There are some forms given that should be useful.

Determining Whether to Use NGT

Your first task is to determine whether nominal group technique is appropriate to the situation. To the extent that the answer to any of the following questions is *yes*, there is some doubt about the advisability of NGT as a group decision mode:

1. At this meeting, is it more important that the group conduct routing business or resolve conflict rather than generate ideas or set priorities?
2. Do a few group members possess knowledge about the issue under consideration that is greatly superior to that possessed by most members of the group?
3. Are there a few group members who have significantly greater power over the decision outcome than that of most participants? If so, are those persons likely to exercise that power to override the group's decision if it is different from their own opinion?
4. If you were to employ an informal group discussion method with the issue to be deliberated, is it very likely that practically all group members would participate as thoughtfully and fully in the decision process as you would like?
5. Is your group comprised of more than nine members who could *not* be feasibly divided into subgroups of five to nine members?

Discussion Box 4.2

Think of an objective that needs to be met in the improvement of the functioning of a familiar agency or organization. State the objective below and comment upon the points regarding the suitability of using NGT to achieve this objective.

While the NGT procedures are not complicated, the conducting of the process requires certain skills of you as the leader. To the extent that the answer to any of the following questions is *no*, you should consider an alternative to the nominal group technique:

1. Do you understand the NGT procedures and the rationale for each?
2. Do you accept the objectives of this process as useful for your group?
3. Do you have confidence in yourself as the facilitator of this group?
4. Does the group recognize your ability to serve as facilitator?
5. Can you demonstrate sensitivity to unasked questions about the NGT process?
6. Can you impose structure on group processes without threatening participants or being intimidated by them?
7. Do you have the ability to prevent a group member from talking too much and keep the discussion moving without stifling participation?
8. Can you avoid the temptation to use your position as leader to attempt to convince participants to view things your way?

Discussion Box 4.3

In regard to an objective that might be achieved through the NGT procedures, which of the above items would likely be the most problematic for you as the leader?

Preparing for the NGT Meeting

In your preparation for the NGT meeting, the first consideration is the question to be explored. You should think carefully and obtain input from others. The question should be one that requires the generation of ideas and the establishment of priorities. It should be clearly focused so there will be minimum confusion among participants. If you are using NGT to evaluate need, you should think of a major question that will capture the essence of what information is needed to improve selected programs. A good example is a question such as "What are the most important unmet needs of our clients?".

The next concern is the meeting room. It is best to seat people around tables rather than having people in chairs where some will be seated behind others. Each group should be limited to nine persons. If you have a larger group and will divide them into groups of nine, the room should be arranged with tables for each group which can comfortably seat five to nine group members. There should be sufficient space between groups to prevent them from disturbing one another. The tables should be arranged to minimize eye contact between groups, especially between the members of one group and the leader of another.

The materials available should include:

1. A flip chart and marker for each group
2. A roll of masking tape for each group
3. An NGT Participant Response Form and pencil for each participant
4. A Tally of Votes form to pass around for the recording of votes

Each idea will be placed on the flip chart. Each page, when full, will be taped to the wall where everyone can see it. An alternative is a white board if one is available.

Convening the Meeting and Introducing the NGT Process

Most persons are not familiar with the nominal group technique. It is your responsibility as leader to facilitate each participant's understanding of the procedure and the importance of the topic under consideration. But first, you should *welcome* group members and provide introductions as needed. Then you should explain the *procedures* to be employed as well as the *purpose* for the meeting. It is also crucial that you explain the *use* that will be made of the group's decisions that result from this meeting.

You should explain that the nominal group technique is designed to maximize the contribution of each participant to the thoughtful generation of ideas around an important issue and the establishment of priorities among those ideas. It involves the silent generation of ideas, the recording of each participant's ideas on a flip chart, the clarification of these ideas, and a vote on the importance of each item.

Step 1: The Silent Generation of Ideas in Writing

1. Pass out copies of the NGT Participant Response Form to all group members.
2. Write the question for exploration on a flip chart and read it aloud to the group.
3. Ask if there is any need for clarification of the question. Be careful not to bias the group's process by giving your responses to the question. Also, be sure that others do not do the same.
4. Ask participants to spend five minutes silently writing responses to the question in brief phrases.
5. Model good group behavior by silently working on the question yourself. If necessary, politely remind participants that they are to work silently throughout the five-minute period.

Discussion Box 4.4

Think of a question to pose to participants using NGT. Identify below both the question and the nature of the group that will participate.

Question:

Participants:

Step 2: The Round-Robin Recording of Ideas

1. Explain that you are going to go serially around the room, asking each group member to report one item from his or her list to be placed on the flip chart. Repeat this procedure until all items from each member's list are included. Remind the group that no debating is allowed and that all participants should present their ideas in their own words.
2. Explain that participants should feel free to add additional items to their lists as they go through this step. Items from someone else's list may stimulate further thoughts.
3. Starting at your left, go around the table asking for one item from each participant. Record the item on the flip chart in a brief phrase in the participant's own words. You may need to ask the participant to provide a concise way to express a long sentence, but avoid rewording the statement yourself.
4. Repeat this procedure until all items are recorded. Group members should be asked not to report items that are duplicates of others on the flip chart.

Discussion Box 4.5

If you have the opportunity to execute the NGT with this question and participant group, indicate what you learned about using NGT from this step (recording of items) in the process.

Step 3: Serial Discussion for Clarification

1. Explain that the purpose of this step is to clarify the meaning of each item, not to debate or resolve differences.
2. Starting with the first item, ask if there are any questions anyone would like to raise. Solicit group involvement in the clarification of the items so that members do not feel put on the spot to answer questions regarding their items. Go to item 2 and so on until all items are covered.

In this step, it is critical that you *pace* the group so that relatively equal time is given to each item. There is an unfortunate tendency for groups to spend considerable time on the first items and have little time for the remainder, especially the last items on the list.

During this step of the NGT process, you may wish to have items eliminated that are similar to others, or to do some grouping of ideas. It is important that each participant be given the right to keep his or her idea as presented, if desired. It is usually wise to avoid the temptation to collapse all items into a few broad categories for the voting procedure which comes next. But it may be useful to place separate items into groups so that participants can see how many of their votes are going into one basic category.

Discussion Box 4.6

If you had the opportunity to execute NGT, indicate the lessons you learned about serial discussion for clarification. Did you combine items? Was this difficult?

Step 4: Preliminary Vote on Item Importance

1. Pass around the NGT Group Tally Form and ask each participant to record his or her votes in one of the columns provided. To promote anonymity, you may want to ask members not to record their scores serially in the columns provided so that, for example, the first person might record his votes in the third column while the fifth person in sequence might use the first column, and so forth. Be sure that each person records votes with 5 points for number 1 and so forth, rather than giving rank numbers like 1 for rank 1 and 2 for rank 2 and so forth. An alternative would be to have each participant record votes on a card and pass them in.

2. Sum the scores for each item and assign ranks accordingly. The highest score is given a rank of 1 and the second highest score is given a rank of 2, and so forth. Display the scores on the flip chart for all participants to examine. You should be equipped with a calculator to facilitate this step.

Step 5: Discussion of the Preliminary Vote

1. Give the group members a moment or two to reflect upon the votes displayed on the flip chart.

2. Ask for discussion about the preliminary vote. If there was a good deal of variance on an item (e.g., votes of 5,5,1,2,1,5,0), you may want to ask for a discussion of these differences. Do some participants have access to more information than others? Are the differences simply an accurate reflection of differences in judgment among group members? Be sure to avoid allowing participants to pressure one another during the discussion. Also, be sensitive to the potential that too much discussion of an item may distort the group's final vote by bringing that item to a greater level of consciousness.

Step 6: Final Vote

Repeat step 4 unless there is very good reason to believe that a revote will be a waste of time.

Discussion Box 4.7

If you had the opportunity to execute the NGT procedures, did you employ step 6? If not, why? If you did employ step 6, did you find it useful?

Forms to be Used with the NGT Procedures

Several forms are presented on the following pages which can facilitate the NGT process. The first one (Participant Response Form, Exhibit 4.1) is used by participants to record their ideas in brief phrases. While not essential, you may want to make a copy of this form for each participant. The second form (Participant Response Form, Exhibit 4.2) is employed to record the rank order of the five items thought by the participant to be of most importance in response to the question. You are advised to make a copy for each person. The final form, Exhibit 4.3, is for tallying the group's votes on the items presented by group members. This form is passed around and each participant is asked to record his or her votes. You are advised to make two or three copies for each group to reduce the time for this recording process and combine the scores of the two or three forms into a master tally form for presentation to the group.

Recording of Ideas from Group Members

After you have been given time to record your ideas, you and the other group members will be asked to present them one at a time in round-robin fashion. When your time comes, you will be asked to offer one idea. Your time will come again, at which you will be asked to offer a second

EXHIBIT 4.1 • *Participant Response Form*

Page 1

Record the question for deliberation:

Regarding the above question, record your ideas in brief phrases below.
Place a number next to each idea.
Please remain silent during this period of the process.

EXHIBIT 4.2 • *Participant Response Form*

Page 2

Ranking of Items

When instructed to do so, select five items from the list on the flip chart that you consider most important as a response to the question. Place the idea number as given on the flip chart in the first column. Then insert a brief phrase that summarizes the idea in the second column. Ignore the last two columns for the present.

Idea Number	Idea	Rank	Points

idea, and so forth until you have offered all of your ideas. During this period, you may have new ideas that are inspired by what others have said. You are encouraged to add new items to your list in this discussion process. Also, you may find that an idea on your list has been offered by someone else, which means you can erase it from your list. During this period, you are asked not to discuss the ideas of others. You especially should refrain from challenging anyone else's ideas or attempting to rephrase their idea into your own words. You will be given an opportunity to raise questions for clarification in the next period in the process.

Your next step is to determine the relative importance of each of the five ideas selected above. Decide which one is the best response to the question and give it a rank of 1. Place this number in the third column labeled Rank. Then select the second most important idea and give it a rank of 2, and so on until you have ranked all five ideas, and have placed their ranks in the third column.

Your final step in this procedure is to assign points to each item by giving 5 points for a rank of one, 4 points for a rank of two, 3 points to a rank of three, 2 points to a rank of four, and 1 point to a rank of five. Place these points in the final column, labeled Points.

Tally of Votes

Record your votes in Exhibit 4.3 for the five items that you selected as being the most adequate response to the question. The item number for each item on the flip chart is presented in the first column. There are several columns next to each item for group members to record the points, if any, that were assigned to each item. Record your points in one of the columns labeled Person 1 or Person 2, and so forth. Do not enter a number in the TOTAL column. Please record the POINTS, not the ranks. For example, if you are person 3 and have given 2 points to item 5, you would insert the number 2 in the cell that is at the intersection of the line that is numbered 5 for Item and the column that is labeled Person 3.

EXHIBIT 4.3

Item	Person 1	Person 2	Person 3	Person 4	Person 5	Person 6	Person 7	Person 8	Person 9	TOTAL
1										
2										
3										
4										
5										
6										
7										
8										
9										
10										
11										
12										
13										
14										
15										
16										
17										
18										
19										
20										
21										
22										
23										
24										
25										
26										
27										
28										
29										
30										
31										
32										
33										

Discussion Box 4.8
_____

If you had the opportunity to execute the NGT procedures, record the highest ranked items in response to your question.

Question posed:

Highest ranked items:

Discussion Box 4.9
_____

What is your overall assessment of the NGT process? Was it useful? Was it difficult? Did you learn how to use it?

Exercise B: Preliminary Examination of Service Process

In this exercise, you will examine a familiar program with regard to the overall service process. Ideally, this process begins with a client recognizing a need, receiving an effective service in meeting this need, and is discharged into an appropriate follow-up plan. But the process can be viewed as more complicated. There are various places in this process that can contribute to the program's success in meeting client need. Here is an outline.

1. Clients must recognize their need. Are those in need aware of their need? If not, what program strategies are used to enhance this awareness? What could be done to improve this awareness?
2. Clients must be aware that a service exists that can help. Are those in need aware of the program? Are they confident this program will meet their needs?
3. The services must be accessible to the clients who are in need. How has the agency addressed this issue? For example, are the agency's hours of operation compatible with prospective clients' schedules? Is the location of the office convenient to prospective clients?
4. New clients must be given an effective intake process. This includes both treating the client with respect and making appropriate intake decisions. Does the agency provide an inviting atmosphere for the new client to apply for service? Are clients properly screened for eligibility? Are clients given appropriate information that assists them in determining the nature of the fit between their needs and agency services?

5. The service must be effective in meeting client need. What does the service look like? Does the structure of the service make sense as a response to client need? For example, if clients with the particular problem have need for information, some form of training would be a logical part of the service. But if clients are most in need of working out a relationship with another person, some form of therapy might make more sense.

We could conceive of two basic forms of justification for a given program's design—logical justification and scientific justification.

- Logical justification is based on whether the design of the program makes sense. If ignorance of the effects of drug abuse is a main cause of drug abuse, some form of training about the effects of drugs would make sense. But if those who abuse drugs have plenty of knowledge about the effects of drugs, training would not make sense.

- Scientific justification refers to the results of studies that have been done on the effectiveness of a given service. Do you have any evidence about the effectiveness of your service?

6. Clients must be given an effective follow-up plan to sustain their growth. What does the agency do in this regard? What information does the agency have on the status of past clients?

These aspects of process evaluation will be examined in more detail, with questions being posed to you to examine each one. There is an infinite variation in level of attention you could give to each of these aspects of process evaluation. At one end of the continuum, you could simply devote a paragraph or two to the presentation of your own opinions based on your knowledge of the questions posed. At the other end of the continuum, you could undertake a comprehensive examination of any given aspect, with details regarding agency policy, agency outcome studies, agency surveys, agency service statistics, and so forth. This end of the continuum could contain either a great amount of detail based on agency documents or a great deal of detail on how you would suggest the agency construct studies to compile the answers to these questions. And, of course, there are numerous places on this continuum between these two extremes. For example, if you select the minimal end of this continuum, you could enhance the level of sophistication of your presentation by the inclusion of selected details from agency documents, client comments, and so forth.

Identifying the Program and Client Needs

Before engaging in the specific aspects of the service process, you need to be clear about the nature of the clients' problems or needs and the nature of the program that is being evaluated. First, what is the program being evaluated? Identify the structure of the program in sufficient detail that the reader can recognize it. For example, the Adult Inpatient Treatment Program for persons suffering from severe depression might be characterized as follows:

> Clients receive 24-hour residential care that includes medication, daily monitoring of health by a nurse, daily group therapy sessions, daily individual therapy sessions, and daily recreational therapy sessions.

A somewhat more complicated description is provided for a program designed to address the needs of persons suffering from chronic and persistent mental illness (e.g., schizophrenia):

This program employs a multidisciplinary team where all clients are served by all members of the team, without specific assignment of an individual client to an individual team member. The team consists of a team manager, a psychiatric nurse, a human services counselor, and a psychologist. The team meets daily to discuss client needs. Members of the team visit each client four times per month. Each visit typically lasts 15 minutes to a half hour. The team assists clients in finding housing, attaining medication, finding transportation, finding social outlets, attending substance abuse support groups, and other activities that clients typically would have to go to various agencies for, to receive help. A key ingredient of this service is one-on-one contact between team members and clients that provides a sufficient bond for the client to be helped in the reduction of barriers to effective use of concrete services.

Discussion Box 4.10

How would you describe a familiar program that will be the focus of your process analysis?

A second preliminary consideration is the identification of the clients' problems or needs. You should focus on client conditions such as poor grades in school, depression, unemployment, repeat hospitalizations that could have been prevented, child abuse, and so forth. You should *not* characterize the client's needs in terms of a lack of a specific service, such as a need for family counseling, a need for in-home care for hospice patients, the need for follow-up services for discharged hospital patients, and so forth. The service is the solution to the problem or a way of meeting need. It is a response to a need, not a need itself.

Discussion Box 4.11

How would you characterize the chief needs of the clients your program serves? Do they need information, social support, or the ability to avoid hostile encounters with others, or …?

Assessing Service Process

Six aspects of process evaluation are presented below. You should consider each of these ideas with regard to your identified program and your identified problem or need, and then select one or two ideas for elaboration in the discussion box that follows.

1. *Recognition of client need.* The first step in the process of improvement for the client is the recognition of the need. Most persons recognize their needs, but there are some clients who need help with this aspect of the service process. A classic example is the initial denial of a problem by a large number of persons with alcoholism. As a consequence, effective alcoholism treatment programs have components of service that are designed to address this condition.

Do clients with your identified problem or need tend to recognize their need? If not, what does your agency do to address this issue?

2. *Awareness of service.* Are those in need aware of your agency's services? If not, what has your agency done to address this problem? If they are aware, are they confident this service will meet their needs? Is the agency doing anything to address this problem?

One clue to difficulty in this area is the discovery that a certain type of potential client is poorly represented in your client population. Is there an ethnic group that is not represented among your clients at a level that represents their proportion of your community? Is there an age category that is underrepresented? Are males or females underrepresented? Low representation is okay if it is clear that this particular type of need (or problem) is not experienced at a significant level for this group. But if you have no such information, you should question why this group is underrepresented in your client population.

3. *Accessibility of service.* How accessible are your services for the target population? Do you have office hours in the evenings or weekends? Is the location of your agency convenient? Do prospective clients have transportation to your facility?

4. *Effective intake.* Clients must be effectively received at intake and screened for the appropriate match of client need to agency service. The typical intake process for the human service agency has the client coming to the agency asking for a service. When prospective clients come to your agency, how are they treated initially? Is there an inviting atmosphere in the waiting room? Are they greeted warmly? Are there any negative messages that are subtly displayed by this atmosphere or greeting? How would this greeting compare to the greeting you get when you go into your bank to do business or enter your favorite restaurant? If it is not equally positive, ask why.

Is there an effective intake protocol that screens in the appropriate clients and screens out the inappropriate ones? By appropriate, I am not referring to such things as client attitudes or client difficulty; I am referring to client need. I would discourage agencies from screening in only those clients who will be easy to serve.

5. *Effective service.* The service delivered must be effective in meeting client need. Some services are illogically designed. If ignorance is not the cause of the client's problem, it does not seem logical that training would be the solution. If the client's problem is multidimensional, it stands to reason that the service should be multidimensional. For example, multisystemic therapy for troubled youth includes interventions in various aspects of the clients' lives.

Some services are not designed to deliver enough service to reach a certain threshold of client impact. Ask yourself just how much one can reasonably expect in the way of client change by the intensity of the service you are offering. A chronic and severe problem is not likely to be ameliorated by weekly therapy sessions over four weeks.

6. *Follow-up plan.* Effective service in the long run normally includes a follow-up plan designed to help clients sustain their growth or continue to grow. What is the nature of follow up for your agency? Is there a plan that is part of the service protocol? Is there any further contact with clients to evaluate adherence to the plan?

Discussion Box 4.12

Which of these six items is best addressed by your selected program? In other words, which one is done the best?

Discussion Box 4.13

Which of these six items is in most need of improvement?

Exercise C: Preliminary Design of an Outcome Study

In this exercise, you will design several parts of an outcome evaluation study for a familiar program or intervention. When we consider the entire process of conducting an outcome evaluation study, we would address each of the following questions:

1. What is the nature of the target behavior being addressed by the intervention? How is it best defined, so that we know how to measure client progress?
2. What are the dynamics of this target behavior? How can knowledge about these dynamics guide the design of the intervention? For example, what are the causes of the problem? What are the special needs of those with this target behavior?
3. What is the intervention?
   a. What are the objectives of this intervention?
   b. How would the intervention be described with regard to structure? What does it look like?
   c. What is the model that serves as the conceptual link between this intervention and the dynamics of the target behavior, and as a guide for the design of the structure?
   d. How would this intervention be described with regard to personnel?
4. What is the study population and study sample? Given the sample selection procedures, how can the results of this study be generalized to persons not included in this study sample?
5. How will client progress be measured? How reliable and valid are these methods of measurement?

6. What is the design of the evaluation study with regard to data collection and the implementation of the intervention? For example, will you measure target behavior once before treatment and once at the end of treatment for a group of clients? To what extent can we attribute measured client gain to the intervention rather than something else (e.g., normal growth and development over time)?
7. How well was the planned intervention implemented?
8. Did the client(s) achieve a measured gain in functioning? Can this level of gain easily be explained by chance?
9. What conclusions can we draw about the effectiveness of this intervention in the improvement of client functioning?

In this exercise, we will address only a few of these aspects of outcome evaluation. You will address the others in future chapters. Before you consider the tasks discussed, you will need to identify a human service program or intervention with which you have familiarity or can obtain information.

Task #1: Identifying the Target Behavior

You need to identify the target behavior in order to identify the objective of intervention and identify a means for measuring client progress. Suppose, for example, that you want to evaluate outcome for an intervention designed to reduce aggressive behaviors for adult criminal defenders. How would you define aggression? You might define aggression as a behavior that is intended to cause harm to another person or damage property. You would need to decide if your definition of aggression includes verbal abuse, threats, or is restricted to violent acts. If teaching anger management techniques is a key service strategy, you may need to define anger as well. You might define anger as a feeling or emotion that ranges from mild irritation to intense fury and rage. You would probably develop a more restricted definition of your target behavior and call it "uncontrolled anger" or "dysfunctional anger" and define it as anger that is disproportionately intense, or felt too frequently, or expressed inappropriately.

If you have a good definition of the target behavior, you will be in a good position to find a means for measuring client progress. In the above case of aggression, you will seek a tool for measurement that includes both physical and verbal acts of aggression, if you have defined the behavior in this way. It is rather common for standardized instruments for measuring behavior to include several distinct components of the general behavior. For example, the Adult–Adolescent Parenting Inventory is designed to assess parenting and child rearing strengths and weaknesses in four areas: (1) inappropriate developmental expectations of children, (2) lack of empathy toward children's needs, (3) belief in the use of corporal punishment, and (4) reversing parent–child roles. If you had a program designed to enhance parenting ability, you would need to define parenting ability. If your definition had each of these four things mentioned in the description of the AAPI, you might chose to use this tool to measure client progress. However, if your only focus was developmental expectations of children, it would be wise for you to include only the items of the AAPI that measured this aspect of parenting. If no part of your intervention is designed to address empathy, or corporal punishment, or reversing parent–child roles, it would be unwise to expect outcomes related to these aspects of parenting. And it would be unwise to measure these things in your evaluation study.

You also need to analyze this behavior in order to find guidance for the design of the intervention. If child abuse is caused by a lack of knowledge of child development and good parenting practices, some form of parent training would be a logical intervention. If it is caused by the stresses of poverty accompanied by a lack of social support, some form of intervention into poverty and social support would be warranted. If it is caused by the psychopathology of the abuser, it would make sense to offer psychotherapy to the abuser as an intervention.

This line of reasoning would be logical as a method of preventing further abuse. However, you also need a strategy for meeting the needs of the abused child. The analysis of causation of child abuse will do you little good in dealing with the needs of the abused child. Instead, you should focus on what this experience has meant and how the effect of this experience can be reduced and the child's development can be enhanced. Does the abused child need interventions to meet their needs regarding self-esteem, trust, or anxiety?

Discussion Box 4.14

Select a program (e.g., child protective services in Hampton County) or an intervention (e.g., family therapy for the Parker family) for an outcome study. What is the name of this intervention or program? What is the target behavior that is addressed by this intervention?

Program name:

Target behavior:

Discussion Box 4.15

How would you define this target behavior?

Discussion Box 4.16

How would you characterize either the causes of this target behavior, or the needs of those who exhibit this behavior?

Task #2: Identifying the Intervention

The intervention or program can be described with regard to objectives, structure, personnel, and model. In this chapter, you will examine all of these except for the model of the intervention, which will be addressed later. The objectives identify the outcomes sought while the structure describes what the service looks like. The personnel of the intervention refers to the characteristics, or qualifications, of those who provide the service. The model of the intervention, which will be addressed later, identifies the conceptual or theoretical basis upon which the service is founded.

The outcome objective specifies the change that is expected in the client's target behavior. It does not focus on the service. An appropriate outcome objective would be "to enhance self-esteem," while an inappropriate outcome objective would be "to provide crisis intervention services to those in need."

Discussion Box 4.17

What is one of the outcome objectives for the intervention (or program) that you have selected for evaluation?

The structure of the intervention specifies its activities. Does it include counseling provided in the office, or training, or something else? Your description should be sufficient to give the reader of your description clear guidance on the replication of this intervention with another set of clients. Both the nature and intensity of the services should be detailed. If you use broad terms like "case management," you should provide some details regarding what this entails. Does it include an assessment interview followed by a formal intervention plan? Does it include referral to other services? If so, what kinds of services typically are included? Does the case manager engage in a systematic process of monitoring the referrals to see if clients followed up and are satisfied with the service? Does the case manager periodically meet with the client for monitoring and further assessment? If so, how often is this typically done? Are there any written protocols that specify certain aspects of case management?

Discussion Box 4.18

How would you describe your selected intervention in regard to structure?

Discussion Box 4.19

How would you describe your selected intervention in regard to personnel? In other words, what kinds of persons provide this service?

Task #3: Identifying the Means to Measure Client Progress

Your next task is to find a means for measuring client progress. You will return to your definition of the target behavior as well as the objective. You should select a means of measuring client progress that is consistent with each of these statements; each of these two statements should be congruent. For example, you should not identify your objective as improving school grades and your target behavior as self-esteem. You might have your treatment goal as improving school grades and your objective as improving self-esteem, because improved self-esteem is considered to be a measured amount of progress toward the achievement of your goal. In this case, you would define self-esteem and find a measurement tool that accurately measures it. Your objective, of course, could be "to improve school grades." In that case, you have a simple means of measuring client progress.

You can develop your own measure of client progress (individualized instrument) or find a standardized tool. Individualized measurement devices are appropriate either for simple behaviors to measure or ones that are not appropriate for any standardized tool. Target behaviors such as self-esteem, anxiety, depression, guilt, loneliness, and marital conflict typically are measured by standardized devices. Such concrete behaviors as grades, whether the client showed up for a medical appointment, or whether the client was reconfirmed for child abuse after a previous incident are not typically measured by a standardized scale. These data can be derived from agency records.

You can find standardized measurement tools in various books. An easy way to explore this task is to use the Internet and enter the words tests in print or something similar. Internet sources often change from year to year so it is not possible to guarantee that a given website still exits. However, one source available in recent years is the Buros Institute for Mental Measurement. Their website is listed as follows: http://www.unl.edu/buros. You can look up titles and brief descriptions of measurement tools on this site. In one experience with this site, I entered the keyword aggression and found both the Aggression Questionnaire and the Behavioral Assessment System for Children. I learned that the Aggression Questionnaire is designed to evaluate an individual's aggressive responses and ability to channel these responses in a safe and constructive manner. I found that the Behavioral Assessment System for Children is designed to identify behavioral disorders in children. If I had an intervention that was highly specific to the treatment of aggression and one's ability to cope with it constructively, I might find the Aggression Questionnaire to be useful. However, you will note that the Behavioral Assessment System for Children is designed to measure behavioral disorders in general, only some of which are related to aggression. So the latter instrument is less specific to aggression than the former. Also, you should note the audience that is addressed by the instrument; the latter is designed for children.

You may be in a situation where you need to develop your unique way of measuring client progress. It could be that your outcome is easy to measure in a concrete way, such as the number of persons rehospitalized after discharge, or the number of children reported for abuse after a prior investigation failed to substantiate that abuse had occurred. You may use a measure like grades in school, or the number of disciplinary actions invoked.

If you are defining the target behavior as a psychological construct like depression, anxiety, self-esteem, or aggression, you should seek a standardized tool like you can find from the Buros Institute. You don't need to reinvent the wheel, and likely a poor one at that, by creating your own instrument. But you may find that your target behavior is not well measured by an established instrument, and you have no choice but to develop your own tool for measuring a social or psychological construct.

Discussion Box 4.20

What is the tool you will use to measure client progress? Identify the behavior the tool is designed to measure, the name of the tool, and give one or two items from it in the box.

Behavior:

Name of tool:

What tool is designed to measure:

Reference

Delbecq, A. L., Van de Ven, A.H., & Gustafson, D. H. (1975). *Group techniques for program planning.* Glenview, Illinois: Scott Foresman.

5

Assuring the Protection of the Rights of Study Subjects

When you use human subjects for research, you must abide by certain ethical principles. In the first chapter, you reviewed three major ethical issues in research ethics—privacy, self-determination, and protection from harm. Your research should not invade a study subject's right to privacy. For example, you would not want to post John Smith's scores on the agency bulletin board next to his name. Your research also should respect the client's right to self-determination. This means you would not use client information without the client's informed consent. Finally, you would want to avoid placing the client in harm's way regarding damage that might be done to the client's emotions or financial risk, and so forth. You returned to these issues in Chapter 2 when you were asked to participate in a study because you were the study subject and I wanted to assure that your rights and welfare would be protected.

In this chapter, you will return to this subject in more depth. The focus will be on those principles and procedures that are most relevant to evaluation research. When you complete this chapter, you should have fundamental competence in the consideration of ethical principles for your research study and be prepared to deal with the organizational body that must review your research protocol for ethical concerns.

At the completion of this chapter, you will be able to:

1. Distinguish between those research studies that do and do not normally require institutional review for ethical concerns.

2. Explicate the three major principles that guide institutional review for research ethics.

3. Identify how to address the issues of privacy, informed consent, risk, and justice in regard to your research study.

4. Identify the types of institutional review for research ethics and where your own study fits into this typology.

5. Identify which ethical issue is most salient to a given research study.

Overview

Our first step is a reminder of the principles for research ethics given in Chapter 1 from the Code of Ethics of the National Association of Social Workers. Six of the items in that code related to research ethics are as follows:

1. The social worker engaged in research should consider carefully its possible consequences for human beings.
2. The social worker engaged in research should ascertain that the consent of participants is voluntary and informed, without any implied deprivation of penalty for refusal to participate, and with due regard for participants' privacy and dignity.
3. The social worker engaged in research should protect participants from unwarranted physical or mental discomfort, distress, harm, danger, or deprivation.
4. The social worker who engages in the evaluation of services or cases should discuss them only for professional purposes and only with persons directly and professionally concerned with them.
5. Information obtained about participants in research should be treated as confidential.
6. The social worker should take credit only for work actually done in connection with scholarly and research endeavors and credit contributions made by others. (National Association of Social Workers, 1980, *Code of Ethics*, Silver Spring, MD)

The most profound requirement is that research participants must be protected from any harm that might come from the research experience. This is seldom an issue in human service evaluation because the participants are typically asked only to supply information. Medical experiments that put people into hypnosis or administer drugs or electric shocks are in an entirely different arena as far as this issue is concerned.

In evaluation research, confidentiality is an important consideration. Persons who are called upon to answer research questions are normally informed that their responses will be treated confidentially, meaning that their identities will not be revealed in the report that emanates from the research. It is even better if their responses can be anonymous, because privacy is assured in this way and research subjects do not have to worry about whether confidentiality will be violated.

Another issue is voluntary participation. It is important that each study subject's participation be voluntary. This means that your agency should not ask clients to participate in a way that might be perceived as coercive. This also means that your agency should not conduct studies where clients are made to feel that their eligibility for continued service is dependent on their participation in research. If this is true, it cannot be said their participation was truly voluntary. In the study conducted in Chapter 2, you were asked to participate but you were given the option of turning in a blank form to the instructor of the course so that your choice not to participate would not be apparent. In this way, you were truly given the option to participate or not to participate. If the instructor had a way of knowing who had participated, your right to voluntary participation might have been compromised to a limited degree.

This issue of voluntary participation is more complicated than it first appears. There are study protocols that require that study participants not be aware that they are being observed. In these studies, you cannot say that the study subjects offered to participate voluntarily. When this situation is encountered, the critical question is whether the benefits of the research outweigh the risks to the study subjects.

There are several online courses on the protection of human subjects in research. One that informed the present chapter is by CITI. For more information on this course, see www.citiprogram.org.

The issue of protection of human subjects in research is monitored by the institutional review board (IRB) in major institutions like universities or governmental bodies. There are other titles for mechanisms that serve the same purpose for other agencies. It might be the agency's research committee or it might be an assigned responsibility of an individual with administrative duties. The purpose of this review mechanism is to protect the rights of human subjects in research. Full review of details by the IRB is required in some types of evaluation studies, while a more limited review is required by certain other types of evaluations. There are some situations that do not require review at all. These types of reviews will be discussed later in this chapter.

Your next task is to think of an evaluation research study you would like to conduct and identify the organizational body that should review your study protocol to determine if there are ethical concerns that must be addressed. If your study is in the institutional context of a university, your university should have an institutional review board. But you cannot make this assumption. You must check it out and find out the beginning procedures for getting your protocol to this body. For example, you might find that the review group is called _____ and the procedures for submitting a protocol can be found on the website _____. If you are in a human service agency, there may be a research committee or an individual with review responsibilities. Who is this person and what does this person require? You are not asked to get a lot of specifics, only to get a basic question or two answered.

Discussion Box 5.1

Briefly identify the evaluation study you would like to conduct and provide some preliminary information on the organizational body or person who would need to review your proposal for ethical concerns.

What Types of Evaluation Studies Must be Reviewed?

Institutional review boards (IRBs) examine the proposals of researchers who plan to use human subjects in research. A human subject in research is a living individual from whom a researcher collects information for research purposes. Some forms of human service evaluation would not be classified as research. To necessitate a formal review, your evaluation study must collect information from clients in a systematic fashion for the purpose of developing knowledge that can be generalized to others. Systematic collection of information entails such things as administering a pretest and posttest instrument for the purpose of determining treatment effectiveness. It does not refer to spontaneous observation of client behavior during treatment.

To say that the knowledge you generate will be generalized to others means you plan to use the information derived from the investigation to contribute to our general knowledge. Are you conducting this study to develop generalizations about practice effectiveness that will be shared with others through publications, reports, and so forth? For example, you may be testing the effectiveness of a treatment model with a given target behavior and you believe the results will be useful for others in the evaluation of this model. If this is true, your study would fall into the category of one that is intended to be generalized.

The information you obtain from one client that is designed to help you to better treat that client would not qualify for formal review. The information derived from a client satisfaction survey that was used only on an internal basis would also not qualify for formal review. By "internal basis" it is meant that only those in the program will review the information, and will do so only for the purpose of improving this service in this agency. As a rule of thumb, the broader the audience of any report generated by an evaluation study, the more likely it will be viewed as subject to formal review.

Research using existing data normally does not require formal review. An exception would be data where the individual can be identified by his/her data. If there is no way for the researcher to identify the data for a given subject, the study normally would not be subject to review. However, the researcher must also be sensitive to the display of data that readers might be able to use for this purpose. For example, if there was only one faculty member in your college who was listed as American Indian, you would not want to display data that was broken down so that this one person's information could be identified.

Discussion Box 5.2

Let's return to the example of the evaluation study you previously indicated you would like to conduct. Does your study qualify for some form of organizational review for research ethics?

Protection of Human Subjects in Research

There are several major principles that the IRB will employ to evaluate a proposal to determine if it should be approved. According to the CITI online course (www.citiprogram.org) on the protection of human subjects in research, the National Commission for the Protection of Human

Subjects in Biomedical and Behavioral Research met in 1979 and prepared the Belmont Report. This report identifies three principles that underlie all human subject research:

1. Respect for persons
2. Beneficence
3. Justice

The principle of respect deals with autonomy and self-determination. People should be allowed to choose for themselves the risk they will undertake. Study subjects have full autonomy when they can understand the risks involved and have the freedom to volunteer without coercion. Informed consent and privacy are two themes that will be discussed below.

The principle of beneficence requires that we minimize harm and maximize benefits. Risk assessment is a key theme. The principle of justice requires us to design research that does not unduly target its risks to certain groups of people and fails to treat different types of people equably or fairly.

Informed Consent and Privacy

For most research studies, informed consent is required. This means that study subjects have given their consent and they were clearly informed about risks and were truly given the opportunity to refrain from participation without coercion. In this process, no information about risk should be withheld. There are a few exceptions where consent is not required but these situations rarely refer to human service evaluation studies, so they will not be discussed here.

A key issue is the subject's ability to give informed consent. Research using children as research subjects always require formal review because children are not in a position to give fully informed consent. Research involving persons of limited literacy or intellectual ability requires more care in the assurance of this consent.

Not only must subjects give their consent, they must be given the opportunity to withdraw from participation at any time. In this regard, the subject must be notified that there will be no penalty for withdrawal, such as losing service benefits.

Privacy refers to our ability to control access to information about ourselves. *Confidentiality* refers to implied or explicit contracts between individuals about the sharing of information one person may have about another. The regulations of the Health Insurance Portability and Accountability Act (HIPPA) have provided new restrictions on how health information can be shared by health providers. They generally require no release of health information without the explicit permission of the patient and provide guidelines on how agencies can protect unauthorized review of such information by individuals. While this act does not deal only with research, it has major implications for the use of human subjects in research.

There is a distinction between private and public behavior. Public behavior can be observed for research purposes without the need for formal review of research proposals, but private behavior cannot. Private behavior is that behavior that one would normally expect to be private. This would include a conversation between two people alone on a park bench where there is no one within hearing distance. The use of an electronic device for hearing conversations from someone 30 yards away could be interpreted as a violation of privacy, because it would be reasonable for these individuals to believe their conversation was private. However, the behavior of a group of people playing football in a park would be considered public behavior.

Discussion Box 5.3

Let's return to the example of the evaluation study you previously indicated you would like to conduct. How should you deal with the issues of informed consent and privacy?

Risks and Benefits

A risk is a disadvantage to the study subject, while a benefit is an advantage to either the study subject or society in general. Risks normally fall in the category of either invasion of privacy or the harm from study procedures. Examples of the latter are procedures that place study subjects under stress or risky procedures like administration of drugs. Asking a client to complete a scale designed to measure target behavior normally holds no risk of harm from the procedures, so the issue of invasion of privacy is the only category of risk to address in your study protocol.

When there are risks, the IRB will review the balance of risks with benefits. Sometimes the risk is held only by the study subject, and the benefit is to society in general. In this case, the IRB must determine if the benefit warrants the risk; this is not often easy to address.

An issue the IRB will consider when facing risks is whether the researcher has available procedures that are less risky. Even if one could cogently argue that the benefits of this study will outweigh the risks, the IRB may require a less risky procedure that will achieve equal benefits. Whatever the risks, they should always be minimized to the extent feasible.

Discussion Box 5.4

Let's return to the example of the evaluation study you previously indicated you would like to conduct. How should you deal with levels of risk?

Justice

The key issue with regard to justice is whether certain vulnerable populations are being singled out for inordinate burden from the study being undertaken. This is not likely to be an issue for human service research for the day-to-day practitioner dealing with clients who have asked for service. If you were conducting a different kind of study with a national sample of persons from low-income communities, the question would be raised as to whether your study purpose necessitates that data be drawn only from this type of population. It might seem unfair to target governmental housing projects, simply because it is well known that persons in these homes feel they must answer anyone's questions because their housing is subsidized. If your study is about people in subsidized housing, this would be okay. But if it is about a general topic that has nothing specific to do with subsidized housing or poverty, your IRB might raise a question about using only such communities for your study subjects.

Discussion Box 5.5

Let's return to the example of the evaluation study you previously indicated you would like to conduct. How should you deal with the issue of justice?

Types of Review

There are three research situations for the consideration of formal review:

1. Those situations where data are collected but the procedures do not necessitate a review at all because they do not qualify as research studies using human subjects (e.g., the administration of a self-esteem scale to an individual client strictly for clinical purposes where there is no study being reported to others)
2. Expedited review, where the IRB will collect limited data and give a quick response
3. Full review, where the full IRB will review the research study protocol and make a decision if the study should go forth

You read about the first situation in the section of this chapter on what types of studies should be reviewed. The second and third situations require some form of review by the IRB. The expedited review is one where there is only minimal risk to study subjects, or the data are collected in routine situations like educational testing or existing databases where individuals cannot be identified by name. The full review covers other situations where there is some notable risk and the IRB must give careful consideration to the risks and benefits of the proposed study.

In order to avoid common mistakes by novice researchers when dealing with the IRB, there are two things you should consider. First, it is the IRB that will determine whether your study is in the expedited category. You will submit the necessary information to your IRB and it is possible that this body will return a decision to you positing that your study requires full review and further information. Second, you must submit your request to the IRB before you begin collecting your data. If you have already begun collecting data, whatever harm that might come has already been done before the IRB has a chance to stop it.

Summary

In this chapter, you have reviewed several key principles of ethics in the use of human subjects in research. After a review of the Code of Ethics of the National Association of Social Workers, you were subjected to an examination of how the Institutional Review Board (IRB) operates to protect human subjects in research. Then, three key principles that guide the IRB was examined in some depth—respect for persons, beneficence, and justice.

Quiz

The following questions provide a review of the contents of this chapter. Answers are given at the end.

1. Which of the following situations is/are considered research on human subjects and require(s) full review by the IRB or its equivalent in your agency?
   a. You ask one client to respond to a depression scale on a weekly basis for several weeks of treatment and you expect to employ these measurements for clinical purposes, but you do not expect to include this information in a report.
   b. You will conduct an anonymous client satisfaction survey where the data will be used only on an internal basis for program improvement, and you do not expect to include this information in a report to be distributed for general understanding of the nature of the treatment and/or target behavior.
   c. Both of the above.
   d. None of the above.
2. Which of the following situations is/are considered research on human subjects and require(s) either expedited or full review by the IRB or its equivalent in your agency?
   a. You are examining whether the support model of treatment will reduce caregiver

burnout for those caring for relatives suffering from seriously debilitating illnesses. You will administer a stress scale to a group of persons before and after treatment, and will use the data in a report on the effectiveness of this treatment model for caregiver burnout.
   b. You are testing whether a new drug will reduce depression for those suffering from AIDS by administering this new drug during a treatment period when you will also regularly conduct blood tests.
   c. Both of the above.
   d. None of the above.
3. Which of the following statement is/are true?
   a. Children are not considered capable of giving informed consent to engage in research as human subjects.
   b. Studies employing existing databases normally do not require full review by the IRB if individual names of persons are not listed in the database.
   c. Both of the above.
   d. None of the above.
4. Which of the following statements is/are true?
   a. Under no circumstances may you conduct research using human subjects without the

written consent of the person who provides the information for the study.

b. If you wanted to conduct a study of social norms that are prevalent in public housing projects, you would not be able to collect data only using people from public housing projects because of the issue of justice.

c. Both of the above.

d. None of the above.

5. Which of the following statements is/are true?

a. Sometimes the IRB will approve a study proposal that entails notable risk to study subjects because the benefits to society outweigh the risks to the individual study subject.

b. If a study procedure is available to the researcher that is less risky than the one planned, the IRB will usually require its employment in the study.

c. Both of the above.

d. None of the above.

6. Suppose a researcher has proposed to conduct a study on the natural responses to stressful encounters by faking a heart attach on a busy street corner while another researcher observes the behavior of people who react, not knowing the apparent heart attack is a fake. The observer will make notes about the behaviors of the bystanders but will not know their identities.

Which issue in research ethics would be most problematic for this study? (*Note:* The question is not whether this study is so problematic it is unlikely to be approved by the IRB. The question focuses your attention on the issue most likely to present questions for closer review.)

a. Confidentiality

b. Voluntary participation

c. Harm

d. Justice

7. Suppose a researcher wishes to conduct a study on the validity of astrology by gaining information on each study subject's astrological sign (Leo, Virgo, etc.) and asking questions of that person to determine if the information from astrology accurately predicts the answers the individual gives to questions about his or her personality. This study will be conducted in eight prisons, some for males and some for females. A total of 1,200 prisoners will be asked to volunteer for this study. The data will be collected anonymously. Which issue in research ethics would be most problematic for this study?

a. Confidentiality

b. Voluntary participation

c. Harm

d. Justice

Reference

National Association of Social Workers. (1980). *Code of Ethics*. Washington, DC: National Association of Social Workers.

Answers to the Quiz

1. d

2. c

3. c

4. d

5. c

6. b

7. d

6

Process Evaluation and Qualitative Research

In this chapter, you will examine key concepts and issues in process evaluation, with special attention to qualitative research. The natural connection between process evaluation and qualitative research will be illuminated as you examine such subjects as approaches to qualitative research, data collection in qualitative research, and data analysis in this form of research. Finally, you will be given a step-by-step format for conducting a content analysis of qualitative data.

Upon the completion of this chapter, you will be able to:

1. Distinguish between input, process, output, and outcome as forms of potential evaluation.
2. Identify a focus for a process evaluation study for a familiar agency.
3. Identify whether a qualitative method of measurement would be more appropriate than a quantitative one when given an example.
4. Describe ethnography, grounded theory, and the case study approach as examples of types of qualitative research.
5. Identify key guidelines for interviewing, focus group dialogue, and direct observation of behavior as examples of approaches to data collection in qualitative research.
6. Describe the essential nature of content analysis as one approach to data analysis in qualitative research.

This exploration will begin with a revisiting of the systems model for viewing human service evaluation as discussed beforehand. There is a quiz at the end of the chapter which you may want to use as an exemption quiz if you think you may not need to examine the content of this chapter, or as a final test to determine how well you understand this content.

The Systems Model Revisited

The systems model for viewing human service evaluation was presented in a previous chapter as follows:

Input → Process → Output → Outcome

A client comes to the agency with a need (input) and receives a service (process) which can be quantified in concrete terms (output) and achieves an improvement in functioning (outcome). In Table 6.1, you can see some examples of how this works.

In the previous chapter, you reviewed one technique for evaluating the extent of unmet client needs, you reviewed how the service process should work in regard to many different aspects, and you engaged in a preliminary exercise in the evaluation of outcome. In previous chapters, you also reviewed two forms of information—qualitative and quantitative. You saw that qualitative data takes the form of words expressed by people, whereas quantitative data are in the form of numbers or concrete categories.

This chapter will focus on process evaluation and qualitative research, because of the natural fit between the two. When you engage in process evaluation, you are normally seeking ideas on how services can be improved. The flexible nature of qualitative research is especially useful in this situation. However, note that both qualitative and quantitative means of measurement are used in both process and outcome evaluations.

Discussion Box 6.1

Would either (or both) of the following be examples of the evaluation of process?

1. You send out a questionnaire to clients asking for suggestions on how to improve the intake process for a service they have received.
2. You send a questionnaire to clients asking the following question:
   Did the service you received help you in achieving the goals that you had hoped to achieve through our service? _____ Yes _____ No

---

An Overview of Process Evaluation

For a service to be effective there is a process that normally must take place for the individual client. You reviewed this process in one of the exercises in the previous chapter. First, the client must recognize the need. A classic example of a problem with this is the alcoholic's tendency to deny there is a problem. A response to this situation is the idea of an intervention whereby the alcoholic is confronted by relatives and friends. For many people suffering from alcoholism, this is a necessary first step. You could conduct a social survey to assess the extent to which such

TABLE 6.1 *Illustrations of Input, Process, Output, and Outcome*

Input	Process	Output	Outcome
A single client, Ms Fox, is depressed.	Cognitive-behavioral therapy is offered.	Eight therapy sessions are provided.	Ms. Fox's depression level is reduced by 40 percent.
Twelve middle school students have low school performance.	School social work service is provided.	A total of 12 students are served.	The average grades improve by 25 percent but disciplinary actions are not reduced.
Children are reported for child abuse and neglect.	A new protocol for child protective service investigation is implemented.	67 child abuse investigations were completed in the first quarter of the year.	The incidence of repeat offences of child abuse is lowered by 42%.

interventions are necessary. How many people in the community know of a person with an alcohol problem who denies this problem?

The second thing necessary for effective service is that the person in need must be aware there is a service that can help. How many people in your community are aware of the special initiative regarding respite care for caretakers for disabled relatives? A social survey could be helpful in answering this question.

If needy people are aware of their need and are aware of the service, it still will not be an effective response to the social problem unless the services are accessible. This is the fourth consideration in the examination of the service.

The fifth consideration is that the model of service must be an effective model for the given need or problem. Services are designed to achieve certain objectives through designated activities. The organization of the activities is based on a model of treatment. The model of treatment should be based on logic and evidence regarding social behavior with special attention to the dynamics of the problem being addressed. A parent support group would be a logical service to meet the need for social support, which is associated with social isolation as a cause of child neglect. Evidence regarding service effectiveness is perhaps the best source of information on the assessment of the potential effectiveness of the model. If this model has been tested with other populations and found to be effective, it makes sense for you to try it with your population.

A sixth consideration is the extent to which the model of treatment was actually implemented by service staff. Patton (1997) warns us that a label is not sufficient for us to know what happened in treatment. It is much easier to find a label for a given service than it is for us to assure that the model of treatment is being implemented. He gives the example of an evaluation of a foster group home program for juvenile offenders.

> The theory undergirding the program was that juvenile offenders would be more likely to be rehabilitated if they were placed in warm, supportive, and nonauthoritarian environments where they were valued by others and could therefore learn to value themselves. The goals of the program included helping juveniles feel good about themselves and become capable of exercising independent judgment, thereby reducing subsequent criminal actions. (Patton, 1997, p. 210).

The evaluation measured both outcomes and treatment environments. The evaluation of treatment environments revealed great variation in the extent to which the model was being implemented by the sample of 50 group homes being studied.

> In terms of treatment specifications, these data demonstrated two things: (1) in about half of the county's group homes, juveniles were not experiencing the kind of treatment that the program design called for; and (2) outcomes varied directly with the nature and degree of program implementation. Clearly it would make no sense to conceptualize these 50 group homes as a homogenous treatment. We found homes that were run like prisons and homes in which juveniles were physically abused. We also found homes where young offenders were loved and treated as members of the family. Aggregating recidivism data from all 50 homes into a single average rate would disguise important environmental variation. (Patton, 1997, p. 210)

So the design seemed to be working just fine as long as it was properly implemented. But implementation failed in about one-half of the agencies delivering the program.

The final consideration in the quest for a systematic evaluation of a given service is the appropriateness of discharge and follow-up. Many human services are designed to make a dent in a problem or achieve some temporary respite from the condition. When is it appropriate to discharge a client? What happens after discharge? If they achieved the objectives, is this achievement maintained in the future?

It should be reasonably easy to see that both quantitative and qualitative methods of measurement are relevant to process evaluation studies. In this chapter, however, we will focus on qualitative research.

Discussion Box 6.2

Identify how you would evaluate one aspect of the service process for a familiar human service program or intervention. For example, you might conduct a survey of all pregnant women to determine how many are aware of your prenatal service, or you might analyze the clinical notes of psychotherapists to determine if they were adhering to each of several aspects of the protocol for the delivery of cognitive-behavioral therapy, or you might evaluate the discharge component by collecting data on the number of formerly discharged clients who returned for service with unresolved issues from the past service, and so forth.

Evaluating Treatment Sessions

A great deal of research on the outcomes of therapy suggests that the nature of the helping relationship between client and therapist is critical. In fact, it is more important than the choice of a particular treatment model or technique (Hubble, et al., 1999). You are more likely to achieve your treatment goals by having a therapist who demonstrates warmth, empathy, and genuineness than one who is best trained on the latest therapeutic techniques. One of the process variables that you may want to evaluate is the degree to which the treatment session was viewed by the client as helpful and responsive. This is different from outcome, which focuses on change in the target behavior.

The directors of talkingcure.com have developed a session rating scale that can be used for this purpose (see www.talkingcure.com). This approach calls upon the client to answer a very brief questionnaire at the end of each session. There are only four items on this scale. One measures the therapeutic relationship as evidenced in the session. This item asks the client to indicate, on a scale, the extent to which the session can best be characterized as one in which the client felt heard, understood, and respected, or one in which the client did not feel these things. The client can place a mark on a line, with each end stated in the extreme, to indicate the extent to which one or the other statement best reflected the session for the client. Another item on this scale asks the extent to which the session focused on the things the client wanted to work on, while a third item asks whether the approach taken by the therapist is a good fit with the client. The final item is one that asks for an overall reflection on the session.

One practical use of this tool is the monitoring of client perceptions and the prediction of potential for the client prematurely dropping out of treatment. The client's ratings of sessions should be a good predictor of client outcome, given the nature of the scientific evidence on what works in therapy. You may want to conduct some of your own research to test this proposition. And you might want to consider the process variables most relevant to your service and develop a process evaluation instrument specifically designed to ask for client feedback on these variables.

An Overview of Qualitative Research

You reviewed the concept of qualitative and quantitative measurement in the first chapter. When you have completed the *qualitative* measurement of social phenomena, you will have words rather than numbers or uniform categories. These words may come from various sources such as the direct quotes from your study participants or your own field notes from your observations. These words will be examined for themes and will be coded accordingly. As you can see, qualitative measurement is more flexible, and characterizes each study subject in a more unique format. The examination of concepts and ideas is at the center of your qualitative analysis.

On the other hand, when you have completed the *quantitative* measurement of a study variable with your study subjects, you will have either a category or number to assign to each study participant for each variable. Each person may be categorized as male or female. They may be assigned a number that represents their age. They may have been given a score based on their responses to the Adult-Adolescent Parenting Inventory. All study subjects are measured in a uniform way in quantitative measurement.

In both qualitative and quantitative research, your methodology must have a certain level of **transparency** to be legitimate as a scientific approach to inquiry. You will need to be quite clear about the measurement method you used. This is an easier task in quantitative research. In quantitative measurement, for example, you may report that you gave your clients the Beck

Depression Inventory at intake and again six weeks later. This is quite clear and the reader of your report can draw any number of conclusions about the suitability of your methods. They may think your methods are quite good or rather mediocre, but they will not be in the dark about what you did.

But what if someone conducts interviews with open-ended questions? This is more difficult to make transparent. Suppose someone said she had conducted interviews of 12 clients and concluded that your agency's practitioners are not sensitive to the needs of clients. Wouldn't you want to know what questions were asked of clients, something about this person and potential biases about your agency, and more about how the qualitative data from those interviews were analyzed in such a way as to justify this conclusion? If you are to claim to have engaged in a research study using qualitative methods, it is not sufficient to say you have conducted interviews and here are your conclusions; your methods must be more transparent than that.

Besides transparency, both qualitative and quantitative research methods must be recognized as legitimate by others. There is a wide array of models and techniques of qualitative analysis that have been developed in accordance with the spirit of scientific inquiry. One is simply the tallying of the number of persons interviewed who make a reference to a given point (enumeration). This number should be discussed in relation to the total number of persons who were interviewed in order to report what percent of persons focused some attention on this theme, as compared to the same information for other themes. Another technique is seeking disconfirming evidence once an observation has been derived from the qualitative data. If your data seem to suggest that women are more likely than men to talk about relationships and men are more likely to talk about work, you would examine your data, from beginning to end, to find instances where men talked about relationships and women talked about work so that this information could be reported in the context of the general statement. There are, of course, many more techniques that are employed in a wide array of general models of qualitative analysis. The more sophisticated your qualitative methods, the more your conclusions will have credibility.

Discussion Box 6.3

With regard to the conditions for good evaluation research, what is wrong with the following situation:

An agency consultant says "I have interviewed many of the clients of this agency and found that this agency's intake system is insensitive to the diverse needs of persons who seek your help." This is all that is said by this person in a letter to the agency's director.

Can you both describe what is missing from this statement and label it?

Quantitative vs. Qualitative Approaches

The choice of a qualitative or quantitative means of observation (measurement) should be guided by the nature of the research question and existing knowledge about it. You should not begin the research experience with the idea of conducting a quantitative study or a qualitative study. Methods of observation spring from the nature of the study subject, not the other way around. Remember—don't put the cart before the horse!

In the first chapter, you reviewed some guides for choosing either qualitative or quantitative means of measurement. You learned, for example, that a qualitative method is typically more appropriate if you are seeking to develop theories or new ideas, whereas a quantitative means of measurement is usually more appropriate if you are testing a theory or proposition. If you wish precisely to measure a social phenomenon, you would be wise to use a quantitative method, but a qualitative means of measurement would be better if you wish better to understand the subjective meaning of behaviors or social processes. Precision is better achieved with quantitative measurement; broader understanding is suited to the qualitative method. The more that is known about your study variables or themes, the more that a quantitative method is appropriate.

Discussion Box 6.4

Would either, or both, of the following research studies best utilize a qualitative method of measurement rather than a quantitative one?

1. You are investigating the process of moral decline over time for persons convicted of a felony. You wish to know the nature of the stages one goes through to get to a point of committing a crime of a serious nature. As far as you know, the specific description of these stages has not been done before.
2. You are investigating whether your client's level of self-esteem is higher at the end of treatment than before.

Qualitative Research for Human Service Evaluation

An evaluation of service outcome typically takes the form of measuring the client's target behavior before and after treatment using quantitative means of measurement (e.g., the Beck Depression Inventory). In this example, you have a hypothesis to test—clients will have lower depression after treatment than before. The key variable—depression—can be measured quantitatively with a standardized depression scale, of which there are many available. You are not seeking the subjective meaning of depression; instead, you simply want to measure it at two points in time and you believe you know enough to measure depression by a standardized scale, which points to a quantitative type of study.

You may discover, however, that standardized measures do not work for your particular client. Some people have trouble understanding the language of a scale; thus, you cannot be confident that their score truly measures the thing you are trying to measure. When you select a scale, you need to keep this in mind. Some people may be excessively influenced by the social desirability bias—the desire to say things that will be socially desirable whether or not they are really true; the client may select answers that are socially desirable and avoid a true measurement of the condition under study.

In these situations, a qualitative means of measurement may be warranted. This could take the form of asking clients to describe the target behavior in their own terms, such as "the cloud over me was so dark that day I wanted to die," "the cloud was really heavy that day but it didn't make me want to die," "the cloud was a little heavy but I was able to get through the day okay," and so forth. You could engage in a content analysis of the client's descriptions before and after a period of treatment. You could seek ideas that seem to reflect more or less depression at these two points in time. Or you could use the client's words to develop a unique scale that was individualized for this client. You would be using a quantitative measure because you would have concrete categories into which the client's feelings would fall as they were measured at different points in time.

For the most part, however, you will find that quantitative measurement suits outcome evaluation quite well. This is especially true to the extent that you have clarity on the expected outcomes of intervention.

Some evaluative research focuses upon processes. A question may be raised about why certain types of clients improved more than others. In this case, you may be lacking in a theory that explains this fact and you will use qualitative research to develop a theory. A practitioner might want better to understand the processes of recovery for a typical client with a given problem. The well known stages of death and dying—from denial to anger to bargaining—were developed from interviews of persons going through this experience. Once a theory has been developed, such as the one about death and dying, you could use quantitative research to test it. But before the process is well known, you would use qualitative research to better understand it.

While you are more likely to find qualitative methods used in process evaluation and quantitative methods more used in outcome evaluation, there are many exceptions. There is no reason to believe that quantitative research must be used for outcome evaluation or that qualitative research must be used for process evaluation.

Approaches to Qualitative Research

Characterizing qualitative research as to category is no easy chore. Books which claim to cover the territory of this method have a diversity of labels for various approaches. For example, the *Handbook of qualitative research* (Denzin & Lincoln, 1994) provides chapters on case studies, grounded theory, ethnography, historical methods, biographical methods, and clinical research, among others. On the other hand, *Qualitative research in social work* (Sherman & Reid, 1994) divides qualitative research into the categories of ethnographic methods, heuristic methods, grounded theory methods, narrative methods, discourse analysis, and clinical case evaluations. One of the problems with classification is that there is much overlap among the techniques and objectives used by these various types of qualitative research.

Three of these major types of qualitative research are ethnography, grounded theory, and the case study. These three will be described in more detail because they are widely used. Ethnography is best suited to in-depth description because its methods require keen observation of a culture. Grounded theory is best suited for theory development because it starts with observation from which theory is derived, rather than the other way around. The case study approach is well suited to the comprehensive examination of a program because it normally combines qualitative and quantitative observations about a wide array of subjects with regard to a common case, which could be defined as a program. Of course, the case can also be defined in many other ways. For our purposes, it is given attention because of its relevance to program evaluation.

Ethnography as One Approach to Qualitative Research

Ethnography refers to the study of a culture in its natural setting. The purpose is to describe the way of life of a group from within. This is accomplished by researchers by gaining entry into the field through methods designed to gain acceptance and to open their own minds to messages of the group as meanings are held internally. The question focuses upon the meanings of things to the culture; thus, preconceived ideas and biases held by the researcher should be dealt with to the extent that this is feasible (Fortune, 1994).

A distinguishing feature of ethnography is that the process of inquiry begins with the selection of a culture to study rather than the articulation of a research problem to solve or a research question to answer. Problems and questions may emanate from the data analyzed; thus, problem analysis and data analysis are not lined up in the same manner as is typical of quantitative research. While some inquiry into the culture and its problems may precede data collection and analysis, the ethnographic researcher is advised to avoid entering the field with a restricted view. One writer offers the following warning:

> Because the intent of ethnography is to comprehend, without judgment, alien ideology, ritual, behavior, and social structure, one of the most important aspects of such fieldwork is that the investigator's attitude not be 'loaded' before entering the field. (Goodson-Lawes, 1994, p. 26)

Ethnographic researchers immerse themselves in the culture being studied. Methods of observation include participant observation and interviewing. The participant observer interacts with the persons being studied as they go about their daily activities. Observations are made and recorded for analysis. Interviews are more structured interactions between the researcher and the study participant.

Data is collected in ethnographic research through the observations of the investigator, which are recorded in carefully detailed journals. These observations may be organized according to such phenomena as a particular aspect of the culture (e.g., social relations, material culture, religious activities), the autobiographies of individuals, the intensive study of a particular event, detailed observations of a typical day, and so forth (Goodson-Lawes, 1994). Some of the data analysis techniques of grounded theory are employed in the reduction of the volumes of narrative information into themes.

You will not find many examples of ethnography in human service evaluation. It is not well suited to the evaluation of outcome where your concern is highly focused on a program or clinical intervention. It might be useful for process evaluation if you wanted to understand the interplay of culture and professional helping. Perhaps its best use is early in the history of designing interventions because the better you understand the culture of the target audience, the better you will be able to design an effective intervention.

Discussion Box 6.5

How might ethnography be utilized in an evaluation of a familiar program?

Grounded Theory as One Approach to Qualitative Research

Grounded theory is a second major type of qualitative research. The person using grounded theory will have a more focused study at the beginning of data collection than will the ethnographic researcher. A research topic or theme will be developed from the existing knowledge base. The purpose of this method is to develop explanations, hypotheses, or theories that are grounded in observations of social behavior. Some researchers will avoid being immersed in the existing literature before data collection out of fear of being restricted to it. But most will employ the literature review to achieve a focus for the beginning of their inquiry.

The methodology of grounded theory is somewhat more structured than that of ethnography, although some ethnographic researchers borrow from the methods of grounded theory. In a nutshell, this methodology entails the careful recording of observations or quotes from study subjects, the coding of this information in several stages of analysis, and the drawing of connections between themes which serve as the basis for the theory that is developed.

An illustration can be taken from the work of Belcher (1994) and his colleagues, who studied the homeless in the city of Baltimore in the summer of 1989. The study was conducted over a three-month period during which the researchers immersed themselves in the homeless community by familiarizing themselves with the providers of services to the homeless and focusing particular attention upon a particular health care facility. A group of homeless people was identified for a series of informal interviews that took place in surroundings familiar to the study participants.

The researchers used an eight-step process for study:

1. Open-ended questions were asked which emanated from the literature review.
2. Responses from these questions were recorded after each interview into a case file for each respondent.
3. The files were reviewed by using the constant comparative method. This method entails the comparison of files on respondents over and over again until the researcher feels that all possible themes have emerged.
4. Themes were noted and a second set of questions was developed accordingly.
5. These questions were posed to the same respondents in a second set of interviews.
6. Responses were recorded in the individual case files and the constant comparative method was employed once again.
7. A set of working hypotheses was developed.
8. The working hypotheses were discussed with the respondents to test their accuracy. (Belcher, 1994)

One of the questions we need to address in qualitative research is the reliability of our data analysis. To what extent can we depend on our analysis as accurately reflecting reality? According to the spirit of scientific inquiry, accuracy is enhanced by consistency. The more consistent our observations, the more we can depend on them to reflect reality.

In quantitative research, this task is easier. Methods of observation are submitted to the tests of reliability and validity. For example, a set of persons may be administered a scale at two points in time to see if the responses are consistent. Inconsistent responses would suggest some problem with the ability of the instrument clearly to measure what it was designed to measure. This provides for a means for establishing the credibility of the observations.

For the qualitative study reported by Belcher, this basic issue was addressed in three ways: prolonged engagement, persistent observation, and triangulation. The first strategy was achieved by the fact that the interviews took place over a three-month period, sufficient to obtain entry into the lives of the study subjects and overcome normal barriers to understanding the full meaning of behavior. The second strategy was achieved by the extensive eight-step process of observation.

The third strategy for establishing credibility was **triangulation**, the use of multiple sources of data collection. For example, if respondents in this study stated that they had been thrown out of a shelter, the researchers would verify this information with the shelter operators.

From this study, the phases of drift among the homeless were enumerated. Phase 1 is the beginning phase of homelessness and is characterized by movement in and out of the homeless status as friends and relatives help out. At this phase, the study participants did not typically classify themselves as homeless. They generally maintain good contacts with sources of support and service providers. After several months of homelessness, people tend to drift into phase 2, in which an identity as a homeless person is not very strong, but persistent problems such as substance abuse seem to prevent their emergence from the status of the homeless. At the third phase, persons have come to accept themselves as being homeless and have lost hope of a different style of life. These persons typically have been homeless for a year or more and have a great deal of social distance from the mainstream of society.

This characterization of the phases of homelessness led to ideas about the importance of prevention because the longer one's homelessness, the greater the problem of achieving a change. Drift from one phase to another was found to be accompanied by an increase in substance abuse, loss of relationships, loss of income, and loss of hope (Belcher, 1994).

While this study was classified as an example of grounded theory, it could be argued that it illustrates some aspects of ethnography. In some ways, it is a better description of a culture than a basis for the development of new theory. The more important thing, however, is that it illustrates a qualitative approach to research.

Cultural Competence and Grounded Theory

In their book on cross-cultural practice, Harper-Dorton and Lantz discuss naturalistic research (grounded theory) as the preferred method of understanding cross-cultural curative factors. Their description of naturalistic research is instructive:

> Naturalistic research is a form of qualitative research that occurs "in the field," using a "flexible human instrument" to gain and evaluate data . . . Naturalistic research is done in the field so data can be observed and evaluated in terms of connection with social environment. Conducted in natural settings, naturalistic research is different from experimental research, as experimental research flows from theory and confirms or disconfirms theory. Naturalistic research flows from data observed in the field, the result that theory is created from the data observed. Theory evolving out of naturalistic research is called "grounded" theory, as it is grounded in the themes that emerge during observation in the field. (Harper-Dorton and Lantz, 2007)

Naturalistic research was employed to discover eight cross-cultural curative factors. According to Harper-Dorton and Lantz, an understanding of these curative factors can aid the worker in developing helpful and culturally appropriate intervention activities with special populations and clients from different cultural backgrounds. "Each culture's helping processes incorporate culturally significant sources of help or problem solutions" (Harper-Dorton and Lantz, 2007, p. 3).

One of these factors is worldview respect. Culture influences one's view of religion, art, politics, and science, and other key aspects of one's world view. My world view will influence my answer to such questions as "Who am I? Where am I? What's wrong? And what's the remedy?" According to Harper-Dorton and Lantz (2007), worldview respect refers to your respect for other worldviews, and is the most important factor in gaining cultural competence as a social work practitioner. An example was given by these authors of a social worker respecting a client's worldview which incorporated natural healers by referring the client to a natural healer.

A second curative factor is hope. The more hope the client has that a helping relationship will work, the more hope he or she will have for the outcome, and this hope will influence outcome. Helper attractiveness is a third cross-cultural curative factor according to Harper-Dorton and Lantz (2007). This refers to the client's perception of the helper's ability to facilitate a good outcome. This factor is dependent upon culture and worldview respect.

A fourth curative factor is control. "In Western helping practices, it is considered important that the client learn something from the helping intervention and that what has been learned be used after termination to prevent problems in the future" (Harper-Dorton and Lantz, 2007, p. 6). Psychoanalytic practitioners help the client to use insight to gain control, while cognitive therapists help the client to use different thinking patterns. In some cultures, people are taught to pray correctly, or to engage in a certain ritual in accordance with a strict protocol. These accepted means of personal control are grounded in culture.

Among the other curative factors are rites of initiation (helping people make a transition from old behaviors to new ones), cleansing experiences (e.g., catharsis), existential realization (achieving new meaning), and physical intervention (e.g., massage, medication, surgery). Each of these eight cross-cultural curative factors can inform any efforts to engage in process evaluation for people of a given culture.

Discussion Box 6.6

How might you utilize the concept of triangulation in an evaluation study?

The Case Study Method as One Approach to Qualitative Research

The **case study** method is appropriate when you wish to investigate a single individual, event, or social setting (e.g., a single organization) in sufficient intensity to obtain an in-depth understanding of how it operates or functions.

> The approach of case studies ranges significantly from general field studies to the interview of a single individual or group. Case studies may focus on an individual, a group, or an entire community and may utilize a number of data technologies such as life history, documents, oral histories, in-depth interviews, and participant observation. (Berg, 2001, p. 225)

According to Yin (1984), the case study is a way of investigating an empirical topic by following a set of prespecified procedures. It is recommended for use when the research question is about How or Why and the researcher has little control over events. It is also appropriate when the focus is on a contemporary phenomenon within some real-life context. The case study method normally uses multiple sources of data, both quantitative and qualitative. (Yin, 1984)

Yin (1984, p. 25) has noted several applications of the case study approach to program evaluation. One application would entail the examination of the causal links in situations too complex for survey methods or experimental strategies. A second application is to use this approach to describe clearly the experiences of clients as they move from contemplation of service to access to service to receipt of service and discharge, in order to gain insight into how this process could be improved. Another application is the assessment of the program that has unclear goals and objectives and you need a comprehensive examination of a wide array of outcomes, both intended and unintended.

There are five major components of the case study design:

1. The development of the study's questions
2. The development of study propositions
3. The determination of the unit of analysis
4. The development of the logic that links selected data to the propositions
5. The development of the criteria for interpreting the findings

The first consideration is that your study question be a good fit with the case study method. The case study is best when you have a complicated question that could be best addressed by multiple sources of data, including both qualitative and quantitative. The second consideration is the study's propositions. A study proposition is a little like a hypothesis, but is more general and likely to be lacking in empirical support. The type of proposition appropriate for the case study is one born of a logical observation of the phenomenon under study by the research stakeholders or users. The third consideration is the unit of analysis.

Basic Components of the Case Study Design

A list of the components of the case study design according to Yin (1989):

1. A study's questions
2. Propositions (if any)
3. Unit of analysis
4. Logic linking data to propositions
5. Criteria for interpreting the findings.

The first component is the *study question*. According to Yin (1984), the case study approach is better suited to questions of How and Why rather than questions of Who, What, or Where. You might want to know how your program's services achieve their outcomes. This would require information on the components of the service that are most emphasized, the relationship between service emphasis and service outcome, and so forth. You may want to know why certain clients achieve better outcomes than others. This might require information on the characteristics of clients, the relationship between client characteristics and client outcome, the opinions of practitioners about clients that do best in treatment, and so forth.

In case study terminology, a study **proposition** is a theoretical guess about the phenomenon under study. It is your preliminary attempt to explain. It provides guidance on the places you need to go to find relevant information. For example, you may have little reason to measure whether your clients are left-handed or right-handed because it does not make sense that this variable influences client response to treatment. So you would not have a study proposition about being left-handed, but you might have one about the environmental stresses faced by clients.

The **unit of analysis** is the entity on which you will collect your data. In case study terminology, it refers to how you are defining your case. A case could be a single individual. If it is a single case, you would collect all your data on this individual case. You could define your unit of analysis as an event, such as an election, and you would collect data on that election. The unit of analysis could be a program. If so, you can collect any amount of information that seems relevant to this program with regard to your study question.

Another component of the case study design is the *logic that links data to propositions*. In this endeavor, you need to think of the kinds of data that would support your propositions, and, conversely, the nature of the data that would refute these propositions. You should derive these ideas before you collect your data.

The above is also relevant to the *criteria for interpreting your findings.* On what basis will you believe you have sufficient evidence to reach noteworthy conclusions?

Discussion Box 6.7

Think of a case study you might undertake with regard to a familiar program or intervention. What is the research question and the unit of analysis?

Desired Skills for the Case Study Researcher

The basic skills for the case study researcher listed by Yin (1989) are as follows:

1. Ask good questions.
2. Be a good listener.
3. Be adaptive and flexible.
4. Have a firm grasp on the issues being studied.
5. Be unbiased by preconceived notions.

According to Yin (1984), an inquiring mind should characterize the case study researcher both prior to data collection *and* during data collection. A major strength of the case study approach is its flexibility. What will be observed does not have to be determined completely ahead of the beginning of the time frame for collection data. You should be a good questioner. Being a good listener is the second skill of the case study researcher. Do not ignore information simply because it was not on the list of things to record.

Adaptability and flexibility is a key ingredient of the good case study investigation. Go where the data leads. You must also have a firm grasp of the issues being studied so you will better understand what you have received in the way of information. Finally, you should be unbiased by preconceived notions. That is easier said than done. A method of achieving this state is to list your ideas about the thing you are evaluating prior to your study and continually ask yourself if there is evidence that these ideas are overly influencing the direction of your inquiry.

Discussion Box 6.8

The case study method may not be best suited to the highly concrete individual who needs clear and concrete guidance on the steps to take in conducting a study. How about you? Do you think this method is well suited to your personality?

The Case Study Protocol

The **case study protocol** provides information on the investigative procedures and the rules that will govern the inquiry. According to Yin (1984), the protocol should include the following:

1. An overview of the case study project (objectives, issues, auspices, etc.)
2. Field procedures
3. Sources of information
4. Case study questions, along with the possible sources of information for answering each question
5. A guide for the case study report

Sources of Evidence in Case Studies

One of the advantages of the case study approach is the multiplicity of information that can be used. Six sources of evidence were noted by Yin (1984):

1. Documents
2. Archival records
3. Interviews
4. Direct observation
5. Participant observation
6. Physical artifacts

The first two on this list refer to existing documents that may be searched for information. Quantitative data from records can be easily recorded. Qualitative data needs to be analyzed for content using a method of content analysis. Interviews will be discussed in some detail in the next section of this chapter. Direct observation refers to the fact that the researcher can observe what is going on in the behavior of others and make notes. Participant observation is the situation where the researcher is a part of a group that is being observed. Physical artifacts can be anything physical that can provide evidence.

Principles of Data Collection in Case Studies

Three principles of data collection were offered by Yin (1984) as follows:

1. Use multiple sources of evidence.
2. Create a case study data base.
3. Maintain a chain of evidence.

Multiple sources of evidence is sometimes known as triangulation. It is better fulfilled in case study research than most other approaches. The idea is that no single source of evidence is sufficient to answer our questions. A good example is the fact that client satisfaction surveys typically indicate a high level of overall satisfaction with agency services. Does this tell us enough? Is this information subject to the social desirability bias?

A case study database is important, particularly because of the complex array of information that often is collected. This information needs a method of organization and maintenance.

Maintaining a chain of evidence is not easily explained. Some arguments can be made like links in a chain. If one link is broken, that affects the entire chain. Thus, evidence that refutes one part of the chain renders the total argument invalid. But most social inquiries are not that simple.

Discussion Box 6.9

A simple illustration of the concept of chain of evidence is the assumption we normally make that people will tell the whole truth when asked to offer information for a research study. This assumption is a link in the chain between the question and the answer we receive. Can you think of an example where this assumption might be questioned?

Data Collection in Qualitative Research

There are several common methods of collecting data in qualitative research. One is the survey method, whereby study subjects respond to a questionnaire with open-ended questions. The client satisfaction survey is perhaps the best example of the use of the survey in human service evaluation. The individual interview is a second means of data collection in qualitative research. The focus group interview is a third method. With this approach a group of persons is interviewed together rather than individually. Some qualitative researchers use a fourth alternative—the direct observation of behavior. Observations are recorded as the process of behavior unfolds. Sometimes the research is a member of the group being studied. This is a special form of direct observation known as participant observation. The examination of existing records constitutes a fifth alternative for gathering qualitative data.

The Interview as One Method of Data Collection

In this book, an interview is defined as a personal encounter between persons in which one person (or persons) is seeking information from another person (or other persons). It can take place face to face or by way of another mode of personal interaction, such as the telephone. It is distinguished from the social survey in which researchers are asking respondents to answer questions by way of a written instrument such as a questionnaire.

The interview is purposive interaction. It goes beyond informal conversation, suggesting that different persons play different roles in the encounter. The main purpose of the encounter is for one or more persons to obtain information from another person (or persons).

We can conceptualize different types of interviews according to structure. A highly structured interview is one in which there is a precise set of questions which are to be asked in a given sequence with some pre-established categories for response. The highly structured interview may use quantitative means of measurement. In this chapter, we will focus upon interviews that are qualitative in nature, which means that there is a minimum of openness in the structure in which the study subject can respond in their own words to the questions.

The extent of the structure is exemplified by the number and specificity of questions posed and the existence of preconstructed categories into which respondents may fall. It is determined by the specificity of the study question and the specificity of the study subject that is apparent from the knowledge base which supports the research question.

Fontana and Frey (1994) provide the following guidelines for the structured interview:

- Never get involved in long explanations of the study; use standard explanations provided by the supervisor.
- Never deviate from the study introduction, sequence of questions, or question wording.
- Never let another person interrupt the interview; do not let another person answer for the respondent or offer his or her opinions on the question.
- Never suggest an answer or agree or disagree with an answer. Do not give the respondent any idea of your personal views on the topic of the question or survey.
- Never interpret the meaning of a question; just repeat the question and give instructions or clarifications that are provided in training or by supervisors.
- Never improvise, such as by adding answer categories, or make wording changes.
  (p. 364)

This level of structure may not be appropriate for the typical interview for a qualitative research study in human service evaluation because of the imprecise nature of the concepts under exploration in such studies. Yet, these guidelines provide assistance with gaining an understanding of means used in qualitative research to reduce human error in observation. In particular, it is important that the interviewer not express opinions on the topic because of the likelihood that such expressions will influence the response of the study subject.

Discussion Box 6.10

Let's suppose you are conducting a study of the service process of a familiar program using interviews of clients as the method of gathering information. One of your questions is "How can we improve access to our services?" One person you interviewed replied "Don't you think it would be better for the agency to have neighborhood offices?" How would you reply?

The Semistructured Interview   The semistructured interview is one with predetermined questions with an open-ended format which are asked of all respondents in the same manner. Examples include the following:

1. What does stress mean to you?
2. How do you experience stress?
3. What are the three things you are most likely to do when you are under stress?
4. What do you find has been the best way to cope with stress?

Each of these questions would be asked of each respondent and would be asked in the same sequence.

With the semistructured interview, you should follow several guides. First, *be aware of your own predispositions* about the subject under study. You should, of course, avoid revealing these predispositions to the person being interviewed. It is also important that you engage mechanisms to avoid allowing these predispositions to influence your observations. Reflect upon what kinds of responses support or refute your own predispositions and force yourself to pay attention to all that is said, not just to those statements that are congruent with your own views.

A second recommendation is that you *engage the interviewee in the validation of your notes.* You might repeat what you have heard to the persons being interviewed and provide them with the opportunity to correct it or place it more appropriately in their own words if you have inaccurately reworded their thoughts. When recording statements from the interviewee, you should use the interviewee's words as much as possible. You can re-examine these words later and decide upon the broader concepts that may have been expressed. You might want to say something like "Are you saying that you are more likely to use exercise to relieve stress or relaxation techniques?" By presenting options, you relieve the interviewee of the temptation to agree with you even though there may be some reservations about how you are perceiving these thoughts.

A third recommendation is to *seek disconfirming evidence of your initial impressions.* If you believe that the person being interviewed is focusing the most attention upon spirituality as a means of relieving stress, you might want to count the times that this theme was mentioned and compare it to the times that other themes were mentioned. You might want to ask the interviewee to recount the number of times that spirituality was used in the last two weeks as compared to the number of times that something else was used.

A fourth recommendation is to *engage in note-taking methods that place minimal burden upon your memory*. There is a lot of information that might be portrayed in an interview. Our long-term memories can be in error. You might want to take notes in stages with the first stage being the interview and the second stage taking place immediately after the interview. During the interview, you will not be able to record every word spoken by the interviewee. Instead, you will want to quote things that seem to be especially poignant and take rather sketchy notes otherwise. The sketchy notes will contain words or phrases that represent certain responses by the interviewee. However, a few days later, you may not remember what these words mean. Therefore, you should undertake the second stage right after the interview. In this stage, the unwritten words are filled in so that you will be able to return to these notes at any later date and fully understand them.

Discussion Box 6.11

Suppose someone is conducting a study with the purpose of identifying barriers to the receipt of services related to problem pregnancies where abortion is one option. You have been asked to contribute to this research by conducting interviews of 12 persons. Can you identify one or more predispositions you have about this theme that would need to be addressed by you in order for you to be fully prepared to undertake these interviews? If so, how would you address them?

Phases of the Interview Process   After the questions have been determined and a prospective interview subject has been identified, there are several natural phases of the interview. First, we must introduce the purpose of the interview and ourselves and seek permission for the interview. In this phase, it is important that the purpose of the interview be stated, but not any conclusions that might have been drawn from the literature about any aspect of the research question. In other words, you do not want to influence the interviewee's thinking about the questions under study. We also must introduce ourselves and we must indicate how the information from the interview will be used, including assurances that their identities will not be revealed in any report on the interview.

In this first phase of the interview process, the researcher should be sensitive to gender or cultural differences between the interviewer and the interviewee which might influence the responses of the interviewee. How open and honest will this study subject be with this particular interviewer? Sometimes women will express themselves differently to another woman than to a man. The key outcome of this first phase of the interview process is the development of trust and rapport between the interviewer and the interviewee.

The next phase is the presentation of the questions and the recording of the information. We should ask the questions in the same way to each person we interview. We should consider beforehand how to define key terms so that we can use a uniform definition to our study subjects.

The third phase is the analysis of the results. We must make sense of our notes. We do this by looking for themes that are common between persons being interviewed. We need to be attentive to the different terms that can be used to express the same thought. And we should be clear on the level of generality of our conceptions of the subject. Are we looking only for rather broad themes, or more specific themes?

In the analysis of data in qualitative research, numbers often get ignored because they are associated with quantitative research. But numbers are an essential component of the qualitative analysis of information. We count such things as the number of references to a given theme or the number of study subjects who mentioned a given theme.

The next chapter contains an exercise on content analysis in qualitative research. This exercise will take you through several aspects of qualitative data analysis, including enumeration (counting) and bracketing (setting aside your own opinions), both of which have been mentioned here.

The Focus Group as a Data Collection Method

The **focus group** is a method of gathering qualitative data that entails a group interview. The group interview can be more or less structured depending on the context and research issue. Most applications of the focus group can be characterized much like the semistructured interview because there normally is a clear focus for the questions, but there is a need for sufficient flexibility in the questions to obtain a full picture of the phenomenon under study. In fact, it is not easy to envision a situation in which the highly structured format would be used with a focus group.

With an individual client, the helping professional may undertake an unstructured interview, especially early in the helping process, because it is important to allow the client to control the focus of the dialogue. This format, however, would likely lead to confusion and inefficiency with a focus group because you employ such groups when you have a set of focused questions you want answered. The highly structured format would typically be inappropriate for the focus group because it does not lend itself to the stimulation of dialogue—an essential feature of the focus group advantage.

An important distinction between the focus group interview and the individual interview is the opportunity to observe interactions among individuals with regard to the issue under investigation. The individual interview may permit more depth of expression, but the focus group interview reveals how individuals of a certain group coalesce around certain positions on a topic. The interaction among individuals provides new insight on the topic and reveals how the group operates to persuade. Our opinions and attitudes are constantly influenced by our normal interactions with our peers on a daily basis. Perhaps this is why so many market researchers have used focus groups to test new products.

A typical focus group session consists of a small group of individuals responding to a set of semistructured interview questions delivered by a moderator who facilitates discussion. According to Krueger (1994), the size of the group should be kept to a maximum of seven for complex questions.

Key Elements of the Focus Group Experience   There are a number of topics to be addressed by the person who is planning the use of the focus group. It begins with the kind of question that can be best addressed with the focus interview and ends with the analysis of data.

The focus group should be focused on questions that are suitable for the semistructured interview. The ethnographic study attempts to describe a culture in some depth. This normally requires more flexibility than is present in the focus group experience. Broad questions are not suited to the focus group, such as the following:

1. What are the stages of moral regression for the young adult who is a repeat offender?
2. In general, how does the client experience our services?

The above questions require a more flexible format than the focus group. You would need to have multiple sources of information collected at multiple time periods to move seriously toward answers to this type of question. Highly specific questions would also be inappropriate to the focus group experience, such as:

1. Do our clients like our new intake system better than the old one?
2. What proportion of our staff is satisfied with their jobs?

These questions are too specific. They can be answered by structured interviews or a survey.

Suppose, however, you wished to know certain things about your recently changed intake procedures for the admission of clients into service in your agency. You might ask a series of questions related to this experience, such as:

1. What was the first contact with the agency like for the client in the previous system?
2. What was the first contact with the agency like since the change?
3. How did the client feel after leaving the agency on the day of first contact prior to the change, and after the change?
4. To what extent did the client feel well informed about agency services prior to the change, and after the change?
5. What recommendations does the client have about improving our intake system?

These questions could be posed to a group of clients or a group of staff who work with clients. Thus, the focus group is best suited to the situation where the moderator can think of a set of open-ended questions that will stimulate dialogue on a key issue being addressed.

Discussion Box 6.12

Think of a set of questions that might be posed to a focus group with which you might work. Identify the group by type and size, and present the questions for dialogue.

Group members should be in a position to answer the key questions without hesitation or intimidation by others in the group. You need group members who are knowledgeable about your study subject. You also need people who feel free to participate. It is a key task of the moderator to assure good participation by calling on persons if needed. It is best to avoid having one or two highly domineering individuals in a group with some who are rather quiet by nature. This may pose too much of a challenge to the moderator, who, of course, does not want to offend anyone. Some questions are best answered with the homogenous group, while others are better answered by the heterogeneous group.

The moderator should establish ground rules and maintain a functional climate for dialogue. The dialogue is best facilitated if participants are not worried about confidentiality or other such consequences of participation. While a rigid set of rules is not normally warranted, it is a good idea, according to Berg (2001), that the moderator address such issues with the group. It is also important that good rapport be developed among group members and between the group and the moderator. Some form of ice-breaking discussion or exercise may be useful.

The moderator must be a good listener. The role of the moderator is to listen more than to talk because this is a situation that calls upon group members to supply information, rather than being a situation in which the objective is for the leader to engage in persuasion. As noted by Berg (2001):

> Facilitators . . . must listen to what the subjects are saying . . . It is important to have a schedule or agenda during the focus group; however, it should never be so inflexible that interesting topics that spontaneously arise during the group discussion are shortchanged or unnecessarily truncated. Because of the nature of group dynamics, it is possible that topics and issues not originally considered by the researcher as important surface as very important. (Berg, 2001, p. 124)

The moderator should give structure and direction to the dialogue but should avoid offering opinions. According to Berg (2001, p. 124), "While the facilitator should guide the group's discussion, he should avoid offering opinions and substantive comments. With any interview, the ideal product is 90 percent subjects and 10 percent researcher."

The moderator should have the assistance of a note taker during the dialogue. The group moderator can and should make notes during the dialogue but will normally need the assistance of someone who can focus only on taking notes. The note taker should place major emphasis on direct quotes from participants. This will be less necessary if the group dialogue is taped and transcribed for analysis. If you have the luxury, you could have two note takers working with the moderator who also takes notes. These three persons share notes as a method of validation.

The dialogue should be analyzed for content. The principles and procedures of content analysis are appropriate for the analysis of the qualitative data that comes from the process group dialogue. Ideally, the dialogue will be taped and transcribed.

Discussion Box 6.13

One of the qualities needed by the focus group moderator is to be able to maintain ground rules, such as, for example, "People should show respect for the thoughts of others". Another quality is to keep the group focused on the questions being asked. Another is to be a good listener. How would you rate yourself on these qualities if you were asked to moderate a focus group?

Direct Observation as One Approach to Data Collection

Some qualitative researchers use direct observation of behavior as a means of collecting qualitative data.

> One of the hallmarks of observation has traditionally been its nonintervention. Observers neither manipulate nor stimulate their subjects. They do not ask the subjects research questions, pose tasks for them, or deliberately create new provocations. This stands in marked contrast to researchers using interview questionnaires, who direct the interaction and introduce potentially new ideas into the arena, and to experimental researchers, who often set up structured situations where they can alter certain conditions to measure the covariance of others. Simple observers follow the flow of events. Behavior and interaction continue as they would without the presence of a researcher, uninterrupted by intrusion. (Adler & Adler, 1994, p. 378)

Direct observation is a more naturalistic means of measurement than the interview because the researcher has not altered the natural environment. It is the most flexible means of measurement because there are no predetermined questions or variables in observational research. One form of direct observation is participant observation, where the research is a member of the group being observed. In that form, there is some degree of intervention by the researcher who is doing the observation; therefore, it is slightly less naturalistic than when the observer is not interacting with the people being observed.

The method of direct observation will vary greatly from one research experience to another because of the extreme flexibility of this form of data collection. However, there is a method if the researcher is serious. Adler and Adler describe one example regarding the observation of behavior in tearooms:

> The concrete products of observations may vary; some observers record written text that follows a free-association form, whereas others incorporate more structure. In his "tearoom" observations, Humphreys (1975) used sheets that he designed specifically for the project, featuring divided pages: On one part of the page the layout of the tearoom was depicted, and he used that to draw simple diagrams of the interaction; the rest of the page was devoted to explicit descriptions of participants' appearance, clothing, modes of transportation, roles, interactions and exits. (Adler & Adler, 1994, p. 380)

A key issue with the direct form of observation lies in validity. How can the reader of the report make an independent judgment of the credibility of the methods employed and judge the likelihood of human error in the interpretation by the researcher of what is going on in the environment observed? A method for dealing with this potential flaw is the use of multiple observers who cross-check what they have observed.

The direct observation of behavior is not as often used in evaluation research as other methods, such as interviews, focus groups, open-ended questions on surveys, and so forth. For this reason, the direct observation of behavior will receive less attention in this book.

The Survey as One Approach to Data Collection

While we often think of social surveys as being tools for quantitative research, we can employ this tool for qualitative research as well. The distinction is whether the questions on the survey are open-ended (e.g., What are your most important needs?) or close-ended (What is your gender—male or female?). The survey is a more efficient method of data collection than other methods because it takes less time. You can mail a survey out and review the results in less time than it would take to conduct interviews or focus groups or engage in direct observation.

When Should You Use Each Approach to Data Collection?

When you consider the question of which method of data collection is best for your situation, you will want to consider the issue of data collection structure which is dependent on the nature of your question and the information that is needed. When you employ the social survey, you will need to form each question carefully prior to data collection. This is a rather structured situation and will be best when you have clear questions and feel that your total control over the forming of the inquiry is appropriate. The individual interview can be structured at various levels, so you need to decide the level of that structure beforehand. You can engage in an interview with questions similar to the social survey, which means you have substantial control, or you can use an unstructured format where the respondent has substantial control, or you can compromise with the semistructured interview format. The focus group normally uses the semistructured interview format, which falls somewhere between high interviewer control and high interviewee control. The direct observation of behavior normally is highly unstructured where the study subjects have complete control over their own behavior.

A key to this choice of a data collection method is the nature of the question you are posing. If you wished to learn about the stages of moral regression for youth whose behavior has evolved from compliance to deviance, you may not be able to develop a set of structured questions ahead of time. You may have a few specific details you need to understand about the nature of the crimes committed but you will likely be in the dark about how one moves from one stage to another. This is a situation that suggests a highly flexible format for understanding behavior. A highly structured interview is not likely to work well for you. In fact, the focus group interview may be of limited value as well because you may not know how to form specific questions. However, if others have investigated this issue, their work may provide the basis for the use of the focus group interview. This choice, therefore, really depends on the extent to which knowledge has already been gained on the subject as well as the extent to which the study question is narrow or broad.

Discussion Box 6.14

Think of a process evaluation that should be undertaken for a familiar human service program. Restrict your example to one that would best utilize a qualitative means of observation. Consider the formats of social survey, interview, focus group, and direct observation. What are your preliminary thoughts on which format would be most suitable?

Data Analysis in Qualitative Research

There are many techniques for data analysis in qualitative research, depending upon the nature of the study and the specificity of the questions being asked. A key distinction in data analysis between quantitative and qualitative methods is that the means for measuring variables is determined before the collection of data when quantitative methods are employed. For example, the decision to undertake a correlation between self-esteem and depression would be made before data were collected and you would know you needed to measure both self-esteem and depression. When you employ qualitative methods, the structure of your analysis determines the variables to be observed. In other words, the variables are determined after data are collected. You will not know what themes will emerge until you have examined the information that is pertinent to your study subject. Three approaches that facilitate data analysis in qualitative research will be examined in the following pages: (1) content analysis, (2) levels of coding, and (3) analytic comparison.

Content Analysis as a Method of Data Analysis

In **content analysis**, researchers examine artifacts of social communication in order to make inferences about the messages inherent in that information. Attempts are made systematically to identify the special characteristics of the messages (Berg, 1994). Content analysis can be undertaken with any written form of communication: newspaper articles, public records, transcripts of interviews, and so forth.

The basic task of content analysis is to reduce words to themes or concepts which have meaning to the observation of the phenomenon under study. In this endeavor, the researcher must take precautions to avoid the selective recording of information according to some preconceived hypothesis. All the information available should be objectively analyzed for relevance.

Berg (1994) refers to two types of content analysis—manifest and latent. Manifest content analysis is restricted to the primary terms being used in the source, whereas latent content refers to the broader themes or issues underlying the manifest content. For example, an entire speech may be classified as "radical" or a novel could be considered in regard to how violent it was. As one moves from manifest to latent analysis, it is important that the original data not be dropped. One way of verifying a manifest analysis is for it to be tested by others using the same data.

Qualitative studies include data of a more subjective type than is the case with quantitative research. Words or concepts are collected as a means of aiding our understanding of our subject. But counting of things takes place in both qualitative and quantitative observation. The qualitative researcher will often note how many times a certain word or concept was expressed by the sources of information being examined. Certain words will be portrayed by the researcher as being indicative of a certain theme. Words such as *up-tight* or *tense* may both be classified as representing stress. Manifest and latent analysis of content is a form of coding of data from qualitative research. In the next section, you will view a similar conceptualization of this theme.

Coding in Content Analysis

According to Miles and Huberman (1984),

> A code is an abbreviation or symbol applied to a segment of words—most often a sentence or paragraph of transcribed field notes—in order to *classify* the words. Codes are *categories*. They usually derive from research questions, hypotheses, key concepts, or important themes. They are *retrieval and organizing devices* that allow the analyst to spot quickly, pull out, then cluster all the segments relating to the particular question, hypothesis, concept, or theme. (p. 56) [emphasis in original]

Strauss (1987) describes three main types of coding in qualitative research—open, axial, and selective. A discussion of these types of coding can be found in Neuman (1994). According to Neuman, open coding takes place in the researcher's first pass through the data being examined (e.g., a first review of the transcript of a recorded interview). The task of this type of coding is the location of key concepts which bind certain words together. As illustrated above, such words as up-tight and tense might be coded as *stress*. In this phase of coding, the researcher might write the word stress next to each line of data that contains such words as up-tight or tense.

Axial coding takes place in a second pass through the data. During this phase of coding, the researcher "asks about causes and consequences, conditions and interactions, strategies and processes" (Neuman, 1994, p. 408). Can concepts be divided into smaller divisions, or enlarged into larger categories? Can concepts be organized into a sequence?

Selective coding is the final phase of the coding process. In this phase, the researcher is looking selectively for cases that illustrate themes and makes comparisons and contrasts to identify further causal connections in the data or patterns that are broader than those identified in the previous phase. Neuman (1994) uses the example of a study of working class life in the tavern where marriage was noticed as a theme that emerged in much conversation. In the previous phases of coding, marriage was identified as a theme and was divided into major stages such as engagement, weddings, extramarital affairs, and so forth. In the selective phase of coding, a focus turns to differences in the views of men and women. This analysis compares men and women on their ideas about each of these phases of marriage.

In summary, we have viewed three levels of coding. You should conceptualize these as levels of coding. Perhaps you will find it more feasible to think of these as first, second, and third levels of coding rather than remember the labels given above (open, axial, and selective).

Analytic Comparison in Content Analysis

Another helpful tool in qualitative research can be drawn from the work of early philosophers on the nature of logic. Neuman (1994) discusses the method of agreement and the method of difference in logical inquiry and refers to this as analytic comparison. The method of agreement draws the researcher's attention to what is common across cases so that cause–effect relations can be explored. If several different cases have a common outcome (e.g., high stress), the researcher looks for other commonalities that might be candidates for the cause of the outcome. For example, let's suppose that our study of stress among graduate social work students revealed that each of our first four interviewees had a high level of stress and that they mentioned that they had an extra long distance to drive from home to class. Each person has both high stress and a long commute. This provides the beginnings of an exploration of the causal connection between commuting distance and stress. But we might find that many of those with low stress also had a long commute. This is where the method of difference comes into play.

With the method of difference, the researcher seeks information on cases with a different outcome from the initial cases and different causes. If four persons have *high* stress and a *long* commute and another four persons have *low* stress and a *short* commute, we have more evidence for hypothesizing a relationship between commuting and stress. But if we find that persons with low stress are about as likely to have a long commute as persons with high stress, we have little evidence of a connection between these two variables.

One Suggested Format for Content Analysis

You have reviewed the ideas of several persons regarding content analysis. In this section, I will suggest a step-by-step set of procedures for content analysis. You should consider this approach to be only one format for this experience. There are many other ways you could go about this task.

Step one: Clarifying your Basic Research Question Before you engage in content analysis, you need clarification on your major research intent and the nature of the information you should be collecting and analyzing. Consider the following research questions:

1. Does the psychotherapy service of the Adult Mental Health Program of the Parker County Mental Health Clinic improve the happiness of persons diagnosed with borderline personality disorder?
2. Are the services of the Brown County Department of Social Services meeting the needs of its clients?
3. Do the parents of our foster children believe that having only one social worker from intake to discharge is better or worse than having more than one social worker who specializes in selected aspects of service?
4. Has our change in intake procedures been successful?

These questions have been posed at different levels of generality. The more general the question, the more we need either to break down the broad question into more specific questions, or employ a highly flexible format for data collection and analysis. The last question (changes in intake procedures) could be pursued in any number of ways, including the following:

1. Has our change in intake procedures improved our clients' satisfaction with our service?
2. How should we best characterize the experiences of our clients before and after our change in intake procedures?
3. In what ways do our clients believe our change has been helpful? In what ways do they believe it has been unhelpful?
4. What suggestions do our clients have about how our intake procedures could be improved?
5. How has our staff experienced the change?
6. How does our staff evaluate the change?
7. What suggestions do our staff members have for improvement?

One of the reasons for this clarification is to obtain guidance on the type of data collection and analysis procedures you need to employ.

Step two: Selecting the Study Sample   In quantitative research, the logic of sampling suggests that one group of persons or things can represent a larger group of persons or things. The ideal in quantitative research is the random sample, where every entity in the study population has an equal chance of being selected for the sample. Whatever you discover from your study of the sample can be generalized to the population, providing that you have a sufficient sample size and use random sampling.

Qualitative research is less likely than quantitative research to employ a random sample. However, whenever possible it is useful to do so because of the issue of generalizing your findings to a larger group. More likely you will employ a convenience or purposive sample when you are studying service process using qualitative methods. A convenience sample is one drawn of convenience. You may select your class of students because they are convenient. You may select your present clients because they are convenient. The purposive sample is drawn by selecting special persons who are in a better than normal position to offer information on your study topic. This group of persons would not be selected randomly because you have purposefully selected only certain types of people from your population.

The reason you should address the topic of sampling is to help you deal with the issue of generalization. To the extent that you are trying to find suggestions and examples of experiences from persons, you have less need to worry about generalization. That issue can be better addressed when someone wishes to take your suggestions or ideas from your qualitative study and test a relevant hypothesis, most likely with a quantitative study.

In qualitative research you may sample comments or records rather than people. When doing so, you can employ random sampling procedures. But the same issue applies. The question is whether you have qualitative data that sufficiently represents a larger population of ideas.

Discussion Box 6.15

Think of a basic research question that could be answered by qualitative data drawn from either your classmates in this course, or the staff of your agency, or a group of your friends. Identify the sample of persons from whom data will be collected, and the general question to be examined (Specific questions will come later).

Step three: Determining the Method of Collecting Data You should select an appropriate method of data collection based on the degree of specificity of your research question. The interview can be useful for varying levels of specificity, while the focus group is better suited to the medium level of specificity. Direct observation is well suited for the nonspecific question.

Step four: Analyzing Data There are many models for content analysis; I will suggest one. The following will enumerate the steps of this particular model one by one. The example that will be used to facilitate these instructions is an open-ended question that was posed to a sample of social workers by a university social work department. The question was "What is the most important advice you can give to those who are planning a new MSW (Master of Social Work) program?" Their responses were content analyzed for critical information needed in the planning of this program. This analysis is the subject of the exercise in the next chapter. In that chapter you will engage in your own analysis, with the assistance of many concrete suggestions and examples.

 1. Determine the *conceptual framework* that you will use for examining your qualitative data. The extent to which you will have a framework will depend on the structure of your inquiry. With the most general types of grounded theory, you enter the data analysis step with only a rather broad framework because you are being careful not to allow present theory to overly restrict the nature of your inquiry. I would think that most studies in ethnography would use only a broad framework. But you may be engaging in a highly structured inquiry with rather restricted questions which will serve as the guideposts for determining how to analyze the data. In that situation, you would have a more specific conceptual framework from which to operate.
   To illustrate this idea, let's consider two questions. The first question focuses on how to characterize the initial approach that human service practitioners take when they encounter a client in the human services. Some researchers will enter this study with a very broad conceptual framework. They might ask practitioners to state their initial thoughts about a hypothetical client and then examine the data for themes. The second question in this illustration is more focused—Do human service practitioners demonstrate adherence to the strengths perspective in their initial approach to clients? This second study is more focused and requires more in the

way of a conceptual framework. What, for example, is meant by *strengths perspective*? What are examples of statements supportive of this perspective? What are examples of statements that are contrary to this perspective?

2. Engage in a **bracketing** exercise by listing your own ideas about the study question and place this list in a prominent place for your continued notice during the data analysis exercise. Bracketing refers to the separation of selected information for special attention. The idea of this part of the exercise is to heighten your awareness of your own biases about this study subject in an effort to reduce the error that might be introduced into your analysis by these biases. It is natural for you to place more emphasis on those ideas in your review that are consonant with your own opinions. But the data analysis should be of the comments made by others rather than your own opinion, even though it is not possible to remove our biases totally from the experience.

3. Undertake the *first level of coding* (usually called open coding) which requires that you place a word or phrase that captures the basic idea of each individual statement. For example, here are examples of statements in response to the inquiry about advice for planning a new Master of Social Work (MSW) degree program::

"Very selective criteria for enrollment."

"Emphasis on clinical techniques in classroom settings via role playing, case scenarios, videotapes."

"In-depth education on 3 theories as opposed to brief overview of many."

You should place a word or phrase next to each of these three statements that captures the essence of the statement. For example, you might want to code the first statement *selective enrollment*. The second statement could be coded *practice techniques* while the third may be coded *in-depth education*. There is, of course, a variety of words that you might want to use to code these statements. This is an illustration of how the instructor might have done it, but there is no "correct" word for coding each statement.

Repeat this coding procedure for each statement.

4. Undertake the *second level of coding* by determining the major themes that combine many of these statements. Prepare a report that has each theme underlined, with the relevant comments beneath. In the example of asking for advice about planning a new MSW degree program, for example, you might want to consider what the following statements have in common:

"Psychopathology needs to be a primary subject to be studied; more than just one class. Students need to be very comfortable with DSM-IV."

"Emphasis on clinical techniques in classroom settings via role playing, case scenarios, videotapes."

"Have a little more insight into working specifically with behavior problems, substance abuse, and taking LCSW exam."

Is the common theme "preparation for clinical practice"? Or, can you think of a better statement of the theme? If you accept the former, you would underline that theme statement and place each of these statements beneath that heading. And, of course, you would look over the other statements to see what others would logically fall into this category and include them in this list.

It is possible that a given statement has two themes. What if one person said you should offer depth in learning about treatment techniques and another person said you need to offer depth of understanding of community practice? A common theme of these two statements is the importance of depth in education, but these two also offer other ideas—one about clinical practice and the other about community practice. So it is possible to have the same statement in two different lists.

   5. Engage in *enumeration* by counting the number of comments made on a given theme and the number of persons who mentioned this theme. These two lists portray the priorities among the themes. If 25 people mention the importance of clinical practice and 5 people mention the importance of community practice, you can see that the former was given more emphasis than the latter.

   6. Engage in the *third level of coding* by examining relationships between messages or variables. You may have noticed that certain themes tend to be stated by similar people, so there is something these two themes have in common that may not be apparent at first glance. Strauss and Corbin (1990, p. 108) use the example of a content analysis where the topics of pain and pain management were related. You might find that persons suffering from arthritis report different methods of managing pain than those suffering from pain of another source. This is a situation where you are finding relationships between themes rather than simply discovering the main themes, as is the intent of the second level of coding. (Strauss and Corbin, incidentally, refer to this example as existing in the axial level of coding, which is the second level for them. I have distinguished the coding levels in a slightly different way, and I have tried to avoid jargon like "axial coding" or "manifest content analysis" and "latent content analysis" because it is my intent to provide a basic lesson in qualitative analysis. This lesson calls for a certain level of simplicity with attention to manageability.)

   7. Test for **saturation,** or data adequacy, by dividing your qualitative data into segments and reviewing whether the second segment of data provided significant new insights into your study theme. If the second segment revealed the same message about something, you have less reason to continue to pursue this theme with additional segments of data.

The concept of saturation was discussed by Morse in the following way:

> Adequacy [of data] refers to the amount of data collected, rather than the number of subjects, as in quantitative research. Adequacy is attained when sufficient data have been collected that saturation occurs and variation is both accounted for and understood. (Morse, 1994, p. 230)

For example, if you are examining suggestions for how to improve services to clients and both the first segment of responses said the intake system should be changed in a certain way and the second segment of responses seemed to say the same thing at about the same level of priority, you could conclude that you had achieved data saturation, which reduces your need to examine this theme any further with additional data. The assumption is that if the first 25 client responses provided support for a certain suggestion and this same message was found in the words of the second group of 25 client responses reviewed, you would expect the same message from the next 25 and the 25 beyond that group and so forth. Therefore, you do not need to expend precious time and energy with this same theme through additional qualitative data analysis—you have gotten the message!

It is important to exercise good judgment in the determination of how much data you need in each segment. I would not normally divide comments into segments of only 10 or 15 unless the nature of the content was quite specific and focused. I do not, however, have a numerical guide that can be used to determine what this figure should be for your particular data.

Suggested procedures for saturation assessment

a. Your first step in the saturation assessment is to determine how to divide your qualitative data into segments. As a rule of thumb, I would suggest that you have segments that contain at least five comments that fall into each of your most dominant themes (minimally at least five persons in at least one theme). If your first 25 comments have at least one theme with a minimum of five comments for that theme, you have achieved this minimum standard and you can use the number 25 as the number for each segment. This is only the suggestion of one person and should not be treated as having a solid scientific basis. There is plenty of room for argument with regard to the question of how many comments should be on one segment of qualitative data.

b. Your second step is to undertake the first and second levels of coding for your first segment of data. Then undertake the same level of coding for the second segment, making sure you distinguish the comments between these segments. One technique I suggest is to print your first segment in black and white, then enter the comments and themes that arise with your second segment in blue, using either blue letters from your printer or a blue highlighter pen.

c. Your third step is to examine the first two segments for saturation. What was different between the two segments? Did the blue remarks suggest a different set of themes or a noteworthy difference in priority among the themes than was apparent from the first segment? If there are noteworthy differences, you should engage in the analysis of a third segment of data. This may require interviewing more people or going into more records, depending on the nature of your data collection procedures. If there are not any noteworthy differences, you can consider your data analysis to have achieved a minimum level of saturation.

d. Your next step, if necessary, is to continue with a third segment of data, but this would be suggested only if you found noteworthy differences between the first and second segments.

8. Engage in a **credibility assessment** exercise by comparing your list of themes and comments with that of a fellow researcher to determine if there should be revisions of your list. This should be done after the two of you have *independently* completed your lists. You should *not* do the list together. Instead, you should compare your lists after completing the two levels of coding illustrated above.

To illustrate, your fellow researcher may have found two different themes, where you combined these two into a more broad theme. Your fellow researcher may question the listing of a given comment in the list of a given theme, saying that it is actually rather different from other comments in that theme heading, or that it better fits into a different theme. You are not required to agree with your fellow researcher—only to take into consideration this individual's comments.

If you do not have another researcher working with you on your project, you could select a sample of your data and ask the other person to engage in first and second level coding of that sample of data and compare this analysis with your own to determine the level of congruence between the two.

This exercise is designed to provide evidence of the credibility of your data analysis. For this reason, a sample is sufficient to alert the reader of your report to the level of credibility that should be accorded to you as a qualitative researcher with regard to this particular set of qualitative data. One of the most basic ideas in scientific research is that two heads are better than one. To the extent that different observers independently observe things in the same way, they are both in a better position to appear credible to others who may wish to read their studies.

In quantitative research, a measurement device like the Beck Depression Inventory would be subjected to a test of credibility through an assessment of the extent to which it was reliable and valid. The question is whether this tool does a good job of accurately portraying the concept being observed, such as depression. If you were to administer the Beck Depression Inventory and another depression scale to the same people and found a strong positive correlation between the two, you would have evidence of the reliability of the Beck scale.

As a qualitative researcher, you are not using a standardized tool like the Beck Depression Inventory to make your observations. Instead, you are relying on your ability to see things accurately. Thus, your approach needs to be subjected to a test of credibility. How else can others have confidence that your thoughts should be treated as wisdom rather than the peculiar ideas of one person?

Prepare a statement about the credibility exercise. That statement should make some numerical reference to the extent to which the two persons were congruent. It is not sufficient to say that the two of you looked over your separate analyses and concluded that they were "generally congruent." You might, for example, refer to the proportion of themes that were found in common and the proportion of comments within themes that were common. Here is a formula:

$$A - D / A + D$$

where A = number of agreements
D = number of disagreements

For example, if you and the other observer each found 5 themes in common and one not in common, you have 5 agreements and 1 disagreement. This would represent 66.6 percent agreement because $5 - 1 = 4$ and $5 + 1 = 6$ and 4 divided by 6 = 0.666.

9. Prepare a **summary** of your report on these comments by respondents.
   a. What are the main themes from these comments?
   b. What is the priority among these themes—are some themes mentioned more prominently than others? Prominence can be ascertained by numbers of comments in a given theme, by the proportion of persons who mentioned the theme, or by the passion that might be displayed by the words used.
   c. Are there any noteworthy relationships among the themes?

    d. Are there any underlying messages from this analysis that are not readily apparent from the listing of the themes? This would be a message that binds a dominant number of the themes.

    e. In a nutshell, what you have learned?

This is one guide that might be useful for those who are in need of a recipe for content analysis. There are many other ways one can undertake this task.

Summary

The purpose of this chapter has been to illustrate how qualitative research methods are especially well suited to the evaluation of service process. In this endeavor, you have reviewed the nature of process evaluation, the nature of qualitative research methods, and related topics. You have reviewed various approaches to qualitative research such as ethnography, case study methodology, and grounded theory. The interview, the focus group, and direct observation were examined as the various approaches you might use for data collection in qualitative research. Finally, data analysis in qualitative research was examined, with particular attention to one suggested approach to content analysis. In the next chapter, you will be guided through this approach to content analysis with an example that calls upon you to engage in your own research on a particular body of qualitative data.

Quiz

The following is a quiz on the contents of Chapter 6. You have the option of taking it as a pretest, to see if you need to read this chapter, or as a posttest to examine your need for further review of these contents. The answers to these questions can be found at the end of the reference list.

1. Which of the following is/are examples of *process* evaluation?
   a. The examination of your clients' most important unmet needs.
   b. The determination of the extent to which the staff of the Willow Oaks Mental Health Center are implementing the cognitive-behavior model in the treatment of depression.
   c. The examination of the extent to which your clients have improved in their functioning as a result of your agency's services.
   d. All of the above.
2. Which of the following are examples of *process* evaluation research questions?
   a. Are persons in need of our service aware that our service exists?
   b. Are persons properly screened at intake?
   c. Are clients properly followed-up after discharge?
   d. All of the above.
3. Which of the following are examples of questions that would generate qualitative data rather than quantitative data?
   a. What is your age? _____ years
   b. What is your gender? _____ male _____ female
   c. What is your most important unmet need?
   d. All of the above.
4. Which of the following would be considered legitimate descriptions of qualitative research methods in regard to the issue of transparency?
   a. We interviewed 10 clients and here are our conclusions regarding what we learned.
   b. We employed nominal group technique with eight clients who responded to the question "What are your most important unmet needs?" Here is the list of items ranked by priority by these clients.
   c. Both of the above.
   d. None of the above.

5. Which of the following are examples where qualitative means of measurement would normally be more suitable than quantitative means?
   a. You are seeking to measure precisely your clients with regard to demographic characteristics.
   b. You are seeking to test a theory rather than to develop a new one.
   c. Both of the above.
   d. None of the above.

6. Which of the following would be most amenable to the methods of ethnography?
   a. You wish to develop a theory that explains why Hispanic persons are disproportionately underrepresented in your client population.
   b. You wish to evaluate the child protective services program of Howard County in a comprehensive fashion.
   c. You wish to better understand the culture of your clients who refer to themselves as born-again Christians.
   d. You wish to determine the extent to which your clients have improved in self-esteem by employing the Hare Self-Esteem Scale.

7. Which of the above would be most amenable to the methods of the case study?
   a.
   b.
   c.
   d.

8. Which of the following would *not* be included in a case study?
   a. The study's research questions
   b. The study's propositions
   c. The identification of the study's unit of analysis

   d. All could be included.

9. Which of the following formats for the interview is most compatible with the focus group interview?
   a. The highly structured interview format
   b. The semistructured interview format
   c. The unstructured interview format
   d. All of the above

10. Which of the following statements is/are true?
    a. Reliability is an issue in measurement in quantitative research, but not in qualitative research.
    b. When you have achieved saturation in content analysis, you need to examine more data because the picture is not yet clear.
    c. Both of the above.
    d. None of the above.

11. Which of the following statements is/are true regarding content analysis?
    a. The first level of coding is the one that is most directly taken from the words of the study subject. Higher levels of coding constitute ways to conceptualize these words into more broad themes.
    b. Enumeration in coding refers to the frequency by which a certain word or theme is mentioned.
    c. Both of the above.
    d. None of the above.

12. Which of the following statements is/are true regarding content analysis?
    a. Credibility in content analysis refers to trustworthiness or reliability.
    b. Saturation is achieved when you find you need to engage in the collection of further data in the pursuit of your research question.
    c. Both of the above.
    d. None of the above.

References

Adler, P. A., & Adler, P. (1994). Observational techniques. In Denzin & Lincoln (Eds.), *Handbook of qualitative research* (pp. 377–392). Thousand Oaks: Sage Publications.

Belcher, J. R. (1994). Understanding the process of social drift among the homeless: A qualitative analysis. In Sherman, E., and Reid, W. J. (Eds.) *Qualitative research in social work* (pp. 126–134), New York: Columbia University Press.

Berg, B. L. (1994). *Qualitative research methods for the social sciences*. Boston: Allyn & Bacon.

Berg, B. L. (2001) *Qualitative research methods for the social sciences* (3rd ed.). Boston: Allyn & Bacon.

Denzin, N. K. & Lincoln, Y. (Eds) (1994). *Handbook of qualitative research*. Thousand Oaks: Sage Publications.

Fontana, A., & Frey, J. H. (1994). Interviewing: The art of science. In N. K. Denzin & Y. S. Lincoln (Eds.), *Handbook of qualitative research* (pp. 361–376). Thousand Oaks, CA: Sage Publications.

Fortune, A. E. (1994). Commentary: Ethnography in social work. In E. Sherman & W. J. Reid (Eds.), *Qualitative research in social work* (pp. 63–67). New York: Columbia University Press.

Gordon-Lawes, J. (1994). Ethnicity and poverty as research variables: Family studies with Mexican and Vietnamese newcomers. In E. Sherman & W. J. Reid (Eds.), *Qualitative research in social work* (pp. 21–31). New York: Columbia University Press.

Harper-Dorton, K. V., & Lantz, J. E. (2007). *Cross-cultural practice: Social work with diverse populations*. Chicago: Lyceum Books.

Hubble, M. A., Duncan, B. L., & Miller, S. D. (Eds.) (1999). The heart and soul of change: What works in therapy. Washington, DC: American Psychological Association.

Krueger, R. A. (1994). *Focus groups: A practical guide for applied research* (2nd ed.). Thousand Oaks, CA: Sage Publications.

Miles, M. B., & Huberman, A. M. (1984). *Qualitative data analysis*. Thousand Oaks, CA: Sage Publications.

Morse, J. M. (1994). Designing funded qualitative research. In N. K. Denzin & Y.S. Lincoln (Eds.), *Handbook of qualitative research* (pp. 220–235). Thousand Oaks, CA: Sage Publications.

Neuman, W. L. (1994). *Social research methods* (2nd ed.). Boston: Allyn & Bacon.

Patton, M. Q. (1997). *Utilization-focused evaluation*. Thousand Oaks: Sage Publications.

Sherman, E. & Reid, W. J., Eds (1994). *Qualitative research in social work*. New York: Columbia University Press.

Strauss, A. (1987). *Qualitative analysis for social scientists*. New York: Cambridge University Press.

Strauss, A., and Corbin, J. (1990). *Basics of qualitative research*. Newbury Park, CA: Sage Publications.

Yin, R. K. (1984), *Case study research*. Beverly Hills: Sage Publications.

Answers to the Quiz

1. b
2. d
3. c
4. b
5. d
6. c

7. b
8. d
9. b
10. d
11. c
12. a

7

An Exercise in Content Analysis

In this chapter, you will engage in a content analysis of suggestions by social workers on how best to plan a new graduate social work program. Parts of this analysis are done for you and you are asked to complete many of the steps in the process of determining the most salient recommendations from this sample of key informants. There are many ways you could structure a content analysis. The process employed here is just one model for doing so. It is a very elementary model that is designed to introduce you to qualitative data analysis. For models of content analysis that provide more depth and potential for publication of results, you should consult texts that are designed to provide a comprehensive view of this task. At the completion of this chapter, you should have gained familiarity with the key ingredients of content analysis, and you will have a step-by-step process for engaging in this process for another set of data you might acquire on your own.

This exercise can be employed in a research class where you submit your information to the instructor. If you are not using this book in a class, you could engage in this exercise with others interested in learning more about research, using these individuals as your consultants.

Your first task is to examine the background of the study. Then you will go through numerous steps in the analysis of the responses to one open-ended question from the survey related to that study.

Overview

The University of North Carolina at Wilmington undertook a survey of members of NASW in the Fall 2001 in order to collect information on the need for a new MSW program at this university. A random sample of members of the southeastern district of the North Carolina Chapter of the National Association of Social Workers (where the university was located) was mailed a questionnaire. Only those who held the MSW degree were asked to reply because the researchers wanted persons who had experienced graduate social work education as respondents.

These individuals would be in a position to offer expertise on this issue from the perspective of the student who had completed this type of education.

The faculty of the Social Work Department of this university wanted advice on the form a new MSW degree program should take. Information was collected from this survey about the type of practice for these respondents based on the assumption that the nature of current practitioners will reflect the job market of the near future as well as it can be determined. That information was quantitative in nature. One of the questions on that survey was qualitative in nature: *What is the most important advice you can give to those who are engaged in the planning of a new MSW program?* The information in the three tables of qualitative data for this exercise is drawn from the direct quotes of 45 persons drawn at random from the 131 questionnaires returned by the respondents. These 131 persons represented 47 percent of all persons who had been mailed the questionnaire—i.e., the response rate was 47 percent. The data in Table 7.1 were taken from the first segment of persons selected at random from the pool of 131 questionnaires. The data in Table 7.2 represent the comments of the next segment, as do the data in Table 7.3. The data in these tables are random.

The first question on this questionnaire asked for the respondent's primary job position. That response is given in the three tables along with the comment so that this information can be considered.

Overview of the Exercise

Your assignment is to engage in a qualitative data analysis exercise related to these comments and respond to the questions contained in it. This exercise will utilize the data from the three tables which are given at the end of this file. The model for the content analysis you will undertake was discussed in the previous chapter.

Content analysis is a method for analyzing text derived from the direct comments of study subjects about a question or set of questions. Among the kinds of questions that can be answered by content analysis are:

1. What are the messages from the data?
2. What are the priorities among these messages? Do some messages seem to be more important than other messages?
3. To what extent do the study subjects speak with a common voice? If there seem to be multiple voices, what best characterizes them? Are young respondents different from older ones? Are men different from women? Do some people seem to speak with more of a conservative voice than others, so those with the most passionate comments seem to be offering a different message than those with less passionate comments?

These are among the questions that might be answered in our data analysis. There are several preliminary steps in the content analysis procedures suggested in the previous chapter. One is the clarification of the study question. Another is the description of how the study sample was selected, while a third is the articulation of the method used to collect data. A fourth preliminary task is the bracketing of preconceived notions about the research question which you will refer to as you undertake your data analysis. The final task is the clarification of any conceptual models that guide the analysis, if there are any such models. Then you begin your data analysis. In the sections that follow, you will go engage in each of these steps.

Preliminary Steps in the Study

Each one of these preliminary tasks is addressed below. You will be asked to respond to questions about these tasks by commenting in the box beneath the question.

Discussion Box 7.1   The Study Question

Indicate your understanding of our research question.

Discussion Box 7.2   The Study Sample

The next step is the selection of the study sample. How would you characterize the sample for the present study? Is it a sample of key informants who have special knowledge in the field, or a sample from the general population? What was the population from which the study sample was drawn? Was the sample drawn at random from that population?

Discussion Box 7.3   The Method of Collecting Data

The third step is determining the method of collecting data. What method was used for collecting data for this study? Were the data collected from interviews, a social survey, or direct observation of behavior? Does this method seem appropriate to the purpose of the study?

Bracketing of My Own Ideas on This Subject

The next step in this approach to content analysis is the acknowledgement of the ideas you have on the topic under study. This is known as the procedure of *bracketing* because it can facilitate the separation of the ideas of the researcher from the ideas presented by the study subjects. The idea is to place your opinions in brackets rather than incorporating them in the analysis of the data from your study participants. The acknowledgement of your preconceived ideas about this subject can help you to avoid allowing these ideas from overly influencing your analysis. You don't want to give more credence to thoughts from the study subjects that are congruent with your preconceived ideas than those ideas that are not congruent with you thoughts on the subject.

Discussion Box 7.4

List your main thoughts on the question posed to the study subjects—What is the most important advice you can give to those who are engaged in the planning of a new MSW program?

You should keep these thoughts in a convenient place and refer to them occasionally to see if they have influenced your analysis of the qualitative data. Ask yourself if you agree with certain statements offered by respondents to our study and disagree with other statements. Then ask yourself if you are treating these statements differently in your analysis.

Identification of Conceptual Frameworks

The final preliminary step in this procedure for content analysis is the identification of any pertinent conceptual frameworks that serve to guide the data analysis. In our case, there is no major conceptual framework. The intent of the study was to assess need for a new MSW program and to collect advice about such a program. So our answer to this question is that there is no major conceptual framework that will guide our analysis.

Data Analysis

Following are the steps in the analysis of the data from the social workers who participated. In these steps of the exercise, you will undertake a qualitative data analysis of the statements of 45 respondents to the survey about the need for a new MSW program. These statements are given, in their entirety, in Tables 7.1 through 7.3. In other words, these person's expressions have not been reduced to more concise terms, but are given entirely as they appeared on the questionnaire from the respondent.

The comments of each respondent are given in a single cell with a number attached, such as 1a for the first person's comments that are displayed in Table 7.1, 1b for the second person's comments in this table, and so forth. Therefore, each respondent has been given an identification number that begins with the number of the table where this person's comments are displayed.

These tables are given at the end of this chapter. In this part of the exercise, you will be given certain observations about the data in these tables and you will be asked to respond with your comments in the boxes following the questions. For each table, you will engage in first-level coding, second-level coding, and enumeration as detailed below. Then you will engage in a saturation assessment by examining commonalities and differences in these three tables regarding the enumerated themes. Finally, you will consider the issue of credibility (or trustworthiness) by comparing your exercise with that of a fellow researcher.

Following are the steps in this analysis:

1. Code the comments for the data in Table 7.1, determining which word or expression captures the essence of each comment. There may be more than one code (expression) for each person's statements. This is first-level coding.
2. Engage in a credibility assessment of your coding of data by asking a fellow researcher to share his/her coding of the last statements and comparing your two approaches to coding.
3. Determine the themes that bind the codes (expressions) together for Table 7.1. This is second-level coding.
4. Engage in enumeration for Table 7.1 by counting the number of persons who made a comment that fell into each respective theme (i.e., each second-level code).
5. Undertake the first level coding of data in Table 7.2, as noted in step 1.
6. Undertake the second level coding of data for Table 7.2, as noted in step 2.
7. Engage in the enumeration of data for Table 7.2, as noted in step 3.
8. Engage in first-level coding of data in Table 7.3.
9. Undertake the second-level coding of data in Table 7.3.
10. Complete the enumeration procedure for the data in Table 7.3.
11. Engage in a saturation assessment of data in the three tables. To the extent that you have achieved saturation, you will find less need to engage in the collection of data from more persons in order to obtain a fundamentally complete picture of the basic answers to your research question. If you have achieved saturation, you have enough data and should feel comfortable drawing conclusions.
12. Engage in third-level coding by examining relationships between variables. In your case, you have the recommendations of persons in two work categories—direct practice (clinical social work, case management, etc.) and indirect practice (administration, supervision, and other). The key question here is whether there is a difference in the messages given by these two types of study participants. Do they speak with a common voice, or did you find noteworthy differences?
13. Determine your conclusions. In other words, what were the major themes in response to the research question? How should these themes be prioritized? Did the direct and indirect practice persons in this study speak with a common voice?

1. First-level Coding of Data in Table 7.1

In each table, each person is given an identification number in order to facilitate this exercise. The first person is number 1a. This individual only had one comment: "Good field placements." Your first task is to give a label to this idea. How about "Good field placement" as our code? This seems clear and captures the essence of the comment. In fact, this code is the actual comment in its entirety.

Now, let's code the other ideas in Table 7.1. The statement for person 1b was coded by me as "Hire qualified staff." This closely resembles the actual comment, with only a few words left out. This idea and the previous one should be noncontroversial. The third statement (1c) is more complicated. It is as follows:

> I believe it is important to maintain the integrity of the social work profession by offering courses that will establish and enhance one's understanding of social work and its ethics. Also, many MSW students are nontraditional in terms of having already begun their careers and possibly having families. Therefore, it is important to include a certain degree of flexibility in the program by offering courses in the evening and on weekends.

There are several different ideas in this statement. I have given the following codes to the ideas in this person's statement:

1. Social work identity
2. Ethics
3. Be student-friendly
4. Appreciate nontraditional student needs

Perhaps there are other ideas you may have for coding this statement. You might have included "Integrity of the profession" in addition to my comment on the identity of the students with the profession. Numbers 3 and 4 are derived from the same basic comment, so you might argue that they do not deserve two separate notations. But it seemed to me there were two ideas—the idea of being flexible to meet student needs and the idea of being especially responsive to the special needs of the nontraditional student. There are other ways the school could be student friendly and these other ways may be noted by other study subjects.

Discussion Box 7.5

What are your thoughts on the way of coding the statement from study subject 1c?

Now examine the next few statements and determine if you agree with me about how the statement should be coded.

Discussion Box 7.6

With regard to statements 1d, 1e, 1f, and 1g, do you agree with the codes displayed below?

Statement Number	My Code	Your Comments
1d	Marketing of social work	
1e	(1) Recruit good students (2) Student empowerment	
1f	Exploratory semester	
1g	(1) Good field placements (2) Long field placements	

There is room for discussion about how these statements should be coded, so don't be shy about disagreeing. For example, you might have found yourself coding person 1g as "Long field placement" and left out the idea of good field placements. Both statements, of course, fit into the general category of field placements, so the coding of this person's statement only as "Long field placement" could be easily argued. One might assume that a person who says there should be long field placements is suggesting an emphasis on field instruction, much like the person who said "Good field placement." So, it is not necessary to code this statement in two ways.

Your next task is to code the remaining statements in the discussion box. As with the current example, use numbers to set aside different ideas from the same person.

Discussion Box 7.7

Offer your code in the middle column. If you have any comments you would like to offer, provide them in the next column.

Statement Number	Your Code	Your Comments
1h		
1i		
1j		
1k		
1l		

2. Credibility Assessment

Credibility refers to the degree to which others can have confidence that your qualitative data analysis can be trusted (in some texts, you will see the term "trustworthiness" to refer to this concept). If you undertake a highly biased analysis, your results will not be credible or trustworthy.

The examination of credibility in qualitative data analysis deals with the same issue as the examination of the reliability and validity of the means of measurement in a quantitative research study.

Your next task in content analysis of our data is to examine the credibility of your analysis. You are asked here to conduct a very limited credibility assessment with reference to your data in the previous table (persons h, i, j, k, l). Ask a fellow researcher to examine these five statements and determine how they should be coded. Compare your codes with those of the other person.

Discussion Box 7.8

Did you find major differences in the ways these statements were interpreted by you and the other person?

The issue of credibility (or trustworthiness) in qualitative research is similar to the issue of reliability and validity in quantitative research. When you find a lack of congruence between different ways to observe the same thing, you have reason to question the validity of either or both approaches. If they are congruent, we have evidence of the validity (credibility) of your approach to observation (measurement).

3. Second-level Coding of Data in Table 7.1

The second level of coding calls upon you to group ideas into themes. Table 7.1 gives the comments of 12 individuals. This is a slightly small number of persons to constitute a segment of data, but we will go with it just the same so we can get this particular experience. Consider the following codes from my own analysis of these data:

- **a.** Good field placements (1a)
- **b.** Long field placement (1g)
- **c.** Strong supervision in field (1h)

I suppose the common theme is rather obvious—field instruction should be a primary focus of attention. There are, however, two types of statement—one that focuses on the importance of the field placement in general and one that focuses on field supervision per se. You will need to decide whether this difference is sufficient to place these ideas into two categories. I tend to think that one category is sufficient, because it goes without saying that strong supervision in the field is one component of a good field placement (internship).

Now let's consider the following codes from my list:

- **a.** Be student friendly (1c)
- **b.** Nontraditional student needs (1c)
- **c.** Recruit quality students (1e)

> **d.** Student empowerment (1e)
> **e.** Psychological needs of students (1l)

What do these ideas have in common? How about "Focus on student needs"? However, you could argue that there is more than one theme here. Is being student friendly a common theme with recruit quality students? These two statements have the concept of student in common but they have two different aspects of students, so you would need to determine if these statements should be in only one theme category or two theme categories.

Discussion Box 7.9

What do you think about this question? Should "Recruit quality students" be placed in the same category as the other statements?

Consider the following codes from my list:

> **a.** Sound theory, not just techniques (1h)
> **b.** Technical skills, not overview of theory (1j)
> **c.** What works best with a given diagnosis (1j)
> **d.** SA screening assessment (1j)
> **e.** Include mental treatment techniques (1l)
> **f.** Include assessment and diagnosis (1l)
> **g.** Include group work (1l)

Discussion Box 7.10

Would you say there is a common theme here? If so, what is it? If you believe there is more than one theme, identify it.

After you have answered this question, return to the preliminary consideration of bracketing your own ideas about this study subject.

Discussion Box 7.11

Was your thinking (coding of responses) influenced by preconceived ideas about social work education? If so, what do you plan to do about it? If not, explain.

---

4. Enumeration for Table 7.1

The task of enumeration calls upon us to count things. We can count the number of persons who mentioned a given theme or the number of different ideas presented in a given theme. In my enumeration experience, I noted there were three people who mentioned the importance of field instruction, four persons who suggested a special focus on student needs, three persons who suggested a focus on clinical practice, and three persons who mentioned the importance of identity with social work as a profession. I had no other themes with more than two persons who offered suggestions. This approach to enumeration only referred to the number of persons who offered a suggestion in the given category. You also could enumerate the total number of comments offered in a given category. In some cases, the same person offered more than one idea in the particular category.

Discussion Box 7.12

What was your experience in this regard? Did you have a similar enumeration experience? Did you have other themes with more than two persons giving suggestions?

---

5. First-level Coding for Table 7.2

Now, we turn our attention to the first-level coding for the data in Table 6.2. There is no particular reason that a given person was in Table 6.2 rather than Table 6.1 (or Table 6.3); it is a random assignment. The data were placed in three tables both for convenience and for a saturation assessment procedure that will be discussed later.

The statement of person 2a was "provide training, exposure, and educational preparation focusing on community based treatment of mentally ill, substance abuse, and developmental disabilities." One of the themes I saw in this statement was the importance of preparing students for clinical practice. Specific mention was made of three client populations related to mental illness, substance abuse, and developmental disabilities. How to handle this second part of the statement is not as clear as the first. Should we divide this statement into four themes—clinical practice, special attention to mental illness, special attention to substance abuse, and special attention to developmental disabilities?

Discussion Box 7.13

What do you think? Should we code this statement only as "Prepare students for clinical practice," or should we divide it into several themes? If we do the latter, we can always regroup them at the next level of coding.

The following box gives my codes for the next few statements.

Discussion Box 7.14

Offer your notes in the comments column. Do you agree, or do you have a different way to code these statements?

Statement	My Code	Your Comments
2b	Communicate with students.	
2c	(1) Recruit experienced faculty.	
	(2) Weed out bad students.	
	(3) Good field placements—don't allow students to be exploited.	
2d	Recruit good people to social work.	
2e	(1) Good field placements—don't allow students to be exploited.	
	(2) Emphasize clinical practice.	
	(3) Stress the "how to" of practice.	

Discussion Box 7.15

Now offer your codes and comments for the remainder of the table.

Statement Number	Your Code	Your Comments
2f		
2g		
2h		
2i		
2j		
2k		
2l		
2m		
2n		
2o		
2p		
2q		
2r		

6. Second-level Coding for Table 7.2

Now it is time to decide how to group the codes for Table 7.2. My coding of the statements in Table 6.2 resulted in the greatest number of comments in the category of clinical emphasis. I had eight statements from six people in the category of clinical emphasis. Here are my results:

Person	My code
2a	Treatment for mentally ill
2a	Treatment for substance abuse
2a	Treatment for developmental disabilities
2e	Clinical focus
2g	Clinical focus
2o	Specialized training in clinical
2r	Clinical emphasis
2g	Include psychopharmacology

Discussion Box 7.16

What are your reflections on my codes?

Another theme I noticed with the data from Table 7.2 was the importance of focusing on student needs. In the box, offer your codes for the persons designated. Focus on the theme of student need. Some of the persons made comments about more than one theme.

Discussion Box 7.17

What is your code for each of the following persons' statements insofar as they deal with student needs? Do you agree that each of the statements below are related to student needs? Do you have additional statements that should be included?

Statement	Your Code
2b	
2c	
2h	

The next box is a list of numbers associated with selected statements. You job is to determine how each should be coded and whether there is a theme here.

Discussion Box 7.18

Enter your codes for each of the following statements.

Statement	Your Code
2c (1)	
2j	
2m	

Discussion Box 7.19

How would you characterize this theme?

Discussion Box 7.20

Did you see any other themes from these data? If so, list them and designate the person whose statement could be coded as representing this theme.

7. Enumeration for Table 7.2

Now it is time to count the number of persons with a comment in each of the themes identified in the previous step. List your themes from the data in Table 7.2 and the number of persons with a comment regarding that theme. For example, if you agree with my coding you will have 6 persons who made comments in the category of "clinical emphasis." If so, you would insert the number 6 below in the second row, first column and you will insert the words "clinical emphasis" in the second row, second column.

Discussion Box 7.21

Present your themes and numbers below.

Number of Persons	Theme

8. First-level Coding for Table 7.3

Enter your codes for each of the statements in Table 7.3. Offer your code in the middle column. You may have more than one code for a given person; if so, place the number (1) by the first code, the number (2) by the next code, and so forth. If you are having some difficulty with any of your codes, make a comment about it in the comments column.

Discussion Box 7.22

Enter the number assigned to the statement in the first column, your code for this statement in the second, and your comments (if any) that you have about your decision in the third.

Statement	Your Code	Your Comments
3a		
3b		
3c		
3d		
3e		
3f		
3g		
3h		
3i		
3j		
3k		
3l		
3m		
3n		
3o		

9. Second-level Coding for Table 7.3

Now consider the themes represented by your codes for the qualitative data in Table 7.3. Table 7.4 is an example from my coding of the data.

Now it is your turn. Complete the discussion box by inserting the name of the theme in the first column, the person with the idea in the second column, and your coding of that person's idea in the third column. You may insert my codes above in the table below, or you may choose a different path for coding the ideas of these persons. But be sure to include all the themes you have witnessed in this table. A theme should have at least two persons listed, preferably three.

TABLE 7.4

Theme	Statement	My codes
Focus on student needs	3d	Self-awareness for students is critical
	3f	Self awareness cannot be overemphasized.
	3n	Screen students for psychological health.

Discussion Box 7.23

Identify the theme in column 1, the statement number in the second column (3a, 3f, etc.) and your code for the statement in column 3.

Theme	Statement	Your Codes

10. Enumeration for Data in Table 7.3

Now count the number of persons with a comment for each of the themes in Table 7.3 and insert that number next to the theme in the discussion box given in the previous step.

11. Saturation Assessment

The key question in saturation analysis is whether you are likely to find notable differences in the messages given by your respondents if you were to continue your collection of data. If the themes that arise from the second set of data (Table 7.2) were identical to the themes for the first table, this might suggest that additional review of data is not warranted. Perhaps you already have all the themes you will get from this study population. But if you get a few additional themes, you may decide that further analysis is needed. If the third set of data (Table 7.3) provides little additional information, you could say that you have achieved a reasonable level of saturation of your data and it would not be necessary to solicit additional information from this study population.

Suppose you were conducting a study of adults who had been sexually abused as a child and have started to interview a sample of such persons. Suppose further that after completing 20 interviews, you examined your data and found that the second 10 persons you interviewed added a few new themes to your message, in addition to reinforcing many of the same messages as the first 10 persons interviewed. But suppose further that you had found that the third set of 10 persons merely reinforced the themes of the first and second set of interviews. Do you need to select an additional 10 persons for interviews? Probably not, because you seem to be at a state of saturation with regard to the particular questions you were pursuing with these individuals. This does *not* suggest that you have declared there is absolutely nothing new you will ever find from further interviews. It simply means that you have clarified a number of messages and feel confident you have gained major insight into your research question, an insight that can be further tested by other research. In other words, you have gone beyond the discovery of idiosyncratic ideas of a selected few that cannot be generalized to others.

In our study, you have examined the qualitative data from three tables which contained the ideas of 45 respondents drawn at random from 131 persons who responded to a mailed survey. Each table contained one segment of the data from these 45 persons. These segments were randomly assigned. There is no known basis in which we would believe the ideas from these tables would be notably different, one from the other. If we had chosen to separate the tables between those in different positions or different fields of practice, we would have a different kind of analysis at this juncture. But we did not do this; instead, we randomly assigned comments to three tables. So we have no basis for expecting differences between the ideas contained in them.

What should be our response if we were to find the themes from these tables to be quite different? For example, what if the greatest emphasis from the first table was clinical practice while no one mentioned social justice as the emphasis, and we found that the greatest emphasis from Table 6.2 was social justice but no one mentioned clinical practice? Suppose further that almost no one from the third table mentioned either clinical practice or social justice, but we found a third theme as the greatest emphasis, such as the importance of working with the mentally ill? What would we do?

TABLE 7.5

Theme	Number of persons from each data segment		
	Table 7.1	*Table 7.2*	*Table 7.3*
Emphasize clinical practice (n = 13)m	3 [h, j, l]	5 [a, e, g, o, r]	5 [f, g, h, m, j]
Focus on individual student needs (n = 13)	3 [c, e, l]	6 [b, c, d, l, p, h]	4 [e, d, f, n]
Emphasize field instruction (n = 10)	3 [a, g, h]	2 [c, e]	5 [b, d, e, h, i]
Focus on the real world of practice (n = 9)	2 [g, j]	4 [c, f, j, m]	3 [c, e, o]
Maintain high standards (n = 6)	3 [c, e, I]	0	3 [f, i, n]
Emphasize generalist social work (n = 5)	2 [k, l]	0	3 [c, h, l]
Emphasize the importance of social work as a profession and its uniqueness. (n = 4)	3 [c, d, j]	0	1 [a]
Prepare for concerns of macro practice such as social justice, diversity, client advocacy, etc. (n = 4)	1 [j]	1 [f]	2 [j, k]
Be specialized. (n = 3)	1 [j]	2 [q, o]	0
Prepare for rural practice (n = 2)	0	2 [I, k]	0

In this situation, we would conclude that we have failed to achieve saturation, meaning that we should not terminate our collection of data and draw conclusions. We could mention at this time that three different themes emerged but we would not be in a position to put these themes into perspective with regard to emphasis.

Let's examine the issue of saturation by reviewing my assessment table. In this table are my data on the themes with the number of persons from each segment who made a comment in that theme. Examine this table and see if it seems generally appropriate, given your own data analysis.

Let's discuss Table 7.1. For the theme of *clinical practice*, you can see a total of 13 persons with comments and you can see that these persons were somewhat evenly divided between the three segments, with the numbers of 3, 5, and 5. It would seem that saturation has been achieved on this theme. The same is true for *emphasize field instruction* (3, 2, and 5 persons from these three tables), *student needs* as a theme (with the numbers of 3, 6, and 4) and *the real world of practice* which had 2 statements, 4 statements, and 3 statements for these three tables.

Discussion Box 7.24

Do you agree that saturation has been achieved on these four themes?

The next theme in my saturation table is generalist practice. The idea here is that the school should not emphasize specialization, but should prepare students for practice in a variety of jobs and settings. Here we might find ourselves in a dilemma. There were 6 persons who mentioned this theme and they were scattered among the three segments of data. This contrasts with the opposite recommendation from only a few persons who mentioned specialization. However, one could argue that the persons who mentioned an emphasis on clinical practice were giving one version of the need for more specialized education, as contrasted with more generalized education. A clinical focus is only one possible form of specialization in social work. Others include community organization and human service administration. It seems that if you suggest a primary emphasis on any one of these concentrations, you are suggesting a more specialized approach to the curriculum design than a generalist approach.

Discussion Box 7.25
_____

What do you think? Should a recommendation for a focus on clinical social work be grouped with others who suggested specialization? If so, the numbers who recommended specialization will far outnumber those who suggested a more generalist approach to preparation for practice.

---

12. Third-level Coding

There are several additional avenues you can take when you go beyond the second-level of coding. For one thing, you could collapse the second-level themes into fewer themes. In this process, you might even be able to identify an over-arching message in your data. Another avenue you could take is to examine relationships among the data. With our data on suggestions about the development of a new graduate social work program in a university, we collected information on the practice position of the individual who supplied the suggestion. A question that could be posed is whether there is a relationship between position category and message. In other words, do these different types of people offer the same message, or are there major distinctions between the messages of these groups?

Are there major messages that bind the themes together? One of the tasks of the third level of coding entails looking beyond basic themes to broader themes that bind various themes together. The greater the number of items of qualitative data, you more likely you will need to engage in this level of coding. We had a set of relatively simple statements from 45 persons. Some of these individuals had statements that could be coded in more than one way, so we have more than 45 codes to organize. In fact, you can see that there are 69 coded statements in the previous table that were organized into 10 themes. You could examine these 10 themes to see if they could be grouped into fewer themes, but you would normally engage in this level of coding if you had more than 10 themes. Whether they could be organized more or not, you could look at the data to see if there was an overarching message.

Discussion Box 7.26
_____

Do you believe these 10 themes should be combined into fewer themes? If so, what themes? Do you see an overarching message in these statements?

Are there noteworthy relationships among messages or themes? Do people who offer ideas regarding one particular theme tend to be more likely than others to offer ideas in a certain other theme? This would suggest a relationship between these themes. Do respondents of a certain type tend to offer different ideas from the respondents as a whole? This would suggest a relationship between type respondent and message.

In our exercise, we have one distinct variable that was identified that could facilitate this type of analysis—the work position of the respondent. The question to be posed is whether persons employed in different work positions offer different ideas about the basic research question. If persons employed in one type of position tended to emphasize specialized clinical practice while those in a different type tended to emphasize generalist practice, you would want to report this finding.

Our data are dominated by those serving in direct practice positions. Of the 45 persons in our sample, 29 reported direct service as their primary work position. Only 7 reported administration as the primary job, with an additional 5 indicating supervisions, and 4 reporting to be in training or education jobs. Only one person reported community social work, so this category is clearly not sufficient to examine any trends. In fact, all of these categories outside of direct practice are small. This makes the task of relationship analysis a little challenging.

We have seen that clinical practice, field instruction, and student needs were the dominant themes in our data overall. Do the persons in these minority groups (administrators, supervisors, and trainers) pose any major differences from this pattern in their ideas? My examination of this task revealed that administrators offered one idea in the category of field instruction, three ideas in the category of student needs, and one idea in the category of clinical practice. In addition, one administrator offered a suggestion in the category of rural practice and another administrator offered a suggestion in the category of the real world of practice. My analysis revealed that one supervisor's comments fell in the category of clinical practice, two fell in the category of student needs, one fell in the category of the real world of practice, and one was unusual (in that no one else offered an idea in this category). One of the trainers offered an unusual idea, so this person can be dropped from this analysis, leaving only three for examination, a number that is too low to serve as a reasonable view of differences.

So, what do we make of this? Do our respondents from different positions speak with a common voice? I would reply with a tentative Yes because those in the minority groups did not have a pattern that was distinctly different from the overall responses. I say tentative because the number of persons in the minority groups was quite small.

Discussion Box 7.27

What do you think? Did our respondents speak with a common voice?

13. Drawing Conclusions

Your final task is to summarize your findings and draw any conclusions that are suggested by your analysis. This summary should begin with a restatement of the central research question being pursued in this study. Next, you should summarize the major themes that arose with regard to the answer to this question and the priorities that were evident among these themes based on the number of persons with an idea congruent with each theme. You may want to provide any especially poignant quotes from the study subjects in this section. Then you should refer to minor themes that had enough salience to be offered as additional ideas for further analysis. Another issue to be addressed is whether you found noteworthy differences in the messages offered by those in different work positions. Finally, you should indicate if there is an overarching message that might be used to best characterize the advice of these individuals.

In this summary, you should not list the actual numbers of persons for each theme—that level of specificity is reserved for the data analysis sections of the report. Given the small sample size, I would also suggest that themes with small differences in numbers not be treated as different. Suppose, for example, that theme A had 11 people with a comment and theme B had 9 people with a comment, and these were the two themes with the highest numbers. I would suggest that you treat these two themes as comparable and conclude that these two themes were the most dominant, and leave out any reference to these small differences in numbers.

Discussion Box 7.28

Offer your summary.

TABLE 7.1 *Responses from 12 MSW Social Workers*

Position (ID)	Comment
Direct practice (1a)	Good field placements
Administration (1b)	Locate and hire qualified and enthusiastic staff
Direct practice (1c)	I believe it is important to maintain the integrity of the social work profession by offering courses that will establish and enhance one's understanding of social work and its ethics. Also, many MSW students are non-traditional in terms of having already begun their careers and possibly having families. Therefore, it is important to include a certain degree of flexibility in the program by offering courses in the evening and on weekends.
Direct practice (1d)	Explore how to reach as many candidates as possible because colleagues are not aware of higher education options.
Administration (1e)	Screen applicants carefully—constantly evaluate with them if their needs are being met and what changes/additions they recommend.

TABLE 7.1 *Responses from 12 MSW Social Workers* *(continued)*

Position (ID)	Comment
Supervision (1f)	? exploratory semester which offers potential students intro courses MSW program and permits student/UNCW to gauge readiness for rigor of grad school.
Direct practice (1g)	I believe *strongly* that practicum placements need to be designed with the students and the agency clients' needs in mind—not the university calendar nor the program should dictate. Therefore, I suggest nice *long* placements. Having been a field placement supervisor for many years, I'd recommend no more than 2 practicum placements and preferably one during the graduate program. This provides the best opportunity for a supervisor to observe and teach in the field and for students to apply their theory and practice. I would never take a student for less than a year.
Direct practice (1h)	A *sound* theory base and not just "techniques" in isolation. Strong supervision. Appropriate field placement experience with strong supervisor here as well.
Community social work (1i)	We need professional well educated MSW who are proud of their work and will help make this field more appreciated and more accepted so that the community not only seeks our help but is willing to pay a living wage for it. There should be a *huge* difference between someone with a MSW and someone without—so much so that the community easily recognizes the difference.
Direct practice (1j)	More technical skills rather than an overview of theory. How it actually works—the techniques. Only complaint I have with my education is that I didn't have the techniques of the theories (the working skills) to apply with the direct practice face to face with clients. Nor did I know which worked best for what diagnosis—i.e., dialectical with borderline.
	Also believe SA screening during assessment should be stressed. Also, wish someone would advocate for social workers (especially clinical) to be on same list as doctors and teachers for educational loan reduction for working in depressed areas. 30% of your clients are on indigent med programs. 50% are on Medicaid. Without these two programs there wouldn't be a chance of helping these people.
	More advocacy for clients for med coverage and to include MH and medicine coverage is desperately needed.
Direct practice (1k)	(a) Don't be too specialized. (b) Don't foster elitism. People often need social workers to help them with accessing services to meet basic needs as a prelude to a concurrent to improving psychosocial functioning. Case management and information and referral is not beneath the LCSWs functions when that is the need.
Direct practice (1l)	Keep it a *generalist* perspective. Curriculum needs to include ethics, cultural diversity, mental treatment techniques, assessment and diagnosis, group work (I *currently* do not do a lot in this area but there is a huge need and social workers are able and known for being effective group workers). Some programs require ther students to actually attend their own therapy. I think this is an *excellent* idea now that I have been in the field for over 4 years now post masters. I have seen some individuals who have graduated from different MSW programs who are in need of therapy themselves and do not realize how they are effecting their clients.

TABLE 7.2   *Responses from 18 MSW Social Workers*

Position (ID)	Comment
Administration (2a)	Provide training, exposure, and educational preparation focusing on community based treatment of mentally ill, substance abuse, and developmental disabilities
Direct practice (2b)	I suggest a concerted effort to coordinate the communication provided to the candidates. Work diligently to make as much reliable information regarding the curriculum, schedules, and costs readily available as early in the process as possible. Balance the need to inform of changes in these areas quickly, with the need to make the information accurate. Persistent changes result in a sense of being "jerked around" which increases stress and lowers morale. Both of these reduce the likelihood of retention of the candidates until the completion of the program.
Direct practice (2c)	(1) Provide expert instructors who have served their time in the "trenches." (2) Have the courage and integrity to weed out "unfit" candidates (e.g., igotists, non-empathic, unresolved personal pathologies, etc.) (3) Provide challenging & well-supervised practicum settings vs places seeking free no-patient-contact labor.
Supervision (2d)	Please actively recruit. We need more MSWs @ our agency.
Direct practice (2e)	Ensure the field placement sites can offer the MSW students a well-rounded, hands-on, meaningful experience. *Not* only filing, notewriting, etc. Also, put as much clinical (the "how-to") education in the curriculum (especially in the mental health direct practice concentration)
Direct practice (2f)	I commend the faculty for doing a needs assessment related to the development of the MSW program. I hope the profession will not only respond to what services the public is currently willing to support. The MSW program should also insure students to work for social development and social transformation—to promote a more just and caring society.
Direct practice (2g)	Include psychopharmacology, increase clinical coursework, training to be a therapist
Direct practice (2h)	Preach flexibility
Education/training (2i)	Good luck! I think such a program will provide opportunities in surrounding rural areas to recruit MSW level social workers.
Direct practice (2j)	Present realistic views of practice.
Administration (2k)	Please include *rural* practice settings.
Direct practice (2l)	Understand applicants are from various fields of study and not only BSWs and to tailor the program to that understanding. Allow for different disciplines in SW (elderly, family, indirect)
Administration (2m)	Continue to seek input from practitioners
Education/training (2n)	Include UNCP [University of North Carolina at Pembroke]

TABLE 7.2 *Responses from 18 MSW Social Workers (continued)*

Position (ID)	Comment
Direct practice (2o)	I was fortunate to earn a degree in a direct practice emphasis leading to a position as psychiatric social worker. I had the opportunity to take undergrad and graduate courses that were specifically related to all of the positions I have held in the past 18 years. I felt having a strong background in training gave me a leading edge over and above many other interns and recent grads I worked with who went into a psychiatric field but lacked the coursework needed. My point is we have a need in S.E.N.C. for well trained grads in the mental health field. As a supervisor I have worked with many different colleges and the lack of good academics is a problem so I think having a strong clinical emphasis is needed!
Supervision (2p)	Create the program with consideration of the professional—i.e., flexible, laid out in advance.
Direct practice (2q)	Focus on few things well to meet student's needs.
Direct practice (2r)	Beef up the clinical aspect with instructors who are willing to teach group by conducting groups. Also, more emphasis on clinical practice in general.

TABLE 7.3 *Comments from 15 Respondents*

Position	Comment
Direct practice (3a)	One of the most valuable things I learned in my MSW program was what I might label a social work attitude. I went into the program while working as an educator and counselor in a Planned Parenthood clinic. I was specifically interested in training to become a therapist, but what I learned was to be a good social worker in all sorts of venues. It has been helpful in every aspect of my life including my personal life. I notice that many therapists whose training originated in psychology or education don't see their job as broadly as I do. They are less interested in the whole life experience and relationships of the people they see.
Direct practice (3b)	Adequate (extensive) professional on-the-job supervision for students in field work.
Supervision (3c)	Be broad based; ask advise of new graduates of MSW degree and how well it prepared them to get a job in the field and adjust curriculum accordingly.
Direct practice (3d)	I completed advanced standing therefore I would have enjoyed participating in more than one field placement. I feel that hands on experience is a wonderful experience. I feel that individuals (students) need to take a close examination of their selves—whether this means brief counseling sessions or personal interviews.
Direct practice (3e)	Make it available and make it current/timely and challenging material. Of equal significance is the development of a comprehensive internship program coord. With individuals in the field

TABLE 7.3 *Comments from 15 Respondents*

Position (ID)	Comment
Direct practice (3f)	Ensure that your program has a strong clinical orientation as many MSW graduates pursue work as clinicians and are ill-prepared if the program they attend doesn't provide adequate training in this area. Encourage students to do their own therapeutic work to foster self-awareness as they can separate their own issues from those of their clients. This cannot be overemphasized!
Direct practice (3g)	Get your LCSWP immediately, then take the exam.
Direct practice/Education-training (3h)	The program must be diverse; group, individual, family, special ethnic group, gays, children. Also: caring supervision, program planning, marketing, research and theory and behavioral techniques.
Direct practice (3i)	Ensuring integrity of MSW degree by providing appropriate field placements with high standards of practice for students.
Administration (3j)	A focus for a program should center around the impact of managed care in today's environment.
Direct practice (3k)	Secure local and state support for such a move and do aggressive planning and make certain you can justify such a move.
Direct practice (3l)	Provide a program with scope and options. Avoid one "cookie cutter" program that forces everyone down one path.
Supervision (3m)	Psychopathology needs to be a primary subject to be studied; more than just one class. Students need to be very comfortable with DSM-IV
Administration (3n)	Hold students to appropriate standards. Screen for psychological stability as well as intellectual ability.
Education/training (3o)	Make it practical and experiential.

8

Phases of Outcome Evaluation

In this chapter, you will examine the process of outcome evaluation, with an emphasis on how each phase links with other phases of the process. For example, you will explore how a good definition of target behavior, included in the first major step in outcome evaluation, will help in the choice of a means of measuring client progress, a later step. A few major concepts in outcome evaluation will be presented in this chapter; more specific concepts will be examined in the chapter that follows. And you will return to these concepts in later chapters that focus on specific parts of the evaluation process. This procedure of reinforcement of learning (concepts being presented more than once) is a major feature of this book.

At the completion of this chapter, you will be able to:

1. Identify the chief questions to be answered in each of the major phases of human service evaluation.
2. Define the target behavior in a human service evaluation example.
3. Identify the essential connection between a target behavior analysis and a selected intervention.
4. Identify the model for a selected intervention and its link with the target behavior analysis.
5. Explain the essential connection between causation and the choice of a research design.
6. Identify the abstract definition of target behavior in an example.
7. Identify the method used to measure client progress in an example, and the form of data extracted by that particular measurement method.
8. Identify the role of treatment protocols and manuals in the evaluation process.
9. Identify the hypothesis in an example.
10. Identify whether data supports the hypothesis in an example.
11. Distinguish between statements of conclusion in a research example that are and are not consistent with the results of the data analysis.

If you believe you already have acquired these competencies, you can go to the end of this chapter and take the quiz. It is designed to serve either as a means of determining whether you need to review this chapter, or as a mechanism for testing your success after you have completed this experience.

Overview

In a previous chapter, evaluation was described as a judgment of worth. In evaluation, comparison is a key. We cannot evaluate without applying some standard of propriety or efficacy. Statements regarding basic client characteristics of your agency would not constitute an evaluation report. In fact, it would not be a full statement of evaluation if you claimed that 61 percent of your clients said, in a survey, that they would recommend your agency to a friend. Why? This would not be a complete statement because you have not included a basis of comparison. On what basis would you claim that this fact is good news? It might be that clients of other similar agencies had figures higher than 61 percent on this question.

The systems model of evaluation was discussed in a previous chapter as a useful way to conceptualize types of evaluation. This model has reference to input, process, output, and outcome. Clients come to your agency with a need (input) and receive a service (process) which can be quantified with regard to amount of service (output), which should lead to the achievement of client goals (outcome).

The purpose of outcome evaluation is to determine the extent to which the objectives of intervention were achieved. It focuses on client conditions and client progress. In this chapter, you will examine the steps in the process of outcome evaluation. Let's assume you have a client who comes for therapy. Following an initial assessment session, you note the client has the symptoms of depression and expresses the need to overcome these feelings. Following this assessment, you need to examine this target behavior. What is depression? What causes it? What are the special needs of persons with this target behavior?

The experience of finding answers to these questions constitutes the first step in outcome evaluation—the assessment of the target behavior. Your next step is the selection of an intervention. That intervention must be congruent with the analysis of the target behavior. If depression is caused by distorted thinking about stressful events, you would seek an intervention like cognitive-behavioral therapy because this model addresses distorted thinking patterns.

Your next steps refer to the methodology you will employ in the evaluation of this intervention. These steps include the selection of the sample, the selection of the means to measure client progress, and the selection of the research design. In our present example, the sample has been selected because you have a client whose progress you wish to evaluate. You will need to determine how to measure client progress. In our example, a depression scale should be selected that is congruent with our definition of the target behavior. Depression is a concept with such familiarity that there are numerous sources for helping us with our definition. Simply using such a definition would normally be a good course of action. There are other target behaviors that may need some work on your part to determine its conceptual boundaries—how to define it. Another step in the methodology is the determination of the research design. If you are evaluating a single client, you will select one of a number of alternative single-system designs. The research design enumerates the procedures for measurement of progress and the delivery of the intervention. If you can measure the client's target behavior several times prior to intervention and several times during intervention, you will have a better design than one that has no measurements before treatment begins.

Another major step in outcome evaluation is monitoring of the intervention. The task here is to assess the extent to which the selected intervention was actually implemented. There may have been major deviations from the strict rules of a given intervention. One of the reasons you will evaluate outcome is to determine which interventions work best for achieving certain outcomes. If you don't know what was implemented, you will not be in a position to draw conclusions about what worked.

Analyzing data and drawing conclusions are the final two steps in outcome evaluation. In the example of the treatment of depression, you will collect data using your selected depression scale and you will analyze it to determine if it suggests that your intervention was effective in achieving the intended outcomes. Appropriate conclusions will be drawn based on that data analysis. In the next sections, you will examine each of these steps in more detail.

Discussion Box 8.1

We could conceptualize outcome evaluation as having five major steps—assessment of target behavior, selection of an intervention, development of a study methodology (design, measurement, sampling), analysis of data, and drawing of conclusions. Suppose you saw the following summary of an outcome evaluation study:

The Dropout Prevention Program is designed to reduce risk factors associated with dropping before high school graduation. The risk factors associated with dropping out are low self-esteem, poor grades, and disciplinary action. Program strategies are aimed at each of these risk factors. The study found an improvement on all risk factors; thus, it was concluded that the program was effective.

Which one of the five major steps is the least well addressed in this description?

Identification and Analysis of Target Behavior

The first major phase of the research process is problem formulation leading to the development of the research question. In outcome evaluation, this question is more simple to develop than in most other forms of research. We want to know if the treatment was effective in achieving its objectives. In this task, we must address two central questions:

1. How is the target behavior defined?
2. How is the target behavior analyzed?

The answer to the first question provides a clear basis for the selection of the means to measure client progress. If we view self-efficacy as somewhat different from self-esteem and we develop a clear definition of self-efficacy, we will find an instrument that measures self-efficacy rather than self-esteem.

The answer to the second question is helpful in our guidance regarding the selection of the intervention. If our literature review provides evidence that depression is caused by distorted thinking in response to life events, we would be wise to select an intervention that addresses thinking patterns about life events. Your literature review should also examine evidence regarding how well specific interventions have worked in response to your selected target behavior. If cognitive-behavioral therapy has been found effective in the treatment of depression, you would be wise to consider this option if your target behavior is depression.

Definition of Target Behavior. For many forms of target behavior, there are several ways the behavior can be defined. How would you define spouse abuse? Would your definition include both verbal and physical acts of violence, or just physical? If they included both, you would, of course, need to be careful to find a measurement method that included both.

How many of the following behaviors would be included in your definition of depression—feelings of sadness, feelings of worthlessness, feelings of guilt, feelings of hopelessness, disturbances of appetite, disturbances of sleep, disturbances of general activity level? Each of these are included in many depression scales. However, it is important to note that depression is a syndrome rather than a set of independent conditions. In other words, sleeplessness alone is a poor basis for determining that one is depressed. It is when a number of the above conditions are present together that one should recognize depression.

The Clinical Anxiety Scale (Corcoran, 1987, p. 123) is designed to measure the amount, degree, or severity of clinical anxiety. Clinical anxiety apparently refers to the type of anxiety likely to reflect a need for psychotherapy. Items on this scale refer to feelings of being nervous or scared for no clear reason. But the Achievement Anxiety Scale measures anxiety about academic achievement, something that we can see is clearly distinguished from clinical anxiety.

Discussion Box 8.2

What's wrong with the following situation?

A college professor is teaching a course on interviewing skills which is designed to improve the student's ability to demonstrate selected skills related to preparing for the interview, beginning the interview, exploring client questions and feelings, assessing client needs, contracting for clinical service, implementing the contract, and evaluating the results. To measure effectiveness, this professor selects a social skills inventory that measures general social skills related to self-awareness, impulse control in social situations, persistence, self-motivation, and social deftness.

Analysis of Target Behavior.　An examination of the dynamics of the target behavior provides a rationale for the selection of the intervention. If training is a solution to the problem, it stands to reason that ignorance of some kind must be the cause of the problem. Do people abuse drugs because of ignorance? Or, do they do it because of peer pressure, or parent–child conflict, or something else? If it is something else, then our intervention should address the something else.

If the causes of child abuse lie within the pathologies of the abuser, it follows that some form of therapy into these pathologies is the solution. But if we view child abuse as being caused by societal inadequacies, such as acceptance of violence in our culture, or poverty, a different solution would naturally emerge.

This should not be interpreted as a suggestion that there is only one cause for our client's target behavior. If we believe that both individual pathology and societal inadequacies contribute to child abuse, it is perfectly legitimate for a given intervention to address only one of these causes, or to address more than one. But if there is no evidence that ignorance contributes to drug abuse, we would be standing on thin ice to suggest training for the objective of reducing drug abuse.

Discussion Box 8.3

Think of a target behavior of a typical client in a familiar human service program. What is the target behavior and what is one cause of it?

Basic Design of the Intervention

The intervention can be described in many ways. The key to the description is that it should be sufficient to facilitate replication by others. In this section, we will discuss the intervention in regard to:

- Goals and outcome objectives.
- Structure.
- Personnel.
- Model.

Our emphasis, however, will be upon the model of the intervention because of its role in the connection of the intervention to the problem analysis. The other ways to describe the intervention are mentioned here, but will be considered in greater detail in later chapters.

We will start with the critical definitions:

- The goal of intervention is the ultimate statement of client outcome.
- The objective of intervention is a statement of a measured amount of client progress toward the achievement of the goal.
- The structure of the intervention specifies the form and intensity of the services to be provided.
- The model of the intervention identifies the conceptual link between the structure of the intervention and the problem analysis and serves as a logical justification of the intervention design.
- The personnel of the intervention refers to the types of practitioners who will deliver the services to the clients.

Let's suppose you are dealing with the problem of high school dropouts and you wish to prevent this occurrence by interventions for middle school students who are at risk for dropping out. Your goal would logically be the prevention of dropping out of school before graduation. One of your objectives might be to improve the self-esteem of middle school students at risk of dropping out because you have found that self-esteem is related to high school completion. The structure of your intervention might include weekly group counseling sessions for 6 weeks, weekly individual counseling sessions for 12 weeks, and weekly tutoring sessions for 8 weeks. The model of this intervention might describe how students become at risk by having poor study habits, poor social support, and the negative influence of peers. This description would justify the inclusion of group work that is designed to change the nature of the peer influence, counseling that builds self-esteem, and group work that improves social support. You might also report that these services are being delivered by school social workers who hold the Master of Social Work degree.

You should note that neither the goal nor the objective is service oriented (e.g., to deliver counseling services). Instead, they both focus on client conditions. You should also notice that the description of the structure of the intervention specifies both the form and intensity of the intervention. This description noted such things as a weekly counseling session for 12 weeks. This helps you to know that counseling is one form the intervention takes, but it also lets you know there are 12 such sessions that are planned for the typical client.

Discussion Box 8.4

Are each of the following okay as statements of outcome objectives?

1. To provide crisis intervention services to the victims of rape.
2. To assure that each rape victim is administered the rape kit, a protocol guiding the initial response of the program to the rape victim.
3. To reduce the emotional distress experienced by rape victims in the month following the incident.

Model of the Intervention

The **model of the intervention** is the theoretical or conceptual framework that illustrates the dynamics of the target behavior in such a way as to illustrate the essential connections between cause and effect or the special aspects of need being addressed by the intervention. Figure 8.1 is a graphic depiction of a model dealing with stressors and stress and their consequences. The arrows denote causation between variables (or factors) in the model, with the direction of the arrow noting the direction of causality.

According to this model, a stressor is an event or environmental condition that can cause stress. Stress is defined as state of psychological tension exemplified by such concepts as *uptight* or *tense*, which stand in contrast to such states as *relaxed* or *calm*. Stress buffers are things that can mediate the effect of stressors upon stress. An example of a stress buffer would be social support because persons with high social support are likely to experience less stress following a major stressor event in life than those with low social support. A person with high support will likely become less debilitated by depression following a divorce than would someone with low support. A framework like this above could be the underpinning of an intervention designed to help people cope with stressors.

We could apply this model to the topic of stress among graduate students, as I did a few years ago. If the model is correct, you would find a positive relationship between stressors and stress and a positive relationship between stress and health problems. You would also find that stress buffers like social support mediate the relationship between stressors and stress. Thus, the degree of correlation (empirical relationship) between stressors and stress would be lower for persons with high support, because stressors would have less effect. And you would find a negative relationship between social support and stress, meaning the higher your support, the lower your stress.

The reason for depicting the model that explains the essential connections between factors of concern is the guidance a model can give for the design of an intervention. Suppose, for example, that the clients' treatment objectives are related to the reduction of health and emotional problems associated with stress. The model could justify the development of a social support program for clients who are experiencing a large number of stressors because support can be a stress buffer, which could reduce stress, which causes health problems. It could justify an intervention designed to reduce the number of stressors in the client's life because stressors lead to stress, which leads to health problems.

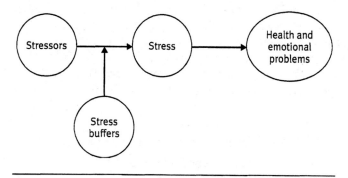

FIGURE 8.1   *Theoretical Model of Study Variables*

Would this depiction of health and emotional problems justify the provision of a training program for clients? If so, what kind of training? This model says nothing about the role of ignorance in the promotion of stress. If ignorance plays a role, then training might be justified. But this should be a part of the model if training is to be justified.

The description of the intervention helps us to determine what worked or didn't work. With this information, we can better generalize the results of one study to another situation. Interventions should be described with enough detail that the reader would know the same intervention if he or she saw it somewhere else. In a later chapter, you will examine the intervention in greater detail with regard to goals, objectives, structure, and personnel. This chapter examined the model of the intervention to illustrate the connection of the problem analysis with the selection of the intervention. The more you know about the target behavior, the better you would be able to develop a model for the intervention.

Discussion Box 8.5

Locus of control is a personality trait that deals with the extent to which individuals view themselves as being in control of their own fate or being controlled by external sources over which they have little control. Persons with an internal locus of control view themselves as being in charge of their own fates. It has been found that persons with an internal locus of control are better able to cope with stressors than persons with an external locus of control. Given the theoretical model depicted above, how would you classify locus of control—stressor, stress buffer, stress, or a consequence of stress?

Selection of the Study Sample

A sample is a portion of a larger entity, the population. In evaluative research, this issue is less difficult than in some other forms of research. Often, our study sample consists of all clients served by your program at a given point. In single-system evaluation, you may select the only client you are serving who is exhibiting a special problem you want to learn more about. In such a case, the sample selection comes first in the evaluation process.

Your study **sample** consists of all persons from whom data were collected. Your study **population** consists of any group of persons that includes all of the persons in your sample. You can define your study population in any number of ways, but your study sample will always be those persons from whom data were collected. Consider the following example:

- ❏ 350 persons are estimated to be abusive husbands in this community.
    - ❏ 143 men sought information about the program for abusive husbands.
        - ❏ 107 men signed up for the program.
            - ❏ 81 men started the program and took the pretest tool.
                - ❏ 62 men completed the program and took the posttest tool.

What is the study sample? It is the last figure—the 62 men who took the posttest, because this is the group of persons from whom you have data. What is the population? Well, you can define it in any way noted, and you might even want to define it more broadly, but you cannot define it in any way that would exclude any person in your sample from that population. For example, you could not define your study population as left-handed men who have abused their wives, because some of those in your study sample would not fit into this category.

You would be wise, however, to define the population closely to the sample, because the closer this group to your sample, the more safe are the grounds on which you are generalizing your findings from the sample to the population.

The key function of sampling procedures is to provide guidance on the extent to which the results of your study can be generalized to persons not in your study. There are several things that assist the reader of your report with the answer to this question. One is the way the sample was selected. A random sample is a selection procedure whereby every person in the study population has an equal chance of being selected for your study sample. Random sampling would be exemplified by drawing names from a hat, but there are more sophisticated methods for doing this. The **random sample** is the only type of sample whereby you can safely generalize your study's findings to persons not include in the study. Safe generalization means there are scientific ways to estimate sampling error. The random sample is also known as a **probability sample**.

However, you will inevitably engage in speculative generalization because you will apply common sense to your findings. If you have no good reason to believe the persons in your study sample are different from the larger group of persons in need, you will likely feel you can generalize your findings to the larger group. In other words, you will see no reason to assert that your findings are relevant only to your present clients. If the intervention worked with your study subjects, you will be confident in trying it with others.

But you will note any major distinctions between your clients and the larger group and will be cautious in your generalization the more you find important distinctions. Consider the example of the program for abusive husbands. To whom do you believe the findings of the pretest and posttest comparisons can be generalized? This is not an example of a random sample, so your generalization will fall in the category of speculation. Your speculation will be safer the closer your definition of study population is to the study sample. Consequently, you would be on the most unsafe ground if you generalized to the 350 persons estimated to be abusive husbands.

Discussion Box 8.6

Let's suppose you selected the 20 psychology students taking a course in research at a given point as your study sample. Which of the following would *not* be a legitimate definition of the study population?

1. Psychology students
2. Left-handed psychology students
3. Psychology students in this university

Selection of the Means for Measuring Client Progress

Defining the Target Behavior. Before you select the means for measuring client progress, you need to define your target behavior. This topic was addressed in a previous section. You should refer to this task before seeking a measurement tool. Be sure you know whether you are seeking a tool for measuring self-esteem or self-efficacy. Seek a tool that measures both verbal and physical violence if both of these are included in your definition.

The conditions identified in the treatment objectives serve as the focus of our definition of variables. We should define these conditions carefully before seeking a means of measurement. What does self-esteem mean? What constitutes an act of child abuse? Is stress a psychological condition or a condition of the environment that creates discomfort?

What are the concepts that are to be included in your broad definition? Typically, concepts that are addressed in a treatment objective can mean different things to different people. It is not essential that you define your concepts just like certain other parties have defined them, but it is essential that you specify just what you mean by the critical terms.

Measuring Study Variables. Perhaps the most fundamental issue in measurement is whether the nature of the variable is such that a qualitative or a quantitative means is more suitable for measurement. A *qualitative* means of measurement is more open and flexible and is exemplified by open-ended questions given in interviews or by the direct observation of behavior. This form of measurement is most suitable when the study question is exploratory in nature, where the definitions of key study variables are not very concise, and we are attempting to develop new theories rather than testing existing ones. *Quantitative* measurement, on the other hand, is more suitable when we are attempting to test a theory and we can find or develop an instrument that measures our variables with precision.

Outcome evaluation normally employs quantitative means of measurement. This is particularly true if the evaluation study attempts to measure the outcome of treatment rather than the process of treatment. In evaluative research, we are usually testing the theory that treatment works. Our research will help us to find out if it does.

In quantitative research, we should select means of measuring our variables that are congruent with our specific definitions of the variables. Existing instruments are recommended for measurement because they have normally been tested by others. Sometimes, however, we will have to develop our instrument. When we examine an existing instrument, we should see if it includes the concepts in our definition.

It is essential that you be aware of the form taken by your measurement method. Is target behavior measured simply by a recording of YES or NO in regard to a question such as whether the client was found to have a clean drug test? Was behavior measured by a scale that has a potential range of scores from 0 to 25?

While quantitative measurement is normally used in evaluation research, the qualitative measurement of client progress is not out of the question. But it would be critical to have a protocol for determining how to establish a category or score for each client when qualitative methods are used. For example, you might review a process recording for all statements by the client that indicated a certain stage of movement toward suicide. In this example, the number of such statements would constitute the means used to measure client progress.

Several issues are considered in the task of selecting a means for measuring client progress. One is *relevance*. Making sure the tool measures your concept precisely is a way to assure relevance. Another issue is *credibility*. Does your tool truly measure your concept for this particular clientele? Some instruments have been developed for children of certain ages, or persons with a certain level of reading ability. Some tools are better than others at the avoidance of the socially desirable response, a response that is based on what the client thinks is the socially desirable answer rather than the true answer for herself. Standardized tests have normally been tested for reliability and/or validity, two ways of testing for credibility.

Validity refers to the accuracy of a particular means of measurement. Does the Beck Depression Inventory accurately measure the concept of depression as we know it? Or does it more accurately measure self concept or some other concept? If the mental health center's clients who were being treated for depression did not score higher on the Beck Depression Inventory at intake than persons being treated for some other condition, we would have reason to question the accuracy of this instrument.

Reliability refers to the consistency of a means of measurement. If a group of social work students had scores that fluctuated wildly from day to day on a self esteem scale, we would have reason to question the consistency of this instrument. An instrument must be reliable in order to be valid, but an instrument can be reliable without being valid. In other words, an instrument can be consistently inaccurate. But if it is not consistent, we don't know just what it is measuring.

Discussion Box 8.7

Think of a target behavior for a familiar human service program, such as child abuse, medical noncompliance, depression, marital conflict, inadequate social support, unemployment, school grades, and so forth. How would you measure this behavior? What is your initial assessment of the credibility of this means of measurement?

Selecting the Research Design

The research design specifies the procedures for measurement and implementation. You might measure the target behavior before and after treatment for a group of clients. You might compare your clients' gain in functioning with the gain of a nontreated group. These are examples of research designs. The research design should be distinguished from the design of the intervention, the latter depicting the type of treatment being offered.

The research design in evaluative research is critical to the question of **causation** in the interpretation of our data. If we merely ask our clients after treatment if they are satisfied with the service, we are engaging in a study that best fits into the category of descriptive research, because we are only describing their opinions. If we measure their condition, such as self-esteem, only after treatment, we do not have a basis of determining how much good the intervention did because we do not know their level of self-esteem before treatment.

If we measure their conditions before and after treatment, we are beginning to develop a basis for gauging the effect of treatment. If they are better off after treatment than before, perhaps we can attribute the change to the intervention. But we know that there are other things that potentially effect the client's conditions. How do we know, for example, that the client would not have improved through normal growth and development through the time period of the intervention? Perhaps the typical adolescent achieves a 20 percent gain in self-esteem in the normal course of development in three months' time. If our treatment lasts for three months and we achieve a 20 percent gain, we will not be confident that our treatment made the difference under these circumstances.

The more we know about the normal course of development, the better we will be able to judge what other variables might effect the client's conditions. When we use the simple before-and-after design (also known as the pretest–posttest one group design), we make the assumption that there are no variables other than treatment that affect the client's target condition. For example, we assume that the clients would not improve significantly on the target behavior during the period of the treatment without the treatment that was given.

But we know that some people do improve over time on their own. We can apply logic to determine the extent to which we should be concerned with this issue in our own situation. We can logically expect a women to be less depressed six months after her husband has died than three weeks after this event. But we would not expect a neglectful mother, who has been neglecting her children for five years, to improve on her own over a period of three months. Perhaps she would improve on her own over a longer period, such as a year or two. But if she has been neglecting her children for five years, we can reasonably expect that her behavior is not going to change in only three months without some form of intervention in her life.

A design that is superior to the before and after approach is the pretest–posttest comparison group design, wherein a group of clients is measured before and after treatment and a nontreated group is measured at the same two times. In this design, we compare the growth of our clients on the target condition with that of a group of persons who did not receive the treatment. We attribute the differences in growth to the treatment. We can have more confidence in this design if we have reason to believe that the two groups are similar except for the fact that one group received the treatment. However, the only way to be truly confident is if we have assigned these study subjects to their respective treatment and comparison groups on a random basis. There are several types of experimental designs that employ random assignment. These designs will be discussed in a future chapter.

Another design that is superior to the before and after design is the AB single-subject design. This is the most popular of the single-subject designs. It entails the repeated measurement of a single client's target behavior over a baseline period which takes place before treatment and the continued measurement of this behavior during the treatment period. The treatment recordings are compared to the baseline recordings to see if they indicate significant improvement. This design is superior to the before-and-after design because the baseline recordings constitute a measurement of the progress that might be underway in the client's behavior. If the treatment trend is superior to this trend, the difference is attributed to the treatment. In other words, it is assumed that the baseline trend would continue in the absence of treatment.

Discussion Box 8.8

Let's return to the example you used in the previous discussion box regarding the measurement of a selected target behavior that is addressed by a familiar human service program. What research design would you use in the evaluation of the effectiveness of this program? How well does it control the things outside of intervention that are likely to affect the target behavior?

Implementing the Intervention

The key evaluation research issue in the task of implementation is whether the service was delivered according to plan or protocol. If clients were supposed to receive ten training sessions but only received three, you have a problem with implementation. If the clients were supposed to receive therapy from certified clinical social workers, but received it from persons without this credential, you have a problem with implementation. If your monitoring of services indicated that half of the case managers did not embrace the strengths perspective, a critical part of the intervention, you have a problem with implementation.

If things do not go according to plan, you should report the pertinent facts in your write-up of the evaluation. And you will need to admit that your study was a limited test of the proposed intervention.

Analyzing the Data

The first approach to analysis of data in evaluative research is *descriptive* in nature. The question is whether the data revealed a better condition as a result of treatment. Were scores better after treatment than before? Did the treatment group have better scores than the comparison group?

The second approach is the examination of **statistical significance**. How likely is it that the results we obtained could be explained by chance? Is a mean gain of only 3.2 points on a 20-point scale potentially the result of chance? If so, we cannot have confidence that our treatment really made a difference. We might have found this small a gain is within the normal fluctuations on this scale and does not represent a gain that we could bet would be repeated with another sample of clients given the same treatment.

The concept of chance is relevant to the study **hypothesis**. The hypothesis is a precise statement of the expected results of the study. Your hypothesis might be that your clients will have a greater improvement in self-esteem than the comparison group. This statement clarifies that your treatment group will be compared to another group in regard to self-esteem. Chance is the rival hypothesis. If chance can explain your data rather easily, you cannot assert that your intervention was effective, and you cannot say that your hypothesis was supported.

Statistical tests reveal a value for p, the number of times in 100 that your particular array of data would occur by chance. You will see the notation $p < .05$ in study reports. This means the statistical test revealed the likelihood of this data occurring by chance as less than 5 in 100. When you submit your data to statistical analysis, you are testing your hypothesis. Only when you achieve statistical significance can you declare that the data supported the hypothesis. This means that you will sometimes find the clients' posttest scores to be better than their pretest scores, but you still have to say your data failed to support the hypothesis because you failed to achieve statistical significance. The standard for determining statistical significance, however, is arbitrary. In the social sciences, it usually refers to the 0.05 standard ($p < .05$), meaning if this would occur by chance less than 5 times in 100, you have statistical significance. But there is no scientific basis for asserting this standard. An alternative like 0.10 could easily be argued as a reasonable standard. But the higher you go, the thinner is the ice upon which you are standing. Few would accept an argument that .30 would be acceptable because this is nearly one time in three. This is too close to chance as the explanation.

Discussion Box 8.9

Consider the following example:

The 23 clients presently served by the Dropout Prevention Program were administered a self-esteem scale two times, once at the beginning of treatment and again at the end of the treatment period. On this scale, higher scores represent higher self-esteem. According to the hypothesis, clients will receive higher self-esteem scores at the end of treatment than at the beginning. The mean pretest score for these clients was 21.5, while the mean posttest score was 18.9. This difference was subjected to statistical analysis with the t test for paired data, and was found to be statistically significant ($t = 2.14$; $p < .05$).

Was this hypothesis supported? Explain.

Drawing Conclusions

In outcome evaluation, several issues are relevant to the drawing of conclusions. One is the issue of **practical significance**. Was the gain noteworthy enough to be treated seriously? We have already addressed the issue of statistical significance in the data analysis section. We might return to this issue in the conclusions phase when we talk of practical significance. It is possible that a gain in functioning was measured that was statistically significant but was not a big enough gain to be declared to be of practical significance.

There is no easy answer to the question of how we determine practical significance. Ask yourself how much gain is considered clinically noteworthy. A place to start is the measurement device. Some scales that measure target behavior have thresholds of functioning such as, for example, a level that indicates mild depression, a level that represents serious depression, and so forth. Another alternative is to examine what one point of gain looks like on the scale. For example, there is a scale for measuring parenting ability that is comprised of items in a Yes-No format, each of which represents a good form of parenting. Each point on this scale represents the presence rather than absence of this parental behavior. For this scale, a change of only a few points may be considered noteworthy if each behavior is considered significant.

Another issue is our ability to generalize our results, a topic which was examined in the discussion of sampling above. To whom can our results be generalized? What other populations should be included in other studies in order to better answer this question?

Another task in the drawing of conclusions is the development of potential explanations of why these particular results were obtained. What might explain the successes or failures as reflected in the data?

The most critical issue here is that your conclusions must be consistent with your data. If you tested three hypotheses and found support for two but not the third, you must be careful to avoid suggesting the third hypothesis is true when you are drawing conclusions. You have the right to believe it is true, but you should not state it in your conclusions section unless your data provided support for this statement.

Discussion Box 8.10

Consider the following description of a scale designed to measure psychological abuse between partners:

This scale has 10 statements like the following:

> My partner frequently yells at me.
> My partner often belittles me intellectually.
> My partner gets really upset when I spend time with my friends.

The respondent answers either YES or NO to each of the 10 statements on this scale.

Suppose this scale was used in a treatment of a married couple and it was administered at the beginning and end of a treatment period of 10 weeks. How much of a change in score on this scale would you consider to be of practical significance?

Quiz

The following is a quiz on the contents of this chapter. You may take it as a pretest to determine the extent to which you understand this content prior to reading the present chapter, or you may use it as a posttest to determine how well you understand these concepts at the end. Answers are given after the references.

1. Which of the following statements is/are true?
   a. A deductive process of inquiry, where the researcher starts with general ideas that are tested through observation, has a more natural fit with quantitative means of measurement than qualitative means.
   b. When you have completed the qualitative means of observation, you typically have placed study subjects into categories or given them a number that represents their value on the variable being measured.
   c. Both of the above.
   d. None of the above.

2. Under which of the following conditions would you normally be better advised to employ a quantitative means of observation rather than a qualitative means?
   a. When you are testing an existing theory rather than developing a new one
   b. When you are seeking an understanding of the subjective meaning of behaviors or social processes rather than the precise description of social phenomena
   c. Both of the above
   d. None of the above

3. Which of the following steps comes first in the research process?
   a. Determining if you should undertake a qualitative study or a quantitative study
   b. Determining the instrument to use for measurement
   c. Determining the purpose of the study
   d. Determining the sample you wish to study

4. Where would you find your best guidance in the selection of the means to measure client progress?
   a. The sampling method employed in your study
   b. The research design employed

   c. The definition of the target behavior
   d. The analysis of the target behavior

5. Where would you find your best guidance on whether you can generalize your study findings to persons not included in your study?
   a. The sampling method employed in your study
   b. The research design employed
   c. The analysis of the target behavior
   d. The description of the intervention

6. Where would you find your best guidance on the question of whether your intervention was the cause of the client's change in target behavior rather than something else such as normal growth and development over time.
   a. The sampling method employed in your study
   b. The research design employed
   c. The description of the intervention
   d. The method chosen for statistical analysis

7. Which of the following would provide clear evidence that the method you have chosen to measure target behavior is reliable or valid?
   a. The finding that the clients' scores on your measurement scale were better at the end of treatment than before
   b. The finding that your scale was positively correlated with another scale that was designed to measure the same target behavior
   c. Both of the above
   d. None of the above

8. Statistical significance refers to:
   a. The extent to which your method of measurement is reliable or valid.
   b. The extent to which you can rule out chance as the explanation of your clients' measured growth rather than the intervention.
   c. The extent to which you can generalize your findings to persons not included in your study.
   d. The extent to which you can replicate your study with other persons.

9. A *p* value of 0.50 means that:
   a. Your data would be expected to occur by chance 5 times in 100.
   b. Your data would be expected to occur by chance 50 times in 100.

c. Your data are statistically significant.

d. Your data cannot be used to test for chance.

10. Suppose you are treating a group of 20 clients for depression, and you find that these clients had a mean posttest score on the Beck Depression Inventory that was better than the mean pretest score (the posttest scores indicated a lower level of depression). Suppose further that you found these differences in mean scores not to be statistically significant. Can you say your data supported the hypothesis that clients would have better scores at posttest than pretest?

a. Yes, because the posttest scores were better.

b. Yes, because statistical significance was not achieved.

c. No, because statistical significance was not achieved.

d. No, because you should not use scales to measure depression.

Reference

Corcoran, K., & Fischer, J. (1987). *Measures for clinical practice*. New York: Free Press.

Answers to the Quiz

1. a

2. a

3. c

4. c

5. a

6. b

7. b

8. b

9. b

10. c

9

Case Example: Outcome Evaluation—Is the New Hope Treatment Program Effective in Reducing Depression?

In this chapter, you will examine the treatment of depression using an example which employs the one group pretest–posttest research design. This example is reported in York (1997). While the data and the situation are from a real example, the name of the agency has been changed. In this example, an emphasis will be placed on the interplay of the parts of the evaluation research process. For example, you will encounter the topic of how a clear definition of the target behavior aids in the selection of the means of measuring client progress.

The New Hope Treatment Center is an inpatient psychiatric treatment program designed to treat depression as well as other acute mental health conditions. The study reported here included the 15 clients served by this agency during a one-month period. Each person was tested for depression once at intake and again at discharge.

Target Behavior of the New Hope Treatment Center Clients

In this section, we will discuss the definition of the target behavior and the analysis of this behavior. Your target behavior definition should be sufficiently clear that you would be in a good position to select a means of measuring client progress. Your target behavior analysis should be sufficiently clear that you would be in a position to select a program or intervention.

Definition of Target Behavior

Each person in this study was being treated for depression. The following statement illustrates how this condition was defined.

> Depression is a feeling or emotion that involves sadness, feelings of worthlessness, or even guilt. This feeling is accompanied by a desire to be alone rather than with others, and disturbances of appetite, sleep, and general activity. (York, 1997, pp. 99–100)

Several levels of depression were conceptualized. Two of these were as follows:

> One level might be characterized as normal. It is the emotional state that appears following the loss of a loved one, or the failure to achieve a strongly desired goal. This type of depression is clearly tied to an event in the environment, so we usually know why we are depressed, and we take steps to get out of it. Major depression, on the other hand, is a state in which people have given up trying. The view people have of themselves in this type of depression is uniformly negative; they feel that life is meaningless and that nothing can be done to improve the situation. This major form of depression often involves thoughts of suicide. (York, 1997, p. 100)

This definition of the target behavior provides clarity on the condition being treated. We can anticipate that the objective of treatment will focus on depression and that client progress will be measured on an instrument designed to measure this condition as defined here.

Did the above description clearly define the target behavior? In other words, would you be able to articulate the intervention objective and select a means for measuring client progress based on this definition? Consider, for example, the following sets of items from different clinical measurement scales. Examine the following items in Table 9.1 from two different scales and consider their appropriateness as a means for measuring client progress for the New Hope Treatment Center.

Discussion Box 9.1

Do you believe that Scale A has items that seem to measure the target behavior? Explain.

TABLE 9.1   *Examples of Items from Two Scales*

SCALE A	SCALE B
I feel tense.	I feel sad.
I feel nervous.	I have crying spells.
I feel suddenly scared for no reason.	Lately, I don't seem to be able to get going.

Discussion Box 9.2

Do you believe that Scale B has items that measure the target behavior? Explain.

A few Reflections on Your Answers.   Did you notice that the second set (Scale B) was from a depression scale? It was. Did you figure out what the first set was designed to measure? It is anxiety, which is often experienced by depressed people but is not the same thing as depression. Precision in measurement is accomplished when you select a method that measures precisely what you need to measure, not something that is related to this behavior but not distinctly the behavior you are trying to measure.

Analysis of Target Behavior

In the report of this study, problem analysis was presented, in part, in the following way:

> There are several types of theories about the causes of depression. One type focuses upon physical factors such as brain chemistry. Because depression often appears to be accompanied by changes in brain chemistry, there are biological theories about its causation. . . . Another type of theory focuses upon intrapersonal factors. The psychodynamic model views depression as emerging from a sense of loss early in life. . . . The cognitive model of depression views this problem as a product of distorted thinking.
>
> In a general sense, one might say that there are two basic strategies for treatment of depression. One entails the administration of drugs which bolster the elements that are lacking in the brain of the depressed person. However, this is not usually considered to be sufficient

---

Discussion Box 9.3

Did the target behavior analysis explain the dynamics of the behavior in such a way as to provide guidance in the determination of the appropriate intervention? To what extent did this analysis provide support for treating depression in any of the following ways?

Training on the chemical causes of depression.

The 12-step model of treatment for substance abuse.

The use of insight-oriented psychotherapy, with emphasis on thinking patterns.

Which of the above, if any, are supported by the problem analysis?

for long-term rehabilitation, even though it may be helpful. A second general strategy is the promotion of insight into the causes of one's depression. If a person can learn that his distorted thinking has contributed to his depression, he can perhaps learn how to change his thinking patterns. Repairing relationships damaged by past behaviors and gaining support from family and friends is a necessary part of this treatment process. (York, 1997, p. 100)

Did you select the last one as most appropriate? Training on the chemistry of depression is not likely to improve one's condition. The 12-step model was not even mentioned in the problem analysis statement. But insight into how one's thinking can contribute to depression might provide the basis for improvement.

Nature of the Intervention Given the Clients

Goals and Objectives

The New Hope Treatment Program is designed to reduce the social and behavioral problems associated with depression. If this program is clearly effective, clients will be able to live a functional life in most spheres of social and behavioral functioning. It attempts to achieve this condition by changing the level of depression experienced by its clients. It does so through an array of services, including psychotherapy, group activities, and medication.

Discussion Box 9.4

Reflect on the instructions given on goals and objectives in the previous chapter. Consider the following statements:

To improve the quality of life

To deliver a comprehensive array of quality services to persons in need

To deliver the following services to persons suffering from depression: process group services, family focus, activity group, individual therapy, specialty group, and medication

Which, if any, of these statements would reflect the goals of the New Hope Treatment Center program?

Reflections on the Goal Statements.   Which is appropriate as a statement of the goal of the New Hope Treatment Program? The first one is too vague. It provides little guidance. The second and third refer to the service rather than an outcome for the client, so they are not appropriate either. So the answer is None of the above.

How about the following statement: To reduce social and behavioral problems associated with the condition of depression? This focuses on a long-range outcome. You could easily identify the reduction of depression as the goal, but this statement is slightly broader. Either one would be fine because you have identified the long-term condition being sought.

What about the outcome objective of the intervention? If you stated the goal in the broader terms above, you could state your objective as reducing depression. The reduction of depression would be a measured amount of progress toward this broad statement. If you stated the reduction of depression as the goal, you might consider thinking of ways people make progress toward the achievement of this end. For example, improving the extent to which the client engages in rethinking exercises that were taught in therapy may be an outcome objective. This is a situation where you may not find it useful to distinguish between the goal and the objective. If you are treating depression as the goal and plan to measure progress on depression, you may find this distinction to be superfluous. An important consideration is that you should have guidance on the search for a means for measuring client progress.

Structure and Personnel

The New Hope Treatment Center utilized a comprehensive array of services as well as residential care. Persons admitted to this hospital unit normally stay two to three weeks for their treatment. This treatment includes medication, individual therapy, group therapy, activity therapy, and family counseling, among other things.

> The interventions employed by the treatment program included process group, family focus, activity groups, individual therapy with their psychiatrist, specialty groups, individual therapy with their therapist, and nurse's medication group. Each subject attended one process group daily, Monday through Saturday, lasting approximately one hour. Process groups offered subjects an opportunity to share and resolve emotional difficulties and learn new ways of interacting with others. Group members shared personal feelings, ideas, problems, and developed new awareness of how their patterns of behavior affect themselves and others. The group sessions allowed subjects to experience and learn within a therapeutic context. Process groups are led by the therapists who are master level social workers (MSW).
>
> Subjects also attended family focus which was held by the therapist on Thursday evenings from 6:30 P.M. to 7:30 P.M. Family focus was offered to subjects and subject's family members as an opportunity to educate and explore the aspects of depression. The meeting was held on a general level discussing signs of depression, coping mechanisms, and how to help the individual family member. Each subject attended two family focus meetings prior to their discharge from the unit.
>
> Subjects attended one activity group daily, Monday through Saturday, lasting approximately one hour. A variety of activities were offered to enhance subject's well being. Daily activity groups included physical exercise, dance therapy, art therapy, and a selection of arts and crafts. Activity groups are led by the occupational therapist and the activity therapist who are trained and certified in their area of therapy.
>
> Subjects met individually with their psychiatrist daily, Monday through Sunday, for at least fifteen minutes to explore and discuss treatment and individual progress. "Subjects also attended one hour specialty groups three times a week. On Monday, Wednesday, and

Friday, the therapist led groups on specific topics asked for by the subjects. During the time of this study, specialty groups were given on assertiveness training, relaxation training, values clarification, communication skills, problem solving, and education on depression. Each subject met with their therapist at least three times a week for an hour each session. (York, 1997, p. 102)

The description of the intervention should be sufficiently clear that you would be able to duplicate it. This means knowing its form and intensity. What form does it take? Is it individual therapy, daily recreational events, medical treatment? What is its level of intensity? Is a given service offered one hour per week for six weeks or three hours per week for ten weeks? Does it entail 24-hour residential care? This latter is relevant to the question of the general level of resources required to deliver a duplicate of this program elsewhere.

Discussion Box 9.5

How well do you believe this description achieves these purposes? Do you have any recommendations about this?

Study Sample and Population for the Study

This study drew data from the first 15 persons who entered New Hope Treatment Center with a diagnosis of depression during February 1992. These individuals constituted the study sample. There were more than 15 persons who sought treatment during this month, but those who followed the first 15 were not included in this study. For the sake of discussion, let's say that the study population was defined as all persons who sought treatment from the New Hope Treatment Center with a primary diagnosis of depression during the two years prior to and including the month of February 1992.

Discussion Box 9.6

The population can be defined in many ways as long as every person in the study sample fits within the boundaries of the definition. Is this true for the definition of the study population?

Discussion Box 9.7

The study sampling procedures determine the extent to which the study results can be generalized to persons not in the sample. Can the results of a study of this study sample be safely generalized to the study population defined earlier?

Discussion of Sample and Population.   The study sample is supposed to be defined as those from whom data were drawn. In our case this refers to the 15 persons who were measured on depression. The issue of how to define the population is open to discussion because we could define our population as any group of persons for whom these 15 people are included. The one requirement is that all persons in the sample must be members of the study population that has been identified. Otherwise, you do not have a proper definition of the study population. All study population definitions, however, should not be considered equal. The closer in space between your sample and your population, the better your ability to generalize, even if that is only on a speculative basis.

The reason to analyze the sampling procedures for a study is to determine the extent to which we can generalize the findings to persons not included in the study. The definition of the population has implications for the question of the group to whom we can generalize our findings. We could say that our data represents these 15 persons in the sample, but that would not be a generalization. Seldom would we conduct a group evaluation project only to determine if a given intervention was effective with this particular group. We want guidance on the future use of the intervention being tested, so normally we want to generalize to some extent.

Does our situation fit into the category of safe generalization or speculative generalization? Do we have a random sample? In other words, was our study sample chosen randomly from the study population as it was defined?

In this case, there is no random sample; we cannot safely generalize our findings because we do not have a scientific means for estimating sampling error. We can, however, engage in speculative generalization, the credibility of which will be determined by the logic of our speculation.

When we engage in speculative generalization we ask ourselves to examine relevant variables that might distinguish our sample from our population. If the intervention was effective with our sample, is it likely to be effective with others in the study population? If not, why not? Do we have reason to believe our sample was different from the population with regard to motivation, degree of depression, gender, age, or anything that might be relevant to the generalization of findings from our sample to our population? If we can think of nothing that is especially relevant, we should consider ourselves to be on rather solid ground in our speculative generalization, but never as solid as the safe ground we would have with a random sample.

Measurement of Target Behavior for Clients

The Beck Depression Inventory was employed in this study to measure depression. This scale is designed to measure the severity of depression. It contains 21 items, each of which asked the respondent to select one of four statements that best characterize themselves at the present time. One of these items included:

[0]   I do not feel sad.

[1]   I feel sad.

[2]   I am sad all the time and I can't snap out of it.

[3]   I am so sad or unhappy that I can't stand it. (York, 1997, pp. 105–106)

The numbers in the margins here indicate the client's score for depression for that item. The score of each item is summed for a total score. The highest possible score would be 63 (21 × 3 = 63), while the lowest possible score would be 0. A score of 17 represents borderline clinical depression. This score would be exemplified by someone who had a score of 1 on about four out of every five items on this scale. Extreme depression would be represented by a score of 40 or higher. This would be represented by someone whose selected statements were like the following:

I am sad all the time and can't snap out of it.

I have lost most of my interest in other people.

The themes on this scale include sadness, pessimism, guilt, blaming oneself, thoughts of suicide, crying, sleep, and so forth. It is a widely used scale for measuring depression for clinical purposes.

The measurement methods should be relevant to the target behavior, and credible; we should have confidence that this method truly measures the target behavior. We should also have clarity on the nature of the measurement in regard to practical significance. Remember that statistical significance refers to the likelihood your outcome data could occur by chance, while practical significance refers to the extent that the gain was clinically significant. How much gain would be noteworthy?

Discussion Box 9.8

In your opinion, does the Beck Depression Inventory adequately measure depression? Explain.

Discussion Box 9.9

Would it have been better for the staff of the New Hope Treatment Center to develop their own scale to measure depression? Why, or why not?

We can address practical significance by examining how good or bad a score might be within certain ranges such as low, medium, or high, or between borderline, moderate, and severe. We should not be left with a report on a mean score that gives us no idea of the seriousness of the condition illustrated by that score. It would be quite informative for a report to say "The average client gained from severe depression to borderline depression during the treatment period." A much less informative statement for the average reader of a report would be the statement "The mean gain on the depression scale was 11.2 points."

Discussion Box 9.10

What would you consider to be an average gain in functioning, as measured by the Beck Depression Inventory, that would be considered of practical significance? Would it be a gain of 5 points, or 10 points, or a gain of 20 percent? What about a gain from one threshold to another (e.g., from severe depression to moderate depression)? There is no right or wrong answer to this question. It is a matter of opinion. The critical question here is the basis for your choice. An answer of "10 points' gain" without explanation will be of little benefit to a class discussion.

Research Design

The research design employed in the present study is the one group pretest–posttest design. This means that we are studying only one group of persons and that we will measure their target behavior at two points in time—before treatment begins (pretest) and after treatment is over (posttest). Data on pretest scores (administered before treatment) will be compared to data on posttest scores (administered at the end of treatment).

The research design gives us guidance on the issue of causation. As you will see in the next section, depression scores for these clients were better at the end of treatment. Can we attribute this improvement to the treatment? Maybe something else caused the change. The research design is designed to address this issue by its structure.

An advantage of the design employed in this study is that client behavior was measured before and after treatment so that we could have a basis for measuring client progress. If clients had been measured only at the termination of treatment, we would have no basis for measuring progress. If the mean score at termination had been 17, how would we interpret this score as a measure of treatment effectiveness? We would know they ended the treatment, on the average, as being in the category of borderline depressed. But where did they start? If we had a threshold score for comparison, we would take one small step toward providing data regarding this question. For example, if we knew from past research that clients who enter this treatment program have average scores that are about 30, we could compare our posttest scores to this threshold.

But we did better than that. We measured each client at intake and at discharge so that we would have a direct measure of progress. But we could have done even better. With our design, we do not know how much progress clients would have made without treatment. A comparison group of nontreated persons with depression would have provided this information because the progress made by the comparison group would be compared to the progress made by the treatment group. This requires that you measure both groups at pretest and posttest times. The effect of normal growth and development over time would be taken into consideration because the gain of the comparison group could be used to estimate the normal gain that would have occurred in the treatment group in the absence of treatment.

A good question for us is whether we really needed to have a research design that addressed normal growth and development, or other things that might explain improvement in depression for our clients. We had a group of persons with a high level of depression who were given a pretest and posttest measure of depression that was only about three weeks apart.

Discussion Box 9.11

Is it logical to assume that these clients would typically have achieved an improvement in depression over three weeks in the absence of treatment? Explain.

Implementation of the Intervention

There was no information given in the report by York (1997) regarding procedures that were used to assure the intervention was delivered according to plan. A good deal of information was given on the plan of treatment. For example, it was reported that specialty groups were given on assertiveness training, relaxation training, values clarification, communication skills, problem-solving, and education on depression. But no information was given on any form of monitoring to assure that assertiveness trainers were truly addressing assertiveness. Even more unclear was the nature of the individual therapy that was offered. So we might say there was good information on the treatment plan, but little information on the monitoring of the implementation of the plan. Such monitoring is seldom done in the human services, unless the practitioners are involved in a major research project.

Collection and Analysis of Data for the Study

In this example, the survey method of collecting data was used. The survey method provides an instrument (questionnaire, scale, etc.) to which study subjects are asked to respond. The subjects' responses constitute the measurement of the variable. Other alternatives for collecting data include interviews, review of documents (e.g., agency records), and direct observation of behavior. One of the advantages of the survey method is that it is inexpensive; another is that it obtains information directly from the study subject.

Discussion Box 9.12

What is your evaluation of this method of data collection for this study? Do you believe the administration of a depression scale directly to clients is a good idea? Do you think there would be other ways to collect this information that would be better?

Data Analysis

The mean score (average) of these 15 patients for the Beck Depression Scale at the time of intake was 34.9. At the time of discharge, the mean score for these 15 patients was 13.8. The mean difference between pretest and posttest scores, therefore, was 21.1. The gain in scores for these patients ranged from a low of 13 (from 33 to 20) to a high of 30 (from 41 to 11). These data were subjected to statistical analysis with the use of the t test for paired data. The difference between pretest and posttest scores was statistically significant ($t = 9.02$; $p < .001$).

In evaluative research, one of the first questions about pretreatment conditions is whether the data represent a serious enough condition to warrant treatment. If these clients had been under the borderline level at intake, we would have reason to question the wisdom of providing intense and expensive inpatient treatment. And we would have little reason to believe they would achieve noteworthy growth as a result of treatment. Recall that scores on this scale can range from 0 to 63; a score of 17 is considered to constitute borderline depression, while a score of 40 represents extreme depression.

The second question is whether the clients achieved a gain in functioning during the treatment period. The mean posttest score was lower than the mean pretest score. Because higher scores represent higher depression, lower scores are better.

Discussion Box 9.13

What is your assessment of these pretest scores?

Discussion Box 9.14

In the case of the New Hope Treatment Center, was there evidence of client improvement?

The third question is whether the gain in functioning can be easily explained by chance. This is an issue for statistical analysis. You will note the p value was given as "$p < .001$."

Discussion Box 9.15

What does the expression "$p < .05$" mean?

The value of p is given as a fraction that represents the number of times a set of data would occur by chance. The value of .10 means 1 time in 10, while the value of .01 means 1 time in 100. In our case, it is 1 time in 1,000.

Discussion Box 9.16

Does this mean we can have confidence that we have found true differences rather than chance?

Drawing Conclusions from the Study

Review the following statement of conclusions:

> The study reported here provides evidence that a comprehensive array of services in an inpatient setting can be effective in the treatment of depression. The clients of the New Hope Treatment Center revealed a noteworthy improvement in scores for depression during a three week period of time. Pretest scores for these clients revealed a serious level of depression, while posttest scores indicated functioning that was even better than borderline depression. This difference was found to be statistically significant, ruling out chance as a serious explanation of the data.

> While a more sophisticated research design would have provided better evidence for this approach to treatment, it was concluded that none of the common alternative explanations for client improvement, such as normal growth over time, was relevant to this study sample. This group entered the program with a high level of depression that had existed for many months for some clients and years for others. It would not have been expected that any of them would have achieved spontaneous recovery in such a short period of time. Thus, it is concluded that the treatment should take credit for the measured improvement.

> The study sample was not drawn at random from a larger group; the results cannot be safely generalized to a larger population. But speculative generalization is warranted because there are no known differences between the study sample and clients who normally seek treatment for depression in the inpatient setting.

> One of the limitations of this study is the absence of an explanation of the model or models of treatment that served as the guide for the specific activities of this program. This hampers replication by other agencies and restricts theoretical guidance that might come from studies of this type.

Discussion Box 9.17

What do you think of this statement? Does it cover what is needed in the conclusion section of an evaluation report? Among the questions to consider are:

Was a clear statement made of the basic study findings? Given the basic purpose of the study, was the study's fundamental question answered in the conclusion section?

Did the conclusion section provide information on both statistical significance and practical significance?

Did the conclusion section address the common limitations of evaluation studies, especially causation and generalization?

Quiz

Each of the following questions refers to the New Hope Treatment Center example. For this reason, this quiz would not serve well as a pretest. You need to go through the example to understand some of these questions.

1. Which of the following would be adequate definitions of depression for the purpose of our evaluative study of the New Hope Treatment Program?
   a. A feeling of being down in the dumps, something that we cannot easily define but something that we know when we see it.
   b. A feeling or emotion that involves sadness, feelings of worthlessness, or even guilt. This feeling is accompanied by a desire to be alone rather than with others, and disturbances of appetite, sleep, and general activity.
   c. Both of the above.
   d. None of the above.

2. The definition of depression was most helpful in which other task in the evaluative research process?
   a. The selection of the Beck Depression Scale for measuring client progress
   b. The selection of the design of the treatment program
   c. The selection of the one-group pretest–posttest research design
   d. The selection of the statistical measure for analyzing data

3. Which of the following statements is/are true regarding the logical design of a treatment program for depression, given the problem analysis that was undertaken for this study?
   a. Because the 12-step program for the treatment of substance abuse has been found to be effective, it stands to reason that it would also be effective for the treatment of depression.
   b. Because depression is caused, in part, by distorted thinking in regard to the stressors of life, it stands to reason that a treatment program for depression would address one's thinking patterns.
   c. Both of the above.
   d. None of the above.

4. Which of the following would be good statements of the goal of the New Hope Treatment Program for depression?

a. To improve the quality of life
b. To provide counseling services to persons with depression that are designed in accordance with the problem analysis
c. Both of the above
d. None of the above

5. Which one of the following statements fits into the description of the structure of the New Hope Treatment Program for depression?
   a. To reduce depression
   b. To provide services that are consistent with the treatment model
   c. Attendance at a family focus group meeting once weekly for one hour
   d. All of the above

6. Which of the following is the proper definition of the study sample?
   a. The 15 persons from whom data were collected
   b. All persons provided services for depression by this program in the past year
   c. All persons who are depressed and seek treatment
   d. All of the above

7. If this study had employed a random sample, you would have been in a better position to:
   a. Declare that the client's measured gain was caused by the treatment rather than something else.
   b. Generalize the study findings to persons not included in the study sample.
   c. Rule out chance as the explanation of the client's measured gain in functioning.
   d. Declare that you had achieved practical significance.

8. Which of the following would be the best way to determine practical significance with regard to the data on the depression scale used in this study?
   a. The number of persons who achieved a measured gain between the pretest and posttest
   b. The proportion of persons who achieved a measured gain between the pretest and the posttest
   c. The mean gain for all clients as compared to the thresholds of functioning (e.g., from severe depression to moderate depression)

d. The number of points of gain on the average for all clients (e.g., a mean gain of 3.4 points on the scale or a mean gain of 5.6 points on the scale, and so forth).

9. Which of the following statements is/are true with regard to the research design employed in this study?
   a. This design controlled for maturation (normal growth and development over time) as an alternative explanation of the client's measured gain in functioning.
   b. This design provided for the measurement of client gain in regard to depression.

c. Both of the above.
d. None of the above.

10. Which of the following statements is/are true with regard to the results of this study?
    a. The measured gain for clients was found to be statistically significant.
    b. Chance was ruled out as a legitimate explanation for the client's measured gain in functioning.
    c. Both of the above.
    d. None of the above.

Reference

York, R. O. (1997). *Building basic competencies in social work research: An experiential approach.* Boston: Allyn & Bacon.

Answers to the Quiz

1. b
2. a
3. b
4. d
5. c

6. a
7. b
8. c
9. b
10. c

10

Understanding Intermediate Concepts in the Evaluation of Human Service Outcomes

In the previous two chapters, you examined the phases in the process of evaluating human service outcomes, along with basic concepts that guide this endeavor. The present chapter will introduce additional concepts in evaluation and move you to another level of understanding of evaluation. In addition, you will see that the content of the previous chapters will be reinforced by new examples and discussion questions.

The chapter that follows the present one will illustrate these concepts with a new example designed to build your level of understanding to the intermediate level. Following this section of the text, which provides an educational foundation regarding outcome evaluation, you will turn your attention to the specific tasks in the process of designing and carrying out an outcome evaluation for your programs or interventions. For example, the next section has a chapter that focuses exclusively on problem formulation and one that focuses on sampling and measurement.

A major feature of this book is the reinforcement of learning through repetition of concepts and the presentation of new examples for further testing of your understanding of evaluation. Because some people learn certain concepts more quickly than others, quizzes are given at the end of concept chapters to facilitate your exemption of certain chapters from your essential reading. If you believe you do not need to review this chapter, you should turn to the quiz at the end to test your understanding.

At the completion of this chapter, you will be able to:

1. Recognize inconsistencies between a target behavior analysis and the design of an intervention.

2. Identify several types of nonprobability samples and several types of probability samples.

3. Identify the level of measurement of a measured variable when given an example.

4. Identify at least two ways to test an instrument for reliability and two ways to test an instrument for validity.

5. Compare several group research designs and several single-system research designs in regard to the extent to which they address two common alternative explanations for evaluation results.

6. Explain the role of statistical significance in one's answer to the question "Did the data support the hypothesis?"

7. Recognize inconsistencies between a given data analysis and a given set of conclusions.

The Evaluation Research Process Revisited

In the previous chapter, you examined several major steps in the process of evaluating human service outcomes. Among the basic things you learned in each of these steps are the guiding principles summarized in Exhibit 10.1 for your review. In this chapter, you will examine additional concepts that build on this knowledge. These concepts will be illustrated with a case example in the next chapter. In that example, you will see how outcomes for a single client can be evaluated.

Achieving the outcomes enumerated in Exhibit 10.1, of course, requires that you have a firm grasp of certain basic concepts, such as target behavior, study sample, statistical significance, and so forth. In this chapter, you will examine this same process and these same concepts, but you will be introduced to additional concepts, all of which will be illustrated with a case example in the next chapter. In this example, you will see how outcomes for a single client can be evaluated.

Identification and Analysis of Target Behavior

In the problem formulation phase of evaluative research, you should find a clear definition of the problem that constitutes the client's target behavior for treatment. The importance of this problem can be addressed by information on its incidence and whether it is growing and, thereby, giving us cause for alarm in the future. The consequences of this problem for human functioning should also be addressed in the quest for information on the problem's importance. The client's problem should also be analyzed in such a manner that the practitioner can be guided in the development of the intervention. Information on the effectiveness of different treatment approaches to this problem can also aid in this choice.

The definition sets the stage both for articulating the treatment objective and selecting the means for measuring client progress. Gordon-Garofalo and Rubin (2004) reported on the evaluation of a psychoeducational group intervention for partners of persons with HIV or AIDS. A portion of their problem analysis is presented as follows:

> Stressors experienced by spousal and partner caregivers include the series of opportunistic infections plaguing persons living with HIV disease and the subsequent caregiving tasks and

EXHIBIT 10.1 • *A Review of Guiding Principles Covered in Previous Chapters*

In the previous chapters, you examined a number of critical concepts in evaluation research. This exhibit will give a brief review for those who believe this will be beneficial. Among the concepts reviewed in the previous chapters are the following:

1. *The identification and analysis of the target behavior* plays the role of assuring that (a) proper objectives are articulated, (b) appropriate methods are chosen for measuring client progress, and (c) the selected intervention is appropriate for the target behavior.
2. *The design of the intervention* should be consistent with the target behavior analysis and should be described in sufficient detail to help others with replication.
3. *The selection of the study sample* should provide guidance on the extent to which the results of the evaluation study can be generalized to those not included in the data analysis.
4. *The means for measuring client progress* should accurately measure target behavior.

5. *The research design* should adequately address alternative explanations for client improvement, so that measured progress can be attributed to the intervention rather than something else.
6. The *intervention should be implemented* in such a way as to assure its design was employed reasonably well, especially in regard to the intended structure, model, and personnel.
7. *The data should be analyzed* in sufficient detail to test for both practical significance and statistical significance.
8. The *conclusions* that are drawn should be consistent with the results of the data analysis and should be discussed in light of the study's major limitations.

Achieving the above, of course, requires that you have a firm grasp of certain basic concepts, such as target behavior, study sample, statistical significance, and so forth.

---

feelings of fear and loss associated with each infection. Other stressors are the effect of social stigma, such as loss of social support and feelings of rejection, and the financial concerns associated with long term illness. . . .

Dealing with the uncertainty that surrounds HIV infection and AIDS is a stressor common to family caregivers. . .Frierson et al. (1987) found that the most prominent psychosocial stressors associated with HIV disease were fears of contagion, stigma, revelation of lifestyle, sense of helplessness, and grief. They note, however, that the most common stressors among family members are the conflicts surrounding care and support provision for the infected family member and responsibilities to other members of the family. (Gordon-Garofalo & Rubin, 2004, p. 14)

These authors went on to connect this analysis with the intervention to be evaluated.

Client concerns in the health care arena generally call for a psychoeducational approach because clients need both education about disease process and treatment and support in dealing with health care issues. Groups can be an effective way for social workers to fulfill these needs, providing a support network, opportunities for members to share problems that arise and possible solutions, and a forum for formal lectures and topics of mutual interest. (Gordon-Garofalo & Rubin, 2004, p. 15)

Discussion Box 10.1

Let's examine the issue of connecting the nature of an intervention with the dynamics of the need it addresses. Write a note that summarizes what you need when you experience a major loss, such as the loss of a romantic relationship or the death of someone close.

Discussion Box 10.2

What kinds of service might be helpful to you in this time of need? How about a support group, or grief counseling, or information about things you need to know?

Do the last two discussion boxes connect? If you feel a need for support, a support group might be a logical solution. If you need to have a sympathetic ear to hear about what you are feeling, some form of counseling would be warranted. If you need ideas about how to change your life or ways you deal with relationships, you might need either counseling or materials to read or exercises to undertake. The key to this exercise is that the dynamics of the target behavior for clients should logically connect with the services they are offered.

The authors of the study of partners of HIV or AIDS provided definitions of concepts when they described their methods of measuring client progress. From the descriptions of their instruments you could extrapolate the following definitions:

Depression was measured by the Beck Depression Inventory, which assesses depression with regard to cognition, affect, overt behavior, interpersonal symptoms, and somatic symptoms.
Anxiety was measured by the State-Trait Anxiety Inventory, which measures situational anxiety.
The Social Support Appraisals Scale was used to measure perceived social support, which measures the degree to which the respondent feels rejected, cared for, and involved.
The Impact of Event Scale was used to measure perceived stress from a subjective standpoint, and is often used to measure post-traumatic stress responses.

What do you think of the adequacy of the above approach to problem definition and analysis? From this information, you should be able to (1) articulate treatment objectives,

(2) select methods of measurement, and (3) justify the selection of different components of the intervention. Let's test out these considerations in a simple format with the following questions.

Discussion Box 10.3

State one treatment objective for this intervention.

Discussion Box 10.4

Give one simple explanation for the use of the Impact of Event Scale for measuring client progress.

Discussion Box 10.5

Give a brief description of one type of service or service activity that would be justified by the problem analysis given.

Description of the Intervention

The description of the intervention should include the following:

1. The goals and objectives of the intervention
2. The model that supports the intervention
3. The structure of the intervention
4. The personnel who deliver the intervention

EXHIBIT 10.2 • *Review of Definitions from Previous Chapters*

The following are definitions of concepts presented in previous chapters that you may want to review before continuing with the lessons of the present chapter.

- The **goal** of intervention is the ultimate statement of client outcome.
- The **objective** of intervention is a statement of a measured amount of client progress toward the achievement of the goal.
- The **structure of the intervention** specifies the form and intensity of the services to be provided.

- The **model of the intervention** identifies the conceptual link between the structure of the intervention and the problem analysis, and serves as a logical justification of the intervention design.
- The description of the **personnel of the intervention** provides information on the types of practitioners who will deliver the services to the clients.

In the previous chapter, you examined goals, objectives, structure, and personnel, but placed more emphasis on the model of treatment because it highlights the connection of the intervention design and the problem analysis. If the problem analysis suggests that lack of information is a cause of the problem, it stands to reason that training would be a service component. If abusive parents are less likely than others to have had good parental role models or good social support, it logically follows that the provision of role models and social support would be among the components of the child protective service program.

In this chapter, more emphasis will be placed on goals, objectives, structure and personnel. Before you continue, you may want to review some critical definitions covered in previous chapters as given in Exhibit 10.2.

In evaluative research, it is critical that the identified intervention comprises all those services or treatment components the client receives concurrent with the evaluation period. If you are the client's individual therapist and the client is receiving group therapy and family therapy during the same period of your individual therapy, you should identify the intervention as including all three things, not just what you are doing. You cannot separate out the effect of your intervention from the effect of the others if they are all being delivered concurrently. If your clients achieve a measured gain in self-esteem when receiving your counseling and two additional services, you cannot conclude that your counseling was found to be effective in the improvement of your clients' self-esteem. It may be that your counseling had no effect at all and all the good came from the other two services. Or, it may be that it was your counseling alone that made the difference. But you cannot determine the answer to this question in this situation. What you can say is that your clients achieved a measured gain in self-esteem during the period they were receiving all three of these services.

Goals and Objectives

A goal is a statement of long-term purpose, whereas an objective is a measured amount of progress toward the achievement of goals. For outcome evaluation, both of these statements should focus on the client's outcomes. You may have a need to state process objectives for other purposes, but outcomes should be the focus of goals and objectives for outcome evaluation. A process objective would specify the "how," whereas the outcome objectives will specific the "what" in terms of client conditions.

Discussion Box 10.6

The following would *not* be appropriate as a statement of a goal or objective—to provide quality services for children at high risk for drug abuse. Why? Think about this and provide your answer before you read further.

Does the previous statement identify a client outcome such as improved self-esteem, reduced depression, or improved knowledge of the health effects of poor prenatal care? No. The statement focuses on process rather than outcome. It says nothing about the outcome to be achieved. Instead, you might state the goal as prevention of drug abuse while two of the objectives might be to improve self-esteem and improve school grades. The objectives would be targeted to the risk factors which represent measured progress toward goal attainment. Self-esteem and grades can be measured in the short term and are believed to be related to the long-term outcome.

What about child protective services? What is the goal? What are the objectives? The long-range outcome is the prevention of further neglect and abuse of children, which means better parenting. The intervention may attempt to improve parenting skills and family relations in order to achieve the long-term outcome. Thus the goal may be stated as the reduction of abuse and neglect while two of the objectives could be to improve parenting skills and to improve family relations.

The objectives serve as the focus of the measurement of client progress. You should state objectives that you plan to measure. If you can measure the goal, you should do so, but the major function of stating goals is to provide a broad conceptual overview of why you are focusing your attention where you are, such as improving self-esteem.

You should avoid vague language in the statement of goals. For example, the statement "to improve the quality of life" is normally too general and vague to provide any useful guidance. Can you name any human service intervention that is *not* designed to improve the quality of life? If not, you can see that such a statement does not distinguish your intent from that of all others.

Discussion Box 10.7

Think of a human service with which you are familiar and provide a statement that fits into the category of a goal of a human service program or intervention and a statement that would be an outcome objective related to that goal. Enter these two statements below.

Share your statements from the discussion box with someone who is familiar with the standards for good goal and objective statements contained in this book, and ask for their feedback.

Structure and Personnel

What does the treatment look like? Does it entail a series of individual counseling sessions or group psychotherapy or training sessions? Does it include residential care? Is it more like talk therapy or play therapy, or something else? Is case management a part of the intervention? How much intervention is given? Is it given one hour a day once a week for six to ten weeks? If it is 24-hour care, how many days are included in the typical service episode for the typical client? These are questions to be answered in the description of the structure of the intervention.

In some cases, the intervention is guided by a set of service protocols or a treatment manual. The function of these instruments is to provide guidance to staff and assure that the design of the treatment is being implemented properly. If this is the case with your intervention, it should be reported in your evaluation study.

Who provides the service? Is service delivered by certified clinical social workers, case managers with BSW degrees, registered nurses, clinical psychologists, or persons with college degrees in just about anything? Is it required that such persons hold any particular form of training for this job beyond college degrees? The answers to these questions provide information on the personnel for the intervention.

Gordon-Garofalo and Rubin, in their study of caregivers, described their intervention in a good deal of detail:

> Following a psychoeducational group intervention model developed originally for caregivers in HIV/AIDS . . . the principal investigator devised an 8-week session outline. Individual and common group concerns were incorporated into the treatment guide and translated into tasks. Although there was a homework-type task for each group session, some were formulated by the facilitator prior to the group's beginning, whereas during the course of the intervention, the group members generated others . . . To the extent possible, group facilitators stayed within the session outlines devised to ensure that the treatment remained the same across all four applications. Group composition and process, however, make it impossible to strictly adhere to a prearranged format . . . Personal issues for group members arising between group sessions would necessitate shifts in focus for particular group sessions. (Gordon-Garofalo & Rubin, 2004, p. 19)

An agenda for each of the eight sessions was presented in a table divided into the categories of educational component, support component, and session task. For example, session six was described as in Table 10.1.

TABLE 10.1 *Components of a Service Program*

Educational Component	Support Component	Session Task
Relationship issues: sexuality, trust, and commitment; blame and resentment; roles; and guilt	Stresses associated with AIDS, recognizing and combating stress, compassion, and fatigue.	Engage in stress reduction exercises and relaxation techniques.

Two master's-level social workers provided this treatment. Each had HIV/AIDS group work experience.

This above description provides information on the structure and personnel for this intervention regarding HIV/AIDS. Even though the goals and objectives were not explicitly stated, one could extrapolate these statements from the information given by the authors. In addition, there is reference to the psychoeducational model in this description. This model, however, was not explicated in the article. A description of the model would have provided information on the basic assumptions about the dynamics of the problem that served as the conceptual foundation of the selection of the service activities.

Discussion Box 10.8

Provide a statement that fits into the description of the structure of a familiar human service program or intervention. First, identify the program or intervention. Then provide the statement related to structure.

Selecting the Study Sample

In evaluative research, the topic of sampling is usually a bit more simple than in some of the other types of research. We typically select current clients as our study sample, and we are left with the task of speculating on the extent to which our current clients represent some larger population. When we do not have a probability sample, we cannot safely generalize our results to persons not included in the study.

In the previous chapter, you encountered the concepts of study sample and study population. If you need some review of these concepts, see Exhibit 10.3.

In the previous chapter, you encountered the concepts of the study sample and study population. You will recall that the study sample comprises those persons from whom data were collected, and the study population is a larger group of persons to whom you wish to generalize your findings. You may also recall that a probability sample is one in which each person in the designated study population has had an equal chance to be included in the study sample. Normally, this is achieved by some form of random sampling procedure.

Random sampling requires a method of identifying all persons in the study population and a special method of selecting persons for the sample from that list of all persons in the population. If you had the membership list of your state chapter of the National Association of Social Workers, you could select a probability sample by selecting persons from that list in a random fashion. If you wished to select one-fifth of all persons for your sample, you could select the first person from the first five on the list by drawing a number from 1 to 5 from a hat, and then selecting each fifth person thereafter.

EXHIBIT 10.3 • *What is a study sample and what is a study population? A Review of Prior Content*

A sample is a portion of a larger entity, the larger entity being known as the population. The study sample consists of those persons from whom data were collected, whereas the study population is a group that is larger than the sample, but contains all those who are in the study sample. In evaluative research, the study sample may be all clients served by your program at a given point, whereas the study population may be clients defined in a broader context, such as all clients served by this agency in the current decade, or all clients who exhibit a particular target behavior. You might conduct a study using the students in your research class. In this case, the study sample would be the students in your class. But these individuals were selected from a larger group. We could conceptualize any number of larger groups within which your research class students resided, such as:

- All students in human service degree programs in the United States
  - All students in the degree program of the study sample

- All students in this class (from whom data were collected)

What would be the study sample? It would be the last item—those in the present class. You could define your study population as either of the first two items, but you would be on safer grounds if you defined it as those students in the same degree programs as your study sample because this group is closer to your study sample and is more likely to share commonalities with it. It is legitimate to define the population more broadly, but you are walking on thinner ice with regard to the generalization of your results.

You can safely generalize your results from your study sample to the study population if your study sample was drawn at random from that specific population. Otherwise, you are walking on the thinner ice of speculative generalization, which requires some analysis of known data about the population and the sample that would support a reasonable conclusion of similarity with regard to the variables of interest to your study.

This procedure is known as the systematic random sampling method. There are other methods for random sampling. One approach calls for you to consult a table of random numbers, which are often found in statistical texts. A special method that might be useful for you is the multistage cluster sampling method (Rubin & Babbie, 2001). This method is useful if you do not have a single list of all population members, but have access to a list of organizations where they can all be found. If you wanted to have a sample of all rehabilitation counselors employed by hospitals in your state, you could obtain a list of all hospitals and select a certain number of hospitals with a random procedure. Then, you would contact those hospitals and ask for the list of all persons employed as rehabilitation counselors. Then, you would select your study sample by drawing a list of counselors randomly from that list.

The concept of sampling can be useful even when you cannot select a random sample for your study. When you are evaluating an intervention for a single client, you could, for example, measure target behavior by selecting time units at random for personal observation, or select days of the month at random for asking certain questions related to target behavior.

Most of the time in evaluation research, you will use a convenience sample. This simply means you are using a sample of persons who are convenient for your study. This might include a single client you are serving with a special problem you wish to study. It might include all those persons presently served by a given program you are evaluating.

The key issue for sampling is generalization of findings. Can you have confidence that your findings would have been similar to another group in your study population if your data had been collected from them? To the extent that you have reason to believe those other persons are different from your study sample, you will be on shaky grounds if you attempt to generalize.

Discussion Box 10.9

Think of a sample of persons who may be the subjects of an outcome evaluation study. Identify how the sample was selected for this hypothetical study and whether this sample would be properly labeled a probability sample.

Measuring Client Progress

In a prior chapter, you examined the importance of clear definitions of target behavior as a guide for selecting a means for measuring client progress. In the earlier discussion of the group intervention for caregivers of persons with HIV/AIDS, you noted the absence of explicit definitions of target behavior, but sufficient clarity regarding measurement that you would develop definitions from those descriptions of measurement tools. Ideally, you will define the target behavior prior to the consideration of measurement tools. This helps you avoid the temptation of allowing the measurement tools to define the behavior rather than vice versa.

In a prior chapter, you examined the two fundamental ways to measure study variables—qualitative and quantitative. With qualitative measurement, you have words to analyze. With quantitative measurement, you have variables measured in such a way as to place persons in your study sample into discrete categories or to give them a number that represents their status, such as age or score on a scale. If you need to review this idea, refer to Exhibit 10.4.

The key issue in measurement is the credibility or accuracy of the method used to measure client progress. Suppose you have identified the client's target behavior as stress, meaning a state of psychological tension exemplified by such feelings as up-tight, tense, and uneasy. You should employ an instrument that measures these states. If you selected a tool that asked how many troubling life events the respondent has experienced, you would be measuring stressors rather than stress.

How do you assess the accuracy of a tool? That is the task of methods for assessing the reliability and validity of a means of measurement. **Reliability** refers to consistency, while

EXHIBIT 10.4 • *A Review of Qualitative and Quantitative Measurement*

Scientific research relies upon two major forms of information—qualitative and quantitative. When you have completed the **quantitative** measurement of a study variable with your study subjects, you will have either a category or number to assign to each study participant for each variable. For example, each study subject may be classified as male or female for the variable of gender. The age for each person may be recorded in its basic form (i.e., 14, 15, 16, etc) or by reference to a category of age (e.g., 0–19; 20–29; etc.). You may have each person in a category according to whether they checked Agree or Undecided or Disagree in response to a particular statement about political ideology.

When you have completed the **qualitative** measurement of social phenomena, you will have *words* rather than numbers or uniform categories. These words may come from your observations of people in action or from the direct quotes from your study participants. These words will be examined for themes and will be coded accordingly. Thus, qualitative measurement is more flexible, and characterizes each study subject in a more unique format. Persons are not placed into preconceived categories but are given the opportunity to express themselves in their own words or actions.

The choice of a qualitative or quantitative means of observation (measurement) should be guided by the nature of the research question and the existing knowledge about it. Thus, one should not begin the research experience with the idea of conducting a quantitative study or a qualitative study. This would be putting the cart before the horse. Methods of observation spring from the nature of the study subject, not the other way around.

While either qualitative or quantitative methods can be applied to a wide variety of purposes and circumstances, there are a few guides which can assist the beginning research student in the choice of an observation mode. For example, a qualitative method is typically more appropriate to the extent that each of the following conditions exist:

1. You are seeking to develop theories or hypotheses rather than testing existing ones.
2. You are seeking an understanding of the subjective meaning of behaviors or social processes rather than the precise description of social phenomena.
3. The concepts of interest are not easily reduced to categories or numbers.
4. There is relatively little that is known about the subject of study from the existing literature or this knowledge base has important missing links.

You could say that the opposite of the above suggest a quantitative method of observation. For example, you would normally use a quantitative method when your are testing a theory, when you wish to precisely measure something, when study concepts are easily reduced to categories or numbers, and when there is a good deal that is already known about the phenomenon under study. Unfortunately, there is no clearcut means of employing the criteria. We cannot say, for example, that if any two of the listed conditions exist you must use a specific means of observation. These are meant only as a general guide.

---

validity refers to accuracy. An instrument must be reliable in order to be valid, but it does not have to be valid in order to be reliable. In other words, an instrument can be consistently inaccurate.

Why would a tool be inaccurate? If it is hard to understand, it would likely generate responses that made little sense to the respondent because he/she does not know what the questions mean. This would produce inconsistent responses. For example, my responses to the questions today would be rather different from my responses a month ago, because both represent my random responses to the unclear questions. A failure of an instrument to be consistent from one administration to another would be evidence against the reliability of the tool.

Another reason a tool might be inaccurate would be explained by the social desirability bias. This bias refers to the tendency of some persons to answer questions according to their idea of the socially desirable choice rather than the truth. There are methods for testing for this bias in a given instrument.

A few means for assessing reliability and validity will be briefly discussed here. One method of testing for reliability is the test-retest method. In this case, you administer an instrument to the same people at two points without administering an intervention in the period between the two administrations of the instrument. If the instrument is reliable, you will get consistent responses from people at two points, assuming nothing has happened to change the thing being measured. A method for testing for validity is to compare the tool to some other way to measure the same thing. You could see if the clinician's rating of clients for depression is positively correlated with the clients' scores on your depression scale. You could see if scores on your anxiety scale are positively correlated with scores on someone else's anxiety scale.

Discussion Box 10.10

When you use the test–retest method of reliability assessment, you make sure you are doing this with a group of people who are not being treated during the period between the first test and the retest. Why?

Selecting the Research Design

In the previous chapter you were introduced to the main reason to be concerned with the design of your evaluation study: If you have a better design than me, you are in a better position than me to attribute the client's measured progress to the intervention rather than something else. You were introduced to a few basic designs for evaluating client outcome. If you need to review these concepts, refer to Exhibit 10.5.

There are two basic types of research designs for the evaluation of human service outcomes. One is the group design and the other is the single-subject design (a.k.a., single-system design). The group design employs measurements of a group of clients being served by a common program or intervention, while the single-subject design employs measurements of a single client being given a tailored intervention. You can employ the methods of single-system evaluation with an entity other than a person, providing you have one indicator of progress that will be repeatedly measured. For example, you could employ the no-show rate for clients of the mental health center as the single indicator of performance and analyze the trends for this indicator.

EXHIBIT 10.5 • *Research Designs and Causation: A Review*

The research design specifies the procedures for measurement and implementation. You might measure the target behavior before and after treatment for a group of clients. You might compare your clients' gain in functioning with the gain of a nontreated group. These are examples of research designs. The research design should be distinguished from the design of the intervention, the latter depicting the type of treatment being offered.

The research design in evaluative research is critical to the question of **causation** in the interpretation of our data. If we merely ask our clients after treatment if they are satisfied with the service, we are engaging in a study that best fits into the category of descriptive research, because we are only describing their opinions. If we measure their condition, such as self-esteem, only after treatment, we do not have a basis of determining how much good the intervention did because we do not know their level of self-esteem before treatment.

If we measure their conditions before and after treatment, we are beginning to develop a basis for gauging the effect of treatment. If they are better off after treatment than before, perhaps we can attribute the change to the intervention. But we know that there are other things that potentially affect the client's conditions. How do we know, for example, that the client would not have improved through normal growth and development through the time period of the intervention? Perhaps the typical adolescent achieves a 20 percent gain in self esteem in the normal course of development in three months' time. If our treatment lasts for three months and we achieve a 20 percent gain, we will not be confident that our treatment made the difference under these circumstances.

The more we know about the normal course of development, the better we will be able to judge

what other variables might effect the client's condition. When we use the simple before-and-after design (also known as the pretest–posttest one group design), we make the assumption that there are no variables other than treatment that affect the client's target condition. For example, we assume that the clients would not improve significantly in the target behavior during the period of the treatment without the treatment that was given.

But we know that some people do improve over time on their own. We can apply logic to determine the extent to which we should be concerned with this issue in our own situation. We can logically expect a women to be less depressed six months after her husband has died than three weeks after this event. But we would not expect a neglectful mother, who has been neglecting her children for five years, to improve on her own over a period of three months. Perhaps she would improve on her own over a longer period, such as a year or two. But if she has been neglecting her children for five years, we can reasonably expect that her behavior is not going to change in only three months without some form of intervention in her life.

A design that is superior to the before and after approach is the pretest–posttest comparison group design wherein a group of clients is measured before and after treatment and a nontreated group is measured at the same two time periods. In this design, we compare the growth of our clients on the target condition with that of a group of persons who did not receive the treatment. We attribute the differences in growth to the treatment. We can have more confidence in this design if we have reason to believe that the two groups are similar except for the fact that one group received the treatment.

Threats to Internal Validity

For all types of designs for evaluative research, there are certain indicators of strengths and weaknesses which have been labeled "threats to internal validity" in the research literature. When we measure client behavior, we make the assumption that observed changes are due to the intervention rather than something else. But we know that other factors may be the cause of these changes rather than the treatment itself. The various threats to internal validity deal with a number of these alternative explanations for the observed behavior of the client.

One of these threats, or alternative explanations, is known as **history**. This refers to the fact that changes in the environment, independent of the treatment, may have caused changes in the client's behavior. If an unemployed client has gotten a job during the treatment period, we may have good reason to believe that it is the job that has increased his or her self-esteem, rather than the treatment. In order to take history into consideration, your research design must have a comparison group or control group that did not get the treatment and whose lives are believed to be consistent with persons in the treatment group with regard to potential environmental influences. In this way, the effect of history is believed to be the same for the two groups; thus, any differences between the groups cannot be attributed to history. For example, it would be estimated that the new factory that opened in town provided as many new jobs for persons in the comparison group as the treatment group; thus, differences in outcome between the two groups cannot be attributed to the new factory. There are some single-subject designs that address history. These designs call for several different treatment periods and several different baseline periods. It is assumed that changes in the environment will not occur only when the treatment is being offered and not when it has been withdrawn, if there are several episodes of this variation between treatment and baseline.

Another threat is that of **maturation**. This refers to the fact that people naturally grow over time and find ways to solve their problems on their own without the help of treatment. We can expect, for example, that the level of depression of a recently separated marriage partner will naturally shrink with the passage of time for most people. If we employ treatment during this period and measure depression before and after treatment, how can we be confident that the treatment was the cause of the reduction in the measured level of depression? There are two basic ways to deal with maturation as an alternative explanation. One is to obtain information on trends in the client's behavior before the treatment began and to project this trend into the treatment period and to compare the treatment measurements to this trend. Another way to address maturation is to have a comparison group that did not receive the treatment. The effect of maturation is believed to be consistent between the two groups; thus, any differences in target behavior gain between the treatment group and the comparison group cannot be attributed to maturation.

There are several additional threats to internal validity which we will not discuss here. They will be discussed later.

Discussion Box 10.11

In your own words, what does the phrase *threats to internal validity* mean?

Most Common Group Designs

We will discuss four group designs for evaluative research in this section: the pretest–posttest one-group design; the alternative treatment design; the comparison group design; and the basic experimental design. These designs vary in the extent to which they address the various threats to internal validity.

We have already discussed the **one-group pretest–posttest** design. It is a better approach to evaluation than the procedure of taking only one reading of the client's behavior after treatment and then speculating on how much credit the treatment should take. But it is inferior to the third and fourth designs discussed here because it does not address either of the two threats to internal validity that were discussed above.

We should be more or less concerned about these threats in accordance with the extent to which we know of information that would logically cause concern about these alternative explanations. For example, just how much would we expect a person to grow naturally on a given condition over a given period of time? If we measure the client's depression and find a serious level of it and we learn that the client has acted very depressed for the past six months, we would not expect this depression to change significantly without treatment in a short period of time, such as, for example, two months.

The shorter the period of treatment, the less we need to be concerned about either maturation or history as alternative explanations for client change. In the case of history, of course, we must be attentive to changes in the environment that we know about. If there are such changes, we must be concerned. The longer the treatment period, the greater is the likelihood that there have been changes in the environment that we do not know about.

With the **alternative treatment design**, we are comparing two treatments to see if there is a difference. It is an extension of the previous design in that pretest and posttest measures of the dependent variable are compared to see if there was a significant gain. What is different is that you compare the gain in functioning for the two treatment periods. This helps us to know what treatment is more effective than another, but we do not have a comparison group which represents no treatment, so we do not know how much change would have occurred in the absence of treatment.

The third group design we will discuss is the **comparison group design**, also known as the nonequivalent control group design. With this design, you have a treated group and a comparison group that did not receive the treatment. They are measured on the dependent variable before and after the treatment period, and their relative gain scores are compared to see if they are significantly different; you would measure both the treatment group and the comparison group before and after the treatment period. For each study subject, a gain score would be computed which reflects the difference between the pretest and posttest measures of the dependent variable. The mean gain score for the treatment group would be compared to the mean gain score for the comparison group to see if there was a significant difference that favored the treatment group.

It is assumed that the two groups are comparable in regard to potential effects of changes in the environment (history) and the effects of normal growth (maturation) and the effects of testing. In other words, whatever is happening with regard to these factors will be evenly distributed between these two groups and, thus, any differences between the two groups cannot be attributed to these factors. This enhances our ability to attribute changes to the treatment.

However, you would be walking on thin ice if you assumed comparability between the two groups when there is a clear reason to expect a difference. For example, if you selected the persons for the treatment group on the basis of a higher motivation for treatment, you would know of a difference between the two groups that might explain differences in gain over a period of time. It seems logical to say that those higher in motivation for treatment are higher in motivation for recovery and persons higher on motivation to achieve something will be more likely to achieve it on their own. This difference would favor the treatment group. But you could make the mistake of a selection procedure that would favor the comparison group and put your intervention at risk of negative findings that are not warranted.

A variation of the comparison group design is the one in which only a posttest recording of behavior is taken. The two groups are assumed to be equivalent at the pretest time; thus, any differences in measurement are assumed to be attributed to the treatment. This assumption is subject to question in many situations. It is clearly better to take a pretest measurement of the dependent variable. In the absence of this opportunity, it is important logically to rule out reasons why the two groups may have been different at the pretest time. The best use of this posttest-only method is when you can randomly assign people to the treatment and comparison groups, but that procedure would put your example in the category of an experimental design as discussed below.

The **basic experimental design** is the final design for evaluative research discussed here. This design is similar to the comparison group design, except that the two groups are assigned to their status as either treatment group or control group on a random basis. The great advantage is that the random assignment of persons to the two groups deals with a host of threats to internal validity. It is assumed that various nontreatment factors which might effect changes in clients' behaviors are evenly distributed between the two groups; thus, any observed differences in gain between the two groups can be attributed to the intervention.

To illustrate the difference between the comparison group design and the basic experimental design, let's examine the use of the waiting list as the comparison group. Persons on the waiting list cannot be considered to be a true control group for the experimental design unless they were assigned to the waiting list on a random basis. If they were placed on this list because they had a less serious problem, we have clear indication of a difference between the two groups (treatment and comparison) that may influence changes in behavior. If they are there on a first-come, first-served basis, we have less concern about differences, but there still could be important differences between the two groups. For example, we might have learned from experience that a certain percentage of clients drop off the waiting list before they are called for treatment. The treated group does not have this segment of potential clients in it, and thus is different.

While it may not be easy to see the advantages of the basic experimental design over the comparison group design, there are several advantages. First, the experimental design does a better job of addressing the two threats to internal validity that have been discussed. Second, it addresses certain threats to internal validity that have not been discussed.

There are several forms of the experimental design. One is the pretest–posttest control group design described above. Another is the posttest-only control group design where people are tested only at the end of the treatment period. There are several additional experimental designs that will not be discussed here because you will rarely see them used in studies by human service practitioners.

Single-Subject Designs

We will discuss four single-subject designs in this section: the B design; the AB design; the ABC design; and the BC design. The designation of the letters for these designs has a pattern. The letter A always represents a baseline period during which the client's behavior is measured repeatedly but no treatment is given. The other letters refer to treatment periods during which the client's behavior is repeatedly measured. The letter B refers to the first (or only) treatment given, while the letter C refers to a second treatment (or a change in the treatment approach). For example, the AB design refers to the situation in which the client's behavior is measured several times before treatment begins and several times while treatment is being given. The BC design is one in which there is no measurement of the client's behavior before treatment. Instead, the client's behavior is measured several times during the initial treatment period and the treatment is changed. Measurement continues during the second treatment period.

With all single-subject designs, the client's target behavior (the dependent variable) is measured during each phase (A, B, C). Normally, the target behavior is measured repeatedly during each phase. In fact, the only exception is the limited AB design when there is only one recording of target behavior during the baseline. This array of measurements is used for the statistical analysis of the data to estimate the likelihood that differences can be explained by chance. It must be understood that statistical analysis depends upon an array of data (i.e., many pieces of data) rather than one or two measurements. With group research designs, you have a group of people who are measured; thus, you have an array of measurements for statistical analysis. When you have only one study subject, you must measure the behavior many times in order to obtain the necessary array of data for statistical analysis. There is no way to assess statistical significance if you only have one baseline recording of target behavior and one treatment recording. This is only two scores, and statistics cannot do anything with it.

The **B design** is the most simple of the single-system designs. With this design you only collect data during the treatment period. The advantage of this design is that you have measurements that can show whether progress is being made and the pattern of that progress. The disadvantage is that you do not have a baseline to show where this behavior was going prior to treatment. For example, you might begin the administration of a self-esteem scale for an adolescent in therapy with the second treatment session and continue to administer this scale each week when the client came for treatment. You may have a total of eight measurements during the treatment period but you have no measurements of self-esteem prior to the beginning of treatment.

The **AB design** has an advantage over the B design in that it addresses the issue of maturation as a threat to internal validity. The baseline period is considered to be a reflection of the pattern of behavior already underway before treatment. If maturation is occurring, it will be reflected in the pattern of measurements during this baseline period. If the treatment period recordings of the client's behavior are significantly better than the projection from the baseline trend, then we would tend to attribute this change to the intervention. In other words, we make the assumption that the trend in behavior demonstrated by the baseline measurements are a reflection of what would continue in the absence of treatment. If the trend shows a gradual improvement, we would chart these scores and extend this trend of gradual improvement into the treatment period and compare the actual treatment recordings to this trend to see if it is better.

The **ABC** design is an extension of the AB design. It simply adds a second intervention (the C phase) to see if it is more effective than the first. The C time period can be compared to both the B period and the baseline (the A period) to see if it is better.

The **BC design** is one that can be used if there is no opportunity to take a baseline set of measurements. It entails the recording of client behaviors during the implementation of the first treatment strategy (the B period) followed by a change in the treatment approach and the continued recording of client behaviors during this second treatment period (the C period). With this design, you are not taking maturation into consideration because you have no baseline of data for estimating the effect of spontaneous development. What you can see from this set of data is whether the two treatments are different in their effects. One might argue, however, that the recordings during the B phase reflect a combination of the possible effect of maturation and the possible effect of the first treatment.

The **ABAB** design is considered by some to qualify as an experimental design. With this design, there are two baseline periods and two treatment periods. The first two phases (AB) are similar to the AB design. The difference is that a second baseline follows the withdrawal of treatment, and a second treatment period follows this second baseline period. If the client's behavior is significantly higher in each of the two treatment periods than in either of the two baseline periods, we would have good reason to have confidence that our treatment was to be credited with the gains.

Consider, for example, the internal validity threat that has been labeled "history." The AB design does not address this threat because it is reasonable to argue that a change in the client's environment during the treatment phase was the cause of the client's gain in functioning rather than the treatment. However, it would be highly unlikely that history is to be credited with client gain if treatment is withdrawn and reintroduced later. How likely is it that changes in the environment would take place only in the two treatment phases of the ABAB design and not influence behavior during the two baseline periods? If there have been changes in the client's environment during the first treatment phase, this change would likely continue to influence the client's behavior during the second baseline as well as the second treatment period. If the client's behavior regresses during the second baseline and improves during the second treatment period, it would be easily argued that the treatment had the desired effect upon client functioning.

A limitation of the designs that include multiple baselines is that you would normally terminate service when you felt the client was prepared to sustain gains in functioning. Thus, you would not expect the client's condition to deteriorate after service is terminated. One of the multiple baseline designs would only be appropriate if you expected this deterioration. Suppose, for example, that you were offering respite care for caregivers of relatives with dementia. These caregivers need some respite from their duties in order to avoid burnout with these heavy responsibilities. You would expect respite care to reduce their feelings of burden. You would also expect their feelings of burden to go back up if respite care is withdrawn. But if you were treating a person for depression, you would normally discharge this person from treatment when you felt their depression would not come back.

Discussion Box 10.12

Let's put to work what you have learned about threats to internal validity and research designs. Think of a human service intervention that might be evaluated through either a single-subject design or a group design. Identify the intervention below. For example, you might refer to the support group for recently divorced women or the therapy offered to a man suffering from depression or the employment support services offered to unemployed individuals or school social work services offered to high-risk high school students.

Discussion Box 10.13

Now think of the threats to internal validity that should be of special concern in the evaluation of this intervention. Would you expect these clients to recover from their problems or have their needs met without receiving the services being offered? This could include normal growth over time (maturation), changes in their environments (history), or something else. Please note that you are not being asked to identify what is *possible* because just about anything is possible. Instead you are being asked to identify what is *probable*.

Discussion Box 10.14

Now identify a research design that would be appropriate for this evaluation study.

Implementing the Intervention

As noted in a prior chapter, the key issue for implementation is whether the treatment plan was carried out. It is perfectly normal for some minor aspects of that plan to be changed during the implementation process. When this happens, you should include this in your report. You may remember the following statement from the previous description of the group intervention for caregivers of persons with HIV/AIDS:

> To the extent possible, group facilitators stayed within the session outlines devised to ensure that the treatment remained the same across all four applications. Group composition and process, however, make it impossible to strictly adhere to a prearranged format. . . . Personal issues for group members arising between group sessions would necessitate shifts in focus for particular group sessions. (Gordon-Garofalo & Rubin, 2004, p. 19)

The essential task here is to report the extent to which the intervention was implemented. If there was substantial deviation from the plan, your study may be in trouble, especially if you are testing a model of intervention and wanted to be able to generalize about its effectiveness.

A key task here is the method used to assure the implementation of the plan. This can take the form of clear treatment manuals for implementation. The greater the clarity of instructions on how the treatment model is to be implemented, the greater is the confidence that it will be implemented properly. Another method for assuring the proper implementation of the model is observation by others of the execution of this plan. You could have treatment practitioners prepare recordings of what happened and these recordings could be reviewed by others. You could have direct observation by others of events selected on a random basis.

Discussion Box 10.15

If you have a good deal of familiarity with the implementation of a human service intervention or program, think of the one thing in the design of this intervention that is most effective in the achievement of the outcome. Then think of how well this aspect of service is actually implemented by the typical practitioner.

Analyzing the Data

There are three key tasks for data analysis in the evaluation of client outcome—description of the study sample, reporting of target behavior, and examining the data for significance (statistical and practical). The first type of data helps the reader of your report deal with the issue of generalization. If all of your clients are senior citizens, a reader may not feel that generalization to teenagers would be appropriate. The second type of data reports on whether the clients achieved a gain. It is possible for them to have experienced a loss. The third type of data helps you to put the results into perspective. The first type of significance is statistical: Can these results be explained by chance? The second type of significance is practical (or clinical): Is the amount of client gain noteworthy, given the amount of need and the amount of resources expended?

Let's return to the study of caregivers of persons with HIV/AIDS. Gordon-Garofalo & Rubin (2004) reported the average age of persons in both the treatment group and the comparison group to be approximately 41 (40.95 and 41.44, to be precise). They were all Caucasian and were rather evenly split between males and females. Most were employed in white-collar jobs. Slightly more than one-half were heterosexual. This description provides information that you could use in determining whether you would be successful using this intervention with your clients. Another use of descriptive data analysis for a comparison group study, such as the one regarding caregivers of persons with HIV/AIDS, is that you can examine similarities and differences between the groups. In the HIV/AIDS study the two groups were found to be quite similar on descriptive characteristics, lending support to the argument that differences between the groups on measured progress on target behavior would be due to the effect of the intervention rather than differences between the groups in their personal characteristics.

The second type of data deals with the study **hypothesis.** The hypothesis is a precise statement of the expected results of the study, given the means used to measure client progress. A vague statement such as "Clients will get better because of treatment" would not be appropriate as a statement of your study hypothesis because it lacks specificity. In the study of HIV/AIDS, the authors spelled out several study hypotheses as follows:

> Specifically, the authors hypothesized that (a) participation in the group would decrease perceived depression, (b) participation in the group would decrease perceived anxiety, (c) participation in the group would increase perceived social support, (b) participation in the group would decrease perceived stress, and (e) participation in the group would decrease perceived stigma. (Gordon-Garofalo & Rubin, 2004, p. 16)

Each of these hypotheses identifies both the independent and dependent variables. The independent variable is the variable believed to cause the dependent variable to change. Each statement identifies both group participation as the independent variable and identifies a dependent variable. You will note there is a separate hypothesis for each dependent variable.

Each dependent variable identified in a hypothesis should be measured in your study. You will note there was not a statement of hypothesis for the HIV/AIDS study such as "Psychosocial functioning will improve as a result of group participation." Why? Psychosocial functioning was not measured as a unitary concept. It was measured in regard to five different variables.

If you could measure your clients' progress in regard to several variables, you would be wise to consider the underlying concept that binds these variables as the focus of the statement of the treatment goal, and the individual variables as the focus of statements of various treatment objectives. Thus, the goal of the HIV/AIDS intervention was to improve the psychosocial functioning of the target population, while one of the objectives was to decrease anxiety.

Before testing your hypotheses, you should examine pretest or baseline data to determine the level of functioning on the scales you have chosen to use to measure client progress. With the study of HIV/AIDS there is a major problem. On the tools used to measure client progress, clients were functioning rather well at pretest, indicating little need for treatment.

For example, the Impact of Event Scale was employed to measure stress. This scale asks respondents to reflect on the major recent event that might have caused stress and to answer a set of questions with the following code:

1 = Not at all

2 = Rarely

3 = Sometimes

4 = Often

The respondent selects one of the above and gets a corresponding score for each item as noted above. Some of the items on the scale are:

I thought about it when I didn't mean to.
I had trouble falling asleep or staying asleep, because of pictures or thoughts that came into my mind.

Because the lowest score you could receive on individual items on this scale was a score of 1, the minimum possible score for this scale was 15 because there were 15 items on the scale. A score of 15 would represent absolutely no stress. The highest possible score was 60, reflecting a response of Often for each item. I would say this means that scores in the range of 45 to 60 would represent a serious level of stress. This means you typically replied Sometimes or Often to these statements.

The mean pretest score for stress for the treatment group in the HIV/AIDS study was 31.21. A score of 30 would be represented by someone who replied Rarely to each statement. This cannot be conceived as showing a problem with stress. So what can you expect with regard to client progress? Very little, if any. And that's what they found. The mean posttest score of 28.05 was better than the mean pretest score, but it reflected rather little gain.

Low scores at pretest were found for the other scales used in this study (in which higher scores represented a greater problem). My reflection on pretest scores indicated little problem with stress, anxiety, depression, perceived stigma, or social support. Perhaps most noteworthy in regard to improvement was the hypothesis regarding depression. It was considered moderate at pretest but achieved a noteworthy improvement in functioning from moderate to normal between pretest to posttest, whereas the comparison group remained moderately depressed at both points. Depression was measured by the Beck Depression Inventory, where scores can range from 0 to 63, with scores above 20 representing clinically significant depression (Gordon-Garofalo & Rubin, 2004, p. 20). The mean pretest score for the clients of the HIV/AIDS study was 14, which represented mild depression according to the authors. However, the posttest score of 8.32 represented no problem with depression, or normal behavior. Perhaps the clinical cutoff score of 20 should not be considered relevant to this study because these individuals were not seeking treatment for depression.

This analysis deals primarily with the issue of practical significance. Statistical significance is the second issue to address with regard to data analysis. You will recall that statistical significance answers the question "Can my data be explained by chance?" There are normal fluctuations in the scores of normal people on any given scale whether or not there is any noteworthy change in their condition. And there are normal fluctuations in our clients' condition that we can expect to happen whether or not they are in treatment. So, can we say our measured progress in target behavior is due to our treatment, or best explained as chance? That is the issue for statistical analysis and is reflected in the value of p that is derived from various statistical tests. You may remember that the normal standard in the social sciences is to have data that cannot be explained by chance any more than 5 times in 100. This would be designated as $p < .05$.

In the study of HIV/AIDS, the statistical analysis produced "inconclusive evidence of the effectiveness of task-centered psychoeducational group intervention for cohabiting seronegative partners and spouses of persons with HIV/AIDS" (Gordon-Garofalo & Rubin, 2004, p. 23). This was because some of the statistical analyses showed significance and some did not. This should not be surprising, given the fact that tools for measuring client progress showed rather few problems before treatment began.

Discussion Box 10.16

Now let's put to use some of the things you have learned in this section. Think of a possible human service evaluation that you might want to undertake. Identify the intervention and state the hypothesis.

Discussion Box 10.17

Identify the dependent variable from this hypothesis.

Discussion Box 10.18

Identify the independent variable from this hypothesis.

Discussion Box 10.19

In the examination of data related to the hypothesis, where would you seek guidance in the determination of statistical significance? What about practical significance?

Drawing Conclusions

In a previous chapter, we examined several issues relevant to the conclusions section of the evaluation research report: practical significance, generalization, and consistency between data analysis and conclusions. Readers of your report will want to know basically what you found with regard to practical significance. Were hypotheses supported by your data? What was the level of gain in practical terms? They also want to know the extent to which your findings can be generalized. And they do not want to see your own biases showing up in the conclusions section of your report, parading as the results of your study rather than your opinion. Statements of your biases may be appropriate, but they should be explicitly stated as opinion and differentiated from the results of your study.

The HIV/AIDS study revealed somewhat inconclusive evidence about the effectiveness of the treatment as indicated in the quote in the previous section. A key limitation of that study was discussed by the authors:

> This group of caregivers entered the group scoring very mild reactions on the psychological outcome measures of coping with the HIV disease, although they entered the group in part to deal with their emotional reactions to caregiving. Being prepared for emotional reactions such as depression, grief, and anxiety and working on management skills to overcome these reactions was an important part of the psychoeducational group process. These were not the only outcomes desired by participants, however, and they are not the only outcomes to the coping model on which this intervention is based. (Gordon-Garofalo & Rubin, 2004, p. 24)

The authors go on to note that cognitive, behavioral, and physical outcomes are often the target of interventions like the one implemented; yet these possible outcomes were not measured in the study of HIV/AIDS. Perhaps they should have been.

Discussion Box 10.20

Suppose that you had undertaken a study of the effectiveness of your support group for grieving widows by measuring depression and perceived social support and found a statistically significant gain in perceived social support but not depression. What do you think of the following statement of conclusion?

It is clear that services that focus on depression, social support, and self-esteem are important parts of any intervention for grieving widows.

Summary

In this chapter, you have examined a number of concepts related to outcome evaluation. You reviewed the definition and analysis of target behavior as instruments for clarifying how progress should be measured and how the intervention should be designed. You reviewed the task of sampling and examined some new material on types of samples. New material was also introduced on reliability and validity in measurement and you were introduced to several new research designs as mechanisms for dealing with alternative explanations for client gain. In a previous chapter, you focused on the description of the model of the intervention, but in this chapter the intervention was described in regard to goals, objectives, personnel, and structure. You reviewed the kinds of data that should be included in the data analysis section of an evaluation report and were introduced to the concept of the study hypothesis. And you returned to the concepts of statistical significance and practical significance as key issues to address in data analysis. Finally, you were reminded that statements in the study conclusions section of the evaluation report should be restricted to the data that were analyzed.

Quiz

The following questions review the material of this chapter. You may use it as a pretest to determine if you need to review this chapter, or as a posttest, which should help you understand how well you read this chapter. Answers are given at the end of the reference list.

1. Barbara has defined the concept of stressor as being an environmental condition or event that

can cause stress and has defined stress as a state of psychological tension characterized by such emotions as up-tight, tense, and so forth. Beth has not defined the concept of stress, but has a general idea of what it means, like most of us do. Both Barbara and Beth have decided that the reduction of stress is the objective for their treatment of groups of single mothers in need of support. What is Barbara in a better position to do?

   a. Select the intervention for achieving the objective
   b. Select a study sample
   c. Select a means for measuring client progress
   d. Select a research design

2. In this example, Beth is using the comparison group design whereby she will compare the gain scores of her clients on anxiety with the gain scores of a group of single mothers on the waiting list for service. Barbara is measuring her clients before and after treatment, and will determine if there is a significant gain, but will not compare her clients' gain scores with another group. In what way is Beth in a superior position in research?

   a. Beth is in a better position to achieve statistical significance.
   b. Beth is in a better position to achieve practical significance.
   c. Beth is in a better position to attribute her clients' gain to the treatment rather than something else such as normal growth and development over time.
   d. Beth is in a better position to select an effective method of treatment.

3. Which of the following would be considered probability samples of the members of the Lions Club of Ohio?

   a. A procedure whereby you selected those persons attending the state convention of this organization
   b. A procedure whereby you reviewed the membership list of this organization and selected your first person by rolling a set of dice and then you selected every fifth person thereafter
   c. Both of the above
   d. None of the above

4. The concept "threats to internal validity" refers to:

   a. Those things that could influence client gain independent of treatment
   b. Those parts of the treatment design that have the highest effect upon client gain
   c. Both of the above
   d. None of the above

5. Which of the following research designs does the best job of addressing threats to internal validity?

   a. The one-group pretest–posttest design
   b. The experimental design
   c. The alternative treatment design
   d. The AB single-subject design

6. Which of the following statements is/are true?

   a. The class of students in Professor Johnson's section of the introductory research course in the MSW Program of Western University constitutes a random sample of students in the MSW Program at Western University
   b. The results of a study of stress among Professor Johnson's class of research students could be safely generalized to all students in this university
   c. Both of the above
   d. None of the above

7. Which of the following would be evidence that your instrument for measuring anxiety was reliable or valid?

   a. The discovery that your clients' scores on this scale were better at the end of treatment than before treatment began
   b. The discovery that scores on your anxiety scale were positively correlated with the ratings of clients by their therapists on depression
   c. Both of the above
   d. None of the above

8. Which of the following statements is/are true?

   a. An instrument for measuring client progress can be reliable without being valid.
   b. An instrument for measuring client progress can be valid without being reliable.
   c. Both of the above.
   d. None of the above.

9. How many different types of treatment are in the ABAB single-system research design?

   a. One
   b. Two
   c. Three
   d. Four

10. Does the AB single-system research design address maturation (normal growth and development over time) as a threat to internal validity (an alternative explanation of client growth)?

a. Yes, because it has two different baseline periods.
b. Yes, because the baseline period serves as an estimate of the effect of maturation.
c. No, because there is no baseline period in this design.
d. No, because there is no comparison group.

References

Gil, E. (1991). *The Healing power of play.* New York: Guilford Press.

Gordon-Garofalo, V. L., & Rubin, A. (2004). Evaluation of a psychoeducational group for seronegative partners and spouses of persons with HIV/AIDS. *Research on social work practice, 14*(1), 14–26.

Rubin, A., & Babbie, E. (2001). *Research methods for social work.* (Belmont, CA.: Wadsworth /Thomson).

Answers to the Quiz

1. c
2. c
3. b
4. a
5. b

6. d
7. b
8. a
9. a
10. b

11

Case Example: Intermediate Concepts in Outcome Evaluation—Is Play Therapy Effective in the Treatment of Attachment Disorder?

The example to be used in the illustration of basic concepts in outcome evaluation was developed by Erin O'Neal, a social work graduate student at East Carolina University (O'Neal, 2004). She used the example of play therapy with a three-year-old child exhibiting the symptoms of attachment disorder. The agency where this practice took place was a family enrichment center that provided childcare services, training, and family outreach. The client was described as follows:

> The client, who will be referred to as "Kate" for the purpose of this paper, came to the [agency] in January of 2004. Kate is a three-year-old girl, who enrolled into the [agency] after she had been removed from the custody of her biological parents. It had been reported that removal was supported by findings of neglect, which included the parents' inability to provide basic needs, such as food, stable housing, and financial support. This was further substantiated by the fact that the family had been living with the maternal grandparents and had been unable to locate and sustain stable housing independently. In addition to these concerns, it had been reported that issues of domestic violence were reoccurring, as well as later speculation of sexual abuse towards Kate. (O'Neal, 2004, p. 4).

In this chapter, you will examine the evaluation research process along with intermediate concepts in evaluation through an example using a single-system research design. This examination will begin with the definition of the target behavior of attachment disorder. A good definition should provide guidance in the selection of a means for measuring client progress.

Another step is the analysis of this target behavior. What are the causes of this condition or the special needs of those who exhibit it? The outcome of this part of the process will aid in the determination of an appropriate intervention. In this case, play therapy was the chosen intervention. A question is whether play therapy makes sense in the treatment of attachment disorder. What is it about this target behavior that justifies play therapy as the intervention?

Another task is the description of the intervention in regard to (1) goals and objectives, (2) structure, (3) personnel, and (4) model. A good description of the intervention facilitates replication. If this intervention is successful, other practitioners likely will want to implement it with their clients. If the intervention is not clearly described, this implementation will be problematic. Others will want to know what play therapy looks like, how much therapy was offered, what types of practitioners provided this service, and what model of human behavior provided theoretical guidance.

The methods of research employed in the study will serve as another major task in the reporting of an evaluation study. In regard to research methods, you will see that O'Neal selected a client for study on the basis of convenience; thus, she employed a convenience sample. You will see that she measured client progress by using special instruments developed specifically for this study. These tools included classroom observations and foster parent ratings that were designed to measure temper tantrums, engagement with other children, and the frequency of nesting rituals. You will also see that this study employed the AB single-system design whereby the client was measured on target behaviors weekly for 10 weeks prior to treatment and the 10 weeks of the treatment period.

The analysis of the data serves as the next step in the evaluation process. You will see, for example, the pattern of temper tantrums during both the baseline period and the treatment period and the statistical analysis that was undertaken to determine whether the differences between these periods could easily be explained by chance. Finally, the conclusions of this study will be noted. To what extent can we declare this treatment to be successful? Included in this analysis are statements about the limitations of the study.

Definition of the Target Behavior

The first task in the presentation of information on the client's target behavior is the *definition of the behavior*. For O'Neal's client, the behavior was labeled attachment disorder and was described for this client as follows:

> Upon entering the program, Kate began exhibiting symptoms of attachment disorder. Symptoms that were observed by staff at the center, as well as Kate's foster parents, included Kate experiencing difficulty transitioning and separating, which often resulted in intensified anxiety and negatively driven behavior. During involvement in her classroom setting, Kate has been observed exhibiting signs of restrictive play and exploration, as well as anxious attachment to teaching staff. In addition to the symptoms being observed at the . . . center, it was reported that Kate was following through with nightly nesting rituals in her current home environment. These rituals consisted of Kate creating 'nests' out of pillows and blankets, which she would place in front of the doorway to her bedroom, making it difficult for anyone to enter. It was also reported that Kate would sleep on these 'nests' every night, often refusing to return to her bed. (O'Neal, 2004, p. 4)

Attachment was defined by O'Neal as a "reciprocal, profound, emotional, and physical relationship between a child and his parent that sets the stage for all future intimate, trusting relationships" (O'Neal, 2004, p. 10, drawing from the work of James, 1989). She went on to explicate this definition, again drawing from the work of James (1989):

> In a typical environment, children will curiously explore their environment, while remaining in close proximity to their parent when stress becomes too great. However, when trauma keeps a secure attachment from forming, such is often the case when a child experiences loss and disruption in their home environment, the result may be an increase in anxiety, an unwillingness to separate or transition, and a lack of exploration of one's environment. In addition to these symptoms, negative behavioral responses are often observed due to the increase of tension felt by the child. (O'Neal, 2004, p. 10)

O'Neal provided a concise definition of this target behavior:

> The target behavior being measured by this study can best be defined as symptoms of attachment disorder. In this particular situation, the symptoms were viewed as maladaptive behavior made evident through Kate's difficulty transitioning and separating, her restrictive play and exploration, as well as the nesting rituals that were reportedly occurring at home. (O'Neal, 2004, p. 14)

Discussion Box 11.1

A good definition of target behavior will provide guidance in the search for a means for measuring client progress. How well does this definition accomplish this objective?

Analysis of the Target Behavior

The second major task in the presentation of information on the client's target behavior is the *analysis of the behavior.* According to O'Neal, a key to the child's attachment to a parent is the stable and consistent guidance provided by the parent, something that is often missing for the neglected child. Consistent guidance leads to trust, a positive self-image, and differentiation between feelings and behavior. The consequence of failure in this area is a disturbance in developmental milestones. This can be manifested in an increase in anxiety, an unwillingness to separate, and a lack of exploration of one's environment. These consequences can lead to negative social behaviors such as temper tantrums.

Play therapy is often used with young children because they are not able to verbalize their thoughts like adults. Instead, they act out their feelings. O'Neal described play as a form of self-expression and a way in which individuals may escape emotionally. It can be effective in establishing trusting relationships, improved self-expression, and a revision of the child's self-image. Some of the themes easily addressed in play therapy are those of power and aggression, family and nurturance, control and safety, exploration and mastery, and alignments that the child may have with others.

Drawing from the literature, O'Neal noted the connection between child neglect and play therapy:

> Children who have experienced neglect often exhibit repressed feelings, developmental delays, and become disengaged with their caregivers. With regard to physical and emotional abuse, many children exhibit signs of anxiety, aggression, withdrawal, and what appears to be an impaired capacity to enjoy life. Therefore, when working with children who have experienced trauma as a result of neglect and/or abuse, it is important for the therapist to approach the child in a non-intrusive manner. In doing so, the child is provided with an opportunity to set boundaries, while moving freely about the room and making choices of their own. (O'Neal, 2004, p. 4)

Discussion Box 11.2

The analysis of target behavior should guide the selection of the intervention. How well was this objective achieved in the analysis?

Description of Play Therapy as the Intervention

Goals and Objectives

The goal of intervention was identified as the reduction of symptoms associated with attachment disorder. The following objectives were articulated:

1. To reduce temper tantrums occurring during periods of transition and separation
2. To increase the amount of times the client appropriately engaged in play with other children in her classroom setting
3. To reduce the amount of nightly nesting rituals in the client's home environment

---

Discussion Box 11.3

Goals should be long-range statements of treatment outcomes, while outcome objectives should represent measured amounts of progress toward the achievement of the goal. How well do these statements adhere to these expectations about how goals and outcome objectives should be stated?

Discussion Box 11.4

Now think of a way to state the goal or objective in a way that would *not* be appropriate according to our standards. A popular form of inappropriate outcome objective would be to focus on the service rather than the client's condition.

Structure and Personnel

The client was observed in her classroom for 10 weeks prior to treatment. During this baseline period, the client's target behaviors were monitored by a graduate-level social worker, who made recommendations to teaching staff and foster parents regarding appropriate ways in which to respond to the negative behavior the client was displaying. The client received play therapy services once a week for an hour each visit. The intervention was implemented by a Bachelor's level social worker with three years of early childhood work experience.

Discussion Box 11.5

The description of the structure of the intervention should reveal the form and intensity of the intervention. The personnel description should report on the credentials of the practitioners. How well are these objectives met with the statement?

The Intervention Model

The description of the model of the intervention should connect with the analysis of the dynamics of the target behavior. The model provides the conceptual or theoretical rationale for the intervention. Much of what could be said in this section of the report is included in the section that portrayed the target behavior analysis. That analysis pointed out the nature of play with the child which logically leads one to suggest something like play therapy as the intervention.

According to O'Neal:

> One way in which to successfully create a non-threatening environment is to utilize the techniques involved in client-centered play therapy. With this approach, children are given the responsibility of developing their own theme in play, while the professional working with the child actively observes and provides verbal affirmation. It is thought that by analyzing the child's play, as well as the manner in which they relate to their environment, insight into the inner conflict that they are experiencing may be gained. (O'Neal, 2004, p. 7)

Client-centered play therapy, according to O'Neal, often parallels the techniques used by Carl Rogers, one of which is the use of unconditional positive regard. Several key components of this model when applied to attachment problems include addressing the issues of avoidance of emotional and physical closeness, and the regulation of affect, cognition, and behavior. Children are able to revisit traumatic issues in a safe environment and learn new ways of coping.

Empirical support for play therapy was noted by O'Neal. She cited evidence from the literature indicating that children had a tendency to feel "less afraid and less agitated" following interventions that involved play-centered approaches. It was discovered that children tended to respond to sessions with an increased eagerness to share their stories. Children were found to express a willingness to address reactions such as fear, worry, and anger in settings that were less directed by supervising staff.

Discussion Box 11.6

Given the above analysis of the model of intervention, would it be considered justified to employ regular office-oriented therapy for this client? In other words, would it be appropriate for the practitioner to schedule hourly therapy sessions with this child in which the therapist and child would discuss various issues that are troubling this client? If so, what is your justification? If not, why not?

Discussion Box 11.7

How well does this description of the model of the intervention achieve the objective of portraying the conceptual or theoretical basis for the selection of play therapy as the intervention?

Description of the Sample and Population

With single-system research, the description of the sample is the description of the client. This has been given above. The issue of generalization of findings from the sample to the population is perhaps less important for this type of research than the group study. For the single-system design, the intent often is to discover better ways to treat an individual rather than generalize to others. However, generalization at some level is always important in evaluative research.

O'Neal described the study sample as follows:

The study sample involved Kate, a three-year-old Caucasian girl receiving childcare and outreach services from the . . . Center. During involvement in this study, Kate was residing with her sibling in a foster care placement, after being removed from the home of her biological parents due to issues surrounding neglect, as well as physical and sexual abuse. This particular sample was a non-probability sample in that Kate was specifically chosen to receive play therapy services after concern was expressed related to the maladaptive behavior that she was displaying. Kate was chosen for this sample from a combination of two three-year-old classrooms located at the . . . Center. Each classroom consists of eighteen children, all of whom are three years of age, though they exhibit a wide range of developmental capabilities. Kate was one of two children in this population that was exhibiting symptoms of attachment disorder, and was specifically chosen due to the severity of her behavior. (O'Neal, 2004, p. 13)

When the treatment of a single client is being evaluated, it is tempting only to describe the particular client. However, what O'Neal did was to go a step further so the reader of the report could get an idea of how this client was selected. You will note this child was in a special treatment agency for children in special need, of whom two were exhibiting symptoms of attachment disorder. Further, she was the one of these two considered most severe.

The major outcome of the sample description for the reader of an evaluation report is to acquire an understanding of the potential of the results to be generalized to persons not included in the study. With the single-system design, the myriad sample types described in traditional research texts does not apply. When only one person is evaluated, the reader of the report will be in the category of speculative generalization. This takes the form of employing common sense in determining whether the results are relevant to your situation.

Discussion Box 11.8

In this case example, was the sample selection procedure described with sufficient clarity to help you do this?

Measurement

Three individualized rating scales were developed to measure the client's target behaviors. One was designed to measure temper tantrums observed during periods of transition. Observations were made during the baseline period while Kate was observed in her classroom setting for one hour a week. Throughout the treatment phase, observations were made during Kate's involvement in weekly play therapy sessions, each occurring for one hour.

A second scale used in measurement pertained to the frequency of the client's engagement with other children and adults in her classroom setting. Teaching staff rated the client on this behavior each Friday during the 20-week period the study was conducted.

The final scale that was created measured the frequency of nesting rituals occurring in Kate's home environment.

> Due to the fact that the client was living in a therapeutic foster care home, it was required that daily progress notes be completed by her foster parents. This provided the observer with an opportunity to review weekly notes, which included the number of times that these rituals were observed. As was the case for the prior two scales, measurements were taken for a twenty-week period so that pre and post intervention phases could be compared in order to determine if improvement was made. (O'Neal, 2004, p. 15)

For each of these scales, a rating system was presented for the respondent that was anchored at each end like the following:

0	1	2	3	4	5	6	7	8	9	10
None										Ten

0 = *Lowest level of problem*
10 = *Highest level of problem*

The first two scales had 10 rating points, while the third had only 7. No explanation was given for this difference.

O'Neal noted that establishing reliability and validity for individualized scales is not as easy as for standardized scales such as the Beck Depression Inventory. The latter is an example of a published scale that has undergone tests of reliability and validity. However, this general issue of credibility was not abandoned. Instead, O'Neal examined face validity by asking for the opinions of professionals working in the agency where the client was served. It was their opinion that these scales did a reasonable job of measuring what was intended.

When you read the measurement section of an evaluation report, you should be able to do each of the following:

1. Visualize the form taken by various measurements tools related to client progress, such as whether the data is categorical in nature (e.g., places the client in the categories of Yes or No) or gives the client a score (e.g., a score from 0 to 25, with higher scores representing improvement).
2. Place various scores on the tool into perspective for determining practical significance (e.g., a score above 20 represents "clinical depression," or a gain of 3 points represents only a 5 percent improvement, etc.).
3. Assess the credibility of the selected measurement tools as an accurate means of measuring client progress (e.g., Was it tested for reliability and validity?).

Discussion 11.9

How well did this report achieve these outcomes for you?

Research Design

O'Neal labeled her research design the AB single-subject research design. She noted there were both baseline and treatment recordings for a single client and there were a sufficient number of recordings of target behavior in each phase to detect trends. There was only one baseline period and only one treatment period; thus, this design, according to O'Neal, fits into the category of the AB single-subject design.

Discussion Box 11.10

Did O'Neal properly label her research design?

She noted various threats to internal validity that might be relevant to her client. One of these is maturation—people naturally grow over time. The AB design, according to O'Neal, addresses maturation because the baseline should reveal the effect of maturation on the client's behavior. A second threat was history—the effect of changes in the environment independent of treatment. This was of concern because there was an incident during the treatment period in which the client was informed that she would be returning to her parents from the foster home. The AB design, according to O'Neal, does not address history as a threat to internal validity.

One of O'Neal's comments regarding these threats is as follows:

> One thing to consider in this particular study is the fact that Kate was having weekly supervised visitations with her biological parents. It is possible that these visitations resulted in an increase of maladaptive behavior being observed at home and in the school setting, thus influencing the outcome of treatment. Kate's introduction into a structured school environment would also be a possible threat to internal validity. With regards to history, it could be said that Kate's daily involvement in classroom activities, as well as interaction with teaching staff and children, was cause for positive change in the maladaptive behavior previously observed. (O'Neal, 2004, p. 18)

A critical piece of information missing from this statement was whether these events took place during *both* the baseline and treatment periods, or just during the treatment period. The question regarding research designs is whether the measured change in client behavior is due to the intervention rather than something else. Anything that takes place during both the baseline period and treatment period is controlled by the AB design, because the only thing different between these two periods is that the client received the intervention during the treatment period, but not the baseline period. Everything else was going on during both periods, so the only difference was the treatment. Under these conditions, you can best argue that the measured change in client behavior is due to the intervention rather than the other things, such as home visits or structured activities in the center. However, we are not sure about this from the report given by O'Neal.

Nevertheless, O'Neal addressed this concern in her conclusion section where she discussed limitations:

> The introduction of an ABAB design was not possible due to time constraints. However, had it been implemented, it is likely that the threat of history could have been addressed. Removing and reintroducing treatment can create parallel changes in behavior, which might have provided more detailed information supporting the hypothesis that treatment caused change in the target behavior. (O'Neal, 2004, p. 27)

The ABAB design is one in which there is a baseline period followed by a treatment period which is followed by a second baseline period (e.g., a withdrawal of treatment but a continuation of measurement). Finally, there is a reintroduction of the same treatment during the fourth phase of the process.

When you have completed your review of the research design section of an evaluation report, you should be able to determine the extent to which you are comfortable attributing the measured progress in target behavior to the intervention rather than something else. In your pursuit of this opinion, you should be able to:

1. Identify the research design employed according to recognized research design protocols (e.g., one-group pretest–posttest design, AB single-system design; comparison group design, etc.).
2. Identify the threats to internal validity that should be of special concern in this particular situation. (For example., maturation would not be of concern for the treatment of chronically depressed individuals when the treatment period is only six weeks but it may be of concern for a study evaluating the effectiveness of parent training for new mothers that lasts for six months.)
3. Identify whether the chosen design addresses the most salient threats to internal validity in the present situation.

Discussion Box 11.11

How well were these outcomes achieved in the description of the evaluation report for play therapy with Kate?

Implementation of the Intervention

No information was presented by O'Neal about means used to monitor the implementation of this intervention. This is rather normal for evaluation reports; information is usually presented in a way that assumes the planned intervention was carried out. O'Neal, however, discussed the need for creativity for anyone implementing play therapy with young children, suggesting that the reader of an evaluation report of such a study should interpret the implementation phase of the process with some caution.

Some forms of treatment are guided by practice manuals that provide details about what to do, when to do it, and under what conditions that certain therapeutic techniques should be used. Interventions that entail structured training sessions typically are accompanied by an outline of the content and training activities to be used in each training session. Monitoring of the implementation of the intervention can include the requirement of detailed notes for each session provided by the practitioner, along with a review of how much the actual implementation deviated from the planned intervention.

Discussion Box 11.12

What is one idea you have about how to monitor the intervention for the client in this study of play therapy?

Collection and analysis of data

Only one study hypothesis was presented by O'Neal—Kate will exhibit reduced symptoms of attachment disorder after ten weeks of involvement in client-centered play therapy. There were three symptoms of attachment disorder that were measured—temper tantrums, engagement with peers, and nesting rituals. In this case, it would have been better if three hypotheses were stated, one for each form of behavior measured.

Discussion Box 11.13

The hypothesis for temper tantrums could have been stated as follows: The client's number of temper tantrums will be lower in the treatment period than the baseline period. Write the hypothesis for (1) engagement, and (2) nesting rituals.

Analysis of Temper Tantrums

During the baseline period, according to O'Neal, the client exhibited a great deal of difficulty transitioning as evidenced by an average of 4.4 temper tantrums each day of observation by staff. This behavior included screaming, crying, throwing objects, and becoming physically aggressive toward other children and adults. During the treatment phase, the client revealed improvement as evidenced by an average of 2 temper tantrums during each observation hour. The scores for each period are displayed in Figure 11.1.

O'Neal explained that the major deviation from the pattern of recordings during the treatment period (4 temper tantrums during week 17) possibly was due to the fact that the client was informed on this week that she would be returning home.

O'Neal applied the standard deviation approach to statistical analysis for her data regarding each of the three target behaviors. With the standard deviation approach, you compute the mean and standard deviation of baseline scores as well as the mean of the treatment recordings. You determine whether the treatment recordings are significantly better than the baseline recordings by determining whether the treatment mean is two standard deviations better than the baseline. The basic standard for the social sciences ($p < .05$) was accepted in this case. Two standard deviations represents the p value of .05. In other words, if a treatment mean is at least two standard deviations different from the baseline mean, you can say that the treatment mean is significantly different ($p < .05$).

There are several steps in computation for determining statistical significance. After computing the standard deviation of baseline scores, you multiply this figure by 2 to obtain the figure that represents two standard deviations. The next computation varies according to whether your objective is to increase the client's scores or to decrease these scores. If the objective is to increase the scores, you would add the two standard deviation figure to the baseline mean to determine the score that is to be compared to the treatment mean. If the objective is to decrease the scores, you would subtract this figure from the baseline mean.

For temper tantrums, the mean for the baseline was 4.4 while the treatment mean was 2.0. In order for the treatment mean to be significantly better than the baseline mean it must be at least two standard deviations lower. The standard deviation of baseline recordings was 0.52 (rounded off).

The computation of statistical significance can be illustrated as follows:

4.4 (baseline mean) – 1.04 (two standard deviations) = 3.36

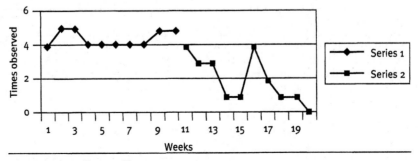

FIGURE 11.1   *Temper Tantrums*

Thus, the figure the treatment mean must beat is 3.36. In other words, the treatment mean must be equal to or less than 3.36. In the situation with this client, the treatment mean was 2.

Discussion Box 11.14

There are two questions to answer in regard to the above information:

1. Did the above data reveal that temper tantrums were significantly lower in the treatment period than the baseline period?
2. What issue in research is represented by the idea of statistical significance? Is it relevance, chance, validity, or reliability?

Data on Engagement

Engagement was measured on a 10-point scale, with higher scores representing better functioning. The baseline mean for engagement was 2.0, while the standard deviation for these scores was .42. The treatment mean was 1.8.

Discussion Box 11.15

Was this hypothesis supported by the data: The client's level of engagement will be higher in the treatment period than in the baseline period? Explain.

Data on the Nesting Ritual

The nesting ritual was measured on a 7-point scale, with lower scores representing better behavior. The baseline mean for nesting rituals for the client was 6.1, while the standard deviation for these scores was .74. The treatment mean was 4.5.

Discussion Box 11.16

Was this following hypothesis supported: The client will have a lower level of nesting rituals in the treatment period than the baseline? Explain.

Drawing Conclusions

O'Neal began the conclusion section of her report as follows: "In this study, it was found that the client being served by the . . . .Center exhibited decreased symptoms of attachment disorder following her involvement in a ten-week period of client-centered play therapy" (2004, p. 25). She went on to discuss the major deviation in target behavior during the treatment period upon the child's learning that she was to return home. She noted that a return to improved behavior followed that one-week deviation, suggesting there was some long-term effect of intervention.

Discussion Box 11.17

Do you agree with O'Neal's basic conclusion?

This beginning was followed by a discussion of the limitations of the study. One of these limitations noted by O'Neal was the sample of one which seriously limits the generalization of results. Another was the research design, which addresses maturation but fails to address some of the other common threats to internal validity. Measurement was also mentioned because an individualized scale was used which had not been subjected to normal tests of reliability and validity, as is the case for most standardized instruments.

Discussion Box 11.18

Do you agree with O'Neal's discussion of the limitations of this study?

Another issue is practical significance. Can you put these results into perspective? Are they noteworthy? Was there enough client gain to satisfy your expectations or justify the resources expended?

Discussion Box 11.19

What are your comments about practical significance? Was there good guidance offered for the determination of practical significance?

References

O'Neal, Erin E. (2004). The effectiveness of client-centered play therapy for a child with attachment disorder. Unpublished paper presented in a graduate course in the School of Social Work, East Carolina University. Used with permission.

James, B. (1989). *Treating Traumatized Children.* New York, NY: The Free Press.

12

Identifying and Analyzing Target Behavior

This chapter examines the identification and analysis of target behavior at a level that exceeds that which has been presented in prior chapters. If you would like to review the previous material, you can turn your attention to the quiz given in Exhibit 12.1. This should give you an idea of how well you have assimilated the basic knowledge already presented about analyzing target behavior.

Identifying and Analyzing Target Behavior

The tasks of identifying and analyzing target behavior are often categorized by the general topic of problem formulation in research. There are three major steps in the natural process of problem formulation in evaluation research. The first is the definition of the target behavior. How are we defining depression? What is included in our definition of family violence—only physical acts, or verbal acts as well? Is our target behavior better characterized as self-efficacy or self-esteem? These are the kinds of questions examined in the first phase of problem formulation.

The second phase is the analysis of the target behavior. What are the causes of depression? What are the needs of victims of family violence? How are stressors, stress, stress buffers, and stress consequences related conceptually? These are the kinds of questions pursued in the second phase of problem formulation.

The third phase is the search for evidence related to responses to the target behavior. What treatment models have worked best for depression? To what extent have multimodel approaches to the treatment of family violence been found to be more or less effective than approaches that focus on one theme such as the psychodynamics of the abuser? These are the kinds of question pursued in the third phase.

EXHIBIT 12.1 • *Quiz Questions that Reflect on the Content from Prior Chapters*

Consider the following questions and determine the answer. Then review the brief discussion that follows.

1. Which of the following are contributions that a clear *definition* of target behavior makes to other tasks in the evaluation research process?
   a. It determines the focus of the intervention goals and objectives and provides guidance on the selection of a means to measure target behavior.
   b. It determines the research design to be employed by its clarification of threats to internal validity.
   c. It determines how well the study findings can be generalized to persons not included in the present study.
   d. It provides guidance on the selection of an intervention—i.e., you have some guidance on whether it is more wise to employ Treatment Model A or Treatment Model B.

2. Which of the following are contributions that a clear *analysis* of target behavior makes to other tasks in the evaluation research process?
   a. It determines the focus of the intervention goals and objectives and provides guidance on the selection of a means to measure target behavior.
   b. It determines the research design to be employed by its clarification of threats to internal validity.
   c. It determines how well the study findings can be generalized to persons not included in the present study.
   d. It provides guidance on the selection of an intervention—i.e., you have some guidance on whether it is more wise to employ Treatment Model A or Treatment Model B.

3. Causation is a major issue to be addressed in which task in the evaluation research process?
   a. The definition of target behavior
   b. The analysis of target behavior
   c. Both of the above
   d. None of the above

Well, how do you think you did? Did these questions seem familiar and easy to answer? Did you find yourself wanting to go back and read the prior chapters?

Let's look at the answers. Problem definition provides guidance on what should be the goals and objectives of intervention as well as how we should measure client progress. So, the answer to question 1 is option a. Problem analysis provides guidance on the selection of the intervention; thus, the answer to question 2 is option d. The answer to question 3 is option b—the analysis of target behavior. If you are confused about these answers, you should review the previous chapters that addressed this theme.

Any time we examine a task in the evaluation research process that has a natural sequence of phases, it is wise to review the old saying "Don't put the cart before the horse!" For problem formulation, we should not start with a treatment model and go backwards. In other words, we should not decide that we are going to use the model known as dialectical behavioral therapy, because we like it, and our next task is to identify the client on which we will use this model. Why? Someone once said "When the only tool in your toolbox is a hammer, every problem looks like a nail." We are more likely to provide an inaccurate, or highly limited, assessment of the client's behavior if we start with the choice of a treatment model.

Discussion Box 12.1

Given this statement, what might be wrong with an agency stating the goal of the agency as "To provide structural family therapy to persons in need"?

Selecting and Defining the Target Behavior

The procedures for selecting and defining the target behavior will vary with the type of evaluation being conducted. If you are evaluating a single client, you and your client will have much flexibility in selecting the targets of change. The client often presents many problems, some of which are selected for your initial focus and others reserved for later. Of those selected initially, you may not choose to conduct an evaluation of all of them. A high school boy at risk for dropping out of school may come from a multiproblem family that presents a multitude of possible targets for intervention. After your assessment, you may choose to evaluate the client's progress in the improvement of self-esteem, school absenteeism, and grades. You may also be treating parent–child relations but chose not to evaluate them. And you may decide that the family's economic condition is a problem that is better handled by other services rather than what you can offer.

If you are evaluating a group intervention, you are probably working with others and with some agency precedent. This means you may have less flexibility in making choices for targets. You may have been assigned to conduct a support group for abused women or a parent education group for abusive parents. These clients have something in common that is the target of intervention. This means your task may be to clarify the definition of the target behavior and choose a method of measurement, but you may not have options for selecting the target behaviors yourself.

If you are conducting a program evaluation, your task may be to examine agency documents and interview staff to ascertain the targets of intervention. A good source of documents would be funding sources and grant applications. Comprehensive program evaluations are more likely to be conducted of local programs funded by grants and contracted for specific periods of time than by ongoing services funded by governmental agencies or the United Way. The latter sources of funds were common in past decades but are becoming less and less the form of funding of human services. For example, the state of North Carolina has diverted mental health funds to local nongovernmental agencies that contract to deliver specific services with specific objectives related to output and outcome. In this state, you do not have the option to become a therapist with a county mental health clinic with a salary and regular working hours and little accountability for output or outcome, as used to be the case. Today, it is more likely that a client "no-show" means less income for the practitioner.

A text by Bloom, Fischer, and Orme (2003) provide suggestions for selecting targets when you are working with a single client. They use the word target to refer to "the specific object of preventive or interventive services that is relevant to a given situation" (p. 87). One initial approach is to have the client take a general test designed to measure a wide range of symptoms or problems. These authors list a number of scales designed to accomplish this task. One example is the Brief Adult Assessment Scale, described as follows:

> The BAAS is a self-report measure that helps you to better assess and understand the severity or magnitude of adult client problems across 16 different areas of personal and social functioning: depression, self-esteem problems, partner problems, sexual discord, problems with a child, personal stress, problems with friends, aggression, problems with work associates, family problems, suicide, nonphysical abuse, physical abuse, problems at work, alcohol abuse, and drug use. (Bloom, Fischer, and Orme, 2003, p. 231)

Another approach is to make a list of common problems identified by your clients. Perhaps most of the problems listed are rarely mentioned by your clients. This would suggest that you develop your own list or have the agency develop one for all to use with the clients of your agency.

Discussion Box 12.2

Think of a familiar human service intervention or program. What framework for problem identification might work well here? Would something like the BAAS be useful? Or should the agency develop its own special list of common client concerns? Or is the problem addressed by this intervention so clear and concrete you already know how to define it and you know of a means of measuring client progress? Indicate your answer.

Another approach suggested by Bloom, Fischer, and Orme (2002) is having the client talk about his or her concerns and making a list, which is discussed and prioritized. If there are five problems and they can be ranked from one to five, you can have a discussion of how far down this list is it realistic to go in the identification of targets for treatment and evaluation. In the selection of targets for treatment, you and the client need to be realistic, given the resources available to you to offer help. From the list of targets for intervention, you select targets for evaluation. You can select all of them, or only a few. You should not, however, select targets for intervention based on their convenience for evaluation. The client's greatest concerns should be the targets for intervention, whether or not they can be conveniently evaluated.

A major task in this process, according to these authors, is the clarification of vague terms such as "My husband is immature," "My wife doesn't care about me anymore," or "My husband doesn't care about what goes on around the house." Upon further discussion, these vague terms are turned into more specific behaviors such as "My husband stays out late at night with his friends," "My husband does not help with chores around the house," or "My wife rarely wants to have sex."

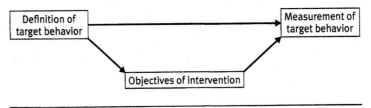

FIGURE 12.1 *Essential Relationships among Definition, Objectives, and Measurement*

A clear definition of the target behavior provides guidance for the determination of the goals and objectives for intervention as well as the methods to be used to measure client progress. A goal is a long-range statement of what is to be accomplished for the client. An outcome objective is a statement of a measured amount of progress toward goal accomplishment. Both statements identify outcomes for the client. For a child at risk for dropping out of school, the goal may be to prevent this behavior, while the objectives may be to reduce absenteeism, increase self-esteem, and improve study habits. The relationships among target behavior definition, treatment objectives, and measurement are displayed in Figure 12.1. Your treatment objectives should focus specifically on the way you have defined your target behavior. The measurement tool you employ should do the same. And, of course, the focus of the objectives should be the same as the focus of the measurement tool.

Discussion Box 12.3

Think of a target behavior that might be addressed by a particular human service. Provide the following information: (a) the label of the target behavior, (b) the objective of treatment, and (c) the concept that should be measured by the selected tool for measuring client progress. This can be simple, and you might think you are stating the obvious, but do so anyway.

    a.

    b.

    c.

The simple purpose of this above discussion assignment is to make sure you are focusing all three of these things on a single concept. If self-esteem is the target behavior, it should be the focus of the intervention, and it should be the thing measured. Don't make the mistake as defining school dropouts as the target behavior, but focusing both your objective and your measurement device upon self-esteem. If you plan to measure the incidence of school dropouts, it would make sense to state your behavior in terms of school dropouts and your objective as the same. But if you are measuring self-esteem, this should be the focus of the target behavior and the objective.

EXHIBIT 12.2 • *Sets of Statements Related to Depression*

Set A

I get upset with myself when I make mistakes.
I have negative thoughts about myself.
I seem to blame myself and be very critical of myself when things go wrong.
Praising yourself is being selfish.

Set B

I may change from happy to sad and back again several times in a single week.
I am frequently "down in the dumps."
I'm not often really elated.
Most people see me as moody.

Set C

I cannot be happy unless most people I know admire me.

If a person disagrees with me, it probably indicates he does not like me.
If a person asks for help, it is a sign of weakness.
If I am to be a worthwhile person, I must be the best in at least one way.

Set D

I feel down-hearted, blue, and sad.
I have crying spells or feel like it.
I feel that others would be better off if I were dead.
I have trouble sleeping through the night.

Clarity in problem definition provides guidance for measurement. Let's consider the category of personal mood as a potential target for measurement. Examine the four sets of statements given in Exhibit 12.2.

In Exhibit 12.2, did you notice the theme that was common for each set? Each is related to depression in some way but only one is viewed as a direct measure of depression. Each set of statements comes from a measurement scale. One scale is designed to measure depression. Another is designed to measure general mood. A third is designed to measure dysfunctional thinking, and the fourth is designed to measure self-reinforcement.

Discussion Box 12.4

Now go back to this list of four sets of expressions and identify (1) which one is measuring depression, (2) which one is used to measure general mood, (3) which one measures dysfunctional thinking, and (4) which one is designed to measure self-reinforcement.

Each of these scales is presented in Corcoran and Fischer (1987). Set A comes from the Frequency of Self-Reinforcement Questionnaire. It is designed to measure a person's tendency to encourage, support, and value themselves. These tendencies are viewed as possible causes of depression. Set B comes from the Mood Survey, designed to measure happy and sad moods as traits. It is designed to measure two dimensions of mood: level of mood, and reactivity to situations. Set C comes from the Dysfunctional Attitude Scale, designed to measure cognitive distortions that are often presented by persons who are depressed. It is designed to represent seven major value systems—approval, love, achievement, perfectionism, entitlement, omnipotence, and autonomy. Set D comes from the Self-Rating Depression Scale, designed to measure depression.

When you responded to the question for the box, you had a distinct disadvantage of not having an operational definition of each of these concepts. So, if you did not do well, don't worry about it.

Scores on these scales would be expected to have a positive correlation with one another because they are related to depression, but only one is a direct measure of depression. People with a tendency to have negative self-reinforcement attitudes are more prone to depression than others. People with dysfunctional thinking are likely to be more depressed than others. And people who are not happy or are moody are more likely to be depressed than others. So, the question to pose for yourself would be "How am I defining my target behavior that should be changed?" Be sure not to define your target as dysfunctional thinking and then chose a depression scale to measure it. And don't define the target as depression and then choose a dysfunctional thinking scale to measure it. Because two psychological constructs are related is not a justification for using a tool for one to measure the other.

Let's review with a little challenge question. Let's define *stress* as a state of psychological tension and *stressor* as an environment condition or event that often leads to stress. Consider the following questions that might be used to measure various behaviors.

1. Do you feel uptight several times a day?
2. Have you experienced a loss of an important relationship in the past month through marital separation, death, and so forth?
3. Have you been highly tense on a regular basis in the past week?

Discussion Box 12.5

Which one of these questions is best suited to be included in your scale designed to measure stressors?

Let's review. The first one would measure stress because it deals with a state of psychological tension. The third one does the same. But the middle one refers to an environmental event that could cause tension, so it is the one you should have selected.

Analyzing Target Behavior

The purpose of target behavior analysis is to obtain guidance on the search for an appropriate intervention. If the cause of the problem is ignorance, a logical solution would be training. If the cause of the problem is dysfunctional thinking patterns, the logical solution would be a model of treatment that focuses on thinking patterns and has a method for changing these patterns. If a cause of a young child's acting out behavior is the lack of a constructive outlet for expression, something like play therapy would be a logical solution.

Sometimes the behavior analysis is best served by the examination of causation. Other times, it may need a different emphasis. For example, it would do little good for you to examine the causes of mental retardation when you are working with people with this condition because it cannot be reversed. Instead, an analysis of the needs of persons with this condition would be more appropriate. In fact, the analysis of needs is always appropriate regardless of the type of target behavior you are addressing.

In the book *Treatments that work* is an article on psychosocial treatments for conduct disorder in children and adolescents (Kazdin, 2002). This article has a table that lists factors that place youth at risk for conduct disorder. These factors could be viewed as causes and a guide to needs, both of which should be addressed in the design of an intervention. Among the factors listed in this article is a difficult child temperament, characterized by negative mood and low adaptability to change. This is a factor that might be genetic or generated in very early socialization. Thus, it may not be an appropriate target for change. Instead, it perhaps should be the focus of strategies that help the child and others to adjust to this reality. Another factor listed by Kazdin is intellectual deficiency, another factor not easily changed by an intervention. Among the other risk factors are:

- Poor bonding or attachment to conventional values.
- Criminal behavior of the parents.
- Harsh parental discipline.
- Inconsistent parental discipline.
- Low affection and warmth displayed by parents of the child.
- Socioeconomic disadvantages, such as poverty, poor housing, etc.
- Various forms of family dysfunction.
- Exposure to violence.

Discussion Box 12.6

What does this suggest to you? Should the child with this condition be subjected to psychotherapy? Or should the parents and other caretakers be given more attention so they can learn ways to help the child?

The latter has been the focus of interventions. Not surprisingly, the most widely supported intervention by evidence is one known as parent management training. This intervention focuses on training the parent to alter behavior toward the child.

It might be useful for you to chart the things that contribute to a particular condition and the things that are the consequence. In an earlier part of this book, a stressor was defined as an element in the environment that can cause stress, while stress was defined as psychological tension. Stress buffers are those things that can alleviate stress. Problems caused by stress would be viewed as the consequences of stress. This model of analysis can be depicted in Exhibit 12.2.

From Figure 12.2, you can see how losing a job would be an example of a stressor which could lead to stress, but which could be reduced by a stress buffer such as social support. Thus, we would expect someone who lost a job but had good social support to have less stress than someone who lost a job but did not have good social support. The more stress you experience, the more likely you are to suffer from minor health problems such as headaches, sleeplessness, and so forth.

When you have completed your analysis of target behavior, you should be in a position to engage in an informed dialogue about what interventions would be expected to have the best chance of working. And you should be able to select one that works for your client.

Discussion Box 12.7

Provide a statement about the analysis of a selected target behavior that makes sense to you. This analysis can focus upon the causes of this behavior, or the needs of persons experiencing this behavior, or both. If you want to be really sophisticated, you can draw a causal chart like you see in Figure 12.2.

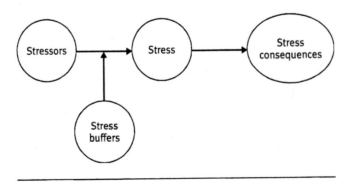

FIGURE 12.2   *Causal Chart for Stress*

Seeking Evidence

The literature is replete with sources of evidence regarding treatment effectiveness. Before we encounter "evidence" in a formal sense, let's examine a few related concepts. **Best practice** usually refers to interventions that are believed by the experts to have the most promise of being effective. Sometimes these practices are founded on good scientific evidence, and sometimes they are not. The term **science-based intervention** is sometimes used to justify a program design on the basis that it is a logical solution to a given problem, given our understanding of the dynamics of that problem. Parent management training may have been designed on the basis of an understanding of risk factors for youth with conduct disorder. If so, it could be labeled a science-based intervention. However, it is not considered to be an evidence-based intervention until it is specifically tested with clients and has data showing that it is effective.

In a broad sense, evidence may be viewed as any information that is employed in determining action. For the purposes of evaluation research, however, we will define *evidence* as information collected from sources external to the decision maker's intuition that are deemed credible by key actors in the social system. Evidence may refer to one specific piece of data. A body of evidence, however, normally refers to evidence that has been systematically collected in accordance with the spirit of scientific inquiry. Thus, a body of information that has been gathered for the purpose of proving a point is inconsistent with this definition. For example, a report would *not* be considered credible if someone had found 10 studies on the effectiveness of a model of treatment but only reported on the 3 studies that had the preferred outcome.

The above definition of evidence clearly excludes the intuitive judgment of decision makers. The statement "My 20 years of clinical experience is my evidence" would be inconsistent with the definition of evidence given in this book. The clinical judgment of an individual may be quite accurate in setting the proper course of action, but it would not constitute "evidence."

Evidence-based practice is the explicit use of the best available evidence in making decisions about the care of individuals. The concept of evidence-based practice, as well as the definition given here, is substantially credited to Sackett and others from the field of medicine (Sackett, Richardson, Rosenberg, and Haynes, 2000). It is generally recognized that evidence-based practice requires the following behaviors of the practitioner:

A clear statement of the research question that addresses the practice goal to be achieved
A search of the literature for the answer to the question
The critical review of the literature as applied to the practice goal
The sharing of information with the client in the determination of the course of action

A very useful source of information on evidence is the book *Treatments that work* (Nathan & Gorman, 2002). This book has 25 chapters, each of which is devoted to a specific clinical condition such as attention-deficit hyperactivity disorder, alcohol use, depression, schizophrenia, bipolar disorder, and so forth. Each chapter is written by set of authors familiar with the particular condition. These chapters provide a summary of various studies that have been conducted of different treatments for the particular condition.

In this book, individual studies of treatment success are classified into categories according to their level of methodological sophistication. Level 1 represents the most sophisticated studies. These entail the use of experimental designs where treated clients are compared to nontreated clients, each of whom has been assigned to a group on a random basis. In these studies, special attention is given to validity of measurement and methods for assuring the consistent application of intervention methods. Statistical assessment, of course, is also included.

Level 2 studies are those with an identifiable flaw that is not considered fatal. This includes studies without the opportunity for random assignment of persons to the treatment and control groups. Level 3 studies have significant limitations, but their results are considered worthy of use as exploratory studies—i.e., providing guidance on the direction for more sophisticated studies, but not for major clinical decisions or policy choices. Three more levels of studies were conceptualize for this book, but they were not levels normally considered to be examples of research studies. This would include papers that offered clinical opinions and suggestions but no empirical data.

One example from this work is a chapter on psychosocial treatment for alcohol use disorder (Finney & Moos, 2002). This chapter presented a review of 15 different approaches to the psychosocial treatment of alcohol abuse, each of which had been subjected to at least 3 studies of Type 1 (highly sophisticated) or Type 2 (studies with minor limitations) varieties. Among the conclusions supported by this review are:

- Approaches to treatment in the general category of cognitive-behavioral (e.g., social skills training, motivational counseling, behavioral marital therapy) were among those approaches rated most effective.
- Confrontational approaches, general education, and general counseling were among those rated least effective.
- There seems to be a negative correlation between the cost of the treatment approach and treatment success—that is, the most expensive models do not do as well as less expensive models.
- Lower intensity treatment over an extended period is more effective for most patients than higher level intensity over a brief period.
- Persons with severe problems and dual diagnosis need treatment of a higher intensity than others.
- Relationship-oriented treatment is more effective for patients who are functioning better, while cognitive-behavioral therapy works better for those with antisocial personality disorders.
- In general, the lower the level of psychosocial functioning of the patient, the more useful are treatments that are highly structured.
- Therapist characteristics seem to have a stronger effect on treatment outcome than the type of treatment applied. In general, patients of therapists who are more interpersonally skilled, less confrontational, and/or more empathic experience better outcomes.

Let's review these generalizations from the evidence regarding the treatment of substance abuse with some examples. One of the approaches that has been common for some substance-abuse counselors in the past is the confrontation of the client's denial of a problem, a condition that is rather common in persons with alcoholism. When the client says something that suggests the denial of an alcohol problem, for example, the counselor would confront the client with the evidence of their problem with drinking.

Discussion Box 12.8

What do you think of this technique given the evidence mentioned?

Discussion Box 12.9

If you were reviewing several candidates for the position of substance-abuse counselor, upon which of the following would you place more emphasis—the model of treatment the candidates are most likely to employ, or the extent to which the candidate exhibited empathy and interpersonal skill?

Another useful source of evidence is *Evidence-based social work practice with families* by Corcoran (2000). This book has sections on family treatment with children, family treatment with adolescents, family treatment with adults, and family treatment with the elderly. Treatment approaches regarding child abuse, conduct disorder, attention-deficit hyperactivity disorder, eating disorders, family violence, and caregivers for the elderly are among the themes of chapters in this work. *What works in child welfare* (Kluger, Alexander, & Curtis, 2000) is another source that can be useful for the practitioner seeking evidence. This book has 36 chapters, including those on family preservation, child sexual abuse, residential care, adoptions, and child care, among others. A collection of articles on various aspects of evidence-based practice, including chapters on evidence regarding selected conditions, can be found in the *Evidence-based practice manual* by Roberts & Yeager (2004).

Discussion Box 12.10

Find one piece of evidence that supports, or discredits, a particular program or intervention. List the evidence and offer your thoughts on its level of credibility.

Cultural Diversity and Problem Analysis

This chapter deals primarily with problem formulation as a general task without reference to any particular population. However, the implications of culture upon problem definition and analysis cannot be overlooked because one must understand both the overt and subtle dynamics of the population being studied. This understanding informs both problem definition and problem analysis. For example, Taylor and others (1997) draw our attention to the overemphasis upon selected social problems when researchers study African Americans. This book moves from the deficit perspective to one that examines issues such as cohabitation, parenting, grandparenting, mate selection, and so forth. The perspective here is that members of this population have issues related to general development rather than simply exhibiting certain social problems. As you seek research questions, perhaps you should be cognizant of this issue.

The analysis of problems for research purposes relies upon a keen understanding of the dynamics of the population under study. You should avoid relying on too much of a generalization about the population in general when your study group includes members of minority groups because there may be differences between subgroups within your study population that should be considered. A book by Jackson (1988) provides an example. In this book, you can review similarities and differences in aging processes between African Americans and others. A book by Neighbors and Jackson (1996) focuses on unique aspects of mental health for the African American. Examples include hypertension and stress denial. The potential misdiagnosis of African Americans through the DSM diagnostic system was discussed by Taylor (1997).

The key points here are that you should consider culture when selecting a research question and studying the dynamics of the population under study. You should avoid stereotypes in this regard. This includes overreliance on literature written by and for members of populations different in culture from those in your study population. This means, by inference, that all major groups in your study population should be considered and you should not rely on literature especially relevant only to one of these groups.

Summary

In this chapter, you have examined the evaluation tasks associated with the definition and analysis of target behavior. You have seen that clear definition guides both the articulation of outcome objectives and the selection of the means for measuring client progress. You have seen that your level of clarity of behavior definition can vary greatly from rather vague to highly specific. You have seen that the analysis of this behavior can guide both the selection of the intervention and the evaluation design. If lack of knowledge is a major cause of your target behavior, it stands to reason that some form of training would be successful. If dysfunctional thinking has caused your depression, it makes sense that a form of treatment is employed that addresses this type of thinking. You have examined the concept of evidence as a topic of particular importance to the analysis of the target behavior because you want to know what kinds of interventions have worked better in the past.

Quiz

The following is a quiz which may be used as a pretest, to determine if you need to read this chapter, or as a posttest, to determine how well you read it. Answers are given at the end of the reference list.

1. There are three steps in the natural process of problem formulation with clients. One is the analysis of the target behavior with regard to such topics as its causes and needs associated with it. Another is the search for evidence regarding the treatment of this behavior. Which of the following is the other step in this process?
   a. Selection of a research design
   b. Definition of the target behavior
   c. Selection of the intervention
   d. None of the above

2. Which of the following statements would be most helpful in the selection of target behaviors for evaluation with a single client?
   a. My husband is immature.
   b. My husband is not sensitive.
   c. My husband doesn't help with chores around the house.
   d. Both a and b above.

3. The Dysfunctional Attitude Scale is designed to measure cognitive distortions often exhibited by persons who are depressed. Which one of the following items is on that scale?
   a. I am not often really elated.
   b. I have crying spells or feel like it.
   c. If a person disagrees with me, it probably indicates he does not like me.
   d. All of the above.

4. Concepts such as practice wisdom, practice intuition, evidence, evidence-based practice, best practice, and science-based practice can add to our confusion if not properly distinguished conceptually. Which of the following is the best definition of the concept of evidence?
   a. Information that clinicians consider helpful to making practice decisions, including their own practice experiences
   b. Information from the opinions of professional peers about what works

   c. Information collected from sources external to the decision maker's intuition that is deemed credible by key actors in the social system
   d. Information collected from randomized controlled trials (using only experimental research designs) regarding the effectiveness of a particular intervention regarding a particular target behavior

5. In research, the concept of evidence has special meaning that may be different from how this term is used in fields other than research. We can also think of the concept of "body of evidence" as reflecting a reasonable collection of evidence. Which of the following statements is/are consistent with the concept of body of evidence?
   a. My 20 years of clinical experience is my evidence. It has taught me valuable lessons about what works and what does not work in the treatment of aggression in adolescent males. For example, I have learned that confrontation is not effective.
   b. From my review of the literature, I was able to find only 18 studies that reported evaluations of multidynamic therapy in the treatment of aggression in adolescent males, of which 10 reported success in that treated clients had lower aggression than nontreated males in comparison groups.
   c. Both of the above.
   d. None of the above.

6. Which of the following would be legitimate ways to identify client problems?
   a. Administer a multiproblem scale to each client.
   b. Develop a list of common problems of agency clients and develop a scale from this list to administer to clients.
   c. Ask the individual client to list problems they are encountering and discuss priorities among these problems.
   d. All of the above.

7. We can distinguish between the concepts of best practice, science-based practice, and

evidence-based practice. Evidence-based practice refers to:

a. The use of information collected from sources external to the decision maker's intuition that are deemed credible by key actors in the social system.

b. The use of interventions that are believed by the experts to have the most promise of being effective.

c. Using a process that seeks scientific evidence about what treatments have worked with the given client's target behavior, sharing that evidence with the client, and collaborating with the client on the choice of an intervention plan.

d. Designing an intervention or program based on what is known from scientific research on the dynamics of that problem (For example, if depression is caused by distorted thinking, we will design an intervention that addresses thinking patterns.)

8. Consider the human service agency that establishes the mission (or goal) of delivering cognitive-behavioral therapy to those in need. Which of the following common-sense principles of science are violated by this statement?

a. Two heads are better than one.

b. Don't put the cart before the horse.

c. Some things happen just by chance.

d. When you wear the research hat, you should be cautious in your conclusions.

References

Bloom, M., Fischer, J., and Orme, J. G. (2003). *Evaluating practice: Guidelines for the Accountable Professional (4th ed.)*. Boston: Allyn & Bacon.

Corcoran, J. (2000). *Evidence-based social work practice with families*. New York: Springer.

Corcoran, K. (1987). *Measures for clinical practice: A sourcebook*. New York: Free Press.

Finney, J. W., and Moos, R. H. (2002). Psychosocial treatments for alcohol use disorder. In Nathan and Gorman (Eds.), *A guide to treatments that work (2nd ed.)* (pp. 157–168) New York: Oxford University Press.

Jackson, J. S. (1988). Mental health problems among black Americans: Research needs. Division of Child, Youth, and Family Services Newsletter, 11 (2). American Psychological Association.

Kazdin, A. E. (2002). Psychosocial treatments for conduct disorder in children and adolescents. In Nathan and Gorman (Eds.), *A guide to treatments that work (2nd ed.)* (pp. 157–168) New York: Oxford University Press.

Kluger, M. P., Alexander, G., and Curtis, P. A. (2000). *What works in child welfare*. Washington: CWLA Press.

Nathan, P. E., and Gorman, J. M. (Eds). 2002. *A guide to treatments that work (2nd ed.)* New York: Oxford University Press.

Neighbors, H. W., and Jackson, J. S. (1996). *Mental health in black America*. Thousand Oaks: Sage Publications.

Roberts, A. R., and Yeager, K. R. (2004). *Evidence-based practice manual: Research and outcome measures in health and human services*. Oxford: Oxford University Press.

Sackett, D. L., Straus, S. E., Richardson, W. S., Rosenberg, W., and Haynes, R. B. (2000). *Evidence-based medicine: How to practice and teach EBM (2nd. ed.)* New York: Churchill Livingstone.

Taylor, R. J., Jackson, J. S., and Chatters, R. M. (1997). *Family life in black America*. Thousand Oaks: Sage Press.

Taylor, R. J. (1997). *African American research perspectives, 3*(2), 1–74.

York, R. O. (1998). *Conducting social work research*. Boston: Allyn & Bacon.

Answers to the Quiz

1. b

2. c

3. c

4. c

5. b

6. d

7. c

8. b

13

Describing the Intervention or Program

In this chapter, you will review an elaboration of the content about interventions that was introduced in the first few chapters of this book. In previous chapters, you were introduced to the essential components of the description of the intervention. In this chapter, you will develop more specific competence in this endeavor, by reviewing more guidelines and examples and being called upon to articulate various aspects of a familiar intervention yourself. If you would like to review that basic material given in prior chapters, turn your attention to Exhibit 13.1.

What follows is a presentation of the objectives for the present chapter. As with other chapters, there is a quiz at the end that can be used either as an exemption device or as a posttest which can measure how well you have acquired the knowledge offered in this chapter.

At the completion of this chapter, you will be able to:

1. Distinguish between a clinical intervention and a human service program.

2. Describe the model of a familiar intervention or program sufficient to facilitate replication by others.

3. Describe the structure of a familiar intervention with regard both to form and intensity.

4. Articulate both the goals and outcome objectives of a familiar intervention or program in accordance with selected standards that assure guidance in the selection of the means to measure client progress and the methods of analyzing data.

5. Describe the personnel of a familiar intervention or program that facilitates replication by others.

EXHIBIT 13.1 • *Reflecting on Content from Prior Chapters*

Prior to this elaboration, let's examine a few questions that were covered before. What is the answer to each of the following questions?

1. Which of the following are things are included in the description of the intervention?
   a. The structure of the intervention (therapy sessions, training sessions, daily residential care, etc.)
   b. The goals and objectives of the intervention
   c. The model that guides the intervention
   d. All of the above
2. Which of the following is the missing piece of the description of the intervention in this list?
   a. The design of the research study
   b. The personnel who will deliver the intervention
   c. The study sample to be employed
   d. None of the above
3. Which of the following is a good statement of one of the goals of the Adolescent Parenting Program?
   a. To improve the quality of life
   b. To provide quality services to adolescent mothers
   c. To reduce the incidence of child abuse and neglect
   d. All of the above
4. Which of the following would be the best statement of one of the outcome objectives, rather than one of the goals, of the High School Dropout Prevention Program delivered to at-risk students in a middle school?
   a. To improve the quality of life
   b. To reduce the risk factors of poor self-esteem and poor study habits
   c. To reduce the incidence of high school dropouts
   d. To attempt to get parents to be more sensitive to their children's needs
5. The Adolescent Parenting Program employs support groups for adolescent mothers along with individual counseling and parent training sessions. Which of the following would best characterize the structure of this program?
   a. To prevent further adolescent pregnancies
   b. To reduce child abuse and neglect

   c. To provide support group services on a monthly basis, counseling on a weekly basis, and parent training sessions on a bi-weekly basis
   d. To provide quality services to adolescent mothers
6. Cognitive-behavioral theory might be described in which of the following parts of the description of the intervention?
   a. Structure
   b. Model or content
   c. Personnel
   d. Goals and objectives

Let's look at these questions. There are four parts to the description of the intervention that were described in previous chapters—structure, goals and objectives, model (or content), and personnel. Thus, the answer to question 1 is "d—All of the above" and for question 2 the answer is "b—The personnel who will deliver the intervention."

The best answer for question 3 is "c—To reduce the incidence of child neglect and abuse" because it specifies the long-range outcome expected from this program. Option "a" is too broad to provide guidance, while option "b" is process-oriented (in other words, it speaks of services to be delivered rather than outcomes to be achieved).

For question 4, the correct answer is "b—To reduce the risk factors of poor self-esteem and poor study habits." This is a statement of a measured amount of progress toward the goal, which is "To reduce the incidence of high school dropouts" (option c). If the question had asked for the goal of the intervention, option "c" would have been the correct choice. Option "d" has the flaw of using the term "to attempt to," which does not require outcome accountability. This option is also a bit vague. If I were called upon to determine how to measure client progress, given this statement of objective, I would have great more difficulty than with option "b," which clearly spells out self-esteem and study habits as targets.

For question 5, the correct answer is option "c". The structure statement should spell out the nature and form of the service. Options "a" and "b" refer to outcomes rather than service structure, while option "d" is the vague "quality services" statement

(continued)

EXHIBIT 13.1 • *Continued*

that provides little information. As a general rule of thumb, the word quality should not be included in a statement either of the goal or objective of an intervention, because it is too vague.

For question 6, the answer is "b". The theory behind the intervention is the subject of the description of the model that provides guidance.

Overview

The *intervention* or program is the process used to bring about the desired change in target behavior. The intervention may be tailored for the individual client or it may be characterized as a program given to a large number of clients. In the first case, the practitioner designs the intervention for a specific client within broad boundaries set by the nature of the program that is funded. A therapist may decide to use cognitive-behavioral therapy for the treatment of Ms. Johnson's depression. While this intervention would follow certain guidelines useful for all applications of cognitive-behavioral therapy, the design of the intervention for Ms. Johnson may be a little different from the treatment of Mr. Parker for the same target behavior. For one thing, it may be decided that Mr. Parker needs ten to fifteen weekly treatment sessions, while Ms. Johnson will be given only five to eight sessions. It is possible that more training will be used with one client than the other because of differences in capacities and needs.

Both of these clients will be served under a broad program of services offered by the agency or service system. You could define the terms intervention and program in similar ways. Each could be characterized as a set of prescribed activities that are designed to achieve a broad goal or set of objectives. A program is broader. You might characterize child protective services

---

Discussion Box 13.1

Examine this list and determine which statement is best characterized as a program, which is best characterized as an intervention, and which is best characterized as neither.

1. The provision of medical counseling to patients who are trying to cope with serious illnesses, the provision of discharge planning services to patients to assure follow-up medical treatment, and the provision of family assessments to assist physicians to develop appropriate medical plans for patients.
2. To attempt to put more emphasis on communication between personnel in different professional categories.
3. The provision of medical social work services to the Johnson family.

Provide your answers in the box. Enter the numbers 1, 2, and 3, and place the appropriate words by each. These words are "program," "intervention," and "neither."

as a program, and a support group for abusive parents as an intervention within that program. You might characterize adult mental health services for the Hampton County Mental Health Clinic as a program and the use of cognitive-behavioral therapy for the reduction of Ms. Johnson's level of depression as an intervention.

The terms used to label a set of activities as an intervention or a program are less important than the conceptual distinctions of activities by level in the system. Programs are likely to be aimed at broad goals that provide general guidance for all services delivered. Interventions should have specific objectives that provide guidance on the way that success will be evaluated for a client or group of clients. Both programs and interventions should be evaluated. The methods will vary a little based on the level of the activities. One of the goals of the Adolescent Parenting Program in one state is to reduce child neglect and abuse. The program can be evaluated by a comparison of clients of this program and nonclients on the incidence of repeat pregnancies while an individual client of this program might be evaluated in regard to the reduction of risk factors associated with abuse and neglect. The percent of clients of this program with a repeat adolescent pregnancy would be an indicator of the program's effectiveness, while the improvement of self-esteem and school absenteeism may be a useful indicator of success for an individual client. Information on self-esteem and absenteeism for all clients could also be used in an evaluation of the entire program.

Model of the Intervention or Program

The model of the intervention is the theoretical or conceptual framework that illustrates the dynamics of the target behavior in such a way as to illustrate the essential connections between cause and effect or the special aspects of need being addressed by the intervention. It also provides guidelines regarding aspects of treatment that have been found to be more effective. Sometimes the practitioner has a well defined theory that serves as the model. Other times, there may be guidelines from the analysis of studies regarding the treatment of the given target behavior.

Based on the work of Kumpfer, Molgaard, & Spoth (1996), Royse, et al. (2001) summarized the elements found to be best practices with regard to parenting and family programs:

> The conclusion was that there is no single best family intervention program. . . . However, several principles for best practices in family programs were identified. These included selecting programs that are: (a) comprehensive, (b) family-focused, (c) long-term, (d) of sufficient dosage to affect risk or protective factors, (e) tailored to target populations' needs and cultural traditions, (f) developmentally appropriate, (g) beginning as early in the family life cycle as possible, and (h) delivered by well-trained, effective trainers. (Royse, et al., 2001, p. 110)

You might cite something like this in the description of the model of your intervention, with reflections on each of these elements of best practice as contained in your intervention or program. This can serve two purposes: to describe the model and to justify its choice. You should keep in mind that the concept of model of the intervention does not refer exclusively to formalized conceptions such as "cognitive-behavioral model," but can include your unique depiction of the conceptual framework that supports the design of your practice activities.

This is somewhat broad based in that it provides general guides for best practice. On a more specific level, Nathan & Gorman (2002) describe interpersonal and social rhythm therapy for the treatment of bipolar disorder as follows:

> IPSRT [interpersonal and social rhythm therapy] encourages patients to recognize the impact of interpersonal events on their social and circadian rhythms. There are two goals for IPSRT: (a) to help patients to understand and renegotiate the social context associated with mood disorder symptoms, and (b) to encourage patients to recognize the impact of interpersonal events on their social and circadian rhythms, and to regularize these rhythms in order to gain control over their mood cycling. In OPSRT patients are given the Social Rhythm Metric . . . , a daily self-report on which they record their sleep/wake times, levels of social stimulation, timing of daily routines (eating, exercise, work, etc.) and daily mood. By reviewing data from this assessment device, patients gradually see how changes in their mood states can occur as a function of variable daily routines, sleep/wake cycles, and patterns of interpersonal stimulation, and reciprocally how these factors are affected by their moods. In time, patients become motivated to regulate their rhythms and find balances among these factors as a means of stabilizing their moods. (Nathan & Gorman, 2002, p. 266)

The following are examples of models of programs that illustrate a range of complexity, but serve to exemplify the models underlying various human services.

1. The Foster Care Independent Living Program is designed to prepare older foster children for the transition to adulthood following foster care services. The model can be characterized as strengths based, where the client is viewed as the expert on his or her own needs. In this model, the agency encourages the youth's active participation in decision making. Because it is strengths based, it acknowledges that all youth have strengths. The optimal approach to development is to build on strengths rather than focus on weaknesses or problems. With this model, the agency treats the youth with respect, is supportive, and remains open to new information. It promotes the sharing of power, and engenders partnership between the youth and the agency; the agency and its personnel refrain from taking the role of the expert. A technique of this approach is for the person in the helping role to ask the client to identify how they overcame certain obstacles that have been put in their path, and how this same strength can be used for achieving their goals in various aspects of life.

2. The Housing Department for Winslow County has developed a program for those persons who have not yet learned or experienced how to be self-sufficient. The Self-Sufficiency Program (SSP) is designed to help those who depend on government assistance for everyday necessities to become self-sufficient and obtain home ownership. One of the assumptions underlying the model for this program is that many people fail to find self-sufficiency because they were never taught to be self-sufficient and have lacked good role models for self-sufficiency. This program provides training on credit, budgeting, parenting, and home ownership, and encourages group interaction where self-sufficiency behavior can be demonstrated. Through credit counseling, the clients are told which debts to pay off first in order to raise their credit score. In the budgeting class, residents are shown how to manage their money. They bring in their check stubs and a list of their monthly expenses and they are shown how to budget their money and pay their bills.

3. The Alcohol Rehabilitation Program is offered in a male prison where various services are offered. The program goal is to promote abstinence among incarcerated individuals by means of education, group therapy, and individual counseling. The model is cognitive-behavioral. This model is based on the belief that an individual's thoughts control their behavior, and that teaching new ways of thinking will lead to new behaviors. Achieving this perceptual change is termed cognitive restructuring, and it is hoped that participant offenders will learn consciously to examine their thoughts, and connect them to their emotions, their addictive behaviors, and their criminal behaviors. This model is based on the assumption that maladaptive behaviors are learned and can be unlearned and replaced with more healthy behaviors.

Discussion Box 13.2

Think of a human service program or intervention and briefly describe the model that guides its design. If you have difficulty thinking of a program, you could instead think of an intervention that could improve your life, such as a new method of studying for exams. Think of a strategy or activity that could help and explain why you think this strategy or activity would succeed.

Structure of the Intervention or Program

The structure of the intervention can be described in such a way as to identify both its form and intensity. The form is what it looks like. The intensity of the intervention or program refers to how much service is given. The description of the form of the intervention can be used to determine the unit of service, which can be useful in the examination of efficiency or quantity of service delivered.

Form of the Intervention

What does the intervention look like? Does it entail a series of individual counseling sessions or group psychotherapy or training sessions? Does it include residential care? Is it more like talk therapy, play therapy, or something else? Is case management a part of the intervention?

A good description of the structure of the intervention will facilitate replication by others. If you describe it very well, I will know how to implement the same thing in my practice.

Discussion Box 13.3

Think of a familiar human service program and describe at least one part of its structure.

A good description also will aid in the determination of the resources needed for the use of your intervention or program. Weekly therapy sessions for six weeks will cost less than residential care for six weeks. Group treatment is less expensive than individual therapy on a per case basis.

Intensity of the Intervention

The description of the intensity of the intervention is a second component of a good report of the structure. How much intervention is given? Is individual therapy offered one hour a day once a week for six to ten weeks? In this case, you could report that clients typically receive six to ten therapy sessions. If your service is 24-hour care, how many days are included in the typical service episode for the typical client? An inpatient treatment program for mental illness might typically be offered for a 20-day period. If your service is case management, you might offer a description of the typical service offered and report on the number of persons served.

In a previous chapter, you reviewed a description of the New Hope Treatment Center program for clients suffering from depression. This is an inpatient treatment program offered to clients typically for two to three weeks. The following is an excerpt selected to highlight the structure of this program:

1. Each subject attended one process group daily, Monday through Saturday, lasting approximately one hour.
2. Each subject attended two family focus meetings prior to their discharge from the unit. Each family focus meeting was for one hour.
3. Subjects attended one activity group daily, Monday through Saturday, lasting approximately one hour.
4. Subjects met individually with their psychiatrist daily, Monday through Sunday, for at least fifteen minutes to explore and discuss treatment and individual progress.
5. Subjects also attended one hour specialty groups three times a week.
6. Each subject met with their therapist at least three times a week for an hour each session.

Discussion Box 13.4

Calculate the total number of hours of professional service given to the typical client of the New Hope Treatment Center program and record it.

Okay, let's go through this task and see where we get with this question. As you will see from the following analysis, some of these figures have to be estimated. This means there is no clear correct answer. The purpose of this exercise is to heighten your awareness of the concept of intensity of treatment.

The process group was offered six times per week for one hour each session, or a total of 12 hours for two-week patients or 18 hours for three-week patients. Perhaps we should say the average is 15 hours. Each client received two hours of family focus meetings. Activity groups were structured identically to process groups, so we can say the average was 15 hours. Sessions with psychiatrists were a minimum of 15 minutes, so this is a little more difficult to tabulate, given the fact that some sessions could be more than 15 minutes and we don't know how many were greater than 15 minutes. But, given our knowledge of how long psychiatrists typically talk to individual patients, I think it is okay to say that the vast majority of these sessions were 15 minutes. This means that three-week clients typically received 4.5 hours of treatment by a psychiatrist while two-week clients received 3 hours of treatment. So, we can average that to 3.75 hours per client, or maybe we can round it to 4 hours, in view of the fact that we are not being especially precise anyway. Specialty groups were offered three times per week for one hour each session, or a total of 9 hours for three-week clients or 6 hours for two-week clients. The average could be calculated as 7.5 hours of service. The same pattern was implemented for individual therapy sessions, so this average can also be calculated as 7.5 hours.

So, we now have the following hours:

1. 15 hours
2. 2 hours
3. 15 hours
4. 4 hours
5. 7.5 hours
6. 7.5 hours

Total = 51 hours

Your numbers may be slightly different from these. This is okay because of the estimations necessary and the fact they could be calculated based on different assumptions. So the idea here was not to get a highly precise number, but to get a number that is in the ballpark of what is being offered.

You are entitled to think this obsessive calculation is going too far, but while you will not routinely be expected to calculate such numbers, I consider it a worthwhile exercise to help you gain familiarity with the concept of program intensity. You might find it useful to calculate numbers like this as you consider the issue of practical significance. If your treatment has the effect of improving target behavior 10 percent, it might make a difference to you that your treatment utilized only 10 hours of professional service as compared to 51 hours.

Unit of Service

The concept of unit of service is relevant to the description of the structure of the intervention. The unit of service is more relevant to program evaluation than clinical evaluations of individuals: It is the tangible measure of process employed in the program, and provides the basis for measuring the amount of service delivered. It can take several forms; one is the time unit. For example, you may define the unit of service as an hour of counseling, or an 8-hour day of child care, or a 24-hour day of residential care. Another form is the episode of service. This refers to the completion of a meaningful unit of service with a normal terminal point. A few examples would include a child abuse investigation completed or a discharge plan completed. In some cases, the only practical approach is to define the unit of service as a client served. With increased emphasis on efficiency in human services, this is not likely to be acceptable by most funding sources.

In mental health services, you may find the definition of a billable hour to be a useful way to define the unit of service. This is a definition given by funding sources and describes the way the funding source views the nature of the output that is being funded. Funding sources recognize that therapy requires more work than the one-hour of treatment that is reimbursed. But funding sources normally provide a unit payment that takes these other things into consideration. Often, client contact hours are reimbursed but time spent on record keeping is not.

In some cases, the intervention is guided by a set of service protocols or a treatment manual. The function of these instruments is to provide guidance to staff and assure that the design of the treatment is being implemented properly. If this is the case with your intervention, it should be reported in your evaluation study. If not, you might want to consider creating a manual, not as an intervention straitjacket but as a guide for action and monitoring. Human service practitioners usually need a little flexibility for their creativity, so straitjackets are not warranted. But treatment manuals might curb the incompetence of a practitioner who operates too far away from recognized treatment protocols.

Discussion Box 13.5

Think of a familiar human service program or intervention and identify at least one way to define a unit of service for this program or intervention.

Goals and Objectives for the Intervention or Program

Your intervention is designed to achieve certain outcomes for your clients. These outcomes can be stated in regard to long-range outcomes and short-term outcomes. Goals are statements of long-range outcomes, whereas objectives are statements of measured amounts of progress toward goal achievement. Neither refers to the intervention to be provided, nor do they refer to the standards that will be maintained. They are focused on client outcomes.

Goals should provide guidance on the long-term intent of the intervention or program. There are several options we might consider in our statement of the conceptual level of the statement. Let's suppose you are designing a program for adolescent mothers. The statement "To improve the quality of life" is too general to provide guidance. What intervention would *not* be designed to improve life in a general sense?

What about the statement "To reduce the negative social consequences of adolescent parenting"? This would work because it provides some guidance and focuses on the outcome. However, you might find some statements like the following to be even more useful: (1) To reduce child neglect and abuse among children of adolescent mothers; (2) to reduce public dependency among adolescent mothers; and (3) to enhance self-sufficiency among adolescent mothers. The latter statements provide more specificity than the first one, but any would seem okay, depending on how much specificity is warranted in your situation.

You could provide even more specificity with statements like (1) To reduce the incidence of repeat pregnancies for adolescent mothers; (2) to prevent adolescent mothers from dropping out of school; (c) to enhance job-entry skills for adolescent mothers; and (d) to enhance knowledge of appropriate parenting techniques for adolescent mothers. However, you might find it useful to refer to these statements as objectives of the program because each provides guidance on progress toward the long-term outcomes. A key to this choice is that *progress regarding the objectives should be measured in your study.* You may or may not have information on progress toward the achievement of the goal, but you should have information on progress toward the achievement of the objectives.

Let's take the example of the peer support group intervention offered to female victims of violence. The only measure of outcome included in the evaluation study of this program was the clients' scores on a life satisfaction scale. Given this situation, which of the following should be the statement of the outcome objective of this program?

1. To improve communication skills
2. To improve the management of anger
3. To improve life satisfaction
4. To develop peer support
5. All of the above

You should have noticed that option 3 was the correct answer because this is the thing being measured in this study. The other things may be part of the focus of group discussions or counseling, but they are not being measured.

Discussion Box 13.6

Consider the Anger Management Program for Pendleton High School, which deals with students who have demonstrated problems with fighting and other consequences of poor anger management. Which of the following would be good statements of the *goal* of this program?

1. To provide good quality support services for students with anger problems
2. To increase the students' ability to manage and control their feelings of anger
3. To improve the student's knowledge of coping strategies for anger
4. To enhance the quality of life

You should have recognized the first one as oriented to service rather than outcome, so it is not the correct answer. You should have recognized the last one as too general. So, we must chose between number 2 and number 3. One of these is better stated as the goal and the other as one of the objectives. Improving a student's knowledge of coping strategies could be viewed as a measured amount of progress toward the achievement of the goal of improved ability to cope with anger. So, number 2 is the better statement of the goal while number 3 is the better statement of an objective. This means that you would need to measure progress regarding knowledge of coping strategies. In addition, you could state an objective regarding involvement with incidents requiring disciplinary action and measure the same.

Personnel for the Intervention or Program

The personnel delivering the intervention should be identified. This does not mean the names of the specific individuals, but the credentials they carry into this intervention. This normally would include degrees, special training, and level of experience. In some situations, licensing requirements provide some control over the general credentials of persons employed in certain types of jobs in the helping professions. Clinical psychologists are typically required to be licensed and the same is true for clinical social workers (in most states). Some states provide licensing of counselors of different kinds, such as substance-abuse counselors, school guidance counselors, marriage and family counselors, and so forth.

Many interventions require special training. I doubt that most helping professionals can read a one-page description of an intervention model and know very well how to implement it. An article on the treatment of children with conduct disorders offered the following observations about Parent Management Training (PMT), a potentially effective approach:

> PMT requires mastery of social learning principles and multiple procedures that derive from them . . . For example, the administration of reinforcement by the parent in the home (to alter child behavior) requires more than passing familiarity with the principle and the parametric variations that dictate its effectiveness (e.g., administration of reinforcement contingently, immediately, frequently; use of varied and high-quality reinforcers; use of prompt, shaping). The requisite skills in administering the procedures within the treatment sessions can be readily trained but they are not trivial. (Kazdin, 2002, p. 65)

Summary

A critical issue in the research on evidence regarding treatments of various conditions is whether the planned treatment was carried out. Information on the structure, model, and personnel for a given program or intervention is critical to this form of evaluative research. It is not sufficient for you simply to say you employed cognitive-behavior therapy in the treatment of a client with depression and that your data supported its effectiveness. You must provide information that would give a critical observer the confidence that you did what the model required. If not, your evidence regarding outcome cannot be included among the evidence that supports or refutes a particular model.

Quiz

The following quiz can be used as a pretest, to determine if you need to read this chapter, or as a posttest, to determine how well you read it. Answers are given at the end of the reference list.

1. The concepts of human service intervention and human service program both refer to:
   a. The evidence that justifies the services to be offered to clients.
   b. The process to be used to achieve the outcomes for the client.
   c. The design of the evaluation study.
   d. The types of persons who will receive the services.

2. Which of the following statements is/are true?
   a. The human service program is a broader concept than human service intervention.
   b. Your treatment of Mrs. Jones for anxiety is better characterized as an intervention than a program.
   c. Both of the above.
   d. None of the above.

3. The model of the intervention or program is:
   a. The conceptual model that links the services to the dynamics of the target behavior.
   b. The description of output.
   c. The description of input.
   d. The form of the services to be offered.

4. Which of the following would be examples of the description of the model of your intervention or program?
   a. We will employ cognitive-behavioral therapy in the treatment of depression. Thus, we will assume that depression is caused by distorted thinking about life events and our approach to treatment will address distorted thinking.
   b. Our treatment will be based on the assumptions that (1) early intervention is better, (2) that confrontation is not effective early in the treatment process, and (3) that the family should be involved because the genesis of this problem lies in family dynamics.
   c. Both of the above.
   d. None of the above.

5. The intervention or program can be described in regard to form, intensity, and unit of service.

Which of the following describe the *form* of the Adolescent Parenting Program?
   a. Clients will participate in an adolescent parent support group, will receive parent training, and will have a case manager to deal with various aspects of life management.
   b. This program is based on the assumption that the problems related to adolescent parenthood are multisystemic in nature; thus, services will address various aspects of the client's system.
   c. Clients typically will receive approximately 20 hours of professional service monthly.
   d. All of the above.

6. Which of the above would best characterize the *intensity* of the services of the Adolescent Parenting Program?
   a.
   b.
   c.
   d.

7. Which of the following would be examples of a unit of service?
   a. A child abuse investigation completed
   b. One hour of family therapy
   c. A day of residential care
   d. All of the above

8. Which of the following is the better statement of the *goal* of the School Dropout Prevention Program than a statement of one of the objectives of this program?
   a. To improve the self-esteem of middle-school students at risk of dropping out of school
   b. To provide good quality services to middle school students that adhere to the principles of the strengths perspective
   c. To reduce the incidence of school dropouts
   d. To attempt to provide services that meet client need

9. Which of the following is the better statement of one of the *objectives* of the School Dropout Prevention Program than a statement of the goal of this program?
   a. To improve the self-esteem of middle-school students at risk of dropping out of school.

b. To provide good quality services to middle school students that adhere to the principles of the strengths perspective

c. To reduce the incidence of school dropouts

d. To attempt to provide services that meet client need

10. The description of the personnel of the intervention or program includes:

    a. The educational credentials of those providing the service.

    b. The special training of those providing the service.

    c. Both of the above.

    d. None of the above.

References

Kazdin, A. E. (2002). Psychosocial treatments for conduct disorder in children and adolescents. In P. E. Nathan and J. M. Gorman (Eds.), *A guide to treatments that work (2nd ed).* (pp. 157–168). New York: Oxford University Press.

Kumpfer, K., Molgaard, V., & Spoth, R. (1996). Family interventions for prevention of delinquency and drug use in special populations. In R. O. Peters & R. J. McMahon (Eds.), *Preventing childhood disorders, substance abuse, and delinquency.* Thousand Oaks, CA: Sage.

Nathan, P. E., & Gorman, J. M. (2002). *A guide to treatments that work.* New York: Oxford University Press.

Royse, D., Thyer, B. A., Padgett, D. K., and Logan, T. K. (2001). *Program evaluation: An Introduction.* Belmont, CA: Brooks/Cole.

Answers to the Quiz

1. b

2. c

3. a

4. c

5. a

6. c

7. d

8. c

9. a

10. c

14

Selecting the Sample and Measuring Target Behavior

This chapter deals with sampling (selecting study subjects) and measurement (selecting tools for measuring client progress) in human service evaluation. These topics have been addressed in previous chapters in a limited way and will receive elaboration here. Two of the key questions in evaluation research are:

- Are your study results relevant to anyone other than those in your study sample?
- Did your method of measurement truly measure what was intended?

These are the two questions that are the focus of your sampling and measurement methods. Your sampling method determines the nature of your generalization of your study results. The better your sampling procedures, the wider the population for which your study results can be generalized. Your measurement tools determine how confident you can be that you have measured what was intended. Your confidence in measurement determines, in part, the extent to which you can make the case that your study constituted a fair test of your intervention.

At the completion of this chapter, you will be able to:

1. Distinguish between the study sample and the study population when given a study example.

2. Distinguish between probability and nonprobability samples, with regard both to their nature and their ability to assist with the generalization of study results.

3. Discuss the difference between speculative generalization and safe generalization of study results.

4. Define the concepts of random, sampling frame, unit of analysis, and sampling error.

5. Identify a few types of probability samples.

6. Identify a few types of nonprobability samples.

7. Describe how one would select a random sample using the systematic random sampling procedure.

8. Describe the concept of measurement error.

9. Distinguish between the concepts of reliability and validity in measurement.

10. Identify a few methods of assessing reliability and validity of measurement tools.

11. Articulate the concept of empirical relationship in regard to the assessment of the reliability and validity of measurement methods.

12. Distinguish between individualized measurement tools and standardized measurement tools.

13. Determine whether the individualized tool is more or less appropriate than a standardized tool when given examples.

14. Identify how to evaluate a standardized scale for appropriateness to a study when given examples.

15. Discuss the role of measurement in the determination of practical significance in the examination of evaluative data.

Selecting the Study Sample

The topic of sampling has been addressed previously in this book. In keeping with the developmental perspective on learning, this topic was previously introduced in a general way and selected definitions were given. If you believe you need to review these basic concepts, turn your attention to Exhibit 14.1, where you will find a review of previous discussions.

EXHIBIT 14.1 • *A Quiz on Sampling Based on Content from Prior Chapters*

Let's begin this review by responding to the following questions. Select an answer and then review the discussion that follows.

1. Let's suppose that you collected data from 15 of the 47 men and women presently being served by the Hampton Valley Substance Abuse Treatment Program. You selected these individuals because they are in your caseload. Consider the following groups of individuals.
   a. The 15 persons from whom data were collected.
   b. All 47 persons presently being served.
   c. All persons who have been served by this program in the past year.
   d. All persons who have been served by similar programs in the nation.
   e. All persons who have a substance abuse problem.
   f. All men who have been served by this program in the past year.
   Which of the above would be the study sample?

2. Which of the options in the above question could legitimately be defined as the study population? (You may give more than one answer)

3. Do you have a probability sample? _____ Yes _____ No

4. What is meant by the term "random sampling"?

5. What is the key contribution of sampling to the evaluation research project?
   a. It helps you to determine how to measure target behavior.

b. It helps you determine the extent to which you can generalize your findings to persons not included in the study.
c. It helps you to determine the appropriate research design.
d. It helps you to deal with the issue of causation in evaluation research.
6. How do you distinguish between the concepts of "speculative generalization" and "safe generalization"?

Let's examine these questions. For number 1, the study sample would be option a (persons from whom data were collected). A sample is a portion of a larger entity, the larger entity being known as the study population. You can declare any group to be your study population as long as every member of the sample is a member of that larger group. For this reason, option f is the only one that is illegitimate, because you have both men and women in your study sample. All other options are legitimate as the study population. However, some are better than others for the purpose of generalization. The

closer the defined population to the sample, the better position you are in for speculative generalization.

You do not have a probability sample. A probability sample is one in which every member of the defined population has an equal chance of being selected for the sample. This is done by various forms of random sampling, a method of selection similar to drawing straws or names from a hat. Sampling helps with the generalization of study results to persons not included in the study. Safe generalization is done if you have a random sample. Speculative generalization is when you do not. The latter is helped to the extent that you do not have known biases in your sampling procedure. If you have selected those persons from your waiting list who are most severely impaired, you have introduced a bias into your sampling procedure. If you select those persons with the characteristics believed to make them most receptive to treatment, you have introduced a bias into your sampling procedure. In both cases, you will have problems with generalization.

The Study Sample and the Study Population

A sample, by definition, is a portion of something that is larger. For evaluation research, the study sample is composed of those persons from whom data were collected. The something that is larger is known as the study population. There is only one way to define your study sample—those who offered data. But your options for defining the study population vary with whether you have a probability sample or a nonprobability sample. As previously discussed, the probability sample is one drawn at random from a designated population. In this case, your sample is the group from which data were drawn while the population is the specific group from which the persons in the sample were drawn on a random basis.

When you have a nonprobability sample, there are several options for defining your study population. If you collect data from all 23 women served in your Women's Shelter this month as your study sample, you could define your study population as any aggregate of persons larger than this group that includes each and every one of the persons in your sample. Assuming that you have both women under the age of 30 and women who are 30 or over in your sample of 23 women, you could not define your study population as "female victims of violence who are under the age of 30." This definition would leave out some of the persons in your study sample. But you have several options regarding how you wish to define your study population. As depicted in Figure 14.1, you might define your study population as all persons served this year ($n = 73$), or you could define it as all persons who are in the target population (all female victims of violence). However, the closer the population definition to the sample, the stronger is your case for asserting speculative generalization of study results.

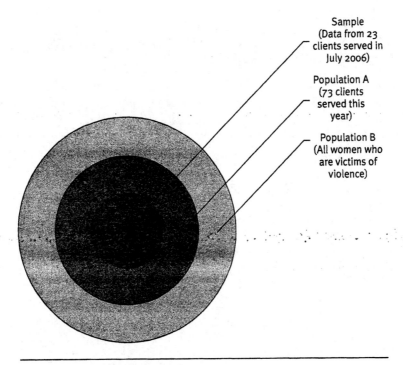

Sample
(Data from 23
clients served in
July 2006)

Population A
(73 clients
served this
year)

Population B
(All women who
are victims of
violence)

FIGURE 14.1 *Options for Defining the Study Population
for Nonprobability Samples*

Sampling Elements, Sampling Intervals, and Sampling Error

When you draw a sample from a population, typically you will be selecting individual clients, but you could be selecting families or records or other things to be your unit of analysis. The unit of analysis is the *sampling element*. For typical evaluation research studies, the sampling element (or unit of analysis) will be individual clients. The *sampling frame* is the list of persons (or records or families) from which the sample will be selected. When you draw a sample using the systematic random sampling procedure, your sampling interval is the number of sampling elements that will be skipped between selected elements. For example, if you wish to draw a 25 percent random sample, you could select each fourth person. In this case, your sampling interval is four.

Sampling error is the deviation between the nature of the sample and the nature of the population. If you find that 28 percent of those in your sample is female but you learn that 32 percent of your study population is female, the difference is the sampling error, or the amount that the results of the sample deviate from what is true about the population. There is some error in all sampling strategies. The purpose of sampling techniques is to reduce the size of this error. You will have less sampling error if you randomly select 250 persons from a list of 1,000 than if you randomly selected only 50 persons from this list.

Nonprobability Samples

For the front-line practitioner, random sampling procedures are often not feasible. Nonprobability samples are those that were not drawn on a random basis. Perhaps the most common type of nonprobability sample used by human service evaluators is the **convenience sample**. The convenience sample is the one selected out of convenience. When you select all your present clients for your study, you have a convenience sample. When you select those who volunteer, you have a convenience sample. The question arises as to whether this sample is representative of a larger group of persons from whom your sample was constituted, such as all clients served by your agency. Without a probability (random) sample, you cannot safely generalize your results from the sample to the population. In our terminology, we will refer to safe generalization as that which accompanies a probability (random) sample. When you lack a random sample, you are in the field of speculative generalization.

Sometimes you will select what is known as a **purposive sample**. This is a sample that is drawn from persons known to have special characteristics that are important to the research study. For example, if you wished to examine the reasons why some clients with substance abuse problems drop out of treatment, you might select substance-abuse counselors with at least 10 years of experience as respondents to your survey. These are persons who have special knowledge of the study topic. This would be a better sample than one for counselors in general.

Snowball sampling can be helpful when the persons in your study population are difficult to identify. With this method, you identify the small number of persons that you know to be members of the study population and you ask them to identify other persons from this population. Then you ask the second group of persons to identify additional persons, and you continue this process until you have a sufficient sample size.

Discussion Box 14.1

In the box below describe an example of a convenience sample, a purposive sample or a snowball sample that you might use in a study. Give the label (i.e., convenience, purposive, or snowball) and briefly describe the nature of this sample (e.g., all the students in your class, all of your clients, all employees of your agency who have at least five years experience as child abuse investigators, etc.)

Probability Samples

If you have a probability sample, all the persons in your designated population have an equal chance of being selected for your sample. Occasionally I have had students get a little confused about this question. For example, suppose your sample consists of all students in your research class. Is this a probability sample of all students in your program? Maybe they all had equal opportunity to sign up for this research class; some did and some did not. In this sense, there was equal opportunity. Does this make your sample a probability one? The answer is No. In order for your study to employ a probability sample, all students in your educational program must have had an equal chance to be selected for this study, not an equal chance of being in a given place at a given time.

Perhaps the simplest means of drawing a random sample is known as the *systematic random sampling procedure*. With this method, we first determine the sampling interval by dividing the number of persons in the population by the number to be selected for the sample (e.g., 1,000 members of your state chapter of the National Association of Social Workers divided by 200 persons to be selected would yield a value of 5, the sampling interval). Once we have secured the sampling interval, we select our first person from among those persons who fall within the first sampling interval. If our sampling interval is 5, we would select the first person at random from among the first 5 persons on our list of persons in our population. Any random procedure will do, such as rolling a set of dice, or using a table of random numbers, or simply saying that the first number between 1 and 5 that you see in the newspaper on your desk will be the first number to be selected for the study. Let's suppose that this number is 3. In this case, person number 3 on the population list would be selected for the study. The second person selected would be the person who falls exactly one sampling interval beyond the first person. In our example, that would be person number 8 (3 + 5 = 8). The next person in our example would be person number 13, then person number 18, and so forth.

The *simple random sample* procedure calls for the use of a table of random numbers. You can find such tables in many books on research and statistics. A procedure that uses random sampling techniques but which yields a greater sampling error is the *multistage random sampling procedure*. To illustrate, let's suppose that you wished to select a sample of social workers who work in women's shelters throughout the state of Pennsylvania. You could first select a list of all women's shelters in this state, and select a random sample of shelters for your study. This would be your first cluster. Then you could secure a list of social workers from these agencies. This would be your second cluster. Then you would select a random sample of persons from this list.

Discussion Box 14.2

In the box below describe the most useful and feasible type of probability sample you could use in an evaluation study of a familiar program or intervention.

Measuring Target Behavior

You have encountered information on measurement in previous chapters. Before we engage in some elaboration of that content, you can take a review quiz related to concepts previously

EXHIBIT 14.2 • *A Quiz on Prior Content on Measurement*

The following is a quiz on concepts covered in prior chapters of this book that relate to the theme of measurement. A discussion of the answers follows.

1. Before you can be expected to do a good job of finding a means of measurement of target behavior, what must you have done beforehand?
   a. You must have carefully selected the study sample.
   b. You must have carefully defined the target behavior.
   c. You must have carefully analyzed the target behavior.
   d. You must have carefully selected the most important client problem.
2. One's score on the Beck Depression Inventory would be an example of:
   a. The quantitative measurement of behavior.
   b. The qualitative measurement of behavior.
   c. Both of the above.
   d. None of the above.
3. Reliability in measurement refers to:
   a. The relevance of the tool to the target behavior.
   b. The consistency of the measurement tool.
   c. The accuracy of the measurement tool.
4. What does validity in measurement mean?
5. What is meant by measurement error?
6. If you found that your clients had better scores for self-esteem after treatment than before, would this be an example of the testing of the reliability of the self-esteem scale?

Let's look over these questions. Before you encounter the task of selecting a means of measuring target behavior, you must have done a good job of defining the behavior. You will find a good number of scales that measure related concepts. The question you need to address is which definition of the concept should I be using. The Beck Depression Inventory is an example of quantitative measurement. This means you are measuring target behavior either in the form of a score or you have placed your clients into discrete categories. Reliability refers to the consistency of a means for measurement, while validity refers to its accuracy.

Measurement error refers to any thing that creates a gap between the measurement tool and the thing being measured. If you understand the concept of validity quite well but you do not get the correct answer to the quiz question on this concept, the question may suffer from a problem that lends measurement error to the grade on the quiz. You might have simply misread the question or the question might be confusing in its wording. Either way, there is measurement error because the tool did not do a good job of truly measuring what it was supposed to measure.

If you found that clients had better scores after treatment than before, you have a measure of the effectiveness of the treatment, not the validity of the scale. To better understand this concept, think of what you would do if the results showed that client scores did not improve. Does this mean you have a bad scale, or an ineffective treatment? The latter is the more logical answer.

discussed on measurement. This quiz is given in Exhibit 14.2. If you feel a need to review, please refer to that exhibit. Otherwise, continue with the content below.

Assessing the Validity and Reliability of Measurement Tools

When you select, or develop, a means of measuring client progress, you want a method that measures what you intended to measure. You might say that various tools of measurement of client progress can be viewed as having varying levels of credibility with regard to this question. Reliability and validity are two forms of credibility. Tools that have stood the test of reliability and validity will give us more confidence that we are truly measuring client progress on our target behavior rather than something else.

Reliability

When we examine reliability, we are assessing the consistency of an instrument or means of observation. One popular means of testing reliability is known as the **test-retest** method. In this method, we give a scale to a group of persons at two points in time and examine the correlation of scores at the two points in time. If John has a higher score than Mary at time 1, he should have a higher score than Mary at time 2. If this does not turn out to be the typical pattern, we have reason to question the reliability of the scale.

Another popular means of testing reliability is through the examination of internal consistency. The question here is whether the items on the instruments seem to be measuring the same thing. One method for this examination is the *split-half* method. In this test of reliability, we split the instrument into two halves and compose two variables, one representing each half. We administer this scale to a group of persons at one point in time and examine whether the two halves correlate. If Barbara's score for the first half of the instrument is higher than Janet's score for this half, she should also have a higher score than Janet for the second half. If this does not turn out to be the typical pattern, we would have reason to challenge the internal consistency of the instrument. This information would suggest that the second half of the items do not seem to be measuring the same thing as the first half. If the two halves are not measuring the same thing, how can we be confident that we know what the instrument is measuring?

In the discussion of the hypothetical scores of Barbara and Janet, we discussed general patterns of responses. There will, of course, be exceptions to the general pattern. The fact that one pair of persons does not conform to expectations does not mean much by itself. What is important is the general pattern and the extent to which there are exceptions to this pattern. The more exceptions, the lower the correlation and the less confidence that we can have that our instrument is reliable. For more details on the concept of empirical relationship and correlation, see Exhibit 14.3.

Discussion Box 14.3

Let's suppose that we have administered a self-esteem scale to a group of persons and have divided this scale into two halves, one for all even-numbered items and one for all odd-numbered items. We now have two variables, one for each half of the scale. We have computed a correlation coefficient between these two halves of the scale. Which of the following values of the correlation coefficient would provide the best evidence of the reliability of this scale?

0.21

0.76

−0.81

EXHIBIT 14.3 • *Empirical Relationships and Correlation*

An empirical relationship between two variables is a relationship that can be tested quantitatively. If John has a higher score than Paul on the first half of the items on the Beck Depression Inventory, he should have a higher score than John on the second half of the items on this scale. This would be logically expected because we would assume that both halves of this scale measure the same thing. If the pattern between Paul and John is the same for all possible comparisons of pairs of persons in your study of the internal consistency of this scale, you would have a perfect correlation between the two halves of this scale. This would be designated as "$r = 1.0$" if you were using the standard correlation coefficient. A perfect correlation between two variables would be indicated as 1.0, while the complete absence of a correlation would be designated as 0.

The absence of a correlation ($r = 0$) would be found if you plotted everyone's scores for two variables on a chart and found no pattern at all. In this latter situation, if Mary's score on one variable is higher than Barbara's score on that variable, there is no more likelihood that Mary's scores on the second variable are higher than Barbara's than it is that Mary's score would be lower. Knowing that Mary scored higher than Barbara on one variable will not help you to predict whether she will have a higher score on the second variable.

Correlations can range from 0 to 1.0, either positive or negative. Higher correlations mean stronger relationships between variables. A correlation of .50 would be higher than one that was .35 and would indicate a stronger relationship. What you should consider to be a strong relationship versus a moderate or weak relationship depends on your opinion. There is no clear-cut basis for answering this question, even though many research texts provide a framework for this determination. However, I can say that when you engage in reliability assessment, you should expect a strong relationship, in the category of .7 or higher.

So far, we have been discussing only the positive empirical relationship. If I am higher than you on one variable I would be expected to be higher than you on the other variable, assuming we are talking about a positive relationship. However, if we have a negative relationship, I would more likely be lower than you on the second variable if I were higher than you on the first. For example, we would expect a negative relationship between self-esteem and depression. If I am higher than you on self-esteem, I would likely be lower than you on depression. If you see a correlation with a negative sign (e.g., $r = -.34$), you will be viewing evidence of a negative relationship between the two variables. If there is no sign, you will be viewing evidence of a positive relationship. You will not see a positive sign.

Validity

Validity refers to the extent to which an instrument truly measures what it is intended to measure. In other words, validity refers to accuracy. An instrument can be reliable without being valid. It can, for instance, be consistently inaccurate. But it cannot be valid without being reliable. Reliability is one basis of support for validity but it is not a sufficient basis for determining it.

There are several methods of examining validity. The most simple form of validity is **face validity**. This refers to whether the instrument seems to be measuring the thing it is supposed to measure. We can examine the instrument and ask ourselves if this is true. Better still, we could ask others to examine our instrument for face validity. We would want to do this with key informants (people who are in a position to understand the nature of the variable we are measuring).

Discussion Box 14.4

We could engage in a test of face validity in several ascending ways in regard to sophistication:

1. We could tell the key informants what our instrument was supposed to measure and ask if they believed it did a reasonable job of doing so.
2. We could give the instrument to our key informants and ask if they believed it did a better job of measuring A (the thing we wanted to measure) or B (something that is similar but different from that which we are trying to measure). In this case, we would not tell the informant what we designed the tool to measure.
3. We could give the instrument to our key informants and ask what they believed it measured and see if they came up with the same concept that we had intended for our tool to measure.

Which of the above options is the weakest as a test of face validity? Explain

---

Of these approaches, the first is the weakest because it tends to solicit a socially desirable response. People often want to please. If they believe we want a particular answer to a question, there will tend to be a bias in favor of that answer. They want to help; they don't want to hinder. So they may not give this task the kind of independent thought that is required for sufficient examination of the issue of validity.

A second form of validity is **content validity**. An instrument has content validity to the extent that it covers the total content of the concept we are trying to measure. If we define depression as including feelings of guilt, we might ask ourselves if a given instrument for measuring depression contains items that are designed to measure feelings of guilt. If not, it is limited in its content validity in this manner. The question being asked is "How well do the items on this scale represent the total concepts included in our definition of the variable?"

Discussion Box 14.5

Let's suppose we wish to develop a scale for measuring marital satisfaction. What would be the categories of things to be included on this scale? Would we want to include something about family values or agreement about finances? Think of the things that should be on the scale and compare your items with someone else to see what you might have left off that you consider important. You don't need to construct the actual questions. You only need to identify the variables such as money management, relations with in-laws, attitudes about child rearing, and so forth.

Both of these forms of validity rely upon the judgments of selected persons. You will typically ask persons with expertise on your topic to judge the level of validity of your instrument. We might refer to this approach as qualitative because you have not reduced your questions to discrete items that can be tested empirically.

Several forms of validity have been categorized as *empirical validity* because they subject the instrument to empirical assessment. You might, for example, undertake an examination of the correlation of scores on your instrument with those on another instrument that is supposed to measure the same thing. If scores do not correlate between these two instruments, the two do not seem to be measuring the same thing. Perhaps one is measuring it accurately and the other is not, but if they do not correlate, you will not know which one is the better one. Of course, it is also possible that neither instrument is accurately measuring the variable in question.

Discussion Box 14.6

If the two instruments for measuring the same thing do not correlate when given to the same people, one of the following is logically true:

1. Instrument A is valid but Instrument B is not.
2. Instrument B is valid but instrument A is not.
3. Neither instrument is valid.

Do you agree with the above statement?

Discussion Box 14.7

Let's consider a fourth option to the above list— "Both instruments are valid." Can this be true? Can both instruments be valid if they do not correlate, and they were designed to measure the same thing?

There are several forms of empirical validity. The distinctions between them are not given considerable importance in this text. Instead, it is suggested that you become familiar with the nature of empirical validity through several examples of it.

We can examine the relationship of our tool to some external criterion that represents our variable in some way. For example, scores on the Graduate Record Examination are supposed to predict performance in graduate school. Are these scores correlated with graduate school grades? If not, we would have questions about the validity of this test for our particular purpose.

We would expect that scores on a marital happiness scale would be a good predictor of whether a person was going to seek a divorce. It is logical to assume that persons who are happily married are not going to get divorced, and that a good number of unhappily married persons will get a divorce. If the scores of persons today on a marital happiness scale are not a good predictor of whether they will get divorced next year, we would have reason to question the validity of our instrument. The key question here is whether our instrument predicts behavior that it should predict if it truly measures the thing it is supposed to measure.

When we endeavor to define our variable, we often find that there are concepts that are close to the one we are defining, but not identical to it. We will also find that there are variables that are naturally related to our variable but are distinct from it conceptually. Does our variable measure something different from the other variable? If not, we have reason to question the validity of our instrument. For example, let's suppose that the instructor for your research course gave you a final exam and also administered a test of IQ and found a correlation of .75 between this exam score and IQ score. You might expect IQ to be correlated with performance on a research test, meaning that those higher on IQ were higher on their test grade.

But let's throw in a challenge. Suppose these same students had been given a research test made by a different instructor that was designed to measure the same type of research knowledge as the one given by your instructor. Suppose the correlation between your instructor's test grades and the other instructor's test grades is only .24. In other words, your instructor's exam correlated much better with IQ than with someone else's test of research knowledge.

Discussion Box 14.8

So, the correlation of my instructor's research exam and Dr. Smith's research exam is only 0.24, which indicates a rather weak relationship, but my instructor's research exam correlates with IQ at a much higher level ($r = 0.75$). What would you make of this? Answer in the box below.

Did your answer raise questions about the validity of your instructor's research exam? It should. These results suggest that your instructor's test is more highly related to IQ than someone else's research exam. Maybe it is doing a better job of measuring IQ than research knowledge. But it is supposed to be measuring research knowledge, not intelligence.

Types of Measurement Tools

There are two major types of quantitative measurement for human service evaluation: individualized scales and standardized scales. A standardized scale is one that has been designed for use with any number of individuals who share a common condition such as depression, anxiety, and so forth. These scales normally have been tested for reliability or validity and have been published. Individualized scales are tailor made for a given client. This is the kind of scale you have to create yourself.

You should choose a standardized scale if you are measuring a general condition like depression, anxiety, self-esteem, and attitudes of various kinds. This is true, however, only if your particular clients are adequately verbal to respond to a standard scale. The standardized scale has the advantage that it is ready made and normally has been tested for reliability and validity. You should develop an individualized scale if your target behavior is not of the common variety, or your client is not adequately verbal to respond to the standard scale.

Individualized Measurement Tools

The individualized scale has the advantage of being tailored to the particular client. In some situations, a client's problems may be unique and not relevant to available standardized scales. In other situations where the individual scale is warranted, the client may not be sufficiently articulate or verbal to respond to the standardized scale and a scale with different words or images may be more appropriate. For a young child, drawing a happy face or a sad face on a picture to show their feelings may be more appropriate as a measure of the condition.

Suppose you had a client who is suffering from depression. This client is not very well educated or verbal. Instead of using the Beck Depression Inventory, you decide to develop a scale using the client's own language to describe the levels of depression that she is experiencing. This client uses the image of a dark cloud to describe her feelings and describes varying levels of this dark cloud to describe how badly she might be feeling at a given time. So a scale is developed with the following points:

1. The cloud was so dark I wasn't sure I wanted to keep living.
2. The cloud was so dark I couldn't get anything done.
3. The cloud was dark but I could get through the day without major problems.
4. The cloud was a little dark but I could get things done without any problems.
5. The cloud was not dark at all.

Bloom, Fischer, & Orme (1999) cite several advantages of the individualized rating scale:

- The individualized rating scale (IRS) may address targets that other measures do not.
- The IRS can be used to assess internal thoughts and feelings, or the intensity of those thoughts and feelings better than standardized scales.
- The IRS can be very useful for charting client progress over time.
- The IRS can be useful for unique situations such as the need to observe selected problematic behaviors in a group of clients during interaction.
- The IRS often has high face validity because it is tailored to the client.

An interesting observation by these authors is the discovery that individualized ratings scales have been found, in many studies, to have acceptable reliability and validity, something that is normally seen as an advantage of the standardized scale.

Discussion Box 14.9

In the box below, identify a variable that would be a good candidate for the individualized scale as contrasted with the standardized scale.

Standardized Rating Scales

The standardized rating scale is one developed for use with many people who share a common condition that is the subject of study. An example is the Beck Depression Inventory. Bloom, Fischer, & Orme described this type scale as follows:

> Standardization refers to uniformity of procedures when administering and scoring a measure, and it implies the availability of existing data concerning validity and reliability of the measure. Thus, a standardized questionnaire is a measure that involves the administration of the same questionnaire items . . . to different people using the same administration and scoring procedures. It typically also involves the collection of information concerning the validity and reliability of the questionnaire during its development. (Bloom, Fisher, & Orme, 2003, p. 212)

Standardized questionnaires (Bloom, Fischer, & Orme, 2003) can be described in terms of six characteristics:

1. What they measure
2. How well they measure it (reliability and validity)
3. How they're structured
4. How many dimensions they measure
5. From whom they elicit information
6. How much time and other resources are required for their use

I will add one more type of information to this list—information that helps you to interpret a given score. Many published scales provide norms that indicate mean scores on groups of individuals who were used to test the scale's reliability and validity. Because many such tests come from the field of psychology, it is not unusual to find that norms were developed with undergraduate psychology students. This information provides guidance on persons who are not necessarily in treatment. If a group of clients served by your program has a mean score similar to the mean of undergraduate psychology students, you would have reason to question whether they needed treatment, especially if you are addressing a serious problem rather than engaging in a preventative or enrichment experience.

Let's go over the seven types of information given for published scales (the above six plus the one I added) using the Achievement Anxiety Scale as found in *Measures for clinical practice* (Corcoran & Fischer, 1987).

What Does it Measure?   The Achievement Anxiety Test (AAT) measures anxiety about academic achievement. It measures both anxiety as a motivator (Facilitating Scale) and the degree to which it interferes with performance (Debilitating Scale).

How Well Does it Measure this Concept?   The AAT has "excellent stability" (Corcoran & Fisher, 1987, p. 82) as reflected in a 10-week test-retest correlation of 0.83 for the Facilitating Scale and 0.87 for the Debilitating Scale. It has good criterion-related validity because it correlates significantly with several measures of academic performance. It has good predictive validity as evidenced by the fact that it predicts grade point average.

How is it Structured?   Respondents are asked to select a number from 1 to 5 with regard to each of 19 statements such as "Nervousness while taking an exam or test hinders me from doing well" (Debilitating Scale) and "I work most effectively under pressure, as when the task is very important" (Facilitating Scale). The ends of the scale for each item are anchored with words like "Always" and "Never." Some statements represent high anxiety (e.g., Nervousness while taking an exam or test hinders me from doing well") while others represent the opposite (e.g., "While I may or may not be nervous before taking an exam, once I start, I seem to forget to be nervous"). Thus, some items are reverse-scored because they have opposite meanings—i.e., "Always" may be scored 1 for a given item but 5 for another item. Each of the two scales is scored separately because they measure distinctively different conditions related to anxiety. The Facilitating Scale has 7 items while the Debilitating Scale has 12 items. Thus, the range of potential scores is 7 to 35 for the former and 12 to 60 for the latter.

How Many Dimensions Does this Scale Measure?   The AAT measures two dimensions: anxiety as a motivator, and anxiety as an interference with performance.

From Whom Does this Scale Obtain Information?   The AAT is self-administered. In other words, it is completed by the person being measured.

How Much Time and Resources Does it Take?   The AAT has only 19 simple statements for response. It should take no more than a few minutes to complete.

What are the Norms for Particular Groups?   The AAT was tested with several samples of undergraduate introductory psychology students. Because they were in introductory classes, these students represented individuals who would major in a number of things, even though you would expect psychology majors to be inordinately represented. The total students included in these tests was 323. For these students, the mean score on the Facilitating Scale was 27.28 while the mean score on the Debilitating Scale was 26.33.

This information tells you the key things to know about this instrument. You should be able to determine if it measures your target behavior reasonably well and how you would interpret a given score. Perhaps the first thing that stood out for you is the fact that this is really two scales rather than one. It would not make much sense to compute a total score for a given individual because the two scales represent opposites to a certain degree. A person with a high facilitating score uses anxiety constructively, whereas a person with a high debilitating score has performance problems due to anxiety. It is the latter type of individual that might need treatment.

Interpreting Individual Scores for a Standardized Scale.   Before you administer your scale, whether it be standardized or individualized, you should get an idea of how to interpret a given score. For the Debilitating Scale, what level of improvement would be clinically meaningful? There are 12 items on this scale, each of which is scored from 1 to 5, with higher scores representing higher debilitation; thus, scores can range from 12 to 60. Someone who replied Never to all negatively worded items and Always to all positively worded items would have no anxiety. This would be represented by a score of 12. A person who marked 2 on the 5-point scale to all items would have a score of 24. (Of course, it is not expected that an individual would mark each item exactly the same.) You would probably not see this score as indicative of a major problem with anxiety. You will note that the mean score for the sample of students in introductory psychology classes was 26.33. A score of 36 would be given to a person who tended to mark the number 3 on the 5-point scale. Being in the middle of the scale is not as easy to interpret as tendencies toward the ends of the scale, but you will note that this score is higher than the mean for the sample of students on whom this scale was initially tested. Scores of 4 to 5 on these items would be viewed as indicating a meaningful problem. This would be represented by scores from 48 to 60.

The above analysis can be useful for determining the client's condition at intake and determining the level of growth from intake to discharge. You may be surprised to find that your client scores low on your scale at intake. Perhaps the client does not have a problem here, or perhaps this scale is not valid for this particular client. When you complete your data analysis, you will address the issue of practical significance. Even if your data are statistically significant, they may not achieve practical significance. Statistical significance refers to the likelihood these results can be explained by chance but it does not directly address the question of whether this level of growth is clinically meaningful for your client.

Determining if the scale is appropriate for your client. An important consideration in regard to validity is whether the scale is appropriate for your clients. In the discussion of individualized scales is an example of a scale developed with the client's own language to describe depression. This was a client for whom a standardized scale may not have been appropriate. The client's age, intelligence, education, and emotional condition are among the things to consider when you select a measurement tool. Most standardized scales have some information to indicate the type of individual for whom the scale would be appropriate. This is especially true for children and adults. The collection of tools in the work by Corcoran & Fischer (1987) are organized by scales for adults and scales for children. Their later work (Fischer & Corcoran, 1994) is organized even further.

You should be careful to select a scale that is sensitive to the kinds of changes that you can expect of your clients in the time frame of your study. For example, locus of control is a psychological construct that refers to the extent to which you view life outcomes to be due to your own efforts or external influences over which you have little control. Locus of control, in a general sense, does not change easily. But health locus of control is more amenable to change. This is the degree to which you view your health as being in your control. There have been scales developed to measure both locus of control in general and health locus of control. You should consider this issue when seeking a scale to measure your clients if the issue of locus of control is of concern. In this case, you may consider that health locus of control can be the target behavior but general locus of control is not appropriate. You might also consider the possibility that health locus of control is not amenable to change from the resources available to you at present, but a certain type of behavior that is related to locus of control is amenable to change. Perhaps some kind of incentive for the behavior would work even though the underlying construct of locus of control does not change for your clients.

Conducting a pilot test of the scale.   One way to test the appropriateness of your instrument is to undertake a pilot test of it. You could give it to a group of persons like your clients to see how it works. You could ask for feedback from individuals to see how they were interpreting the items on the scale. You could review their tendencies to see if they were unexpectedly high or low in their scores, or if they tended to answer each question exactly the same even though the scale was meant to obtain independent responses to individual items. Your first administration of your scale to your clients could be used in this manner as well. You may find unexpected tendencies.

Be sure you clearly understand how a scale is to be scored when you administer it and give your client a score. Most scales have items worded in opposite directions, like the Debilitating Scale and the Facilitating Scale discussed earlier. This means that a response by the client of 5 for a given item should receive the same score as a response of 1 for another item worded in the opposite direction. This is known as *reverse-scoring.* By making this adjustment, you are ensuring that each response is appropriately interpreted. Don't make the mistake of adding up the score for each item without making the reverse-scoring adjustment.

Exhibit 14.4 is an example from a research study presented by York, 1997. The example is a treatment program for sexual offenders who are in prison. The analysis of this target behavior suggested that sexual offenders had three characteristics that distinguished them from others and contributed to the problem—a tendency to engage in cognitive distortions of the meaning of their crimes, a tendency to engage in justifications of their crimes, and a tendency to have low empathy for victims of sexual crimes, especially the victims of their crimes. In addition, this program addressed the issue of motivation for treatment because these characteristics tended to reduce this motivation. If you don't see yourself as having a real problem, why should you be motivated for treatment? This exhibit presents information on treatment objectives, definitions of these target behaviors, and the tools used to measure client progress.

Discussion Box 14.10

In the box below identify a type of client target behavior that would be best measured by a standard scale. Explain why this behavior is best measured this way. Let's take the challenge, however, of not identifying depression or anxiety because they have already been well established and this would be too easy. Think of something else.

EXHIBIT 14.4 • *Objectives, Target Behaviors, and Measurement Tools for the SOAR Program Evaluation*

The four treatment objectives are as follows: (1) To reduce the clients' cognitive distortions about their crimes, (2) To reduce the clients' justifications about their crimes, (3) To enhance the clients' empathy for the victims of their crimes, and (4) To improve the clients' motivation for treatment.

A *cognitive distortion* is defined as an inappropriate way of thinking about sex with regard to the acceptance of personal responsibility for one's actions. It was measured by the cognitive distortion sub-scale of the Multiphasic Sex Inventory (Nichols and Molinder, 1984). This instrument presents a set of statements which depicts cognitive distortions about sex. Examples are "My problem is not sexual, it is that I really love children," and "I feel like a victim as a result of the accusations made against me." The clients marked each statement as being either true or false for themselves. For this sub-scale, there were 21 items. The respondent received 1 point for each statement marked as true; thus, the worst possible score would be 21 and the best possible score would be 0.

A *justification* is defined as an excuse made by the offender for the sexual crimes he has committed. It was measured by a sub-scale of the Multiphasic Sex Inventory which contained statements such as "My sexual offense occurred as a result of my wife's lack of understanding of me and my needs." This sub-scale presented 24 such statements of excuses in the true-false format; thus, the worst possible score would be 24 and the best possible score would be 0.

Motivation for treatment is defined as a recognition of a need for help and a desire to receive such help. It was measured by a sub-scale of the Multiphasic Sex Inventory which presented 8 statements

in a true-false format. An example is "I need help because I cannot control my sex thoughts." The best possible score on this sub-scale is 8 while the worst possible score would be 0.

Empathy is defined as a vicarious emotional response to another person. It is the ability to feel someone's else's pain. The sexual offender tends not to be able to do this for the victims of their crimes. For the present study, empathy was measured by a sub-scale of the Interpersonal Reactivity Index. This sub-scale contains 7 items, an example being "Sometimes I don't feel very sorry for other people when they are having problems." Each statement is responded to with the following scale:

A	B	C	D	E
Does not describe me very well				Describes me very well

The client marked A if the statement did not describe him very well or E if the statement did describe him very well. The client also had the option of marking B, C, or D depending on how well he felt the statement described himself. Respondents were given scores from 0 to 4 depending upon how positive was the response. If the respondent indicated that a negative statement described him very well, he would receive a score of 0. If it did not describe him very well he would receive a score of 4. Scores of 1, 2, or 3 were given for the middle positions on the scale. Scores could possibly range from a low of 0 (the most negative score) to a high of 28.

[The following is taken from York, R. O. (1997), *Building basic competencies in social work research*. Boston: Allyn & Bacon, pp. 233–234.]

Determining Practical Significance

Practical significance refers to the extent that your measured client gain is considered to be noteworthy from a clinical or practical basis. Prior to the analysis of your data from an evaluation study, you should determine the basis for declaring practical significance. How much gain is noteworthy? You could have achieved statistical significance, meaning that you have ruled out chance as the explanation for the clients' measured gain, but failed to achieve practical significance. You would naturally expect a greater amount of client gain from a program with extensive resources than one that offered only a minimal level of service.

One way to examine practical significance is to determine the percentage of gain from pretest (or baseline period for single-system designs) to posttest (treatment period for single-system designs). Prior to this analysis, it would be useful for you to determine the level of change that you would consider noteworthy.

Another way to examine practical significance is with reference to thresholds of functioning according to the scale being employed. A depression score may have thresholds that represent varying levels of depression, from no significant depression, to mild depression, to severe depression. Some agencies have cutoff scores for determining if a person should be treated for a given condition.

Another way to examine practical significance is with the use of **effect size**. The effect size refers to the level of client gain with reference to standard deviations. It provides you with the opportunity to compare different clients who have been examined with single-system designs and with different groups who have been measured by different scales. The effect size is the number of standard deviations of difference between pretest and posttest scores. You might have a scale of marital harmony that is measured on a 100-point scale and another that is measured on a 20-point scale. A gain of 10 points on the former would be far less than a gain of 10 points for the latter. You can compare these two examples with the use of an analysis of percentage gain. However, the standard deviation is useful because it takes variance into consideration, an issue that is at the heart of statistical analysis.

The way to compute the effect size is as follows:

1. Compute the mean of the pretest score (or mean of baseline scores) and the mean of the posttest score (or mean of treatment recordings in single-system designs) and compute the difference to determine the extent of client gain.

   Note: If this comparison fails to show that clients achieved a meaningful gain, you would stop your analysis here, because your data have clearly failed to support your hypothesis.

2. Compute the standard deviation of the pretest scores.
3. Divide the mean amount of client gain (from step 1) by the standard deviation of the pretest scores. This is your effect size.

There is no clear-cut way to interpret the effect size in regard to practical significance. But it is generally considered quite noteworthy if your effect size is 1.0, because this means the average posttest score was one standard deviation better than the pretest scores. For comparison purposes, take into consideration that a standard deviation difference between individuals on IQ is about 15 points. The difference in IQ between 85 and 100 is quite noteworthy to anyone who would be working with such individuals on any challenging educational task. The amount of gain in a typical course in college is between 0.5 standard deviations and 1.0 standard deviations. But 1.0 is not the only score considered noteworthy. Most of the experts consider gains of 0.5 for effect size to be noteworthy at a minimal level.

Discussion Box 14.11

An Exercise on practical significance

Consider the following items on an alcoholism scale.

1. Can you stop drinking without a struggle after one or two drinks? (Y/N)
2. Has your wife (or other family member) ever gone to anyone for help about your drinking? (Y/N)
3. Have you ever neglected your obligations, your family, or your work for two or more days in a row because you were drinking? (Y/N)
4. Do you ever drink before noon? (Y/N)
5. Have you gotten into fights when drinking? (Y/N)

How many YES answers to these five questions would you consider to indicate a need for help with alcoholism?

These items are from the Michigan Alcoholism Screening Test. There is a total of 25 items on this scale, so we only have a few for our exercise and cannot draw definitive conclusions about how you might have answered these questions for yourself. Given the way this scale is scored, a YES response to the first three items above would indicate a serious need for help. But if you answered NO to these three items and YES to numbers 4 and 5, you would not fall into that category, in part because these last two items are given lower severity scores.

If your answer to the question was 3 or more, your response would tend to agree with the creators of this scale.

Cultural Competence and Measurement

If measurement methods are to be valid, they must use culturally sensitive language, perhaps even using non-English translations. A tool will not be valid if it uses words differently from the common usage of a given culture. Keep in mind that means of establishing the reliability and validity of measurement tools typically do not employ samples of persons from minority groups. You should not assume that all cultural groups will respond in the same way as the test sample if that sample does not represent the given group. Often it is advisable to pretest an instrument with the designated population. This will give you some idea if the wording on the instrument is clear and culturally meaningful.

Tools tested with men may not work similarly with women. Measurement devices, however, are typically tested with both men and women. You should keep this in mind as you examine the nature of the data that was generated from validity testing of a given tool. Eichler also reminds us not to make assumptions based on traditional sex roles, such as the man is the head of household. Be sensitive to the female experience when framing the study.

Checklist for Selecting Measurement Tools

Here are some questions to pose for yourself to ensure you have not overlooked major concerns with the measurement of target behavior.

1. *Does your instrument clearly measure the target behavior as you have defined it?* Don't make the mistake of selecting a standardized tool when an individualized tool would be more appropriate for your clients. Be sure there is congruence between the tool and the defined behavior.

2. *Is your tool appropriate for your clients?* If you have a standardized scale, be sure it is worded appropriately for the clients you serve. You should not use an adult scale for children. A scale tested with college students may not be appropriate for adults with a third grade reading level.

3. *Is your tool sensitive to the changes you can expect from your clients?* You must select a tool that is sensitive to change in the short term. You should consider both sensitivity to change and the resources available to you to change that behavior. A given tool may be appropriate if you are giving intensive services over a three-month period, but not appropriate for limited services given in one month.

4. *Does your tool have adequate reliability and validity?* Standardized scales have usually been tested for reliability and validity. But you do not need to consider your individualized scales to be lacking in validity simply because they have not been tested. In fact, some studies have suggested little need for serious concern about this issue with individualized scales. At a minimum, you should test your instrument for face validity. In addition, you should exercise your judgment in your review of the clients' responses to your instrument. It may be obvious that the clients' scores and your clinical assessment are seriously different, suggesting either a flaw in your clinical assessment or the clients' tendency to respond to this particular instrument according to a social desirability bias.

5. *Do you know how to administer the instrument and how to score it?* Carefully adhere to the instructions for administering the instrument. If you are administering the tool to different clients or the same client at different times, be sure it is taken under similar circumstances. It is best to administer the instrument when you have the client handy rather than depend on the client to take it home and complete it later. Be sure you know how to score the instrument, especially with regard to reverse-scoring. This may require that you change the points assigned to the numbers on the scale for given items. If you are administering an instrument to a group of clients before and after treatment, you will need to be able to match the same client's pretest score with his or her posttest score. You can do this while assuring anonymity by asking clients to complete a few questions that will provide their anonymous identification number. (Such questions as "What is the number of letters in your mother's middle name?", "How many siblings does your father have?", and "What is the last digit in your Social Security number?" are the kinds of questions that could serve this purpose. The combination of the client's answers to these questions could serve as his or her identification number. This could be placed both on the pretest and posttest administrations of the scale.)

6. *Do you know what level of gain would constitute practical significance?* You should prepare yourself for the examination of the question of practical (clinical) significance before you examine the data. After you have seen the results, you might develop a bias about this question, because you would normally like to see a gain that is of practical significance. To you, this might indicate success while failure to achieve practical significance would represent failure. Naturally, you want to succeed. But this would be stacking the deck, so to speak. If you adhere to the principles of scientific inquiry, you will determine the answer to this question prior to seeing the results.

Summary

When you consider the topic of sampling, you should know what type of generalization you need to make. If you wish to generalize safely from your sample to a designated population, you will need to employ a probability sample. If generalization is less important, a nonprobability sample just might do fine. This is particularly true if you have little basis for expecting a difference between your sample and the designated population. Do your clients seem quite typical of clients of this particular type? If so, many a convenience sample will be okay.

When you consider the means for measuring client progress, you will find yourself returning to the adage "Two heads are better than one." In the measurement of human variables like self-esteem and depression, we know we cannot be sure that a given tool truly measures what we want to measure. So we develop means of checking this out by looking at consistency and other ways of measuring this variable. The more evidence we find of reliability and validity, the more confidence we can have that we are really measuring our intended variable. Likewise, the more of this evidence you find, the more you can feel that your study was a fair test of our intervention.

Quiz

The following are questions for review of the contents of this chapter. You may take it either as a pretest, to determine if you need to read this chapter, or as a posttest, to determine how well you read it. Answers are given at the end of the reference list.

1. Which of the following are examples of probability samples?
   a. You select all the clients in your caseload to test the hypothesis "Persons suffering from depression will have lower depression after 10 weekly therapy sessions using cognitive-behavioral therapy."
   b. You compose a sample of homeless people by asking clients of your homeless shelter to identify other people they know who are homeless and then you ask each person in this second group to identify other persons who are homeless.
   c. Both of the above.
   d. None of the above.

2. Suppose that you want to select a study sample of 50 persons who are representative of all 450 clients presently served by your agency by using the systematic random sampling procedure. You determine the sampling interval by dividing 450 by 50 and get the number 9 as your sampling interval. You obtain an alphabetical list of your clients and select client number 7 as the first person in your sample by using a random method, such as drawing a number out of a hat. What is the number of the next person to be selected for your study sample?

a. 14
b. 16
c. 23
d. 25

3. Which of the following statements is/are true?
   a. The sample described in the previous question would constitute a probability sample of all clients presently served by your agency.
   b. The sample would constitute a probability sample of all persons ever served by your agency.
   c. Both of the above.
   d. None of the above.

4. Which of the following statements is *not* true?
   a. You can have a scale that is reliability but not valid.
   b. You can have a scale that is valid but not reliable.
   c. You can have a scale that is neither reliable nor valid.
   d. You can have a scale that is both reliable and valid.
   e. None of the above—all are true.

5. Which of the following would be evidence that your anxiety scale was either reliable or valid?
   a. A finding that scores on your anxiety scale were lower after treatment than before.
   b. A finding that scores on your anxiety scale were correlated with another scale designed to measure anxiety.
   c. Both of the above.
   d. None of the above.

6. Which of the following would be evidence of either the reliability or validity of your anxiety scale?
   a. A finding of a positive correlation between scores on the first half of the scale and scores on the second half of the scale.
   b. A finding of a positive correlation between scores on your scale taken at one point in time and scores taken at a later time.
   c. Both of the above.
   d. None of the above.

7. Which of the following would be best measured by an individualized scale?

a. Progress of a spouse regarding helping out with household chores
b. Depression
c. Anxiety
d. Self-esteem

8. Suppose that you had proof that you fully understood the concept of validity but you did not correctly answer a question on a research test about validity. This would an example of:
   a. Sampling error.
   b. Reduction error.
   c. Measurement error.
   d. Procedural error.

9. Suppose you conducted a study of ninth grade students and found a positive correlation between self-esteem scores and scores on a math test that is a perfect correlation ($r = 1.0$). This would mean what?
   a. If a student in this study named John had a higher score on self-esteem than a student in this study named Paul, you would know for certain that John had a *higher* score than Paul for math test grade.
   b. If a student in this study named Barbara had a higher score on self-esteem than a student in this study named Bonnie, you would know for certain that Barbara had a *lower* score than Bonnie for math test grade.
   c. You would know that most, but not all, students in this sample who had higher scores on self-esteem would have higher scores on the math test.
   d. None of the above.

10. What would be the best way to find evidence regarding practical significance?
    a. Conduct a test of statistical significance.
    b. Compare the clients' measured gain in functioning with movement from one threshold on the scale to another.
    c. Ask a colleague if he or she believes your clients achieved a gain that was clinically noteworthy.
    d. Compare your research design to that of another evaluation study.

References

Fischer, J., & Corcoran, K. (1994). *Measures for clinical practice* (2nd ed.). New York: Free Press.

Bloom, M. Fischer, J., and Orme, J. G. (2003). *Evaluating practice: Guidelines for the accountable professional* (4th ed.). Boston: Allyn & Bacon.

Corcoran, K., & Fischer, J. (1987). *Measures for clinical practice*. New York: Free Press.

York, R. O. (1997). *Building basic competencies in social work research*. Boston: Allyn & Bacon.

Answers to the Quiz

1. d
2. b
3. a
4. b
5. b

6. c
7. a
8. c
9. a
10. b

15

Selecting the Research Design for a Single Client

When we evaluate human service outcomes, we typically do so for a single client or a group of clients. Before you select the research design, you should have selected the clients to be evaluated, defined the target behavior, analyzed the target behavior, decided how to measure client progress, and selected the intervention to be employed in the achievement of that progress. Various research designs require different structures for collecting data and administering the intervention.

The topic of research design has been addressed briefly in previous chapters. In this chapter, you will take this learning a step further and acquire basic competence in the selection of a research design for a single client. In the chapter that follows, you will focus on research designs for groups of clients.

There is a quiz at the end of this chapter. You could use this quiz as a pretest, to determine if you need to read this chapter, or as a posttest, to determine how well you have read it. Because you have encountered the concept of research design in prior chapters, the first section of this chapter will provide a review of that prior content. Following this review, you will examine the concept of threats to internal validity. Then, you will review various single-system research designs organized in accordance with how well they address two threats to internal validity. Additional threats to internal validity will be discussed in the next chapter.

At the completion of this chapter, you will be able to:

1. Determine which threats to internal validity should be of special concern in an example of single-system evaluation.

2. Identify at least one single-subject research designs that controls for maturation as a threat to internal validity.

3. Identify at least one single-subject research design that controls for history as a threat to internal validity.

4. Determine the proper fit between the single-system research design and the threats to internal validity that should be of special concern in research examples.

5. Describe the following single-system research designs: the B design, the AB design, the limited AB design, the ABC design, the BC design, the ABA design, and the ABAB design.

Review

You have encountered the concept of research design in previous chapters. In this chapter, you will see an elaboration on that content. Prior to this journey, you may want to test yourself on your understanding of the content offered about research designs in prior chapters. If you feel this need, turn your attention to Exhibit 15.1. In not, then continue with the content of this chapter.

EXHIBIT 15.1 • *Quiz Review of Content on Research Designs*

Select the best answer to each of the following questions. Then, review the discussion that follows.

1. If Study A used a superior research design when compared to Study B, what does this mean?
   a. You are in a better position to generalize the findings from Study A to people not included in your study sample.
   b. You are in a better position to attribute the clients' measured growth in Study A to the intervention rather than something else.
   c. You are in a better position in Study A to select the most relevant client problem.
   d. You are in a better position in Study A to achieve statistical significance.
2. Which of the following statements is/are true?
   a. When you are evaluating the progress of a group of clients, you would employ a group research design.
   b. When you evaluate the progress of a single client, you would employ a single-system (single-subject) research design.
   c. Both of the above.
   d. None of the above.
3. A control group (or comparison group) is:
   a. The group that receives the intervention.
   b. The group that does not receive the intervention.
   c. The group that determines the research design to be employed.
   d. None of the above.
4. The comparison group design is one where you:
   a. Compare the pretest scores of one group of clients to their posttest scores.

   b. Compare the posttest scores of individuals to a norm.
   c. Compare the gain in functioning between a treated group and a group that did not receive treatment.
   d. Compare baseline scores of an individual client who is being treated in a group to that person's treatment scores.
5. Is the comparison group research design better than the one-group pretest–posttest design?
   a. No, because it has only one group.
   b. No, because it compares groups rather than individuals.
   c. Yes, because it does not address any of the threats to internal validity.
   d. Yes, because it addresses normal growth and development as an alternative explanation for the measured progress of clients.
6. You would be using the AB single-system research design if you:
   a. Charted the progress of a single client during the treatment period on his/her scores on your measure of target behavior.
   b. Compared a single client's treatment scores, measured several times, to that client's baseline scores, measured several times.
   c. Compared a single client's pretreatment score, measured once, to that client's posttest score, measured once.
7. Single-system designs are designated with letters, such as AB, ABC, ABAB, and so forth. When does the letter A represent?
   a. Scores taken during a period of time during which the client is receiving treatment.

b. Scores taken during a period of time during which the client is not receiving treatment.

c. Sometimes it refers to scores during treatment and sometimes it refers to scores during a period when the client is not receiving treatment.

d. None of the above.

Let's examine these questions. The answers in sequence are: 1—b, 2—c, 3—b, 4—c, 5—d, 6—b, and 7—b. In the next two paragraphs are brief explanations. If you did not do well, you may want to review previous chapters that addressed the task of selecting the research design.

Question 1 asks about the major contribution of the superior research design to the evaluation process. If Study A has a superior research design, it means that you can better attribute the clients' measured progress to the intervention rather than something else. The research design deals with the issue of causation. Better designs do a better job of controlling for things outside of intervention that might explain the clients' measured progress. Question 2 deals with the fundamentals of single-system and group designs. Single-system designs would be appropriate when you are evaluating a single client. Group designs are appropriate when you are evaluating a group of clients using the same tool for measurement of progress. Please keep in mind, however, that you measure the client's target behavior many times whenever you employ a single-system design. For group designs you typically measure the target behavior two times for several clients.

Question 3 asks for the definition of control group (or comparison group). This is the group that does not receive treatment. When you employ the comparison group design, the progress of the control group is used to gauge the effect of normal growth and development on the client's target behavior. The treatment group's progress is compared to the progress of the control group to determine whether the intervention had an effect on the target behavior that cannot be attributed to normal growth. Thus, the answer to question 4 is option c. The one-group pretest–posttest design, however, does not have a comparison group; thus, the answer to question 5 is option d. The answer to question 6 is option b. Option a of this question is an illustration of the B design, not the AB design. Option c is not a single-system design—you cannot measure a single client once before treatment and once after treatment and do anything statistically with this information. Statistical analysis requires an array of data, whether that data be related to repeated measures for a single client or measurements of a group of clients.

Procedures for Evaluating Outcome with a Single-Subject Design

Some of the procedures you employ will vary by the particular research design you select. Some designs require the recording of client behavior during a baseline period. You have already examined how to analyze the target behavior, how to select the intervention, how to select the sample, and how to measure client progress. These steps will be listed below in order to draw a total picture of the procedures when the single-subject design is employed.

1. Select a client for treatment. Determine the study population from which this client was drawn.
2. Define the client's problem. Use this definition to select a means to measure client progress.
3. Analyze the client's problem. Use this analysis to guide your choice of an intervention.

4. Develop an intervention. Be sure this choice is congruent with the problem analysis.
5. Select the means to measure client progress. Be sure these measurement methods are congruent with the definition of the target behavior and the treatment objectives.
6. Select a research design. Be sure this design addresses the threats to internal validity that should be of special concern in your client situation.
7. Measure target behavior to determine:
   a. Whether the measurements of target behavior revealed growth.
   b. The likelihood that the measured client progress can be explained by chance.
   c. Whether the measured client progress is clinically noteworthy—i.e., of practical significance.
8. Draw conclusions and address the study's limitations. Be sure your conclusions are congruent with your data.

Discussion 15.1

Let's suppose that a colleague has defined stress as psychological tension exemplified by such concepts as *anxious* and *up-tight* and is viewed as the opposite of such concepts as *calm*. Suppose further that this colleague has decided to measure stress by asking clients to identify how many traumatic events they have experienced in their lives such as the death of a close family member, losing a job, being expelled from school, and so forth.

   What is wrong with this scenario?

Discussion 15.2

Let's suppose that a colleague has analyzed the behavior known as ADHD (attention-deficit hyperactivity disorder) and concluded that in children this condition is caused by a difference in the brain of the ADHD child from other children, and that parents need to understand how to employ certain behavior techniques to help the child adjust to this reality. Suppose further that this colleague has proposed psychotherapy for the ADHD child as the treatment. What is wrong with this?

General Types of Research Designs

There are two major categories of research designs for evaluative research—group designs and single-subject designs (a.k.a. single-system designs). With group designs, you are collecting data on the same variable for a group of clients who are receiving the same service. For example, you may measure self-esteem before treatment and again after treatment for all clients using the Hare Self-Esteem Scale. With single-subject designs, you are collecting data on a single subject. For example, you may measure school grades for your client for four grading periods prior to treatment and for six grading periods during the treatment period.

With group designs, typically you will collect data at two points in time—before and after the treatment period—although there are variations from this procedure with different designs. With single-subject designs, you will collect the same data many times for the same client. You *cannot* measure a single client once before treatment and once after treatment and subject these data to statistical analysis; statistical analysis requires an array of data that is larger than two units. You will have the necessary array of data when you either compute scores for a group of clients or repeatedly for a single client.

Discussion Box 15.3

Think of an outcome evaluation study you would like to conduct. For example, you might want to compare the rate of repeat child abuse reports for the past six months as compared to the last six months of last year as an evaluation of the new Rapid Response System that was first implemented six months ago. You might want to evaluate whether one of your clients is improving in regard to daily conduct reports in kindergarten. You might want to know whether the clients of your adolescent mothers' support group have improved in their attitudes about parenting in the six weeks of group meetings.

Briefly describe the nature of the study and identify whether you would use a group research design or a single-system design.

Threats to Internal Validity

In this chapter, you will examine single-subject designs. In the next chapter, group designs will be the focus. With both designs, you must address the concept of **threats to internal validity**. Threats to internal validity refer to alternative explanations for the client's recovery other than treatment. The choice of a research design helps you to determine the extent to which you can attribute the client's progress to the treatment rather than something else.

For example, the group research design that is most famous is sometimes referred to as the "classic experimental design." With this design, you divide your study subjects into a treatment group and a control group (no treatment) on a random basis. With this design, you have a basis of asserting that differences in outcome between the treatment group and the control group can be attributed to the intervention rather than something else, like normal growth and development over time or changes in the clients' environment. Of course, the people in the two groups will have differences that may affect the outcome scores, but these differences between members of the two groups will likely cancel each other out in view of the fact that the only reason one person was in the treatment (experimental) group and another was in the control group was purely random. For every person in the treatment group who has poor motivation for treatment, there is probably a person in the control group with the same characteristic, so they cancel each other out. The only noteworthy difference between the two groups is treatment.

Discussion Box 15.4

Suppose you are conducting a study using the experimental design and Paul tells you he knows there are two persons in your treatment group who obtained employment during the treatment period, and that this probably explains their improvement in the target behavior. For this reason, Paul questions the outcome of your study that revealed a major difference in outcome between the two groups that favored the treatment group.

What would you say to Paul?

There is a variety of single-subject research designs to select from. The choice should be dictated by the particular circumstances you encounter regarding alternative explanations for client growth (threats to internal validity). You want a basis for concluding that the client's growth was due to treatment rather than something else. One of the alternative explanations is normal growth and development, known in research terms as **maturation**. We normally grow over time and we normally find ways to cope with our difficulties. We don't always require treatment in order to recover. Another one of the prominent alternative explanations is change in the client's environment, independent of treatment, which might explain the client's growth. This is referred to as **history** as a threat to internal validity. If an unemployed client got a job during the treatment period, you might have reason to believe that the client's growth was due to the job rather than treatment. In the next chapter, you will view additional threats to internal validity. For now, you will consider only maturation and history, so that you can achieve a basic conceptualization of this idea of alternative explanations for client outcome, without being overwhelmed by detail.

Which Threats Should be of Special Concern to Me?

A critical question to ask is "Which alternative explanations should I be especially concerned about?" If a client's social history clearly suggests she has been clinically depressed for a year without any noticeable change, you might conclude that there is no process of maturation underway with this client. If your treatment period is only three months, you may logically conclude that maturation is not a special concern. This would mean that finding a research design that addresses maturation would be of less need for you than for a researcher who had a basis to be concerned with maturation. If, however, you provided parent training for adolescent mothers for a six-month period, you would likely conclude that maturation is a special concern. You might conclude that new mothers normally learn lessons about parenting over a six-month period without special training; thus, changes in parenting skill may be attributed to maturation rather than the treatment. In this situation, you would seek a research design that addresses maturation. On the other hand, you might have literature that reveals that adolescent mothers with a history of delinquency do not grow in parenting ability over time. In this situation, you would have less reason to be concerned about maturation.

There is a variety of single-subject research designs. These include the AB design, the B design, the ABA design, the ABC design, and the ABAB design. With each of the designations, the letter A refers to a baseline period during which the client is repeatedly measured on the dependent variable but is *not* receiving treatment. All other letters refer to treatment periods, with B representing the first treatment, or the only treatment, and C representing a second treatment given after a period of time in which the client was receiving the treatment labeled as B. For example, the B design has no baseline and only one treatment. The ABC design has a baseline and two different treatments (e.g., medication without psychotherapy and medication with psychotherapy). The ABAB design has two baseline periods (both A phases) and two treatment periods (both B phases) but only one treatment (e.g., cognitive-behavioral therapy).

Discussion Box 15.5

Consider the following outcome evaluation possibilities. You are asked to determine if either history or maturation should be of special concern.

Suppose you have decided to examine growth in reading readiness of clients in your special kindergarten readiness program. You will administer a reading readiness test both at the beginning and end of this year-long program, and you will compute the difference to determine the level of gain. The reading readiness test measures the child's ability to recognize certain things that facilitate reading, such as the fact you read a sentence from left to right, that a period ends the sentence, and so forth. Should you be especially concerned with either history or maturation as threats to internal validity?

If you measure reading readiness for a child who is four years of age and you measure this variable again in a year, would you expect an improvement in reading readiness? Is it likely that a five-year-old child is more likely than a four-year-old to recognize what a period means? If so, you can expect a gain from one's fourth birthday to one's fifth. If you measure this change as a reflection of the effectiveness of your special program, how do you know it is the program that made a difference rather than normal growth and development?

When you consider the topic of history as a threat to internal validity, it is important to consider the question of whether you would normally expect things to change in a child's

---

EXHIBIT 15.2 • *A Review of the Concept of Threats to Internal Validity*

Research designs allow us to make a stronger case for causation (i.e., the treatment caused the client's growth) to the extent that our design addresses issues in causation known as threats to internal validity. Some designs do a better job than others. Another way of understanding the concept of threat to internal validity is to think of explanations of client growth that are different from the effect of the treatment. We might call these alternative explanations, and an example would be a change in the client's environment independent of treatment. In the nomenclature of research, we call this threat *history*. If an unemployed client has gotten a job during the treatment period, we may have good reason to believe that the job has increased his or her self-esteem, rather than the treatment. In order to take history into consideration, your research design must have a comparison group or control group that did not get the treatment and whose lives are believed to be consistent with persons in the treatment group with regard to potential environmental influences. In this way, the effect of history is believed to be the same for the two groups; thus, any differences between the groups cannot be attributed to history. For example, it would be estimated that the new factory that opened in town provided as many new jobs for persons in the comparison group as the treatment group; thus differences in outcome between the two groups cannot be attributed to the new factory.

This example was from a group research design. There are also some single-subject designs that address history. When more than one baseline period is employed, it is easier to detect the effect of environmental changes upon the target behavior.

It is not likely that there will be changes in the environment only during the treatment periods and not during the baseline periods. Thus, multiple baselines can control for the effect of environmental changes. If the client's scores on the Care-given Burden Scale are high during the first baseline but goes down during the first treatment period, but goes up again in the second baseline that follows treatment, you can reasonably assume that the reduction in these scores is due to the treatment rather than changes in the environment.

Another threat is that of *maturation*. This refers to the fact that people naturally grow over time and find ways to solve their problems on their own without the help of treatment. We can expect, for example, that the level of depression of a recently separated marriage partner will naturally lower with the passage of time for most people. If we employ treatment during this period and measure depression before and after treatment, how can we be confident that the treatment was the cause of the reduction in the measured level of depression? There are two basic ways to deal with maturation as an alternative explanation. One is to obtain information on trends in the client's behavior before the treatment began, to project this trend into the treatment period, and to compare the treatment measurements to this trend. Another way to address maturation is to have a comparison group that did not receive the treatment. The effect of maturation is believed to be consistent between the two groups; thus, any differences in target behavior gain between the treatment group and the comparison group cannot be attributed to maturation.

environment that would influence progress on the target behavior. The question is *not* whether it is *possible* for the environment to change, the question is whether it is *probable* that the environment will change. All kinds of things are possible. If you restrict your analysis to those things you can imagine that are possible, you will always conclude that history must be controlled in every study, when, in fact, the truth is that history is probably not of special concern in a wide variety of studies. In other words, it is typical that the client's environment does not change in a way that would influence the target behavior independent of treatment.

Discussion Box 15.6

Suppose that you have decided to administer the Adolescent Anger Rating Scale to 15 middle-school students both before and after a five-week treatment period during which they will attend anger management training sessions twice weekly. These 15 students have been identified by guidance counselors as having a problem with anger management and aggressive behavior. In this situation, should you be especially concerned with either history or maturation as threats to internal validity?

A major influence on your analysis of this question should be the brevity of the treatment period. The treatment period is only five weeks long. Not a lot happens with regard either to maturation or history in brief periods like five weeks.

Single-Subject Designs That Fail to Address Maturation or History

Two of the single-system research designs that address neither maturation nor history as threats to internal validity are described next; these are the B design and the limited AB design. Neither of these designs address maturation (normal growth) as alternative explanations because in neither case are there sufficient data before treatment to establish a trend that can be projected into the treatment period as a basis for considering the process of growth that might already be present for the client. In other words, there is no basis for measuring the effect of maturation on the target behavior. Each of these two designs also fails to address history as an alternative explanation for the client's growth because there is no accommodation for the effect of potential changes in the client's environment during the treatment period. Designs that introduce treatment, withdraw treatment, and re-establish treatment would address history because changes in the environment that influence target behavior are not likely to occur only during the treatment periods in cases where there is more than one such period. In neither of the following designs is there a provision for this procedure.

The B Single-Subject Design

With the B design, there is no baseline, but there are repeated measurements of the client's target behavior throughout the treatment period. In many cases, it is not feasible to measure the client's target behavior before treatment begins. This design does not address either maturation or history as alternative explanations for the client's growth; thus, it would not be appropriate if either of these threats to internal validity were of special concern in a given situation.

If you are not concerned with the examination of statistical significance, you can simply plot the client's scores on a chart and examine the trend to help draw conclusions about treatment effectiveness. Examine the data in Figure 15.1 on martial satisfaction during an eight week period of treatment. These data reveal a score on marital happiness of 15 at the end of the first week of treatment, followed by scores of 17, 17, 18, 19, 19, 19, and 21 in that time sequence. This shows a gradual gain in marital happiness. You can examine these scores from a clinical standpoint and draw conclusions about treatment effectiveness, taking into consideration whatever you know about outside influences on this target behavior. Statistical significance will be addressed in the coming paragraphs.

In order to conduct a statistical analysis of your data with the method included in this text, you must have *at least eight treatment recordings*. It is also necessary that the client's behavior be measured *at the interval level*. There is a statistical test that can be used to determine if the trend in your treatment recordings is significantly different from a horizontal line which would be represented by data that revealed no effect of treatment. But this procedure requires a minimum of eight recordings. The statistic employed here is the C statistic (Tripodi, 1994).

An example of the B design was one done by a graduate social work student who provided cognitive behavioral therapy in an outpatient setting to a 33-year-old male once per week for a nine-week period. The presenting problem was depression. Because no pretreatment recordings of depression were feasible, the B single-subject research design was employed. The client was administered the Beck Depression Inventory each week for a total of nine recordings. The recordings for depression for this client are given in Table 15.1.

From these scores, you can easily see a marked decline in depression. The B statistic was applied to these scores to determine if the downward trend that is obvious from the data constituted a slope that was significantly different from a horizontal line. A horizontal line would be represented by scores that were the same for each recording, or scores that fundamentally showed a horizontal line (e.g., 32, 34, 32, 35, 33, 32, 34). A pattern that is best depicted as a horizontal line would indicate no gain in functioning. As you would expect, these data on depression scores revealed statistically significant growth ($p < .05$); this downward pattern was sufficiently different from a horizontal line to suggest that it is not easily explained by chance.

The data from the B single-system design measures client growth, but does not control for any of the common threats to internal validity. Your choice of this design should be justified with reference to the conditions of the particular client that reflect various alternative explanations for the client's growth on the target behavior. In the example, information about the duration of the depression and trends in these feelings should be ascertained and recorded by the clinical researcher. If this client revealed that he had been seriously depressed for the past six months with no change in his level of depression, you would have little reason to be concerned with maturation as an alternative explanation for the significant improvement that was recorded. If, however, this client had indicated that his depression was much higher a

Scores								
30								
29								
28								
27								
26								
25								
24								
23								
22								
21								X
20								
19					X	X	X	
18				X				
17		X	X					
16								
15	X							
14								
13								
12								
11								
10								
	1	2	3	4	5	6	7	8
	Weeks in the treatment period							

FIGURE 15.1 *Example of a B Single-System Design*

TABLE 15.1 *Client Scores on the Beck Depression Inventory*

Score	35	31	30	23	24	15	11	7	5
Week	1	2	3	4	5	6	7	8	9

month ago and he feels better now, you would naturally be concerned about maturation as an alternative explanation. It could be that the maturation process currently underway would result in the decline that was recorded and that treatment had made no difference. In this situation, a different research design should be employed.

Discussion Box 15.7

Think of a treatment situation and indicate whether the B single-system design would be appropriate. If you cannot think of a client, think of yourself or a friend who was having problems of some kind that might have been amenable to some form of intervention.

The Limited AB Design

The AB single-system design calls for the measurement of client behavior during both the baseline period (before the client was receiving treatment) and the treatment period. The letter A represents the baseline period and the letter B represents the treatment period. I am doing something a little unusual for texts on research when I divide the AB design into two categories—the limited AB design and the AB design. The limited AB design has at least one baseline recording but not enough to detect a trend. The AB design has enough baseline recordings to detect a trend. The question of how many is enough to detect a trend is not easy to answer. I suggest that you use the cutoff point as four recordings. If you have at least four baseline recordings, you are employing the AB design, but if you have one, two, or three baseline recordings, you are employing the limited AB design.

There are two implications of this distinction. First, the AB design addresses maturation as a threat to internal validity but the limited AB design does not. The argument that the AB design addresses maturation is based on the assumption that the effect of maturation would be revealed in the baseline period, so a pattern of scores in the treatment period that is significantly better than the baseline trend would control for maturation. In other words, the client's gain can better be attributed to the intervention than to maturation. But this assumption is dependent on there being sufficient baseline data to detect a trend. I challenge this assumption in cases where there are fewer than four baseline recordings.

The second implication of this distinction between the limited AB design and the AB design is related to statistical analysis. The statistical approach for these two alternatives is different. This issue is addressed explicitly in Chapter 20 of this book. When you have only one baseline recording, you have this one score to use for comparison to an array of treatment scores. When you have two or three baseline recordings, I suggest you use a single score to represent the baseline, such as the mean of these scores. In both cases with the limited AB design, you are using a single score to represent the baseline. When you have trend data in the baseline, you can use different approaches to statistical analysis.

TABLE 15.2   *Client Scores on the Social Avoidance and Stress Scale*

	Baseline		Treatment Period				
Score	20	17	17	14	10	6	8
Week	1	2	3	4	5	6	7

The limited AB design has an advantage over the B design because you do have some pretreatment data for comparison. You do know something about the client's pretreatment functioning. Also, the limited AB design can employ different statistical analysis techniques that provide better information for your analysis. For more information, see Chapter 20 of this book.

A social worker employed the limited AB design in the examination of the effect of dialectal behavior therapy in the reduction of the anxiety and social avoidance of a 32-year-old woman diagnosed with schizophrenia. The Social Avoidance and Stress Scale (SAD) was administered to this client two times before treatment and five times during the treatment period. This scale is designed to measure anxiety in social situations and tendencies to avoid social situations. It gives higher scores for higher anxiety and avoidance. The two baseline recordings were 20 and 17. The mean of these two recordings (18.5) was employed for comparison of the scores in the treatment period. The treatment recordings were as 17, 14, 10, 6, and 8, as depicted in Table 15.2.

When this social worker submitted this to statistical analysis, she discovered that the treatment scores were significantly lower than the mean of the baseline scores ($p < .05$). Thus, the hypothesis was supported.

Two Single-Subject Designs That Address Maturation But Not History

There are three designs that address maturation but not history that will be examined in this section: the AB design, the ABC design, and the BC design.

Discussion Box 15.8

Describe the AB design, the ABC design, and the BC design.

The AB Design

One of the single-subject research designs that address maturation but not history is the **AB design**. The AB design has been described above and was distinguished from the limited AB design. It was explained how maturation was addressed by the AB design. To illustrate, let's suppose that John was measured on a self-esteem scale that gave higher scores for higher self-esteem and we found the following weekly baseline scores—12, 13, 14, 15. John's self-esteem seems to be making steady, but slow progress. If you projected this baseline trend into future weeks, you would expect scores of 16, 17, 18, 19, and so forth—and this would be your expectation without treatment. So your treatment scores would have to be significantly better than this trend for you to assert that you had data that revealed client growth that can be attributed to the intervention rather than maturation. Treatment scores like 20, 25, 27, 29, and 31 just might do the trick. But scores like 16, 18, 19, 18, 20, and 19 would not reveal a change in the trend because this array of measurements is too close to the projected trend. The projected trend is what you would expect in the absence of treatment.

The AB design does not address history as a threat to internal validity. This threat refers to changes in the client's environment that might influence the target behavior independent of the treatment. A client may get or lose a job, break up with a spouse or reconcile with a spouse, and so forth. These things can affect the target behavior. The AB design does not address this threat because the changes can occur in either the baseline or the treatment periods, but it is not likely that they would have happened in both periods with equal effect.

Let's suppose that you are measuring the client's self-esteem using a scale where higher scores represent higher self-esteem. In Figure 15.2, you can see an example of hypothetical data when the AB single-system design is employed. There are four weeks in the baseline period followed by a five-week treatment period. The four baseline recordings are 14, 15, 15, and 13 in that time order. During the treatment period, you have scores of 15, 17, 17, 19, and 21. This indicates an increase in self-esteem scores. Whether this increase can be easily explained by chance is an issue for statistical analysis, which will be addressed in Part IV of this book.

The data in Figure 15.2 reveal a baseline mean of 14.25 and a treatment mean of 17.8. These figures reveal growth. But is this difference easily explained by chance? That is the task of statistical analysis, which will take into consideration the variance in the baseline scores and will determine the likelihood that the treatment scores were within a range of scores that would be too easily explained by chance to be treated as a serious indication of growth.

The ABC Design

The **ABC** design also addresses maturation but not history. With this design, you collect target behavior data during a baseline period (at least four recordings), followed by repeated measurements of target behavior during the first treatment period, which is followed by a change in the form of treatment along with repeated measurements of target behavior during this final phase of the process.

For example, you might collect data on daily conduct ratings of your kindergarten child for five weeks before attempting the use of medication for your child's ADHD (attention-deficit hyperactivity disorder) behavior. Then, you would give the child medication that is designed to help the child control impulses and focus attention better. This would be your first treatment. You could examine daily conduct ratings for four weeks of this treatment period. So far, you have an example of the AB design. You could turn your study into one with the ABC design by adding another type of treatment, such as behavioral techniques administered by the parent. The third phase, or the second treatment period, comprise a combination of the medication and

Score	Baseline Period (A Phase)				Treatment Period (B Phase)				
30									
29									
28									
27									
26									
25									
24									
23									
22									
21									X
20									
19								X	
18									
17						X	X		
16									
15		X	X		X				
14	X								
13				X					
	1	2	3	4	5	6	7	8	9
	Weeks of baseline and treatment								

FIGURE 15.2   *Example of the AB Single-System Design*

Discussion 15.9

The AB design has an advantage over the limited AB design in that the AB design addresses maturation as a threat to internal validity. Explain how this statement is true. Why can it be said that the AB design addresses maturation, but the limited AB design does not?

behavioral techniques. There are two questions being pursued in this example of the ABC design:

- Does medication improve the target behavior?
- Does the addition of behavioral techniques by parents improve the target behavior beyond the effect of medication?

This situation is illustrated in Figure 15.3. The baseline scores are 10, 11, 10, and 11. With higher scores representing more problems, you can see a serious problem with this child's conduct in kindergarten. You can also see that there is rather little fluctuation in these baseline scores. The less the variance in baseline scores, the more likely you will find statistical significance when you compare a set of treatment scores that are better than the baseline. The reason is that statistical tests take into consideration the variance in scores and assumes that variance makes things less predictable.

When you examine data from the ABC design, you have two separate statistical tests to undertake. The first compares the A phase data with the B phase data just as if you were using the AB design. The second analysis compares the B phase data with the C phase data in the same way. In other words, you compare the C phase data with the B phase data the same way you would undertake statistical analysis using the AB design. In all of these cases, you are comparing data from two phases to see if there is a statistically significant difference.

Conduct Problem Scores	Baseline Period (Phase A)				First Treatment (Phase B)				Second Treatment (Phase C)			
12												
11		X		X								
10	X		X									
9												
8					X		X					
7						X						
6								X				
5												
4									X			
3										X		
2											X	X
1												

FIGURE 15.3   *Example of the ABC Single-System Design*

The BC Design

When you employ the **BC** design, you have no baseline measurements, but you have measurements during two different treatment periods using two different forms of treatment. Because you have no baseline recordings, you do not have a clear measure of maturation. So the question of maturation is not easy to address. In many ways, you should look upon the BC design like the AB design. The main difference is that you are comparing the second treatment with the first treatment. You could argue that the BC design addresses maturation in that the recordings during the B phase reflect the combination of the effects of maturation *and* the first treatment. So, if your C phase recordings are significantly better, you could argue that Treatment C is significantly better than the combination of maturation and Treatment B. But recordings during a baseline period (when there is no treatment) would provide for the better argument of controlling for maturation.

Single-System Designs Addressing Both Maturation and History

According to Bloom, Fischer, & Orme (2003), there are several single-system designs that meet the qualifications of being considered experimental designs. This means the issue of causation has been addressed rather fully, if not completely. Most threats to internal validity have been addressed by these designs. Among the designs listed with this qualification are the ABA design, the ABAB design, and the BAB design (Bloom, Fischer, & Orme, 2003).

The ABA Design

The **ABA** design is one in which there are two baseline periods, one before treatment and one after. You collect data on the target behavior during a traditional baseline period (phase A) followed by the continued collection of repeated measures of the target behavior during the treatment period (phase B), which is then followed by the withdrawal of treatment accompanied by the continued collection of target behavior data during a second baseline period. The idea is that the client's target behavior will improve during the intervention period (phase B) over the baseline period (phase A) and that it will return to the baseline level in the second baseline period (The second B phase). If this were to occur, you would have a claim to causation with regard to the relationship between treatment and target behavior.

But many, if not most, situations in evaluation research are not appropriate for the ABA design because they are examples where treatment is terminated because you expect the client's progress on target behavior to be sustained. After all, most human service interventions are not designed to be given to a typical client forever. If you treat a depressed client for three months and she achieves a major reduction in depression, you may find it warranted to terminate treatment. In this case, you expect the reduction in depression to be sustained after treatment is terminated. So it would be inappropriate to use the ABA design, because you would see that the lower levels of depression were evident in *both* the treatment period and the second baseline period. You would not want to argue that this fact eliminated your claim to causation. It would be more logical to assert that the continued gain would be the long-term consequence of the treatment rather than the failure of treatment to affect the behavior.

So when would you employ the ABA design? It would be when you do not expect the gain to be sustained in the absence of treatment. It is when the gain is dependent on treatment for the foreseeable future. An illustration can be given with regard to caregiver burden for caregivers of patients suffering from serious illness or disability. Suppose you were offering an intervention to the wife of a patient with Alzheimer's disease. Your objective is to reduce stress by providing respite care where someone substitutes for the caregiver each day for several hours so that she will have the freedom to do things not possible when she is with her husband, who needs constant attention. You measure stress during a baseline period and find it rather high. You offer respite care and find the stress level goes down significantly. Then respite care is terminated, but you continue to measure stress. If the stress level goes up during this second baseline period, you have reason to argue that the intervention is the cause of the reduction in stress, and there are no other explanations that are clearly evident. This example is illustrated in Figure 15.4, where caregiver stress was measured on a 30-point scale with higher scores indicating higher stress.

You can see from the data in Figure 15.4 that stress went down in the treatment period but went back up when treatment was terminated. This would indicate a causal link between treatment and stress.

Caregiver Stress Score	Baseline Period (Phase A)				Treatment Period (Phase B)				Second Baseline (The second Phase A)			
22												
21			X	X								
20	X											
19		X									X	X
18									X	X		
17												
16												
15												
14												
13						X	X					
12					X			X				
11												

FIGURE 15.4   *Example of the ABA Single-System Design*

The statistical analysis would take two forms—the comparison of the first A phase with the B phase, and the comparison of the B phase with the second A phase. In other words, you would have two data analyses to conduct. In each situation, you are examining whether the two phases are significantly different.

The ABAB Design

When you employ the **ABAB** design, you collect measurements of the target behavior during a period before treatment begins (the first A phase), and you continue to collect these recordings during the first treatment phase (the first B phase). At this point in time, you have the ingredients of the AB design. But you continue by collecting repeated measurements of the target behavior during a second baseline period (the second A phase). Finally, you administer the treatment again during the second B phase, and continue collecting repeated measures of the target behavior. With this design, you are employing only one intervention, but you are administering it two different times.

With the ABAB design you are in the optimal position, for single-subject designs, to attribute the measured client gain to the intervention rather than something else. Maturation is addressed in the first half of this process (the first A and B phases), as was discussed in the section on the AB design. If you are concerned with the influence of changes in the client's environment, you can be comforted in the thought that the client is highly unlikely to have instrumental changes in the environment *only* during the two baseline periods and not either of the two treatment periods. How likely is it that I will have major changes in my environment that enhance my self-esteem during the first treatment period and the second treatment period, but *not* either of my two baseline periods? Not much of a chance—right? So, we will assume the ABAB design addresses history as a threat to internal validity in addition to maturation as a threat.

The statistical analysis of data takes three different forms. One is the comparison of the first A phase with the first B phase. The second is the comparison of the first B phase with the second A phase, while the third compares the second A phase with the second B phase. In each situation, you are determining the likelihood that differences between phases is due to chance.

This design is not feasible for most human service evaluations because of the difficulty of collecting baseline data in two periods and the potential ethical dilemmas of terminating treatment for the sake of research. It might be feasible in situations where data are routinely collected for human performance with or without special interventions. An example would be data collected on a regular basis for school performance. We routinely record grades and data on disciplinary actions. If these types of information can be used to measure your client's target behavior, you may find the ABAB design to be feasible.

The BAB Design

When you employ the BAB design, you start treatment, withdraw treatment, and restart treatment while taking repeated measurements of target behavior during each phase. The only difference between this design and the ABAB design is that you do not administer a second phase of baseline when you employ the BAB design. The second baseline period is one where a return to poor target behavior may be indicated. This event would suggest that the target behavior is dependent on the treatment rather than something else. The same caution that is applied to the ABA design is relevant to the BAB design, because you often have a situation where you expect the client's gain in the treatment period to be sustained after treatment.

Summary

In this chapter, you have examined various single-system research designs in light of how each deals with various alternative explanations for client growth (i.e., threats to internal validity). It was stressed that you should determine which threats are of special concern in your particular situation as you select the design to employ. You should pay careful attention to these threats and do what you can to address them with your design. If it is not feasible to use a design that addresses these threats, you should consider this a limitation of your research design.

Discussion Box 15.10

Think of an example where a single-system research design might be employed in the evaluation of outcome. In the box below, answer the following questions:

- What is the target behavior?
- Which threats to internal validity should be of special concern? (Note: the question is *not* what is possible, but what is probable.)
- What research design would be feasible in this situation, given the practical or ethical constraints of this practice situation? (For example, a withdrawal of treatment may be considered unethical in this situation.)
- Does this design address the threats of special concern?

Quiz

This is a quiz on the contents of this chapter. Select only one response to each question. Answers are provided at the end of the chapter.

1. What is meant by the concept "threats to internal validity"?
   a. The extent to which the client's measured gain can be generalized to persons not in the study

   b. Those things outside of treatment that might be the cause of the client's measured gain
   c. The extent to which the method of measurement correctly measures what you intended it to measure
   d. The extent to which your measurement device operates consistently

2. Which of the following research designs does the best job of addressing maturation as a threat to internal validity?
   a. The B design
   b. The limited AB design
   c. The posttest only one-group design
   d. The pretest–posttest one group design

3. The experimental group research design is optimal in addressing threats to internal validity because:
   a. It employs a random assignment of persons to the treatment group and the control group.
   b. It uses groups for data analysis rather than a single client.
   c. It can be classified as a probability sample selected from a larger population.
   d. It employs better methods of measuring client progress.

4. What is meant by history as a threat to internal validity and maturation as a threat to internal validity?
   a. Maturation refers to changes in the client's environment, while history refers to things that have happened in the past that might influence client growth.
   b. History refers to changes in the client's environment, while maturation refers to the amount of growth in target behavior during the treatment period.
   c. History refers to changes in the client's environment, while maturation refers to the client's normal growth and development over time.
   d. History refers to the client's normal growth and development over time, while maturation refers to changes in the client's environment.

5. How many different types of treatment are in the ABAB design?
   a. One
   b. Two
   c. Three
   d. Four

6. Which of the following statements is/are true?
   a. The B single-system design addresses history but not maturation.

   b. The AB single-system design addresses history but not maturation.
   c. Both of the above.
   d. None of the above.

7. Which of the following statements is/are true?
   a. The AB design addresses maturation, while the limited AB design does not.
   b. The ABAB design addresses both history and maturation.
   c. Both of the above.
   d. None of the above.

8. In which of the following situations should you be especially concerned with selecting a research design that addresses maturation as a threat to internal validity?
   a. You are providing a one-year program of prekindergarten education and your target behavior is reading readiness.
   b. You are providing a one-month intensive outpatient program for the treatment of depression for those who have been chronically depressed.
   c. Both of the above.
   d. None of the above.

9. Which of the following research designs does the best job of addressing maturation and history as threats to internal validity?
   a. The limited AB design
   b. The AB design
   c. The ABCD design
   d. The ABAB design

10. The B single-system research design does not address maturation as a threat to internal validity because:
    a. There are no pretreatment data on the client's target behavior.
    b. There normally are not enough measurements of target behavior to subject these data to statistical analysis.
    c. There are not enough pretreatment measurements to designate a trend in the target behavior.
    d. There is only one baseline period.

References

Bloom, M., Fischer, J. & Orme, J. G. (2003). *Evaluating practice* (4th ed.). Boston: Allyn & Bacon.

Corcoran, K., & Fischer, J. (1987). *Measures for clinical practice*. New York: Free Press.

Tripodi, T. (1994). A primer on single-subject design for clinical social workers. Washington, DC: National Association of Social Workers.

Answers to the Quiz

1. b
2. d
3. a
4. c
5. a

6. d
7. c
8. a
9. d
10. a

16

Selecting a Research Design for Groups of Clients

In the previous chapter, research designs were divided into two categories—group designs and single-subject designs. With group designs, you are collecting the same data on a group of clients who are receiving the same service. This means that we have a group of clients with a common intervention and common target behavior whose progress is being measured by the same instrument. With single-subject designs, you are collecting data on a single subject. With group designs, you typically will collect data at two points in time—before and after the treatment period. With single-subject designs, you will collect the same data many times for the same client.

In this chapter, we will examine group designs. We will discuss only a few of the many group designs that you could employ, with emphasis on practicality. Research designs vary in the extent to which they address various threats to internal validity. Some do not address a given threat at all. Others may address a particular threat in a minimal way while still others may address this threat optimally. A critical question to ask is *What threats to internal validity should I be especially concerned with in my study?* This should serve as a guide to the selection of a research design and to the interpretation of the study results. This issue was discussed in the previous chapter with regard to the evaluation of a single client. In this chapter, we will continue our discussion of this topic using examples of group designs.

The concept of threats to internal validity was addressed in the previous chapter. We will return to it here with some elaboration, including the addition of six new threats. Then we will examine several group designs, after which we will compare these designs with regard to the question of how well they address the most common threats.

Threats to Internal Validity for Group Designs

The concept of threats to internal validity has been addressed in several chapters and you should understand it by now. In the first discussion box, you will be asked to apply your understanding of this concept to an example.

Discussion Box 16.1

Think of an evaluation study you would like to conduct regarding a designated target behavior and a designated intervention. Identify (1) the target behavior, (2) the intervention, and (3) whether you would need to be especially concerned with maturation as a threat to internal validity. Your task in item c is to identify whether it is probable that maturation would occur, not to identify if it is possible that maturation would occur.

1. Target behavior:

2. Intervention:

3. Explanation:

When we consider the research design to employ, we should consider whether a given threat to internal validity should be of special concern to us in our given evaluation study. Take, for example, the possibility that changes in the client's environment will affect the target behavior independent of treatment. When we address this issue, we should not be speaking of all those things that are *possible* (some of our clients might have a marital breakup, might lose their jobs, or might join a religious cult) but instead, we should be focusing on those things that are *probable* (many of the clients are in job training and likely will get jobs during the treatment period which could improve their self-esteem).

If we consider all the possibilities of things that might happen to our clients, we will engage in a trivial pursuit that will render our evaluation process excessively encumbered by things of little relevance to the real world. If your group of clients is chronically unemployed, you might consider that one or two of these 24 persons might get a job during the treatment period and this change could affect their target behavior. But you might reflect on your past experience with this type group of clients and note that it has been quite rare for a client in this group to get a job in the five-week period of the treatment. You know that it is possible, but you conclude that it is not probable; therefore, you will not list history as a threat to internal validity on this basis.

When we consider history as a threat to internal validity, we are speaking only of potential influences upon the target behavior that are *independent of treatment*. If part of your treatment plan for the Jones family is to help a family member to get a job, your success in so doing is part of the treatment, so it should not be viewed as an alternative explanation for the family's growth on the objective of reducing family conflict.

Discussion Box 16.2

Regarding the evaluation research study you identified in the previous discussion box, do you think that history should be considered a noteworthy threat? Remember that history refers to any change in the client's environment, independent of treatment, which is likely to influence the target behavior.

In prior chapters, both maturation and history have been discussed as threats to internal validity. There are several threats to internal validity that have not been discussed before in this book. One of these is **testing**. This refers to the effects of the testing experience itself. Does the fact that I have been tested on my self-esteem last week affect the way I will respond to this same scale this week? Testing is especially important to consider for examinations of knowledge. I may remember the questions asked on the first exam and be better prepared to respond for that reason alone. Maybe I have had time to think about some of these questions and have realized my mistake on the previous test. The question here is whether my posttest grade is a reflection of my gain in knowledge about the subject of the training, or a function of the fact that I remembered the questions from the first test. If it is the former, we have good evaluation data, but if it is the latter, we are in a situation where testing is a threat to internal validity.

In my experiences as a college professor, however, I have seldom discovered evidence that being given a pretest of knowledge will influence knowledge on the posttest. On the occasions when I have tested this proposition, I have found only a very modest influence, perhaps not enough for us to be especially concerned about, unless a high degree of precision in research is our goal.

There are several other threats to internal validity that are presented in Exhibit 16.3. We will not discuss these threats at length here, but you can easily find other texts on research that will do so. The assumption of the present text is that you are seeking practical guidance in conducting evaluative research rather than preparing yourself for doctoral study or becoming a prolific writer of research studies. Being aware of the idea of alternative explanations for client growth and being competent in the application of the three most salient threats to internal validity should work well for you in regard to the achievement of fundamental competence in evaluation research on a practical level.

A key question to answer for your own study is whether you have reason to be concerned with any of these threats. For example, you would expect new parents to naturally grow (maturation) in parenting ability over a six-month period, but their growth over a two-week period would probably be minimal. Does your treatment extend over six months or two weeks? In the former case, you will need a research design that addresses maturation. In the case of history as a threat, you can collect information during the treatment period which considers this factor. Did things in the client's environment change? In the selection of a research design, you should try to predict the potential for such changes in determining the type of design that you will need to employ.

EXHIBIT 16.1 • *Additional Threats to Internal Validity*

Three threats to internal validity were discussed in the body of this text. Several additional ones will be presented here for your reference.

Instrumentation as a threat to internal validity refers to the validity of the measurement devices employed in the study. If these instruments are not valid measures of the dependent variable, you cannot conclude that the treatment was effective. The instruments can be invalid because of a flaw inherent in the tool itself, a flaw that would have been discovered in a good test of validity. Instruments that have been well tested should cause little concern on this basis. However, we can also have an instrumentation problem if we fail to administer the instrument in a proper way.

Statistical regression refers to the fact that people naturally tend to regress to the mean when they stand at extreme positions from the mean. For example, a person who scored lowest on IQ is more likely to score higher the next time than would be the case of someone who scored at the mean. Likewise, a person who scored highest would likely score *lower* the next time, because this person would also be regressing to the mean. In other words, both extremes move toward the mean on subsequent measurements. This is a natural phenomenon; thus, if we select the most extreme clients for treatment, we can expect that their scores will be more likely to improve without treatment than would be the case of less extreme clients. If we select extreme persons, we will need for our research design to address this threat to internal validity.

Selection bias is a third threat to internal validity that will be described here. This refers to the fact that the method used to select the clients for the study may be biased in some way that would effect their measured progress. If we intentionally select only the most highly motivated clients for our study, we would be introducing a selection bias into our study. However, if we divide these highly motivated persons into a control group that does not get treatment and an experimental group that receives treatment, we have a means of addressing this potential problem.

The **reactive effect** of the client to being in treatment is another threat to internal validity. Clients sometimes improve simply because they are being included in a study rather than the fact that the specific treatment protocol is effective in achieving progress. Clients may feel special because they are in a study and this factor may influence their progress.

Mortality is the final threat to internal validity to be described here. Some clients drop out of treatment before it is complete and are removed from the study. Are these persons different from those who remained? If so, in what way? Was it because treatment was not working for them? If this is true, then the persons in your study are restricted to certain persons for whom treatment was effective.

Discussion Box 16.3

Regarding the evaluation research study you identified in the previous discussion box, are there any threats to internal validity, other than maturation and history, which should be of special concern? Why?

Overview of Group Research Designs

Some texts divide research designs into the categories of pre-experimental designs, quasi-experimental designs, and experimental designs. These general categories suggest the level of sophistication of the design in addressing threats to internal validity. The pre-experimental design does not address any of the threats to internal validity, while the quasi-experimental design addresses a few of them. The experimental design does the best job of addressing these threats through the random assignment of persons to treatment and control groups. I will focus more on the particular threats addressed by designs than on which general category they best fit into.

There are two practical questions answered by the research design. First, did the clients improve? Second, to what extent can you attribute the clients' measured growth to the intervention rather than something else? In other words, to what extent can you infer causality?

If you only measure your one group of clients at the end of the treatment period, you do not have any evidence of client improvement. If you did not measure client growth, how can you assert that treatment was effective? There are some conditions that would suggest that posttest-only data can be used for evaluation, and these conditions will be discussed later. The issue of causality has been discussed in previous chapters and is addressed by the concept of threats to internal validity; this will receive elaboration in this chapter.

In the next few sections, you will review the posttest-only research design, the one-group pretest–posttest design, the comparison group design, the basic experimental design, and the posttest-only control group design. In the descriptions of group designs, symbols will be used as to designate a given design. The letter O will represent an observation (measurement of client conditions), while the letter X will represent a treatment. The letter R will represent a random assignment of persons to their group status. For example, the one-group pretest posttest design will be designated as follows:

$$O_1 \qquad X \qquad O_2$$

These symbols tell us that our clients had a measurement before treatment (observation at time 1), followed by a treatment, which was followed by another measurement of their condition (observation at time 2). When the letter R is placed before a line, this means that the group being measured has been assigned to its status on a random basis. If there is no R at the beginning of the line, you can assume that there was no random assignment procedure used.

One Group Posttest-Only Design

When you use the one-group posttest-only design, you will measure the clients' target behavior after treatment but not before treatment. This can be designated by the following symbols:

$$X \qquad O$$

This means the clients received a treatment (designated as X) followed by a measurement of target behavior (designated by the letter O). The clients did not receive a pretest measurement of target behavior.

The key question, of course, is whether you can assume that clients improved if you did not directly measure their gain on the target behavior. You might conduct a client satisfaction survey and ask clients to offer their opinions about their growth. This would be better than nothing. However, client satisfaction surveys have certain problems that have been discussed in previous chapters, and it is advised that measuring actual client growth is much better.

In some cases, it may be warranted for you to assume a certain level of behavior prior to treatment and compare the posttreatment condition to that assumption. It would be proper to assume that people in alcoholism treatment had a drinking problem before treatment began, so the number of persons who are abstinent six months after treatment could be calculated as a measure of success. You might have data reflecting the typical level of functioning of your clients at pretest in the past and may feel that it is appropriate for you to measure your clients only at the end of treatment and compare this level of functioning to the established data.

But most human service evaluations are not in this category, so it is advised that client target behavior be measured before treatment began and after treatment is complete. This is a clear way to measure client growth on the target behavior.

Discussion Box 16.4

Can you think of an evaluation you might conduct where the one-group posttest-only design would be warranted because you have some basis for estimating the client's pretreatment level of functioning? If you can't, maybe you can ask someone in your agency. Make a note about this situation.

One-Group Pretest–Posttest Design

With the one-group pretest–posttest design, you measure target behavior before treatment and after treatment. The following is the symbolic representation.

$$O_1 \quad X \quad O_2$$

The O_1 designation refers to measurement (observation) at time 1 (pretest) while O_2 refers to measurement at time 2 (posttest). The designation X, of course, means that this one group received a treatment.

Your measurement of client behavior before and after treatment can take many forms. You might, for example, tabulate whether or not your clients are employed at each time. But progress more likely will be measured by a scale. One's score on a self-esteem scale or a depression scale would be examples. In this situation, your statistical analysis of data would take the form of a computation of a gain score for each study subject and the statistical analysis of the mean gain score. The gain score is computed by taking the difference between each person's pretest score and posttest score. The gain score for a scale on depression, assuming that higher scores mean more depression, would be computed by subtracting the posttest score from the pretest score. If my depression level is 30 before treatment and 15 after treatment, then my gain score would be 15. This would represent my level of improvement on depression. However, if we are measuring a variable like self-esteem, where higher scores represent better functioning, we would subtract the pretest score from the posttest score to obtain a gain score. Whether the measured client gain can be explained by chance is an issue for statistical analysis of data. The *t* test for paired data is often used for this design and will be discussed in more detail in Chapter 21 of this book.

With the one-group pretest–posttest design, we have a basis for measuring client progress. We know whether clients improved in their functioning, assuming we have a valid means of measuring it. This has a clear advantage over designs that fail to measure client progress, with the exception of the posttest-only control group design that will be discussed later.

With this design, however, we do not have a basis for addressing various threats to internal validity, so its claim to the depiction of causality is weak. For example, we do not have a basis for taking normal growth and development into consideration. If we compared our clients to a nontreated group, we would have such a basis. We would also have a basis for considering maturation if we had collected data repeatedly over time for our clients before treatment.

Discussion Box 16.5

Think of an evaluation you might undertake where the one-group pretest–posttest design would be appropriate because you do not need to be especially concerned with any of the common threats to internal validity. Make a notation here.

Alternative Treatment Design

The alternative treatment design is one where you use different treatments for two groups of clients. With this design, you measure target behavior before and after treatment for a group of clients where one approach to treatment is used, and compare this gain to that of a different group of clients who are being subjected to a different type of treatment.

For example, you might employ medication only for one group of clients and medication plus counseling for a second group of clients. The comparison of the level of gain for these two groups gives you a basis for determining the difference made by the addition of counseling. You might compare the academic achievement of students in two schools that employ different models of education.

The symbolic representation of this design is as follows:

$$O_1 \qquad X_1 \qquad O_2$$

$$O_1 \qquad X_2 \qquad O_2$$

This reveals that each of two groups of clients receives measurement of target behavior both before and after treatment, but they receive different treatments.

The key information from this design is the different levels of effect of two approaches to treatment. You do know how much gain there was for clients in each group. You can assert that these treatments are or are not different in effectiveness. Because you have no comparison group of persons who received no treatment, you do not have a clear basis for controlling for maturation as a threat to internal validity. However, if treatment 2 is superior to treatment 1, you might assert that the gain for treatment 1 is a reflection of the combination of maturation and the effect of treatment 1; therefore, the superiority of treatment 2 is a certain amount better than this combination of treatment 1 and maturation. However, if there is no difference in gain for the two treated groups, you cannot lay claim to the control of maturation. It could be that the comparable gain for each of the two groups is due totally to the effect of maturation.

The same case could be made for some of the other common threats to internal validity, such as history. Without a nontreated group, you do not have clear basis for addressing history. But a result showing a superiority of one type of treatment could indicate a superiority of this treatment over the combination of the other treatment and history. This is slightly nonconventional thinking, so you might want to be cautious in making this assertion with a research purist.

Comparison Group Design

In the comparison group design, also known as the non-equivalent control group design (Campbell & Stanley, 1963), a treated group is compared to another group that did not receive the treatment. In the following designation, there are two groups of persons; one is receiving treatment and the other is not receiving treatment.

$$O_1 \qquad X \qquad O_2$$

$$O_1 \qquad\qquad O_2$$

You will notice that the letter X is on the line for the first group but is absent on the second line, which represents the second group. This means the first group received treatment and the second group did not. You should notice also the absence of the letter R, which means the persons in the two groups were not assigned to their group status on a random basis.

With this design, you have the basis for measuring client progress and the basis for inferring causality to a limited degree. For example, maturation is addressed with this design because the comparison group should be a basis for estimating the amount of growth that people typically achieve in the absence of treatment. In your analysis of data with this design, you would compare the treated clients' level of gain with the comparison group's level of gain.

While the comparison group design does not include the random assignment of people to the two groups, the experimental design does include this procedure. The assumption is that this random assignment procedure assures that the two groups are comparable except for one thing—one group gets the treatment and the other group does not. Thus, a host of threats to internal validity are addressed with the experimental design.

Because the comparison group design lacks this procedure, the extent of comparability between the groups is a question to be addressed. You should be especially carefully to examine this issue. If you know of a clear basis for a difference, such as motivation for treatment, between the two groups, you are in a weaker position to assert causality in regard to the treatment—you will be in a weaker position to assert that the treatment caused the difference in client gain between the two groups. For example, suppose you selected clients for treatment from the waiting list on the basis of motivation for treatment. You could have your intake person rate service applicants on this basis and use this as the method for selecting the persons for treatment. If you selected the others on the waiting list as the comparison group, you would have a known basis on which the two groups were different. The treatment group may get better because of their superior motivation rather than the effect of the treatment.

When you consider the issue of comparability, you should focus your attention on those things that are relevant to the target behavior. It is possible that you could have a comparison group that is completely comparable to the treatment group even when the assignment is not random. There may be differences between the groups that seem unrelated to the target behavior. For example, you may have reason to believe that males and females are similar on their spontaneous recovery from the target problem or that people of different ages do not differ on this basis. In this case, you have little reason to worry about differences between the two groups on gender or age. In general, however, the more differences you can find between the two groups, the more you should be concerned about comparability.

According to Campbell & Stanley (1963), the comparison group addresses several threats to internal validity, including maturation, history, testing, instrumentation, selection, and mortality. This design, however, does not address these threats as well as the experimental design because of the advantage of random assignment for the latter. Again, the greater the comparability between the two groups, the more similar the comparison group design to the experimental design with regard to the argument that the measured gain in client functioning is due to the treatment rather than something else.

The statistical analysis of data for the comparison group design entails the comparison of the mean gain scores for each group, assuming that the dependent variable is measured at the interval level (or you feel comfortable treating your dependent variable in this way). You would create a variable that represents the client's gain in functioning in the same manner as described. The mean gain in functioning for the treatment group would be compared to the mean gain in functioning for the comparison group. If the dependent variable is measured at the interval level, the *t* test for independent samples would be an appropriate statistic for determining significance. This will be discussed in more detail in the data analysis section of this book.

Discussion Box 16.6

Think of an evaluation study you might undertake that would employ either the alternative treatment design or the comparison group design. Identify the target behavior, the intervention, the research design that would be appropriate, and the reason it would be appropriate.

1. Target behavior:

2. Intervention:

3. Design:

4. Explanation:

Basic Experimental Design (Pretest–Posttest Control Group)

There are several variations of the experimental design. The most common is the pretest–posttest control group design and will be referred to here as the basic experimental design. This design is similar to the comparison group design with one important distinction—persons are assigned to their group status on a random basis. This means that a sample of people needing a certain treatment is divided into two groups on a random basis, and that one of these groups receives the treatment and the other does not. The major feature that all experimental designs have in common is the use of random assignment of persons to groups.

Another symbol in our shorthand for designating research designs that has not yet been employed is the letter R, which represents a random assignment of persons to the different groups. In the comparison group example, there is no letter R on the lines. This means that these persons were not assigned to their group status on a random basis. Instead, a client group was compared to another group that was selected on some other basis. In the example below, the persons in each group are assigned to their group status on a random basis.

$$R \qquad O_1 \qquad X \qquad O_2$$

$$R \qquad O_1 \qquad\qquad O_2$$

The random assignment of persons to groups covers a host of threats to internal validity. Furthermore, it addresses these threats in a better manner than such designs as the comparison group design. We can be more confident that the treatment group and the other group are comparable on such things as environmental changes or maturation or testing because the only thing that distinguishes them is their random assignment to their group status.

If we select the students in Ms. Smith's math class as a comparison group for the new teaching technique used by Ms. Jones, we must consider that these two groups of students have different teachers and that Ms. Jones may simply be a better teacher, and that this fact may be the reason her students do better rather than the new technique that she is using. However, if we select 10 teachers at random to be taught the new technique and compare their students with 10 other teachers' students selected at random, we would be in a good position to assume that teaching ability would be comparable between the two groups because the two groups of teachers were selected on a random basis.

It is rare that human service agencies find it feasible to employ the random assignment of clients to a treated group and a nontreated group. Usually agencies encounter clients at a time they need services, so denying them services for the sake of research is often problematic from an ethical standpoint. However, there are situations where this is feasible and ethical. One example that comes to mind is a treatment program for prison inmates that was to be offered in shifts, with one group getting the treatment from September through November and the second group getting the treatment from December through February. The reason for the shifts in treatment was that the prison lacked the resources to provide the treatment to all in need at the same time. In this case, the prospective clients were randomly assigned to their shift and the group to be treated later was the control group for the study of the group to be treated first.

Sometimes the ethical question is addressed by the fact that the new treatment to be tested is currently untested, so we don't know if those in the control group are being denied an essential service. This case can normally be made if the new treatment is supplemental to existing services or its effectiveness is rather unpredictable. Informed consent, of course, is essential when you are making this case.

Posttest-Only Control Group Design

Another experimental design worthy of special attention is the posttest-only control group design. When you are in a position to assign persons on a random basis, you do not have to use a pretest measurement. You can assume that the persons in the two groups are similar at the pretest time. If they are in their groups on a random basis, there is no reason for one group to be significantly different from the other. The symbols for this design are as follows:

$$R \qquad X \qquad O_2$$

$$R \qquad \qquad O_2$$

The statistical analysis of data for the posttest-only control group design takes the form of the comparison of the two groups on the dependent variable at the point in time in which intervention is terminated. If the treatment group (experimental group) has a significantly higher level of functioning than the control group, we would attribute that superiority to the treatment. The statistical test employed would be similar to that for the pretest-posttest control group design except that, with the posttest-only control group design, you would be comparing the two groups on the basis of their level of functioning at one point rather than comparing the level of gain between the two groups. A major advantage of this design is that it controls for the effects of the pretest.

Discussion Box 16.7

Think of an evaluation study you might conduct that could employ one of the experimental designs. Make a note here, including reference to the target behavior, the intervention, the design, and the explanation for it.

Solomon Four-Group Design

The Solomon four-group research design is highly sophisticated, but seldom used. It combines the basic, or classic, experimental design with the posttest-only design and controls for just about everything we can think of needing to control. The graphic depiction of this design is as follows:

$$R \quad O_1 \quad X \quad O_2$$

$$R \quad O_1 \quad\quad\ O_2$$

$$R \quad\quad\ X \quad O_2$$

$$R \quad\quad\quad\ O_2$$

With this design, you randomly assign clients to four groups. The first group gets a pretest and posttest and an intervention. The second group gets a pretest and posttest with no intervention. The third group gets an intervention and a posttest but no pretest, while the fourth group gets only a posttest. This group adds the advantages of both the basic experimental design and the posttest-only control group design.

Comparing the Designs

A summary of these four designs and the three threats to internal validity is given in Exhibit 16.2. As you will see, the one-group pretest–posttest design does not address any of these threats. The comparison group design addresses each of these threats on a minimal level; thus, you must consider those things that might challenge the validity of this design, such as known differences between the comparison group and the treatment group. The two experimental designs address each of these three threats to internal validity at an optimal level.

There are many more research designs than those presented here, and there are other threats to internal validity than those discussed in this chapter. The purpose of the present discussion is to cover the most common designs and the threats that are most likely to be of concern to social work research. Other texts on research can be consulted for a more thorough treatment of these concepts.

EXHIBIT 16.2 • *Research Designs and Threats to Internal Validity*

Research Designs	How well are these threats to internal validity addressed by given designs?		
	Maturation	*History*	*Testing*
Posttest-only one group	Not at all	Not at all	Not at all
One group pretest–posttest	Not at all	Not at all	Not at all
Comparison group	Minimally	Minimally	Minimally
Alternative treatment	Possibly*	Possibly*	Possibly*
Pretest–posttest control group	Optimally	Optimally	Optimally
Posttest only control group	Optimally	Optimally	Optimally

*Note the word of caution about the alternative treatment design because there is not a clear basis for addressing these threats.

Quiz

The following are questions related to the content of this chapter. You may use it as a pretest, to determine whether you need to read this chapter, or as a posttest, to determine how well you read it. Answers are given at the end of the references.

1. The concept of threats to internal validity refers to:
   a. Causation.
   b. Generalization.
   c. Chance.
   d. Measurement error.
2. *Testing* as a threat to internal validity refers to:
   a. The effect of normal growth and development over time.
   b. The effect of changes in the environment.
   c. The tendency of extremes to regress to the mean.
   d. The effect of the measurement experience.
3. Which of the following designs provides for the measurement of client growth?
   a. The one group posttest-only design
   b. The one-group pretest-posttest design
   c. Both of the above
   d. None of the above
4. Which of the following statements is/are true?
   a. Your best use of the one group posttest-only design would be when you have a basis for estimating the clients' pretreatment condition on the target behavior.

   b. The posttest-only design addresses maturation as a threat to internal validity.
   c. Both of the above.
   d. None of the above.
5. Which of the following statements is/are true?
   a. The one-group pretest–posttest design addresses maturation as a threat to internal validity.
   b. The comparison group design addresses maturation as a threat to internal validity.
   c. Both of the above.
   d. None of the above.
6. Which of the following statements is/are true?
   a. The alternative treatment design compares the effectiveness of different interventions.
   b. The alternative treatment design includes the measurement of client growth.
   c. Both of the above.
   d. None of the above.
7. Which of the following designs does the best job overall of addressing threats to internal validity?
   a. The alternative treatment design
   b. The comparison group design
   c. The experimental design
   d. The one-group pretest–posttest design
8. Which of the following statements is/are true?
   a. The position advocated in this book suggests that we should focus our attention on

all those threats to internal validity that can possibly explain the client's gain, no matter how remote its likelihood, not just those things that will probably explain the client's gain. We must select designs that address all threats.

b. One of the bases for our being especially concerned with maturation as a threat to internal validity is the extent of time that passes between the pretest and posttest measurements.

c. Both of the above.

d. None of the above.

9. The posttest-only control group design, which assigns people to the two groups on a random basis, addresses which of the following threats to internal validity?

a. Maturation

b. History

c. Both of the above

d. None of the above

10. What is the thing that all experimental research designs have in common that best distinguishes them from other designs?

a. Random assignment of people to groups

b. The use of random samples of people from larger populations

c. The measurement of client gain using a validated scale

d. The statistical analysis of data that controls for autocorrelation

Reference

Campbell, D. T., & Stanley, J. C. (1963). *Experimental and quasi-experimental designs for research.* Boston: Houghton Publishing.

Answers to the Quiz

1. a

2. d

3. b

4. a

5. b

6. c

7. c

8. b

9. c

10. a

17

Writing the Evaluation Report for the Outcome Study

When you prepare a report on an outcome evaluation study, you will begin with an introduction followed by a literature review that portrays your target behavior analysis. The introduction captures the attention of readers and lets them know where you are taking them. It does not need to be set aside with a separate heading from the literature review; it simply begins the paper. Your literature review of the target behavior clarifies the nature of your target behavior and its dynamics. If it is more than a page or two, it normally should include headings that distinguish the themes being pursued. The same is true for the presentation of the methods section of your report and the data analysis, but the conclusions section is normally without division into sections with headings. It is normally too brief to suggest this kind of division. The methods section will describe how client progress was measured, how the sample was selected and the nature of the research design, while the data analysis section will present the results of the measurement of client progress.

In this chapter, you will be given practical guidelines for writing the report of an evaluation study. This chapter will begin with practical guidelines for writing the introduction to the report, which is followed by guidelines for the analysis of the target behavior. Then you will review guidelines for writing the research methods which will be followed by advice about the presentation of the data. Finally, some suggestions will be presented about the conclusions section of the report.

At the completion of this chapter, you will be able to:

1. Prepare an introduction to your evaluation report that captures the reader's attention through concise statements of the importance of the topic and the nature of the study being undertaken.

2. Prepare a literature review that discusses the relevant literature in accordance with selected principles of organization and presentation.

3. Write a research hypothesis that recognizes the special role of this statement in outcome evaluation research and adheres to basic research standards.

4. Prepare the methods section of an evaluation report that facilitates replication and provides the reader with information that can be used to assess the study's credibility as a means of providing a fair test of the intervention.

5. Prepare the results section of an evaluation report that clarifies the data that tests the study's hypotheses.

6. Prepare a conclusions section of a research report that summarizes the study's results, utility for human services, and its limitations in the pursuit of a definitive answer to the key questions being analyzed.

Writing the Title and Introduction

In this section, you will see guidelines for preparing the title of your research report as well as the introduction. The title should reflect the meaning of your study, while the introduction should entice the reader into a full examination of your results. In the following paragraphs are selected principles for guiding these efforts.

Principle 1: The Title Should Concisely Identify the Essence of the Study

The title for your evaluation report should be meaningful, but concise. It should identify both the intervention and the target behavior. In some situations, it would be appropriate also to identify the study population in the title, but this is less important and should be omitted if it makes the title too cumbersome. Critical information should be included, but unnecessary information should be omitted.

Being cute is not appropriate. For example, I remember an evaluation study of the effectiveness of school social work in the improvement of selected risk factors for middle school youth that was given the title "School Social Work—Are we there yet?" This title did not reveal that this study was an evaluation study regarding school social work's effectiveness in improving risk factors. It could have been the title for an essay on the importance of school social work, and it could have been many more things as well. The key is that this title gave very little information.

Being cumbersome is also inappropriate. Consider, for example, the following title for an evaluation research study:

> A study of the effectiveness of school social work in the reduction of school absenteeism, the reduction of disciplinary episodes, the improvement of grades, and the improvement of self-esteem among a group of 12 students at Walker High School identified as being at high risk for dropping out of school.

Whew! You really don't need that much information in a title. How about the following revision of this title?

> A study of the effectiveness of school social work in the reduction of dropout risk factors for high school students.

This revised title provides essentially the same information with more conciseness.

It is also inappropriate to include the results of your study in the title. For example, the title should not be "School social work is found effective in reducing risk factors for high school students." Try to remember that you are writing a research report rather than an article for a newspaper. The report will provide details to the reader to help that individual to draw conclusions. It is premature to capture the conclusions in the title.

Discussion Box 17.1

Prepare the title for an evaluation research study you would like to conduct.

Did your title (listed in the discussion box) adhere to the principles enumerated? Did it include the identification of both the intervention and the target behavior? Did it reveal that the report is regarding an evaluation study? Did it avoid being cute or cumbersome?

Principle 2: The Introduction Should be Brief; Full Explanation of Theories or Research Findings Should be Reserved for the Literature Review Section

The introduction to your outcome evaluation report should begin with an enticement of the reader into the nature of the study being reported. A brief description of the importance of the target behavior and the need for a study of treatment effectiveness is a good approach to the beginning of the evaluation report. Following this enticement, you should briefly state the nature of the study being reported, including the identification of both the target behavior and the intervention and how the effectiveness of the intervention in the treatment of the behavior was measured in this study. You normally should not, however, state what you concluded from the study. This will be reserved for the last section of the report.

The introduction to a research study should be no more than one page. Details from the literature should be reserved for the literature review section. Quotes from the literature and references to sources should be rather limited, because you will provide such information in the literature review. You should avoid redundancy between the introduction and the literature section, e.g., do not repeat sentences in the literature section that were identically presented in the introduction. Assertions made about the theme of the paper in the introduction, however, should be backed by information in the literature review. Elaborations of what was mentioned in the introduction should be in the literature section.

Principle 3: Begin the Introduction with a Description of the Problem and the Reasons for its Importance

Consider the following description by York (1998):

> The first thing the reader wants to know is "What is this paper about?" The next thing is "Why should I be concerned about it?" Consider the following statement:
>
> Among adolescents in this nation, there are hundreds of thousands of suicide attempts each year, of which about one percent result in death. Of special importance is the fact that suicide is the third leading cause of death for persons between the age of 15 and 24.

What did you learn from this brief sentence? First, you can see that the topic is suicide, but not suicide in general. It is about suicide among the young people of our nation. Next, you learned that there are a large number of suicide attempts each year among our youth and that it is the third major cause of death.

If you begin the introduction with the statement given, it should be followed by brief statements which reveal the major themes of the study such as, for example, the treatment of suicide, or the prevention of it. Then you should state the purpose of the study. For evaluative research, the purpose is normally the testing of the effectiveness of an intervention in the treatment of a given target behavior. So information is needed regarding both the behavior and its treatment (York, 1998, p. 217).

Discussion Box 17.2

With regard to the evaluation study you conceived for the previous discussion box, present the first sentence of the introduction.

Principle 4: Clarify the Purpose of the Study After the Description of the Problem

The purpose statement should be placed early in the paper, but not until you have given the reader a reason to believe that this purpose is worthwhile. Why? It is more effective to entice the reader into the subject before laying out the study purpose. But you certainly want to state the purpose early in the paper. You are not advised to begin your paper with the statement of the study purpose, but this strategy would be superior to one that held the reader in suspense for several pages before the purpose was clear. Consider the following quote from York (1998):

> Recent studies indicate that many first marriages end in divorce, and the average duration of matrimony is quickly declining. Thus, divorce appears to have become a more acceptable alternative for coping with dissatisfaction in marriages. In light of the short duration of so many marriages, it can be speculated that many of these relationships contained the seeds of their own destruction from the pre-marital period of the relationship.
>
> Premarital counseling has long been considered an effective means for preventing marital disharmony and keeping marriages together for the duration of life. The effectiveness of premarital counseling, however, has not been clearly established. While some researchers have reported success, others have produced conflicting results.
>
> The purpose of the study reported in this paper is to examine the effectiveness of one premarital counseling program in the enhancement of marital satisfaction. Several variables considered to be related to marital satisfaction will also be examined to determine if premarital counseling is related to marital satisfaction when other variables are controlled. (York, 1998, p. 218)

In this example, the purpose was stated in the third paragraph, but not until the reader was given a reason to want to read the report. The literature review that follows this introduction should elaborate upon various forms of marital counseling, the objectives of such counseling, and the results of studies that have examined the effectiveness of this form of counseling.

Make sure your stated purpose is consistent with what you intend to study. Don't say that your objective is to examine the relationship between drug abuse and school performance when you are really going to test the effectiveness of an intervention designed to improve the school performance of adolescents at great risk for substance abuse.

Discussion Box 17.3

Let's examine some of these guidelines with regard to a study of the effectiveness of integrated group treatment for depressed assisted living residents, as reported by Cummings (2003). Assisted living is a form of residential care for the elderly who need regular care but not the intensive type of medical care typical of what many still call nursing homes (or rehabilitation centers). Group treatment is a means of reducing depression for people in this type of care who have been displaced from the residences that they had called home for a long time. Your task is to examine the following two statements and decide which one is the better statement for the introduction to the study.

A. Assisted living facilities represent the fastest growing type of senior housing in the United States. Currently, more than one million older Americans live in an estimated 20,000 to 30,000 ALFs throughout the country. Although definitions of assisted living vary, ALFs are generally defined as residential settings that offer a special combination of personal and supportive health care services to meet the needs of those who require help with activities of daily living. The typical ALF resident is female, widowed, in her 80s, and requires assistance with three daily activities. ALFs provide services to compensate for elders' functional disabilities. Much less emphasis, however, is placed on the residents' mental heath. In his 1999 report on mental health, the U.S. Surgeon General noted that a significant percentage of the older population experienced mental health disorders. Depression is particularly prevalent among older adults. Researchers estimate that 8% to 20% of community-dwelling elders and up to 62% of nursing home residents experience symptoms of depression.

B. Growth in the size of the elderly population has spurred the rapid development of the assisted living facility (ALF) industry. As people live to the oldest ages, they encounter greater needs for assistance with everyday activities due to increased chronic conditions and illnesses. Studies suggest that residents of ALFs suffer from a high rate of depressive symptomatology. Thus far, however, little attention has been focused on the mental health needs of assisted living residents and the interventions that might help. In response, this study investigated the efficacy of an integrated group treatment program for depressed assisted living elders.

Is Statement A or Statement B the better one? Indicate your answer.

You may have noted that statement A is better suited for the section of the evaluation report that deals with specific aspects of the target behavior. Statement B, however, is better suited to the requirements of the introduction.

Writing the Literature Review of the Target Behavior

The literature review for a research report provides the conceptual framework upon which the research study is founded. It lets the reader know about the nature of the topic, why it is important, and what needs to be done about it. It covers many of the same points as the introduction, but the introduction covers them in a very concise manner. Furthermore, the introduction will add a brief explanation of the nature of the study to be done.

The basic points to be included in the literature review are:

1. *What is the problem or issue being addressed?* In evaluative research, the problem being addressed normally is the client's target behavior. This might be anxiety for a single client, or marital satisfaction for a spouse group, or recidivism for a delinquency program. The key task for this theme is the definition of the condition being addressed.

2. *Why is this problem or issue important?* In evaluative research, you could address the incidence, prevalence, or severity of the condition being addressed. If this condition is growing in our society, you would point this out. If this condition affects one out of every four families in our nation, you would point this out. If this condition is devastating for those affected, you would point this out.

3. *What do we presently know about this problem or issue from the existing literature?* The evaluative researcher will address the dynamics of the target behavior in such a way as to inform the task of choosing an intervention. What do we know, for example, about child abuse that would be helpful to those who need to design a treatment program for abusers? What causes child abuse? What are the special needs of those who abuse?

4. *What do we know about the effectiveness of the interventions that have been employed to address this target behavior?* There are two tasks here—identifying interventions that have been used, and examining the scientific evidence regarding their effects. You will likely find more of the former than the latter. Both are important. An intervention that has been used extensively, but is untested, has the value of being designed by those with experience and expertise in this field. There are two ways to analyze this information. First, you would want to test the identified interventions logically with reference to the dynamics of the problem. If ignorance is not a cause of the problem, it does not make much sense to employ training as the solution. Second, you would examine empirical evidence about this intervention. A widely used intervention can possibly fail on both counts.

5. *How can the literature be summarized to the best advantage of the task of formulating an intervention?* The section of the evaluative report that follows the literature review normally provides a description of the intervention being tested in the present study. The summary of the literature review should provide a good link between the literature and the intervention. To what extent has the literature been instructive in regard to the choice of the intervention being tested in your study?

Discussion Box 17.4

Think of a target behavior you would like to address in an evaluation study. Identify (a) the target behavior, and (b) a key question that might be answered by a literature review of this behavior.

Principle 1: Select a Target Behavior and an Intervention to be Tested that Can Contribute the Most to the Effectiveness of your Professional Efforts.

Your first task in evaluative research is to identify the target behavior and the intervention that you will evaluate. In some cases, this will be given to you by your supervisor. In some cases, you will have an intervention or program that is the approach taken by your agency, so you do not have the option of selecting an intervention or target behavior. But you may have options regarding what aspect of the intervention or target behavior to address in a study. In many cases, you will want to test your intervention with a single client and the choice will be entirely in your hands.

You should ask yourself what it is you want to know. Are there any types of clients or behaviors or interventions that you feel a need to test? Some interventions have been better tested than others, and you may be confident in your use of these interventions because they have been validated. So why reinvent the wheel? Of course, you may have questions about the effectiveness of a well tested intervention for a particular type of client. But, in most cases, you will want to select an intervention for testing that is not well validated.

When you select an individual client for your evaluation study, be cognizant of the particular reason you selected this client. Be prepared to identify this information when you report your findings to others, because they might have some interest in your sample selection procedures, given the implications of this task for the generalization of results from one study to a given population that is similar to the study sample.

Discussion Box 17.5

Identify a target behavior and an intervention and indicate why you selected this one for an evaluation study.

Principle 2: Develop a First Draft of an Outline of the Target Behavior Analysis Before you Begin Writing

In some cases, you will be conducting an evaluation of your practice with the assistance of rather limited literature and documents to assist with the analysis of the target behavior. For more formal evaluations that might be submitted for review by others or published, you will devote significant time to a review of the knowledge base about the target behavior. This may include the general literature as well as governmental documents or agency publications. Most of what follows will be useful for the person doing the more formal study for review by others or publication.

After you have examined the literature and other documents about the target behavior, you should develop a first draft of an outline of your analysis before you begin writing. This will be a tentative outline and it may not look really good at first, but going through this step can help you organize your thoughts. In most cases, you will revise your outline several times as you write. Do not allow yourself to avoid writing because you do not yet have the perfect outline. For some people, it may be best to start writing before developing an outline. If this is the case, be sure that you develop an outline at some time in the process, so that the organization of your ideas will be evident. Without an outline, you are likely to fall into the trap of moving back and forth between subjects, leaving the reader confused as to where you are going with the topic.

Consider the task of reporting on a study that evaluates a treatment model for the resolution of grief. The following outline (York, 1998, p. 211) illustrates one way you might organize the content.

I. Loss and grief.
   A. What is loss?
   B. Types of loss.
   C. Why is loss important?
      1. Loss leads to grief.
      2. Grief is painful.
      3. Grief can interfere with social functioning and happiness.
   D. The developmental perspective of Kübler-Ross
      1. The stages of grief reaction.
      2. The healthy resolution of grief.
   E. Obstacles to healthy resolution of grief.
      1. Pain of loss leads to avoidance.
      2. Resolving anger is particularly difficult for some.
      3. A healthy view of the future is impeded.

II. How grief can be treated
   A. The special needs of grieving persons.
   B. Two forms of therapy that address these special needs.

       1. Supportive therapy.
       2. Cognitive therapy.
   C. Research on treatment has been inconclusive.

III. The purpose of the present study.
   To examine the effectiveness of a combined model of supportive and cognitive therapy in the reduction of grief symptoms for a sample of twelve adults seeking help from a community mental health center.

The outline begins with a definition of the problem and moves to a discussion of why it is important. Then it addresses theory and research about the problem which justifies the purpose of the present study. Finally, the purpose is stated very clearly.

The literature review should be organized by theme, not by source. You should organize your themes in a logical fashion and present the ideas of various authors around the themes. You should not move back and forth between themes in various parts of your report.

Discussion Box 17.6

Consider the following statements that are drawn from a study of the effectiveness of group therapy in the reduction of depression for residents of assisted living facilities (Cummings, 2003, pp. 609, 610, 611):

    A. Studies indicate that almost 30% of congregate living elders experience depressive symptoms.
    B. Assisted living represents the fastest growing type of senior housing in the United States.
    C. This study explored the effect of an integrated supportive-remotivation group treatment program on the psychological well-being of assisted living residents.
    D. Assisted living makes up 75% of all new senior housing developments.
    E. Four supportive-remotivation treatment groups were offered in two assisted living facilities. Each group had five participants and was led by a geriatric social worker.
    F. Few studies have been reported of the effectiveness of group therapy for elders residing in assisted living facilities.
    G. An analysis of psychosocial interventions for depressed elders concluded that individual therapy and group therapy are equally effective.

Your first task is to identify the statement that does not belong either in the introduction or the literature review of the target behavior. Indicate the letter next to that statement in the box.

Discussion Box 17.7
_____

Your next task is to identify the sequence of the other statements as they should appear in the literature review or introduction. Indicate the sequence of these statement by placing the proper letter of the above statement in the proper space.

   First statement should be statement _____
   Second statement should be statement _____ .
   Third statement should be statement _____
   Fourth statement should be statement _____
   Fifth statement should be statement _____
   Sixth statement should be statement _____

The first thing you should have noticed is that statement E should be included in the section that describes the intervention rather than the section of the report that describes the target behavior. Next, you should have placed statement B first on your list of the sequence of statements that describe and analyze the target behavior. Then you should have statement D, followed by statement A, then G, then F, then C. This is the sequence of the statements as they appear in the article by Cummings (2003).

Principle 3: Divide the Behavior Analysis into Sections with Headings

The part of the evaluation report that presents the analysis of the target behavior should begin with a general heading that is centered on the page, with each word capitalized. If this part of the report is more than five pages long, there should be subheadings that are presented flush with the left margin. The extensiveness of the headings is a matter of individual judgment. In the example by York on a previous page regarding the treatment of grief and loss, let's assume that this literature review was nine pages in length. In this case, the headings in roman numerals should be set aside as special headings, but further breakdowns would not be necessary.

Discussion Box 17.8
_____

Have you ever written a paper more than five pages in length without any headings or subheadings? If so, how many pages long was this paper, and how many headings should you have had?

Principle 4: Use a Reference Format Consistently Throughout your Paper

You will need to cite the sources that you employ in your paper. The APA (American Psychological Association) format has been increasingly used by different journals and schools in the past decade and is employed by many human service journals. Thus, you are encouraged to employ this format. You should do this consistently. A paper that moves between formats is not acceptable for formal reports. Access to this format is easy. Many universities offer this service through the Internet; one example is Purdue University (http://owl.english.purdue.edu/ow).

Principle 5: Use Internet Sources Carefully

Students are increasingly using online sources for literature reviews and target behavior analyses. Many publications available in hard copy are also available online. This is one of the major advantages of the Internet—you can get useful information conveniently. The more difficulty comes with other types of sources. *Do not make the mistake of assuming that something that is officially online at someone's web page has credibility.* Anyone can have a web page and can say anything they want. Thus, you have an extra burden of proof when you select web sources for your literature review. You should be sure to identify the nature of the entity that sponsors the website (e.g., the website of the National Association of Social Workers), the author (if available), the title of the report, the web address, and the date the source was accessed. Overreliance on the web will result in an paper being unimpressive in the eyes of the serious scholar or student.

Principle 6: Use Direct Quotes Sparingly

Be careful not to overdo the direct quotation of material from the literature. You should describe the material in your own words with a reference to the source. Direct quotes should be used for a profound statement or eloquent way of saying something. An example of a good quote (York, 1998, p. 213):

> Chronic excessive drinking, or addiction to alcoholism, with its compulsive character and devastating effect, has become one of the great public health problems of our world. (Block, 1965, p. 19).

An inappropriate quote is as follows: "Several people have studied the issue of what works for chronic alcoholism." This is a statement that should be in your own words. It is not profound or powerful or artistic or especially informative. If you rely too heavily upon direct quotes, you are in danger of presenting an image of not being able to say things in your own words.

Try to avoid quoting someone who is quoting someone else. It is tempting to quote Jones, who quotes Johnson on a given topic. While this is generally acceptable (you are not violating a major principle of writing), it is not in good form. It might give the impression that you are avoiding doing your own research and are depending on others to interpret original sources for you. Better form is to go to the original source. If this is impossible, yet the quote is essential to your review, you should indicate that you received the quote from the second source rather than the original source. For example, you could say the following in parentheses after the quote: (J. M. Turner, as cited in Pearson, 1999, p. 45).

Principle 7: Establish the Authority Behind What You Say

Factual statements should be accompanied by a reference to the source where the information was found. Ideas obtained from your literature sources should be accompanied by a reference source when you paraphrase them yourself. At the end of each paragraph, ask yourself if you need to give a reference to someone for the idea that you are presenting. Direct quotes, of course, should be accompanied by a reference citation, and that citation should include the page number.

Deciding where to put the reference citation is not easy for many people. Sometimes you go back and forth between sources, or refer to a given source for several continuous paragraphs. Here are some suggestions:

> The specification of the reference should be at the end of the idea presented or at the end of the paragraph, whichever comes first. You should present this reference information in such a way that you leave the reader with no doubt about what information is being credited to the particular source. Do not go on for several paragraphs regarding information from a single source without making it clear that all this information is credited to this particular source. If you have such a situation, you could begin by saying something like "According to a theory by Jones (1986), there are two main components of effective treatment for alcoholism. . . ." You could begin the next paragraph by saying "This theory by Jones proposes that the helping person engage in. . . ." In this case, you would not need to enter the year in parentheses after the name of Jones because it is clear that you are making a further reference to Jones who was referenced fully in the paragraph above. However, if you do not refer to this theory again for several pages, you would need to provide the reference information as originally presented with the date along with the last name. (York, 1998, p. 214)

Be sure not to make statements of facts without a reference citation. In some cases, however, you can make it clear that the assertion is based on your own experience. Don't say "Most therapists prefer to use a form of treatment that is comfortable, either because they have special training in it or it fits their personalities." Instead, you could say,

> In my 10 years' experience in a community mental health center, it was my observation that most therapists at this agency preferred to use a form of treatment that was comfortable. Some used models in which they had received special training, while others used models that fit their personalities.

An even bigger improvement would be for you to use some examples from your experience to make your point. Do not offer statistics without a reference citation, unless original to your own data collection.

Discussion Box 17.9

Let's examine the question of what needs to have a reference citation. Consider the following statements from the article by Cummings (2003) discussed in previous exercises in this chapter:

1. The goal of assisted living is to support the capability of frail elders so that they can remain independent as long as possible.
2. Studies suggest that residents of assisted living facilities suffer from a high rate of depressive symptomatology.
3. Currently, more than one million older Americans live in an estimated 20,000 to 30,000 assisted living facilities.
4. Assisted living facilities provide services to compensate for elders' functional disabilities.

Indicate which, if any, of these statements should have a reference citation.

If you are involved in the provision of assisted living services, you may feel comfortable not having a reference for statement 1 because you are living this in your world of work; you are the expert and you can speak from this position. But if you have no major connection with this service, you would normally need a reference because you got this idea from the literature and need to give credit. The second statement needs a reference. It would not be warranted for you to make statement 2 without a resource. You should not say things like this just because you have the impression that this is true. Typically, you have reviewed articles that reported on several studies or have found this statement in an article that reviews many studies. These should be referenced. Statement 3 also needs a reference. How do you know there are one million older Americans who live in assisted living facilities unless you found this in the literature? The last statement is similar to the first one; you normally would not need a reference if you have some contact with this service sector and this is an obvious statement of reality.

Writing the Research Hypothesis

The research hypothesis is a statement of the expected results of a research study on a given theme based upon theory or explanations derived from existing knowledge. The hypothesis should be supported by a knowledge base. You are not at liberty to state a prediction of the results of a study in the form of a hypothesis unless you have a knowledge base to back it up. Thus, the hypothesis does not derive merely from curiosity or a hunch. In evaluative research, the direction of the results of your data analysis is clear—you expect the client's behavior to be better. This means that you expect the single client's treatment recordings to be superior to the baseline recordings, or that you expect the treated clients to have more gain in functioning than the control group who did not have treatment, or that you expect the group of clients' post-treatment scores to be better than their pretreatment scores.

The research hypothesis is distinguished from the *null hypothesis*. The null hypothesis stands in opposition to the research hypothesis. It is a statement that is true if the study results can be explained by chance. Consider the following example: Clients in the treatment group will have no greater gain in self-esteem than persons in the control group. This is an example of a null hypothesis. The null hypothesis has an important role in traditional research methodology. When we apply statistics to data in order to test the research hypothesis, we are dealing with chance as one of the reasons for our configuration of data. The traditional researcher will state a null hypothesis and apply statistics to determine whether the null hypothesis should be rejected. If the null hypothesis is rejected, the research hypothesis is supported. The rejection of the null hypothesis does not provide proof of the truth of the hypothesis; it eliminates one of the alternative explanations for our data.

In this text, emphasis will be placed upon the research hypothesis rather than the null hypothesis. You should remember, however, that if you wish to publish your work in certain journals, you may need to translate your research hypothesis into a null hypothesis in order to conform to the tradition.

Practical guidelines for writing the study hypothesis in evaluative research follow. Many of these suggestions are guided by the work by Pyrczak and Bruce (1992) with specific adaptations peculiar to the evaluative research study. Guidelines for the writing of the hypothesis statement in general can be found elsewhere, including in the text by York (1998).

Principle 1: The Evaluative Research Hypothesis Should Identify the Target Behavior and the Intervention

If one of the treatment objectives for the Adolescent Parenting Program is to improve the self-esteem of adolescent mothers, and you are evaluating this program with the one-group pretest–posttest design, you could state your hypothesis as follows:

> The self-esteem of the clients of the Adolescent Parenting Program will be greater at the end of treatment than before treatment began.

If you were comparing clients of this program with adolescent mothers who were not in this program, you could state the hypothesis as follows:

> The gain in self-esteem for the clients of the Adolescent Parenting Program will be greater than the gain in self-esteem for adolescent mothers in the comparison group.

Notice that both examples provide information on both the target behavior (self-esteem) and the intervention (Adolescent Parenting Program). They also provide information on the nature of the data based on the type of research design employed.

In the first chapter of this book, you were urged not to state the purpose of your study as trying to prove a point. In other words, you were encouraged to say the purpose of your study was to examine the extent to which the program had been effective in meeting client need rather than to say the purpose was to demonstrate that the service was effective in this way. This may make you feel a little uncomfortable with the fact that the hypothesis states a prediction of the expected results. But this is okay. This is what you are supposed to do in the hypothesis, which is a different type of statement from the study's purpose. Also, keep in mind that the hypothesis is a special type of statement that serves a special function in research. It is different from day-to-day conversation.

Principle 2: The Variables Named in the Hypothesis Should be Operationally Defined

The reader needs to know just how the variables were measured. The operational definition, of course, should be relevant to the abstract definition of the concept reflected by the variable. The abstract definition of a variable provides the type of definition that we might find in the dictionary. It provides conceptual guidance about what we mean by the term. The operational definition specifies how we intend to measure that variable in our study. It is not necessary to specify the scale used in our study in your hypothesis as long as you provide a clear operational definition of that variable in your research methodology section of our report. The scale used to measure self-esteem for adolescent mothers was not given in the previous example. However, it could have been stated as follows: *The scores for clients of the Adolescent Parenting Program on the Hare Self-Esteem Scale will be higher at the completion of the program than at the beginning.*

Principle 3: The Evaluative Research Hypothesis Should Avoid Statements about Causation

The purpose of the evaluative research study is to provide evidence regarding causation. The question is whether the intervention had the effect of changing the target behavior. The data examined by the hypothesis will provide evidence of change, but the cause of that change will be determined substantially by the research design employed. The fact that the research study obtained a measured change in the target behavior is not, by itself, proof of the cause of the change. Therefore the following statement is *not appropriate* as a statement of a study hypothesis: The client's level of depression will improve as a result of cognitive-behavioral therapy. Instead, the hypothesis should be stated in the form noted in the previous paragraph.

Discussion Box 17.10
_____

In each pair of statements below, see if you can pick out the one that is the better statement of a hypothesis.

Pair A

a. Participation in the Head Start Program will increase kindergarten readiness in at-risk four-year-olds.
b. Reading readiness scores for at-risk four-year-olds participating in the Head Start program will be higher than reading readiness scores for at-risk four-year-olds who did not participate in Head Start.

Pair B

a. It can be hypothesized that case management and wraparound can be designed to provide long-term supports and services for youth at risk for out-of-home placements.
b. The number of antisocial behaviors of at-risk youth will be lower during the six months of case management and wraparound services than during the six weeks prior to service.

Discussion Box 17.11
_____

Now, see if you can rewrite the following hypothesis statement to make it better.

It thus seems likely that middle and high school student scores on the Adolescent Anger Rating Scale will be affected by the implementation of the Anger Management course of the Mediation Center. (Note: Higher scores reflect improvement.)

Writing the Methods Section of the Evaluation Report

In this section is a discussion of how to write the methods section of the evaluation report. Included are considerations of sampling, measurement, and research design. One part of this section of the report typically will also include the statement of the study hypothesis, a topic that has already been given attention in this chapter. Some of the principles included here were inspired by the book on writing research reports by Pyrczak and Bruce (1992). They have been modified for the specific purposes of this book.

Principle 1: The Basic Study Design should be Presented in Sufficient Detail to Facilitate Replication

In this text, you have been given descriptions of several designs for evaluative research. These included the one-group pretest–posttest design, the comparison group design (nonequivalent control group), and the pretest–posttest control group design. These labels are useful in evaluative research for conveying to the reader the extent to which external influences upon the client's behavior have been controlled in the study procedures. For example, you were informed that the one-group pretest–posttest design did not address maturation as a threat to internal validity.

If you are conducting descriptive or exploratory research, you will not find this classification system to be very useful. Instead, you might find it useful to report whether a cross-sectional survey or a longitudinal survey was employed. This classification system reveals whether data were collected at only one point in time, or repeatedly. But this book deals specifically with the evaluation of outcome, a topic for which the issue of research design is critical.

While the provision of a correct label for the research design can facilitate communication with the reader, it is more useful for the report to include the specific procedures employed. For example, you could say that the one-group pretest–posttest design was employed, but it would be even more important to describe how this worked. For example, you could say "The study subjects were given the Generalized Contentment Scale before and after their participation in the treatment program."

Many traditional texts in research classify research designs into the categories of non-experimental, quasi-experimental, and experimental. I have found that this classification system creates more problems than it solves for students and novice researchers. Further, it is not necessary. If you can describe the design employed and you can identify its limitations, it means very little for you to be able to place it correctly into the category of quasi-experimental or experimental.

Principle 2: Identify the Instruments Employed to Measure Study Variables and the Definition of the Variables They were Designed to Measure

You should provide an abstract definition of any complicated concept that is measured in your study. Such definitions would apply to concepts like self-esteem or extroversion, but not to such variables as gender or age. If you are employing a standard instrument that has been published, you will report what that scale was designed to measure. It is not sufficient to provide the name of the scale, even if the scale title has a commonly known concept such as depression or anxiety. There are various ways to define such concepts. You should specify how you are defining them in your study.

You should describe the format for the instrument and the kinds of response categories that are provided. For example, the Index of Family Relations contains 25 statements such as "My family gets on my nerves" and "I think my family is terrific." Respondents are asked to indicate how often each statement is true and are given response categories on a 5-point ordinal scale from "Rarely or none of the time," to "Most or all of the time."

You should also provide the possible range of scores and provide any information available regarding thresholds of functioning. In the case of the Index of Family Relations, scores can range from 0 and 100 with higher scores providing more evidence of family problems. Scores above 30 are considered to indicate a clinically significant problem.

Principle 3: If You Employ a Published Scale, Identify Whether Reliability and Validity have been Addressed and Refer to the Source of the Instrument

Measures that have been published have normally been subjected to tests of reliability and/or validity. It is not necessary for you to describe in detail how this was addressed. At a minimum, you should indicate whether either the reliability or validity of the instrument has been tested and whether the results were favorable, and you should provide the source for this information.

If you wish, you can specify what types of reliability or validity were addressed, but you are cautioned not to rephrase statements in the published source unless you are familiar with the concepts being presented. I have often seen mistakes made by students who tried to describe such information when they didn't understand it. You could, of course, quote the material right out of that source. That is the safer approach.

Discussion Box 17.12

Consider the following two descriptions of how target behavior was measured in two different studies.

Example A

The Generalized Contentment Scale is designed to measure non-psychotic depression among adults. It focuses primarily upon the affective aspects of clinical depression. Scores can range from 0 to 100, with higher scores representing higher depression. Clients with scores higher than 30 are considered to have a clinically significant problem with depression. This scale has been tested for internal consistency and test-retest reliability with favorable results. In the category of validity, this scale has been found to correlate with several other measures of depression and has been found to effectively discriminate between persons known to be depressed through clinical observations and those not known for this problem (Hudson, 1982).

Example B

Parents fill out a questionnaire asking them to rate their own level of skill. The questionnaire is a ten question form using a Likert scale to determine one's parenting attitudes and personal evaluation of parenting skills. It asks parents to rate themselves from 1-5 (1 being strongly disagree and 5 being strongly agree) on their parenting skills, knowledge of appropriate child development (testing appropriate expectations), and nutrition.

Which of the above is the better?

Principle 4: If You Employ a Nonpublished Scale, Describe the Instrument in Detail and Report on the Ways that Reliability and Validity have been Addressed

If you employ a published scale, you can refer the reader to the source of the scale for details about what it looks like and how reliability and validity have been established. If you develop one yourself, or use one that has not been published, you carry a greater burden to establish its credibility.

Under these latter conditions, you should describe the scale with examples from it, or include the scale as an exhibit or appendix to your report. You should report how reliability and validity have been addressed. For example, if you computed a split-half correlation, you should report those results, including the correlation coefficient and the *p* value.

At a minimum, you should address face validity and internal consistency. Face validity is the weakest form of validity, but it is clearly better than no test of validity at all. You should develop a specific plan for testing face validity. This might entail selecting five persons known to have expertise on the subject of the scale and asking them to indicate whether this scale measures the thing it is supposed to measure. This could include a direct question about face validity (Yes or No) as well as comments about its weaknesses or recommendations for alteration. You should be clear how you plan to use it and the purpose it will serve.

Internal consistency is a simple matter to address because you do not have to collect any additional information; you examine the extent to which responses to the items seem to hang together. One of the primary methods for examining internal consistency is the split-half approach. With the split-half approach, you split the items on the scale (the ones that are supposed to be measuring the same variable) into two halves on some kind of random basis. A popular approach is the odd-even method, in which all odd-numbered items form one subscale and all even-numbered items form another subscale. Then you compute the correlation between these two subscales. You would expect a positive correlation that is rather high and statistically significant. If the correlation is weak, you would not have good evidence that the various items on the scale are measuring the same thing.

Principle 5: Define the Study Population and the Sampling Method Employed

A study sample is a portion of a study population. The study population is that aggregate of persons to whom you wish to be able to generalize your results, however weak or strong your evidence for generalization. If your study purpose was to determine the extent to which the past clients of the Hopewell Family Counseling Center were satisfied with the services they received, your study population would likely be the former clients of the Hopewell Family Counseling Center. However, it is not likely that you would have the ability to include every past client in your study. Instead, you would select a sample of these persons, and you would hope that your sample was representative of the entire population.

In your report, you should define the study population and describe the methods you employed in the selection of a sample. If you are well versed in sampling terminology, you would give a label to your sample, such as convenience sample, probability sample, and so forth. If you describe how the sample was selected, you do not need to worry very much about the label to give it. The reader can draw proper conclusions about generalization without the necessity of a label, providing that sufficient information is given. Do *not* come up with your own terminology in labeling your sample, as for example, one student who decided to label his method a "slice-of-life sample."

A probability sample is one in which every member of the population had an equal chance of being selected for the sample. This is one label that is worth mentioning, because it says a lot about your ability to generalize your results to the population.

You should report on attrition from the sample. For example, if you mail a questionnaire to a random sample of 100 of the 300 persons who comprise the population of persons served by your agency in the past 10 years, you would also report on the proportion of persons who actually returned the questionnaire. If you asked each client to complete a satisfaction survey at the termination of service, you would report how many persons refrained from participation, and the reason why they refrained if that information is available.

When you have completed the description of the sample and the population, you will have given the reader a clear picture of who was included and excluded from the study sample. From that information, the reader can draw conclusions about the generalization of the study's results. For example, a study was conducted by Edleson and Syers (1991) of men who had been in a treatment program for males who had battered their mates. A description of the study sample:

> Over 500 men initially sought service during the study period. Of these persons, 340 completed intake interviews but only 153 completed the program. Of these persons, 70 could be located at the follow-up time period which was 18 months after the completion of the program. These 70 cases constituted the study sample.

With this description, the reader can draw conclusions about generalization. Can the results of this study be generalized to all men who batter, or all men who initially sought help from this program, or all men who completed this program, or all men who could be located at follow-up? You can draw your own conclusions, given a clear description.

Discussion Box 17.13

What is your opinion about the population to whom the study of males who had physically abused their wives could be generalized?

There is no clear answer to the question in the box, 17.13, but a discussion of different answers can illuminate the issue of generalization of study results.

Principle 6: Describe the Characteristics of the Study Sample

The study sample should be described in sufficient detail to give the reader a general picture of what kinds of people were in the study. The particular variables to include will vary by the nature of the study, but you would normally report information on gender and age. Often, you will find it useful to report information on race or ethnic origin, income level, occupational status, and so forth. Of particular concern will be information on the nature of the problem being confronted in the study. For example, among the information given by Edleson and Syers (1991) in the study of men who batter was the following:

> Those for whom data were available ranged in age from 18 to 56 years, with a mean of 33.75 (SD = 8.3). Fifty-one of the men were White, representing 72.9% of the sample. In addition there were 5 Black (7.1%), 1 Hispanic (1.4%) and 1 Asian man (1.4%). The average number of years of education reported by the men in this sample was 13.7 (SD = 2.2). The majority of the men (52.8%, $n = 37$) were reported employed full-time, whereas 22.8% (n = 16) stated they were unemployed at the time of intake . . .
>
> At the time of the intake into the treatment program, almost half of this sample (45.7%, $n = 32$) reported themselves married or living with their partners, and 50% ($n = 35$) of them were single, divorced, or separated. At the 18-month follow-up, however, only 21.4% ($n = 15$) of the men were reported to be married and living with their partners . . .
>
> More than one third of the men (35.7%) reported that they had been court ordered to treatment. Almost two thirds (61.4%, $n = 43$) reported having received mental health services at some point prior to intake, and 47.1% ($n = 33$) reported having been involved in some type of chemical-dependency treatment. (Edleson & Syers, 1991, p. 229)

This information provides a clear picture of the types of persons included in this study, and will facilitate readers' evaluation of the relevance of this study to their situations.

Writing the Results Section of the Evaluation Report

In the results section, information is presented on the results of the analysis of data in the pursuit of the study questions. Information on the characteristics of the sample may be reported in the methods section or the results section, but normally in the latter. The primary focus of the results section is upon the information that was collected in the pursuit of an answer to the research question.

Principle 1: Organize the Presentation of Data Around the Research Questions or Study Hypotheses

If you have three research questions, you should present information regarding question 1 followed by question 2, and so forth. Your information should not move back and forth among the various study questions or research hypotheses. For example, suppose that you had administered pretests and posttests to your clients on (1) self-esteem, (2) self-confidence, and (3) knowledge about the consequences of drug use. Between the administrations of the pretests and posttests for these three variables, you have administered a program designed to reduce risk factors for substance abuse. Thus, you have pretest scores for each of these three variables and you also have posttest scores for each.

Discussion Box 17.14

What do you think of each of the following examples of outlines of the presentation of information for this hypothetical study?

Example A

    Pretest scores for self-esteem.
    Pretest scores for self-confidence.
    Pretest scores for knowledge.
    Posttest scores for self-esteem.
    Posttest scores for self-confidence.
    Posttest scores for knowledge.
    Statistical analysis of pretest and posttest scores for self-esteem
    Statistical analysis of pretest and posttest scores for self-confidence.
    Statistical analysis of pretest and posttest scores for knowledge.

Example B

    Pretest scores for self-esteem.
    Posttest scores for self-esteem.
    Statistical analysis of pretest and posttest scores for self-esteem
    Pretest scores for self-confidence.
    Posttest scores for self-confidence.
    Statistical analysis of pretest and posttest scores for self-confidence.
    Pretest scores for knowledge.
    Posttest scores for knowledge.
    Statistical analysis of pretest and posttest scores for knowledge.

Which of the above examples is better?

In the example in the box, you have three study hypotheses, one related to each of these variables. In this situation, you should *not* present the mean pretest score for self-esteem, followed by the mean pretest score for self-confidence, followed by the mean pretest score for knowledge, and then turn your attention to the presentation of the mean posttest scores in the same sequence. Instead, you should present the pretest and posttest scores as well as the test of statistical significance for the first hypothesis, followed by the second, and the third.

Principle 2: Organize Large Amounts of data into Tables and refer only to the data Highlights in the Narrative

It is boring for the reader to be presented with myriad details from your data analysis. This is a special problem for the descriptive study. Take, for example, the descriptive study of the characteristics and services of the clients of the neonatal intensive care unit of a hospital reported by the author in another book (York, 1997). Data had been collected on the gestational age of the babies, the age of each parent, the education of the mother, the number of parents, the number of siblings, the method used to pay the hospital bills, the weight of the baby, the number of cases with each of six presenting problems, and the disposition of cases for each of these six presenting problem. Altogether, data were collected on 20 variables.

Consider the following way to begin the presentation of the results:

Only one baby had a gestational age of 25 months and this represented 2.2 percent of the total sample. Two babies had a gestational age of 26 months (4.4%) while four babies had a gestational age of 27 months. Twelve babies had a gestational age of 28 months (26.7% of the total) and seven babies had a gestational age of 29 months (15.5%). Of the remainder, two had a gestational age of 30 (4.4%), four had a gestational age of 31 (8.9%), four had a gestational age of 32 (8.9%), six had a gestational age of 33 (13.3%), and three had a gestational age of 34 (6.7%).

If you are not bored yet, just think how you would feel after being subjected to such a report on a total of 20 variables.

The solution to this problem is to organize these data into tables which the reader can review as he or she might wish. The narrative should refer only to the highlights. For example, the writer might point out that 62 percent of these families paid their hospital bills through the Medicaid program, indicating that they were in a low income category. Another fact that would be of special interest was that 71 percent of these babies had a gestational age that was less than 32 weeks, which is a threshold for normal lung development.

Principle 3: Present Explanatory and Evaluative Results with Statistical Details in Parentheses

Data analysis for explanatory research entails the testing of a hypothesis or a set of hypotheses. Evaluative research is a particular type of explanatory research that is treated separately in this text, but is similar in that you are testing a hypothesis. For this type of research, data results should be organized around the hypotheses that are being tested.

In the presentation of your data, you should provide three kinds of information:

1. The descriptive statistics that reveal the outcome data, such as the mean pretest and mean posttest score, the mean gain in scores for the treatment group and the comparison group, the single client's scores on the scale for each measurement period, and so forth.
2. The statistical coefficient, or its equivalent, derived from the statistical measure employed (examples: $r = .31$ $t = 3.56$; $C = .58$; $X^2 = 2.96$).

3. The level of statistical significance achieved (the value of p). This can be reported in two forms. The traditional form is to report whether the level of significance (alpha level) established for testing the hypothesis was achieved. If you established the .05 level as your standard, you could report the p value as $p < .05$ if your hypothesis was supported. If it was not supported, you could report either $p > .05$ or ns, which means "not significant."

   The newer form entails the presentation of the actual p value, such as $p = .02$ or $p = .34$, and so forth. In either case, this information should be given in parentheses at the end of the sentence that presents the descriptive data about the hypothesis or states whether the hypothesis was supported.

Avoid such awkward terminology as "Significance was achieved at the $p < .05$ level." Such expressions as "$p < .05$" should be placed in parentheses. The following are examples for the presentation of data results for explanatory and evaluative studies:

1. The mean pretest score for self-esteem was 9.7, while the mean posttest score was 14.2. This difference was statistically significant ($t = 2.6$; $p < .05$); thus, the hypothesis was supported.
2. The first hypothesis (there is a positive relationship between self-esteem and number of days absent from school) was tested with the Pearson correlation coefficient. The results of this analysis failed to support the hypothesis ($r = .18$; $p = .34$).
3. The mean gain in self-esteem scores for the treatment group was 4.3, while the mean gain for the comparison group was 2.6. The difference in mean gain scores between these groups was found not to be statistically significant ($t = 1.2$; $p = .31$). The hypothesis was not supported.

Discussion Box 17.15

Consider the following statement:

> The mean posttest grade of 82.3 was found to be significantly higher than the mean pretest grade of 77.4 because the t of 2.33 was significant at the $p < .05$ level.

Rewrite this statement.

Writing the Conclusions Section of the Evaluation Report

In the conclusion section, sometimes referred to as the discussion section, the researcher summarizes the results and provides an image of how the results should be interpreted in light of the limitations of the study. In addition, it is customary for information to be presented on the direction of future research on the chosen theme. This last section of the research article is usually given the heading of Conclusions or Discussion.

Principle 1: At the Beginning of the Conclusions Section, Restate the Study Question or Hypothesis and Summarize the Evidence Presented on its Behalf

The last part of the research article provides a synopsis of the study. The reader has been taken through a literature review, a description of the methodology, and the analysis of data. At the end, the reader may have missed a major point regarding the results of the study. For this reason, you need to provide a summary of the findings. For example, the beginning of this last part of the report may begin as follows:

> In the study reported here, a single client received cognitive-behavioral therapy in the treatment of depression. The client's scores on a depression scale revealed significant improvement during the treatment period.

Principle 2: In the Conclusions Section, Present only the Highlights of the Results Rather than Restating them in Detail

You will notice that this example did not repeat the data that was given in the data analysis section, with means, or correlations, or *p* values. That would be repetitious and would get into the way of the major highlights of the study results. In this last part of the article, you want to have a clear focus on the highlights. There is seldom a need to mention specific pieces of data such as means, frequencies, correlations. You would, of course, indicate whether a given hypothesis was supported and indicate what relationships were found between study variables. But repeating correlation coefficients and *p* values would be unnecessary. This information has been presented in the results section and the reader can refer to this section if these details are of interest.

Principle 3: Discuss the Limitations of the Study

You should help the reader place your study into perspective by noting the limitations of the methodology. The key place to find limitations is in the study methodology. Often, you will find that the sample selected for study can be generalized to a limited population because of the sampling methods employed. Another key place for the discovery of limitations is the study design. Did you conduct a cross-sectional survey where a longitudinal survey would have been better? What threats to internal validity were not addressed in your evaluative research design? Are these threats of special importance in your specific situation?

The selection of study variables and the means used to measure them is another candidate for the discovery of limitations. There are many ways to measure client progress; You selected only one or a few. What are the implications of these choices?

Discussion Box 17.16

Should the conclusions section of the evaluation report contain a large number of statements from the literature that require reference citations? Why or why not?

Quiz

The following is a quiz on the contents of this chapter. You may use it as a pretest, to determine if you need to read the chapter, or as a posttest, to determine how well you read it.

1. Which of the following are considered to be solid sources of reference material for a literature review for a research study, in that substantial reliance upon sources of this nature would be considered adequate as a support for the knowledge base that supports your research study?
   a. Articles from newspapers and popular magazines
   b. Information from the Internet
   c. Excerpts from agency manuals and quotes from speakers at workshops or professors in class
   d. Articles from professional and academic journals
   e. All of the above

2. Suppose you are conducting a study of the effectiveness of a treatment program for men who abuse their wives. You have prepared a literature review that is 10 pages in length. Approximately how many headings or subheadings should you have for this literature review?
   a. None
   b. Two or three
   c. Ten
   d. Thirty

3. Which of the following would be examples of appropriate direct quotes for a literature review?
   a. "Chronic excessive drinking, or addiction to alcohol, with its compulsive character and devastating effect, has become one of the great public health problems of our world" (Block, 1965, p. 19).
   b. "Several persons have investigated the effectiveness of Reduction Therapy in the enhancement of self-esteem for at-risk adolescents, including Jamison (1987), Parker (1993), and Benton (1997)" (Harkin, 1998, p. 16).

c. In summary, it can be said that the results of the present study achieved the same conclusions as those by Hemphill (1996), Carter (1989), and Taylor (1998). In other words, "cognitive restructuring can be effective in the treatment of depression" (Carter, 1989, p. 134).

d. All of the above.

4. Which of the following would be the preferable way to describe the study design?

a. A quasi-experimental design was employed in the test of the study hypothesis.

b. In the test of the study hypothesis, clients were given the Beck Depression Inventory before and after treatment, and their gain in scores was compared to the gain in scores during the same time period for a comparison group of persons on the waiting list.

c. The nonequivalent control group design was employed in the test of this study's hypothesis. The quasi-experimental control group utilized the agency's waiting list.

d. A pre-experimental research design was employed in the testing of the study hypothesis.

5. Which of the following study variables would require an abstract definition of the concept?

a. Gender

b. Age

c. Anxiety

d. All of the above

6. Which of the following should be included in the introduction section of the evaluation report?

a. A detailed description of the key theory being subjected to testing in the evaluation report

b. Some of the data revealing the results of the study being reported

c. Both of the above

d. None of the above

7. Which of the following would be good statements of an evaluation hypothesis?

a. The clients' scores on the Beck Depression Inventory will be lower at the end of treatment than before treatment began.

b. The clients' level of depression will improve because of cognitive-behavioral therapy.

c. Both of the above.

d. None of the above.

8. Which of the following would be good statements of the results of an evaluation study?

a. The mean difference between pretest and posttest scores on self-esteem were found to be significant at the $p < .05$ level because the $t = 4.54$ was actually significant at the $p < .01$ level.

b. The mean pretest score for self-esteem was 21.4, while the mean posttest score was 26.7. The difference between these mean scores was found to be statistically significant ($t = 2.11; p < .05$).

c. Both of the above.

d. None of the above.

9. Which of the following statements is/are true?

a. You should not present statistics in your formal evaluation report without a reference citation, unless the statistics originate with you.

b. You should never begin the writing of the literature review regarding your target behavior without first developing a complete and detailed outline.

c. Both of the above.

d. None of the above.

10. Which of the following statements is/are true?

a. There is no difference in the credibility of Internet sources and sources from scholarly journals.

b. If you prepare your own scale for measuring the client's target behavior in a formal evaluation study, you do not need to address the issue of reliability or validity—this issue is addressed only when you are using published scales.

c. Both of the above.

d. None of the above.

References

Corcoran, K. & Fischer, J. (1987). *Measures for clinical practice.* New York: Free Press.

Cummings, S. M. (2003). The efficacy of an integrated group treatment program for depressed assisted living residents. *Research on Social Work Practice, 13* (5), 608–621.

Edelson, J. L., & Syers, M. (1991). The effects of group treatment for men who batter: An 18-month follow-up study. *Research on Social Work Practice, 1* (3), 227–243.

Hudson, W. W. (1982). *The clinical measurement package.* Chicago: Dorsey.

Pyrczak, F., & Bruce, R. R. (1992). *Writing empirical research reports.* Los Angeles: Pyrczak Publishing.

York, R. O. (1997). *Building basic competencies in social work research.* Boston: Allyn & Bacon.

Answers to Quiz Questions

1. d
2. b
3. a
4. b
5. c

6. d
7. a
8. b
9. a
10. d

18

An Exercise in Outcome Evaluation

In this exercise, you will undertake a few of the assignments necessary for the design an outcome evaluation study. This is an exercise designed to focus your efforts in the design of an evaluation study. It is *not* designed to list all the details that should be in a report that presents a design of an evaluation study. In this exercise, you will be asked to:

1. Describe the practice setting where the proposed evaluation will take place.
2. Identify a target behavior.
3. Analyze the selected target behavior.
4. Describe the intervention or program. This can either be a proposed intervention/program or the one that is presently employed by this agency to address the selected target behavior.
5. Discuss how well the selected intervention/program is justified as an effective method of achieving the objectives.
6. Describe the study sample and population.
7. Describe the method of measuring client progress.
8. Describe the chosen research design in light of threats to internal validity of special concern.

When these tasks are complete, you should have a guide for preparing a full report on how the evaluation study should be undertaken.

Assignment A: Describing the Practice Setting

Your first task is to describe the practice setting, the agency and program where you will focus your attention. Some examples:

- This practice setting is the Investigative Unit of the Child Protective Services Program of the Child Welfare Division of the Harper County Department of Social Services. This unit investigates complaints of child abuse, determines if the incident should be classified as confirmed for child abuse or neglect or not confirmed, and offers referrals of the family to other services where appropriate.
- This practice setting is the support group offered to abused women residing temporarily in the Women's Shelter of the Women's Services Center of Wymar County. The purpose of this group is to enhance the women's self-esteem and sense of empowerment in their relationships with their partners and others.
- This practice setting is school social work services offered to middle school students in Johnson County who are at risk for poor school performance and dropping out of school. These services entail case management, peer support group services, and special tutoring. Outcomes expected are increased grades, reduced school disciplinary behaviors, reduced school absenteeism, and enhanced self-esteem.

Discussion Box 18.1

Provide your description of your practice setting.

Assignment B: Identifying the Target Behavior

In this assignment, you will identify the target behavior being addressed in the practice setting that you will propose to evaluate. This refers only to those target behaviors that are the focus of your proposed evaluation study. Because this exercise is designed for the beginning human service practitioner or student, you are advised to select a common target behavior that is presently being treated by an agency familiar to you. You will need to have access to information about this behavior and the intervention that addresses it.

Selecting the Target Behavior

Your first task is to select the behavior. If you are presently in a human service job or internship, you will have your own clients' target behaviors to consider. If not, you can interview persons in human services to help in this endeavor.

Here are only a few of the target behaviors you might consider:

- Child abuse
- Alcoholism
- Problematic school behaviors
- Depression
- Unemployment
- Kindergarten readiness for at-risk children
- Family displacement for children
- Attention-deficit hyperactivity disorder (ADHD)
- Family violence
- Eating disorders
- Noncompliance with follow-up medical treatment of discharged hospital patients
- Severe and persistent mental illness
- Homelessness
- Marital discord
- Parent–child conflict
- At-risk adolescent parenthood

You should note there are no items on this list that focus on a given service. You did not see, for example, need for family counseling service, or need for parent training, or need for parent support group. Instead, you saw a list of possible target behaviors that clients might bring to a human service agency. The service is the intervention that will be addressed later in this exercise. For now, you are asked to focus on the behavior that might be addressed by a familiar intervention.

Discussion Box 18.2

List a few of the target behaviors of special interest to you.

Are any of the items in the discussion box service oriented rather than focusing on the client's condition? If so, strike them. Then select the one of most interest to you and put a check or asterisk next to it.

This target behavior will be the focus of your outcome goal. Your outcome goal will be a guide for the articulation of outcome objectives, defined as measured amounts of progress toward the achievement of the goal. This target behavior should be addressed by a familiar human service, such as school social work, child protective services, family counseling, Head Start, inpatient mental health treatment by the Oak Hill Psychiatric Center, discharge planning services of Memorial Hospital, the Women's Center, etc.

Defining the Target Behavior

This part of the assignment calls upon you to define the target behavior. A good definition will help you later in the selection of a means for measuring client progress. If you have a convenient definition from the literature or an agency document, provide this definition below and identify its source. If not, list the things that are considered a part of this behavior, and design your own definition from this list. A good definition will specify the behavior in clear terms that distinguishes it from others that are similar.

Discussion Box 18.3

Indicate your definition of the target behavior. Start the first sentence with the words "_____ is defined as. . . ," with the blank being the label you are giving to the target behavior.

Identifying Client Need

Most likely your selected target behavior is broad enough that you will find it useful to identify the needs that clients experience with this target behavior. What do abused wives need? Do they need social support, or certain forms of information about legal matters, or economic independence, or a husband willing to enter therapy, or help with decisions about the future?

What does a homeless person need? The quick answer is a home; but is it that simple? Why is this person homeless? Does this individual need better to understand how to get and maintain a job, or to get help finding a job, or to overcome depression, or improve self-esteem?

Note that there is no reference here to the need for job training, the need for a support group, or the need for counseling. These are services that might address a need, but they should not be conceptualized as the client's need. The need for certain forms of information may lead logically to the decision to offer some form of training. The need for social support may lead logically to offering a support group experience. But we should distinguish between these two.

Discussion Box 18.4

Indicate the most important needs of persons with your selected target behavior.

Now go back to the list in the discussion box and identify the needs that should serve as a focus of an outcome evaluation study. Put a star or mark next to each of these needs. These needs should be those that receive a good deal of attention by the intervention that addresses them.

Assignment C: Analyzing the Target Behavior

In this part of the exercise, you will analyze the target behavior either to justify the selected service you are focusing upon or suggesting modifications of it. The dynamics of the target behavior should be congruent with the design of the intervention. If the client needs information, he or she should be given some form of training. If the ADHD child's behavior is caused by brain chemistry, some form of medication would be the logical solution to the behavior, but it might also be necessary for the parent to better understand how to use behavioral techniques especially helpful for the child with this condition. Thus, a combination of medication and parent training (or educationally focused counseling) would be warranted.

Discussion Box 18.5

Your next task is to identify what is known about your selected target behavior. You might focus more on the causes of this behavior or the needs of persons with it. Identify one or more key documents that deal with this subject.

Discussion Box 18.6

Now summarize how well the selected intervention addresses the dynamics of the target behavior as identified in the document. If you do not have such a document, you can offer your own analysis of the dynamics of the selected target behavior for the purpose of this exercise, even though you are advised to conduct a literature review before completing the behavior analysis for an evaluation research study.

Assignment D: Describing the Intervention

In this assignment you will describe the selected intervention with regard to goals, objectives, structure, model, and personnel.

Identifying Goals and Objectives

The first task is to identify the broad goal of your intervention and the outcome objectives that will be measured in your study. The goal is the ultimate outcome you are seeking. It may or may not be directly measured by your outcome measurement tools. The outcome objective, on the other hand, is a measured amount of progress toward the achievement of the goal, and it will be the focus of your measurement of client progress.

For example, the goal of discharge planning services of Memorial Hospital may be the prevention of health problems, while an outcome objective may be to assure that discharged patients follow up with prescribed medications and other forms of suggested care. One of the goals of school social work service may be to prevent at-risk youth from dropping out of school, while one of the objectives could be improved grades, reduced disciplinary problems, or improved self-esteem. The goal of the Women's Center may be to empower women, while one of the objectives may be to improve the women's knowledge of legal matters related to achieving independence from a spouse.

Discussion Box 18.7

What is the broad goal or goals related to your selected intervention?

Discussion Box 18.8

What are the outcome objectives related to this goal that will serve as the focus of your attempt to measure client progress?

Identifying the Structure of the Intervention

The structure of the intervention specifies the form it will take and the intensity of the services for the typical client. Here are a few examples:

- Psychotherapy for the reduction of depression is offered in one-hour office sessions, with the typical clients receiving eight sessions.
- Parent training is to be offered in two-hour weekly sessions for four weeks.
- Discharge planning for the hospital includes assessment, referral, and monitoring which takes the form of (1) the development of a discharge plan for identified patients, (2) referral

of clients to necessary services included in the plan, and (3) monitoring of plan implementation. The assessment process includes interviews with the patient and family members and consultation with medical personnel, which leads to the development of a discharge plan. Referrals typically are made by phone calls to agencies and followed up with necessary documentation. The plan is monitored on a monthly basis through contact between the social worker and key persons.

Discussion Box 18.9

How would you describe the structure of your selected intervention?

If you gave the description in the box to a typical human service practitioner, would this individual be able to recognize it in practice? Would this person be able to give a rough estimate of the amount of service to be supported by the agency's budget? For example, would this individual be able to say the budget needs funds to support 22 hours of the time of human service professionals of a certain type (psychologists, nurses, social workers)?

Identifying the Personnel of the Intervention

Your task here is to identify the type of personnel who will deliver the services included in this intervention or program. If the intervention is complex, you will need to identify what type of practitioner will deliver Service A and what type will deliver Service B. For example, with services that are delivered by social workers, you should identify whether these persons will be licensed clinical social workers, social workers with the MSW degree, social workers with the BSW degree, or persons hired into social work positions without formal training in social work.

Discussion Box 18.10

For your selected intervention, describe the personnel.

Identifying the Model of the Intervention

The model of the intervention identifies the underlying assumptions that are being made about the dynamics of the target behavior. The use of the cognitive-behavioral model for the treatment of depression, for example, is based on the assumption that depression is caused by dysfunctional thinking about life experiences. As a result of this assumption about the nature of depression, the cognitive-behavioral model emphasizes intervention into the client's thinking patterns. Your treatment model for victims of domestic violence may be based on the assumption that such victims typically are lacking in the kind of social support that allows them to make critical choices that could prevent future acts of violence; therefore, your intervention will include a support group. Persons without social support may be more vulnerable to being a victim of domestic violence. It may be that perpetrators of violence try to isolate their victims for this reason. The discharge planning service of Memorial Hospital may be based on the assumption that some discharged patients lack the life organization skills and knowledge of resources to properly follow up on recommended health practices; therefore, the hospital uses medical social workers to provide discharge planning services.

Discussion Box 18.11
_____

How would you characterize the model of the intervention you are addressing?

Assignment E: Describing the Study Sample and Study Population

Your task in this assignment is to identify your study population and your study sample. Your study sample is always the person(s) from whom data were collected. The population can be defined in various ways but must be defined in such a way that all persons in the study sample are a part of that population.

The key purpose for clarifying your sample and population is to help you in the generalization of your study results. If you find that cognitive-behavior therapy has been effective in the treatment of 12 persons in your caseload, can you generalize this finding to other persons who are depressed? Will this form of therapy work with others?

You can safely generalize your study findings from a probability sample to the population from which it was drawn, providing that you have a sufficient sample size; a sample of one is not a sufficient sample size. The determination of what size of sample is appropriate is a complex issue more fully explained in other texts. For our purposes, we will say that a sample of one is not sufficient and that samples of 10 or more are probably sufficient, providing that your study population is not more than 10 times larger than your sample. A probability sample is one that is selected at random from the designated study population.

If you do not have a probability sample, you can engage in speculative generalization. In this text, speculative generalization is distinguished from safe generalization in that the latter is restricted to probability samples. Speculative generalization is a matter of opinion. The key issue is whether there is something different between your study sample and your defined population that would suggest that findings from your sample are likely to be different from similar findings from the entire population.

Discussion Box 18.12

Define your study sample.

Discussion Box 18.13

Define your study population. Your population must be larger than your sample. By definition, a sample is a part of something bigger.

Discussion Box 18.14

Indicate whether you have a probability sample and explain your answer.

Discussion Box 18.15

Indicate whether you believe your study results could be generalized to this study population, either on a safe basis or a speculative basis. Explain.

Assignment F: Selecting a Means for Measuring Client Progress

Now you need to determine how client progress will be measured in your study. You should refer to the definition of the target behavior and to the outcome objectives that were identified. Ideally, each outcome objective would be measured in your study. For this exercise, however, you are asked to identify only one means of measurement. One or more of your outcome objectives may be easily measured by data readily available, such as grades in school, the number of times that referred clients followed up with their appointments to services, or the number of times that previously served families confirmed for child abuse had a repeat confirmation of abuse. Other outcomes may need to be measured by some type of scale, like the ones discussed in many research texts. Examples are depression, anxiety, self-esteem, guilt, family functioning, hostility, phobia, loneliness and stress.

Clarifying What You Want to Measure

Discussion Box 18.16

Identify the outcome objective upon which you will focus your attention.

Discussion Box 18.17

Does your agency already have a tool for measuring client progress on this? If so, identify it. Be specific; describe what it is supposed to measure and generally what it looks like.

If your agency does not have a convenient measurement tool that will work for your purposes, review your definition of the target behavior and identify precisely what the instrument that you select should measure.

Discussion Box 18.18

Identify what your measurement tool should measure? If your agency already has a suitable measurement method, indicate N/A.

Finding a Measurement Tool

Your next task is to find a means of measurement. You will need to choose between a standardized scale and an individualized one. If you have a simple situation (recording school grades, counting the number of failed appointments through the agency's calendar) and no need to measure a psychological construct, you do not need to go through this part of the exercise.

Normally you will want to check out standardized scales first. If there is one for your situation, you will have the advantage of having one already made up by someone who has put a lot of time into deciding what should be on the scale, and you likely will have a tool that has been tested for reliability and validity.

There are numerous books that can be used for this purpose. *Tests in print* is one example. You can find out a lot about scales through the Internet. The following is a brief exercise that might be helpful.

> Go to the Buros Institute for Mental Measurement website, www.unl.edu/buros/bimm/index.html.
> Click on the option Need information about a test.
> Enter the keyword *test anxiety.*

You will see a long list of tests. One of the problems with these searches is that you get a list with many items that are not relevant to your situation. For example, you will see Adolescent Separation Anxiety Test on this list, which obviously does not measure test anxiety. But you will note a test named the Test Anxiety Profile; if you click on it, you will find a description of this test. According to the description, the Test Anxiety Profile measures how much anxiety a person experiences in various testing situations. If this is what you need, you can order that test or perhaps find it in a book that contains various tests.

If you enter *eating disorders* as a keyword, you will find various instruments including the Eating Inventory, which measures three dimensions of eating disorders found to be important in eating-related disorders. These three dimensions include cognitive control of eating, disinhibition, and hunger. If you are looking for a measure of eating disorders and have included these three things as a part of your definition of your target behavior, you will have found a tool.

Discussion Box 18.19
_____

List the name and description of the measurement tool you will use to measure the achievement of the outcome objective you have selected for study.

Assignment G: Selecting the Research Design

In this part of the exercise on outcome evaluation, you will select the research design for your outcome evaluation study. Your first task is to identify those threats to internal validity that should be of special concern in your situation. Then you will identify the research design that would be appropriate.

What is Likely to Influence the Target Behavior Independent of Treatment?

The idea of *threats to internal validity* refers to the question of what might explain changes in the target behavior independent of treatment (things that are not a part of the design of the intervention). If one part of the intervention strategy is to obtain housing in a new neighborhood, this change in the client's environment is a part of the intervention and would not be listed as an example of history as a threat to internal validity. It would be changes in the client's environment outside of intervention strategies that would be considered examples of history as a threat to internal validity.

In this part of the assignment, we are not talking about all that is possible. Instead, we are talking about what is probable. So the question is "What is *likely* to influence the target behavior independent of treatment?" If a client is currently in a job training program that will enhance job skills, you would likely expect the client to obtain a job in the near future. If the client has a long-standing history of allowing an abusive husband to return to the home after only a few months away, you would likely expect this to happen in the next few months. While it is *possible* that a client with a chronic unemployment problem will get a job in the next three weeks, you would probably determine that this is not likely, given this client's history.

Discussion Box 18.20
_____

List the things that might influence the target behavior independent of treatment? You do not need to give these things a label now. If you cannot think of anything, this is okay, as long as you explain why you cannot think of anything.

Discussion Box 18.21

Now identify how data will be collected in your evaluation situation. For example, you might say that a group of 12 adolescent mothers will be given a self-esteem scale at intake and again six months later. You might say that your one client will be given a depression scale once before treatment and again each week for six weeks during treatment.

Discussion Box 18.22

Now give the label for your research design. Some of the common labels are (1) one-group pretest–posttest design, (2) B single-subject design, (3) comparison group design, (4) alternative treatment design, and (5) pretest–posttest control group design (or basic experimental design).

Discussion Box 18.23

Does this design address any threats to internal validity that should be of special concern? Explain.

Now you have information on a potential limitation of your study design. If there are alternative explanations of client progress that are not addressed by your research design, you should discuss this topic in the conclusions section of your research report.

Summary

Now, you have the skeleton of an evaluation study; it will be fleshed out as you pursue this evaluation research study. If you have all the essentials enumerated in this exercise, you are in good shape, providing that you fill in more details in your final report. As noted in previous chapters, there are several avenues for focus when you consider the issue of study limitations in your final section of the research report. These include the type of sample, the measurement device, and the study design. Hopefully, this exercise will help you to organize your research efforts and highlight the strengths and limitations of the approach you are taking.

Reference

Buros Institute of Mental Measurement. How to use tests in print. Retrieved September 16, 2007 from http://www.unl.edu/buros/bimm/html/howtotip.html

19

An Introduction to Data Analysis

In this chapter, you will examine the elementary model of data analysis, basic concepts in evaluation research, and tips on how to use the Excel spreadsheets that are used in the elementary approach to statistical analysis. The elementary approach to data analysis is discussed so that you can see its advantages and limitations. Basic concepts in evaluation are reviewed so that you will be better able to understand the language employed in these chapters. And finally, you will obtain a brief overview of Excel, the computer software used in this approach to statistical analysis; if you are already familiar with Excel, this will not be necessary. There is a quiz at the end of the chapter to help you determine if you need to read this chapter, or how well you read it. The model of elementary analysis is the theme with which you are least likely to be familiar with from previous readings; the others should be familiar to you.

Because this chapter presents a review of concepts previously discussed, there is no breakdown of specific objectives. The goal is to assure that you are prepared to employ the chapters that deal with the analysis of data.

Model of Elementary Analysis

This will be an elementary approach to data analysis in evaluation. It is simple in that it presents methods that are easy for the practitioner to use. It is practical in that it addresses most outcome evaluation situations that confront the front-line practitioner in human services. This approach views chance as an important issue in evaluation, but does not deify statistical tests. For the front-line practitioner, close is good enough; a high degree of precision in statistical analysis is not viewed as necessary.

This practical approach employs Excel spreadsheets because they can be used for most evaluations for the front lines. This approach does not require the purchase of expensive statistical software. Many agencies will have access to software like the Excel spreadsheet that comes bundled with many Microsoft® computer packages loaded onto computers at purchase.

Avoiding the purchase of statistical software not only saves money, but saves time because its use requires a mini-course in the particular software. The approach taken in this book simply requires you to have Excel on your computer and does not require familiarity with specific technicalities associated with this software. All you will need to do is load the Excel software into memory and follow some simple instructions on where to insert your specific data and where to find your results.

Chance is viewed as an important issue in evaluation. When you examine data to determine if there is evidence that the treatment is effective, you should confront the issue of chance. Behavior usually does not stay the same from one week to another. It fluctuates, sometimes in a rather random fashion. A critical question is whether your data is best explained as representing the normal fluctuations in target behavior, or the effect of treatment itself. It could be that a client achieves a 20 percent gain on target behavior from the first to the last recording, but it could also be that the client's recordings of behavior have fluctuated a good deal during the months prior to treatment, including periodic 20 percent gains and losses, suggesting that 20 percent is best explained as chance rather than treatment effectiveness.

The way to address the issue of chance is through statistical tests. You can take a rigid approach to statistical analysis, employing only the most advanced approaches that are known. One could argue that this approach has a tendency to deify statistical tests—to glorify the minor distinctions between statistical tests as though the reduction of error by small amounts has profound meaning in the real world.

But you could take a simple approach, which does not deify statistical tests. It recognizes the limitations inherent in statistical analysis and takes the stance that close is good enough for the real world. The simple approach is taken in this chapter. This approach has a number of limitations because of the following compromises with precision in statistical analysis:

1. A simple test can be used instead of a more complicated one because it is unlikely that this choice would make a difference in the basic conclusions that would be warranted by the data. For example, it is asserted here that the vast majority of times a more complicated statistic is employed, the difference in p value (probability of chance) will not move the researcher from the conclusion that the treatment was effective to the conclusion that it was ineffective. It is asserted here that, for the basic practitioner, p values of less than 0.10 are not very noteworthy. For example, the difference between a value of 0.02 and 0.09 should not change the basic conclusion. A p value of 0.02, of course, is better than 0.09, but is it sufficiently better to suggest that conclusions should be changed? I think not.

2. The choice of the 0.05 level of significance, widely accepted for the social sciences, has no scientific basis, and favors the reduction of Type I error over Type II error. In the front lines of human services it is less dangerous to conclude erroneously that an ineffective intervention is effective than to do the opposite—to fail to recognize an effective intervention. The more restrictive standard of 0.05 favors the former rather than the latter. It would more likely have practitioners rejecting effective interventions in order to make extra sure that an ineffective one is not being accepted. This highly conservative approach does not address the critical needs of human service agencies and the clients they serve because employing the conservative standard is likely to lead to the rejection of a mildly effective treatment in favor of an untested treatment that may not be effective at all. After all, there is a wide array of funded treatments that lack scientific justification.

3. Ordinal data can sometimes be treated as interval. The theoretical distinction between ordinal and interval measurement is more useful in academia than the front lines of evaluation. When you compute the mean for a variable in your data set, the statistical test that computes the mean makes the assumption that the variable is measured at the interval level. Computing a mean score for an ordinal variable is less than optimal, but it makes only a small compromise in the pursuit of perfection. In fact, it is not at all unusual for an evaluation study to use means as measures of intensity of opinion when the variable is measured at the ordinal level, such as, for example, when the instrument offers the response options of strongly agree, agree, undecided, disagree, and strongly disagree. These options are ordinal in nature but often one assigns numbers to the categories in ordinal sequence with higher scores representing higher levels of agreement. When these numbers are assigned to individual items on an instrument, it is not uncommon for these items to be combined into a scale with an overall score for the scale. This is one way that the assumptions of levels of measurement are violated, but it is generally accepted.

4. Tests designed for independent samples can be employed for related samples, providing that one acknowledges this limitation, because the criticality of testing for autocorrelation (in single-system research) is far from clear (See, for example, Huitema, B. E., 1985, Autocorrelation in applied behavior analysis: A myth. *Behavioral Assessment, 7*, 107, 118).

The last point, about autocorrelation, can use further clarification. The vast majority of statistical tests have been developed for data for independent samples. This means that the data are from different people, or otherwise are not dependent in the sense that one score on the test can be predicted by another score.

Single-system data, however, are drawn from related samples because you have repeated measures on the same scale for the same person. Statistical measures such as chi square, the independent samples *t* test, and the standard deviation are examples of tests used for data from independent samples. However, the problem of independence is dealt with if your data are not autocorrelated. In cases where the data are not autocorrelated, you can employ tests that are designed for data from independent samples. But the determination of autocorrelation is problematic for a number of reasons too complicated to discuss here.

For the novice researcher, you can do any of several things:

1. Ignore statistical analysis for single-system data. This means that you do not address the issue of chance as an alternative explanation for your data as you reflect upon whether your intervention is effective.
2. Ignore the issue of autocorrelation, assuming that your data are not autocorrelated and apply statistical tests, keeping in mind the limitation inherent in this assumption.
3. Test for autocorrelation and apply statistical tests only when you fail to find that it exists in your data. This is not easy, given the fact that simple tests for autocorrelation have been reported to be incomplete in the examination of this issue.

The approach taken in my document is in keeping with alternative 2, which means that you will be shown ways to test for statistical significance but you should take the stance that you are dealing with chance as an alternative hypothesis in a limited way. In your presentation of your details for statistical analysis, you should report this to the reader. You might want to quote the following as your defense:

> The statistical test employed in this situation is one that has been designed for data drawn from independent samples. The data in the evaluation presented here, however, are drawn from related samples. This is one of the limitations of the present analysis. However, the present analysis is consistent with the "elementary approach" to data analysis, designed for the human service practitioner who views chance as an important issue but is prepared to make compromises with technical specifications because it is assumed that small differences in technicalities in statistical analysis are not likely to alter basic conclusions.

This limitation is relevant to statistics used for single-subject research designs. It can be relevant to the analysis of group data, but usually is not. In this document, you will find a statement regarding this caveat in each situation that applies.

Basic Concepts in Evaluation

There are several basic concepts in research that you need to understand in order to use this guide. If you already understand the following concepts, you do not need to read this section; You can move to the next part, where the guide for analysis begins.

- What is a hypothesis?
- Under what circumstances can you say your data supported the hypothesis?
- What is the difference between quantitative and qualitative measurement?
- What is meant by *target behavior*?
- How do you distinguish between the nominal, ordinal, and interval levels of measurement?
- What is the difference between the single-subject design and the group design?
- What is the difference between the baseline and treatment periods?
- What is meant by *statistical significance* and *practical significance*?
- In the analysis of single-system data, what is meant by a *slope*, a *pattern*, or a *trend*?

The Hypothesis

The **hypothesis** is a prediction of the results of your study delivered in a special format. The statement "I think my client will get better" is not in the proper form for the hypothesis. The proper format includes reference to the variables in the study and the nature of the predicted relationship between them. It is free of excess words that do not fit this need. Examples of study hypotheses for evaluative research include the following:

- The client's scores on the Beck Depression Inventory will be lower during the treatment period than would have been expected by the baseline trend.
- The clients of the Hope Clinic will have greater gain on self-esteem than those on the waiting list who have not yet been served.

- There will be a greater number of referrals of clients to the Follow-Up Program from nurses who have received the Follow-Up Orientation Training than those who have not had this training.

Support for the Hypothesis.   You can say your data supported your hypothesis when you have achieved statistical significance. If you have not achieved statistical significance but your clients revealed a gain, you can report this fact by saying your average client achieved a gain, but you cannot say your data supported your hypothesis, because of the special role the hypothesis plays in research.

You will see reference to the **null hypothesis**. The null hypothesis says there is no difference between groups or between pretest and posttest measurements. We will not go into detail about this form of the hypothesis, nor do I expect this form to be used by everyday practitioners. I am only making a reference to this form because of the special role the hypothesis plays in research. In terms used by researchers and academicians, you say that you rejected the null hypothesis when you achieve statistical significance. This means you have ruled out chance as the alternative hypothesis. By alternative hypothesis is meant the hypothesis that would be true if chance is a reasonable explanation of your data. So don't say your data supported your hypothesis unless you have tested for statistical significance and have achieved it; you have ruled out chance as the alternative hypothesis. However, in some circumstances, it is appropriate to say your data were not amenable to statistical analysis.

Qualitative and Quantitative Measurement

This section will focus only on **quantitative** data analysis. Quantitative variables are measured as categories or as numbers that reflect either order, from low to high, or scores. When you divide your clients into male and female, you have quantitative measurement. When you ask the extent to which they agree with a given statement and give them the options of disagree, uncertain, and agree, you have quantitative measurement. When you give them an instrument that gives them a score on the scale, you have quantitative measurement.

But when you ask them to answer an open-ended question, you will have words to analyze. When you review progress notes, you have words to analyze. When you have words to analyze, you have **qualitative** measurement.

Levels of Measurement

There are four levels of measurement—nominal, ordinal, interval, and ratio. These four levels form a hierarchy in that a variable can be treated as being measured at a lower level. With **nominal** variables, you have simply placed study subjects into categories that have no order. Gender would be an example. It is divided into the categories of male and female without any order. If the categories have an order, from low to high, you have **ordinal** level measurement. An example:

How much do you agree or disagree with the statement "Most people can get a job if they really want to?"

Strongly agree
Agree
Disagree
Strongly disagree

When you have a score on a scale, you normally have measurement at the **interval** level. The interval level can be distinguished from the ordinal level. With interval measurement, the distance between each adjacent set of values is equal to the distance between any other adjacent set of values. For example, a person who is 10 years of age is one year older than someone who is 9 years of age, while a person 27 years of age is one year older than someone who is 26 years of age. The distance between 9 and 10 is the same as the distance between 26 and 27. Theoretically, the same cannot be said of ordinal measurement, where there is an order to the categories but the distance between categories is not always equal. For example, one can argue theoretically that the distance between "disagree" and "agree" is not necessarily the same as the distance between "strongly agree" and "agree." As noted earlier, the distinction between ordinal and interval measurement draws more attention in academia than the world of everyday human service practice, so compromises with this distinction are okay here.

The same can be said of the distinction between interval measurement and **ratio** measurement; it has little practical utility in the real world of human service practice. The ratio variable has the same qualities as the interval variable, with the addition that the values on the scale of a ratio tool have a fixed zero point. In practical terms, this means you cannot have a negative value for a ratio variable. You cannot have a negative age or a negative height—so age and height are examples of measurement at the ratio level.

These levels of measurement form a hierarchy:

(4) Ratio

(3) Interval

(2) Ordinal

(1) Nominal

In other words, nominal measurement is the lowest on the hierarchy; it is the lowest level of measurement. Ordinal comes next, followed by interval. At the highest level is ratio measurement. This hierarchy is conceptualized to suggest that you can treat a variable as being measured at a lower level than naturally formed but not at a higher level. This is the party line for those who teach statistics and research and work on sophisticated national research studies, where precision is highly valued. But it is less important to the everyday human service practitioner. I would propose only one rule that should never be violated—you *cannot* treat a nominal variable as being measured at a higher level when you engage in the statistical analysis of your data.

The rationale for reviewing the idea of level of measurement is that various statistical tests make assumptions about level of measurement. For example, the Pearson correlation coefficient makes the assumption that the variables in the analysis are measured at the interval level, whereas the chi square statistic does not. You would not, therefore, call upon the Pearson correlation coefficient to examine the relationship between one's party affiliation and one's gender. The correlation coefficient that would be generated by the use of this statistic for this analysis would make no sense.

I would suggest that you pay attention to the distinctions among ordinal, interval, and ratio levels of measurement whenever you feel the audience will appreciate it. If you are on your way to becoming a serious researcher or research consultant, or wish to undertake a national study based on a federal grant, you will need to do this.

The Special Case of the Dichotomous Variable.   An important type of measurement in evaluative research is the **dichotomous** variable. This is the variable that is measured with regard to only two categories, such as Yes or No. This is one form of the nominal level of measurement that lends itself to data analysis employing my elementary approach. Other forms of the nominal variable are not amenable to analysis using this elementary approach. The dichotomous variable can be treated as interval because there is only one set of values—there is only one interval. Therefore, the idea of equality among intervals is moot. However, you should first consider the dichotomous variable, such as gender, to be something measured at the nominal level. It is only when you have an unusual circumstance that you should treat it as interval; I suggest that you seek consultation before doing so.

Target Behavior

The behavior that you are measuring to determine client progress is the target behavior. You need to be clear on how it is being measured and the level of its measurement. If you are using the Beck Depression Inventory, you will have a depression score for each client that is measured at the interval level. If you have classified the target behavior into the categories of improved or not improved, you will have a nominal level of measurement. (Remember: You should treat the dichotomous variable as interval only in complicated situations after seeking consultation from an expert.)

Single-System and Group Designs

There are two general forms of research designs. The **single-system design** is used when you are evaluating a single client, or you are using a single score to represent progress over time. The single-system design uses repeated measurements of target behavior over time as the basis for compiling an array of data sufficient for statistical analysis. The **group design**, by contrast, uses measurements of a number of people on the same scale as the basis for analysis. While the single-system design is normally used with a single client, it can also be used with other units of analysis, such as an organization or a community, providing that you are collecting a single measurement of the dependent variable in your repeated measurements of progress. For example, you might collect data on the absenteeism rate for an agency or the unemployment rate for a state.

One of the most feasible single-subject designs for the everyday practitioner is the **B design**, where there are no measurements of target behavior prior to treatment, but multiple measurements during the treatment period. A second feasible single-subject design is the **limited AB design**, where you have at least one measurement prior to treatment, but multiple measurements during the treatment period. It is often feasible to treat the assessment period of therapy as the pretreatment period because you do not begin a conscious treatment protocol until after you have determined the approach to treatment. In this case, it is often feasible to measure the target behavior once before the formal period of treatment begins. This one measurement serves as the baseline measure.

The two most common group designs are **one-group pretest–posttest** and the **alternative treatment** design. On occasion, the human service practitioner has the opportunity to employ the comparison group design, where there is a comparison group, but this is not often the case in day-to-day human service practice.

When you test a group of clients once before treatment and once at the end of treatment, you are employing the one-group pretest–posttest design. When you are comparing the gains of clients with nonclients, you are employing the comparison group design. When you are comparing clients with one form of treatment with clients using another form of treatment, your analysis of data would take the same form as the one where nonclients form the comparison group. With this design, you are measuring both groups before and after treatment, and you are comparing their levels of gain.

Baseline Period and Treatment Period

When you employ the **AB single-system design**, you will collect measurements of target behavior before treatment begins and during the treatment periods. The measurements prior to treatment are the baseline measurements, while the ones taken during treatment are the treatment measurements. With the **ABAB design**, you have two baseline periods (those lettered A) and two treatment periods (those lettered B).

Statistical Significance and Practical Significance

When you analyze data, you want to draw conclusions. You want to know what to make of the data. You want to know how significant it is. One form of significance is **statistical significance**. This refers to the extent to which your data can be explained by chance. Statistical tests give you a *p* value. The p value refers to the number of times in 100 that your data would be expected to occur by chance. If this value is high, you cannot have confidence that you have witnessed a noteworthy pattern in your data that can give you the ability to draw positive conclusions about your intervention. Instead, you would be encouraged to conclude that your data can too easily be explained by chance to have given you confidence that your treatment was effective.

It is possible for your clients to achieve a gain during the treatment period that is not statistically significant. The lower the level of gain, the greater the likelihood that your data can be explained by chance. The greater the variance in scores, the greater the likelihood your data can be explained by chance. It is possible that your observed changes in the clients' scores are random fluctuations in behavior that do not represent a positive effect of the intervention.

Practical significance refers to the extent to which you can say your client or clients achieved a noteworthy improvement in the target behavior. This is a matter of professional judgment. It is highly influenced by the context of your practice. It is informed by reference to the percent of gain, whether the clients moved beyond major clinical thresholds, and how much gain your client(s) achieved in regard to standard deviations of change.

Data Patterns, Trends, and Slopes

When you examine data in the baseline and treatment periods in single-system evaluation, you may encounter the concepts of pattern, trend, and slope. A *pattern* is any recognizable form of data. The pattern can show that the behavior is not changing, or that it is changing. If the baseline reveals changing behavior, either up or down, you can say you have a *trend* or a *slope*. I will use the term slope because it is clearer to the average person. In my elementary approach to analysis, I declare that you do not have data sufficient to detect a pattern if you do not have at least four baseline measurements. Three or fewer measurements provide the basis for estimating the fixed point of client functioning but not detecting a change (slope) in the target behavior. This is my arbitrary rule; it may not be agreed to by others who teach research.

Using Excel Spreadsheets to Analyze Data

In this chapter, you are given instructions on the use of Excel spreadsheets for examining data using various statistics. Excel is produced by Microsoft and comes bundled with many other Microsoft products such as Word® and Access®. You must have Excel on your computer in order to use this feature of this chapter.

Excel is a spreadsheet type of software. When you load it into your computer, you will see a screen that has columns and rows that look somewhat like Table 19.1.

The table shows columns with letters as labels and rows with numbers as labels. The cells on the screen can be used either for letters or numbers. The files you will be asked to use in this document will have instructions entered in the first several rows. You will be asked to enter your data in selected cells, such as A4, B8, and so forth. The A4 cell is the intersection of column A and row 4, the one that is shaded. Your software, however, will not shade cell A4—the above is done only for illustration purposes.

TABLE 19.1 *Illustration of a Spreadsheet*

	A	B	C	D	E	F	G	H	I
1									
2									
3									
4									
5									
6									
7									
8									
9									

Your tasks in using the Excel files furnished by the author are as follows:

1. Load the Excel software into your computer's active memory.
2. Load the special Excel file, developed by the author, which you need to use.
3. Enter your data according to the directions supplied in this book and the particular Excel file you are using.
4. Examine the cells that tell you what you need to know in regard to client improvement and statistical significance.

Your first task is to load the Excel software into your computer's active memory. A spreadsheet with columns and rows somewhat like a table, will be on your screen as illustrated.

Your next task is to download the Excel file that has been made available by the author of this chapter on elementary data analysis. This is a file, composed with the Excel software, which has been developed by the author for application to many statistical tests useful for human service evaluation. There is a different Excel file for each type of application; each is labeled for that application. For example, the file used for comparing pretest and posttest scores for one group of clients when behavior is measured at the interval level is labeled "one-group, pre-post, interval data." To load this file, click on **File** at the top of the screen and select **Open,** after which you select the appropriate file from your disk that comes with this book.

You will find instructions at the top of each file that explain how the file is to be used. Those instructions will tell you where to enter your data and where to find the value of the particular statistic, and, most important, it will tell you where to find whether the results were statistically significant.

Your final task is to enter your data and examine the appropriate cells to determine whether your data achieved statistical significance. You can print this file or save it on a disk or the hard drive of your computer. Then you can exit by going to the File option at the top of the screen and choosing Close as your next option. You will be asked if you wish to save your file. *When you exit this file, you should* not *save the file*. Saving the file will mean that you have encumbered this statistical file with old data when you want to use the file with a different example in the future. If you do this inadvertently, you can correct it simply by deleting the old data and putting in new data.

Exercise in the Use of the Excel Spreadsheet

This section will provide you with an example that carries you through the steps in the use of the Excel spreadsheet. If you are familiar with this type software, you may not need to undertake this exercise.

The example uses the paired *t* test for the examination of pretest and posttest scores for one group of clients. In this example, lower scores are *better*; therefore, the gain score is computed by subtracting the posttest score from the pretest score. The following are the data to be entered. Be sure to enter negative gain scores with the minus sign.

CLIENT CASE NUMBER	PRETEST	POSTTEST	GAIN
3289	24	29	–5
3144	29	23	6
2675	45	32	13
1773	46	48	–2
2314	33	33	0
2429	42	39	3

First, load the Excel software into your computer's active memory. You must, of course, have this software on your computer in order to use these files for data analysis.

Next, load the file named "one group, prepost, interval data." Your instructions at the top of the file will ask you to enter the data starting in cell A8 for the first client's pretest score, followed by entering this client's posttest score in B8, and this client's gain in C8. You should enter the second client's pretest score in A9, posttest score in B9, and gain score in C9. You should repeat this procedure for each of the other four clients.

To determine whether the posttest scores were generally lower than pretest scores, as would be hypothesized, you should consult cell A37 for the mean pretest score (36.5) and cell A38 for the mean posttest score (34). You can see there was a slight gain on the average, given that lower scores are better. But is this difference statistically significant? For the value of p, you should consult cell A42. In this cell you will see the figure 0.191672. This means the difference did not meet the standard of 0.05 because it is higher than this figure. In fact, it also failed to meet the standard of 0.10 (1 time in 10). You should conclude that no real gain in functioning was observed, because this small difference can easily be explained by chance.

You can now exit this file by clicking on the File option at the top of the screen, and selecting Close as your next option. You will get the message "Do you want to save the changes you made to "One group, prepost, interval data"? You should answer No because you do not want your present data to be on this file when you wish to use it again.

Quiz

The following are questions on the contents of this chapter. You may use this test as a pretest, to determine if you need to read this chapter, or as a posttest, to determine how well you read it. Answers are given at the end.

1. Which of the following are true statements about the elementary approach to statistical analysis used in this text?

   a. You should never treat a nominal variable as though it is measured at a higher level, except for the dichotomous variable.
   b. You should never treat an ordinal variable as though it is measured at a higher level.
   c. Both of the above.
   d. None of the above.

2. Which of the following are true statements about the elementary approach to statistical analysis employed in this book?
   a. It is better to abandon the issue of chance as an explanation of our data than to employ a statistical test that is not perfect for the situation.
   b. Small differences in statistical error are not meaningful to the evaluation of day-to-day human service practice.
   c. Both of the above.
   d. None of the above.

3. Which of the following are good examples of the research hypothesis?
   a. The client will get better on the target behavior because of the intervention.
   b. The clients' scores on the Hare Self-Esteem Scale will be higher at the end of the treatment period than before treatment began.
   c. Both of the above.
   d. None of the above.

4. You can say your data supported your hypothesis in which of the following circumstances?
   a. When your clients achieved a measured gain in functioning
   b. When your clients achieved a measured gain in functioning that was found to be statistically significant
   c. When your clients achieved a gain in functioning that is considered by you to be of practical significance
   d. All of the above

5. Consider the following question on an instrument:

   Look at the list below of life events.
   - Death of someone close to you
   - Loss of a job
   - Moving to a location where you had no familiarity with people
   - Marital breakup or breakup of a serious long-term relationship
   - Getting into a really big fight with someone where the interpersonal conflict has been left unresolved

   How many of these events have you experienced in the last six months? _____
   At what level is this variable measured?
   a. Nominal
   b. Dichotomous

c. Ordinal
d. Interval or ratio

6. The main reason we are concerned with identifying the level of measurement of a variable is:
   a. It helps with the choice of a study sample.
   b. It helps with the choice of a research design.
   c. It helps us to draw conclusions about practical significance.
   d. It helps us to choose a statistical measure.

7. If you measured 10 clients on depression using a depression scale before treatment began and again after treatment, you would be employing which research design?
   a. The B single-subject design
   b. The limited AB single-subject design
   c. The one-group pretest-posttest research design
   d. The comparison group design

8. How do you distinguish between baseline data and treatment data?
   a. The baseline data come from measurements of target behavior when the client is not in treatment, while the treatment data come from measurements of target behavior when the client is in treatment.
   b. The baseline data come from measurements of target behavior when the client is in treatment, and the treatment data come from measurements of target behavior when the client is not in treatment.
   c. The baseline data come from any base that you might use as an estimate of the client's target behavior both during and after treatment.
   d. The treatment data consist of those measurements of target behavior that signify an improvement in the client's functioning, while the baseline data refer to all other data.

9. Where would you seek your best guidance in the determination of practical significance?
   a. The value *p* from the statistical analysis of your data
   b. The value of *t* from the *t* test or the value of chi square from the chi square test, and so forth
   c. The extent of gain in client functioning evidenced by the measurement of target

behavior, such as, for example, the percent of gain, whether the client passed a threshold of functioning, and so forth

   d. The extent to which you have found your measurement tool to have face validity.

10. In order to use the Excel files available with this book, you need to have:

   a. The Excel software available on your computer.

   b. The decision of which Excel file from this book that would be appropriate for your particular analysis.

   c. Both of the above.

   d. None of the above.

Reference

Huitema, B. E., 1985, Autocorrelation in applied behavior analysis: A myth. *Behavioral Assessment*, 7, 107, 118).

Answers to the Quiz

1. a
2. b
3. b
4. b
5. d

6. d
7. c
8. a
9. c
10. c

20

Elementary Data Analysis for Single-System Designs

When you have a single client to evaluate, you can employ any of a number of designs referred to as single-system designs or single-subject designs. You can employ these designs whenever you are treating an entity as a single client. This could include a community or an organization in addition to a single client. The key is that you are using a single indicator of progress such as a score on a test or a mean for some type of condition and you are measuring it repeatedly. With single-system designs you collect several measurements of the same target behavior using the same measurement tool. Group designs, by contrast, call upon you to measure the same target behavior with the same instrument for several different people, rather than many recordings for a single person or entity.

The first part of this chapter will focus on the visual analysis of single-system data. Your first task in this process will be for you to present your recordings of target behavior on a chart or graph. Following the discussion of visual analysis, you will review several specific applications of data analysis for single-system designs. These specific applications will vary by research design and level of measurement of your target behavior.

Upon the completion of this chapter, you will be able to:

1. Visually inspect single-system data to determine its suitability for statistical analysis.

2. Articulate the elementary approach to statistical analysis, with specific reference to selected compromises regarding such issues as level of measurement and autocorrelation.

3. Draw a trend line, both by hand and by use of an Excel spreadsheet, and use the inspection of this line to determine the approach to take to statistical analysis.

4. Select an approach to the statistical analysis of data when the B design is employed and execute the analysis using an Excel file provided with the text.

5. Select an approach to the statistical analysis of data when the AB design is employed and execute the analysis using an Excel file provided with the text.

Visual Analysis of Single-System Data

Visual analysis of single-system data refers to your charting the client's scores and viewing the chart for clues to the client's functioning and the suitability of statistical analysis. In some cases, statistical analysis is not warranted. In some cases, the scale used to measure client functioning is not appropriate for this particular client. Perhaps in rare cases, you will even find the client does not need treatment on the behavior measured by your scale.

Your first task is to chart the client's target behavior. You use a chart that depicts the scores along the side and has a column for each measurement. Examine the chart in Figure 20.1.

In Figure 20.1, the client's score for week 1 was 24 on this scale, while the score of 22 was recorded for week 2, 20 for week 3, 20 for week 4, 20 for week 5, and 19 for week 6. These marks were connected by lines. Usually these are straight lines, but I have used arrows for special emphasis; either is okay.

Before you address the issue of statistical significance, you should engage in a visual analysis of single-system data. This means looking at the pattern of data on a chart to determine what it might mean. This analysis should be especially important in your examination of practical significance. In some cases, your single-system data may not lend themselves to statistical analysis, so the visual analysis is the only thing you can do. It is easier to make the case for practical significance in the absence of statistical significance when your data are not amenable to statistical analysis, and your visual analysis suggests noteworthy client progress that can be attributed to the intervention. Here are some questions to guide this visual analysis:

Baseline analysis

1. What is the level of the target behavior in the baseline phase of the study?
   a. Is this client particularly low or high on this scale?
   b. How does this level compare to norms or thresholds of functioning?

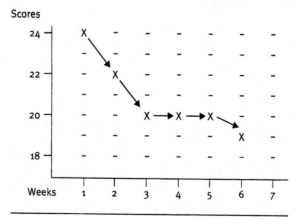

FIGURE 20.1 *Charting a Client's Scores*

    c. Does the level seem accurate for this client? If a clearly depressed client achieves a very low depression score on your scale, perhaps the tool is not a valid way to measure the target behavior for this client.

    d. Does this level suggest the client does not need treatment? Perhaps self-esteem is not a problem for a particular adolescent with disciplinary problems, even though it may be for others.

2. What pattern is suggested by the collection of scores in a given phase? Do the measurements suggest the behavior is stable (level), going up or down, or highly erratic?

- Stable patterns are best for statistical analysis.
- If the behavior is improving substantially, you need to question whether treatment is appropriate, whether you have selected the most meaningful target behavior for evaluation, or if the measurement tool is valid.
- Highly erratic patterns can be analyzed clinically, but not statistically.

Comparison of baseline and treatment

1. Do treatment measurements suggest an improvement in target behavior? If baseline shows gradual improvement and treatment shows the same gradual improvement, you cannot assert that the treatment made a difference because the pattern did not change.

2. How noteworthy is the level of improvement from a clinical standpoint? This question is relevant only if you have treatment data with a pattern that is superior to the prediction from the baseline pattern. In other words, you first should establish that the treatment seems to have made a difference before you address the question of practical (clinical) significance—did it make *enough* of a difference?

Steps in the Visual Analysis of Data with the AB Single-System Design

In this part of the document, you will be led through a step-by-step approach to visual analysis, which should precede statistical analysis. Your first question is whether your baseline seems valid, or believable. If a client appears to be highly depressed, you would not expect really low scores on a depression scale.

    The next question is whether the baseline scores are stable. A stable baseline depicts a clear pattern, whether that pattern be one that suggests the client is improving or deteriorating in functioning, or remaining rather even from one measurement to the next. An erratic baseline depicts scores that are moving up and down demonstratively. An ambiguous baseline shows a pattern that is hard to interpret, such as clear movement up in one part of the baseline followed by clear movement down in a subsequent part of the baseline.

    If the baseline is valid and stable, your next question is whether the baseline scores depict substantial growth. By substantial growth it is meant growth that would suggest the client will do okay without treatment if the baseline growth trend continues in the future. Often this pattern is one in which you could draw a line from the baseline into the treatment period that would reach close to the most positive possible score during the treatment period, and this would be the expected pattern even if the client was not treated.

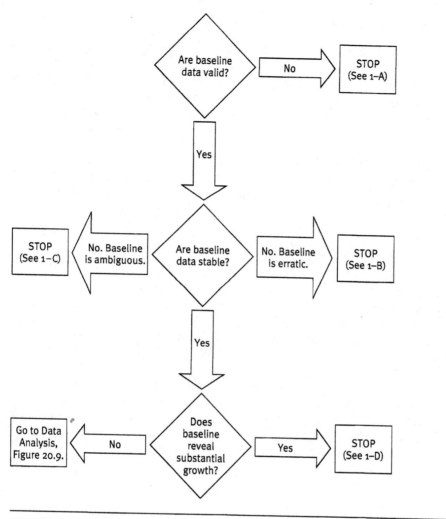

FIGURE 20.2   *Visual Analysis of Baseline Data*

The flowchart in Figure 20.2 covers these questions. Following this flowchart is further explanation for each terminal point on the chart.

Notes for Visual Analysis

In Figure 20.2 you saw a guide for the visual analysis of data when you are employing the AB single-system design. Each terminal point had a reference to a note (1—A, 1—B, 1—C, 1—D) except for the last one that instructed you to go to Figure 20.9, where you can receive guidance in the analysis of your data. The notes (or guides) that follow provide some ideas on each of the terminal points depicted in Figure 20.2. Do not confuse these designations with the section headings and subheadings.

1-A: *Baseline Recordings are Not Valid*

Perhaps the first question to ask yourself is "Are these recordings of target behavior valid (believable)?" Sometimes clients will answer questions on a scale according to what they believe is the reflection of the best behavior rather than the reality of how they feel or believe. A client exhibiting clear signs of depression should answer a depression scale in a way that would depict depression. If such a person had a score that reflected no depression at all, you would have reason to question the validity of this particular recording of this target behavior. In this case, you will need to address this issue with the client, and it would be unwise to record and analyze this client's scores on this scale. Perhaps a different way to measure the target behavior is in order. Perhaps you were not correct to interpret the client's behavior as depicting depression. In any case, you would not want to use these recordings of target behavior for analysis.

1-B: *Baseline Recordings are Erratic*

A second question is whether the baseline recordings are stable. A stable baseline is one that shows a clear pattern that is either level or is rather consistently going up or down. One type of baseline pattern that is not stable is one that is erratic. An erratic baseline is one that jumps all over the place, from very high to very low. Figure 20.2 illustrates this point. On this chart are scores of a client on the Caregiver Burden Scale, where higher scores depict a greater sense of burden and stress regarding the job of caring for an elderly family member with dementia.

The pattern depicted in Figure 20.3 should not be subjected to statistical analysis. It is difficult to interpret and it has much too much variance to lend itself to a possible achievement of statistical significance. Instead, you will need to deal with this pattern clinically; you would need to explore this pattern with the client. A goal could be to stabilize the pattern. In this case, you could examine the chart to see if the pattern did become more stable in the intervention period.

1-C: *The Baseline is Ambiguous*

Another pattern that lacks stability is one that shows different trends in different periods of time, leading to ambiguity in your interpretation of what is happening. In Figure 20.4, the behavior appears to be going up slightly in the first part of the baseline, but is going down in the second part. Computing a mean for these data would be misleading. So, what should you do? The answer is not clear, but your clinical assessment of this situation is essential. If the behavior is going down for a good reason and you have reason to expect it to continue going down, it would be wise for you to redraw the baseline and exclude the early part, where the behavior was going up. Normally, you would not want to employ this entire baseline in your statistical analysis.

1-D: *Baseline Reveals Substantial Growth*

Sometimes your baseline will reveal that the client's target behavior is growing at a substantial rate; the client is likely to achieve his or her treatment goal without treatment, assuming that

Scores on Caregiver Burden Scale

44	44	44	44	44	44	44	44	44	44
43	43	43	43	43	43	43	43	43	43
42	42	42	[42]	42	42	42	42	42	
[41]	41	41	41	41	41	41	41	41	41
40	40	40	40	40	40	40	40	40	40
39	39	39	39	39	39	39	39	39	39
38	38	38	38	38	[38]	38	38	38	38
37	37	37	37	37	37	37	37	37	37
36	36	36	36	36	36	36	36	36	36
35	35	[35]	35	35	35	35	35	35	35
34	34	34	34	34	34	34	34	34	34
33	33	33	33	33	33	33	33	33	33
32	[32]	32	32	32	32	32	32	32	32
31	31	31	31	31	31	31	31	31	31
30	30	30	30	[30]	30	30	30	30	30
29	29	29	29	29	29	29	29	29	29
28	28	28	28	28	28	28	28	28	28

Weeks 1 2 3 4 5 6 7 8 9 10

FIGURE 20.3 *Erratic Baseline*

the baseline trend continues. If your client's scores in the baseline illustrate a good deal of growth, you should draw a line from the baseline throughout the treatment period that best represents the baseline. If this line shows the client will achieve his or her goals in the treatment period without treatment, you should stop your analysis and go back to the drawing board. Perhaps this client does not need treatment on this target behavior.

Elementary Statistical Analysis for Single-System Designs

In the sections that follow, you will see how you can undertake the statistical analysis of data when single-system designs are used. You are reminded, however, of a caveat with regard to this endeavor. Most statistical measures are designed with the assumption that data are drawn from independent samples rather than related samples. Single-system data are drawn from related samples. Consequently, your statistical analysis for single-system data has this limitation. As noted in the previous chapter, the researcher has the options of (1) refraining from statistical analysis of single-system data, relying exclusively on clinical analysis, (2) using statistical tests that are not perfectly suited for the data because you do not want to ignore the issue of chance as the explanation of your data, or (3) dealing with the complex issue of autocorrelation

EXHIBIT 20.1 • *Using Excel to Draw a Trend Line*

You can employ Excel in the drawing of the trend line for your data by using the following procedures:

1. Load Excel into your computer's active memory.
2. Enter your data in Column A in the spreadsheet.
3. Go to the top of the screen and click on the **Chart Wizard** icon.

4. Select **XY (scatter)** by going to this option and clicking on it.
5. Click on **Finish** at the bottom of the screen. You will then see the chart with your data.
6. Go to the top of the screen and click on **Chart**.
7. Select **Add trendline** and click on **OK**.

You now can save this chart or print it.

If you have a slope in the data that is in the right direction, your next question is whether this slope is significant. Statistical analysis is the key to determining if your data are best described as random fluctuations in the target behavior or something out of the ordinary, possibly the effect of the intervention.

The C statistic is a method of examining whether a slope is significant. If the value of C is high enough to represent statistical significance, you can say the slope is significantly different from a level (horizontal) line across the chart. There are two major consideration in the statistical analysis of data—the number of recordings of target behavior, and the extent of variance in these recordings.

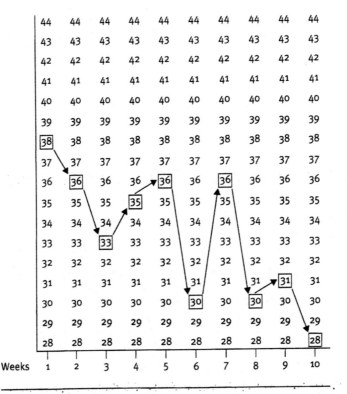

FIGURE 20.6 *Caregiver Burden Scores for Client A*

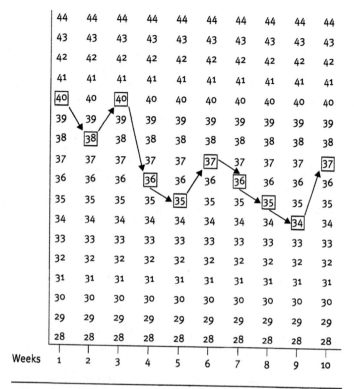

FIGURE 20.7   *Caregiver Burden Scores for Client B*

On the following page is a set of charts (Figures 20.6, 20.7, and 20.8) that depict Caregiver Burden scores for three hypothetical clients. These scores depict the extent to which caregiver of a disabled spouse or parent feels psychologically burdened by the caregiving experience. Lower scores represent progress (lower feelings of burden). Review these charts and determine whether you think the pattern represents a slope significantly greater than a level line.

Which clients had significant progress? The client depicted in Figure 20.6 had scores that began at 38 and ended with 28, a 10-point gain. The client depicted in Figure 20.7, however, only moved from 40 to 37, after detouring to a score as low as 34. The client depicted in Figure 20.8 started at 38 and progressed to 32, a 6-point gain.

So you might be inclined to think that the data for Figure 20.6 was the most significant from a statistical standpoint. If you did, you would be wrong. Why? The key lies in the differences in the variance among these charts. There is only one chart that depicts a gain at a statistically significant level, and that one is Figure 20.8. The main reason is the low level of variance from one score to the next, when this chart is compared to the others. The slant, or slope, of the line that would represent each of these clients is rather similar, but the variance is not.

You should keep this in mind whenever you examine data for the B design. The greater the slope, the greater the significance level. The less the variance, the greater the significance level. You don't need a steep slope to have significance, providing that you have rather little variance.

There is a method of testing for statistical significance with the B design. It is the C statistic (which should not be confused with the contingency coefficient, also noted by the letter C).

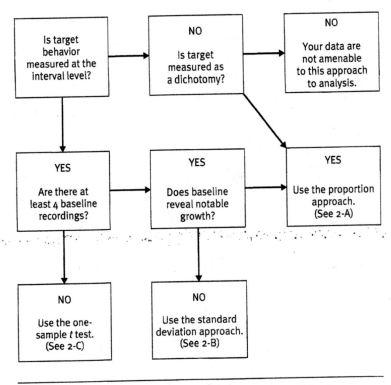

FIGURE 20.9   *Analyzing Single-System Data with the AB Design*

Guides for Statistical Analysis of AB Single-System Data

Specific guides follow for analysis based on Figure 20.9. If you used this figure to determine how to analyze your own data, you will have come to a terminal point with the designation of 2-A, 2-B, or 2-C, or you will have been informed that you must terminate this process because your data are not amenable to analysis using the options found in this chapter. See the guides below for analysis.

2-A: The Proportion Approach

The proportion approach compares the proportion of treatment recordings that are favorable with the proportion of baseline recordings that are favorable. This is applicable in two situations when the AB single-system design is employed: (1) when you have baseline data sufficient to detect a trend but your baseline reveals a slope, and (2) when you have target behavior measured as a dichotomy. This approach is labeled the *proportion/frequency approach* in the text by Bloom, Fischer, & Orme (2003).

As suggested by Bloom, Fisher, and Orme (2003), the binomial test can be employed in this situation. This is a rather simple statistical test that is relevant to the situation where you have a variable that has only two categories and you want to know if the number of recordings in the two categories is significantly different from a given expectation, such as, for example, a 50–50 split between the two categories. You are asking the question "Is the number of things (persons, recordings, etc.) in one category significantly greater than the number of things (persons, recordings, etc.) in the other category?" This distribution of things into the two categories is compared to a selected standard that represents the expected proportion of things in the two categories. For example, if roughly 50 percent of all citizens are female and 50 percent male, you may want to know if your distribution of clients by gender is significantly different from this 50–50 standard. You might have 24 females and 20 males. Is this significantly different from a 50–50 split, which would be represented by 22 females and 22 males? The binomial test can be used to answer this question. In one type of single-system data analysis, you want to know if the distribution of recordings on the favorable side of the trend line in the treatment period is significantly greater than a 50–50 split.

When you have baseline trend data that reveal a slope   In situations where you have interval baseline data sufficient to detect a trend (four or more recordings) in the client's target behavior, and the baseline pattern reveals a slope, you can examine data in the same way as you would for a dichotomous variable; you would compare the proportion of favorable treatment recordings to the proportion of favorable baseline recordings.

Your first task, however, is to draw a line that represents the baseline slope. Instructions were given in a previous section regarding how to draw this line by hand. They are repeated here for your convenience:

> You chart your target behavior for both the baseline and treatment periods. Next, you separate the baseline period into two halves and compute the mean of each half. Then you place a dot at the middle of each half that represents the mean of that half. You use these dots to help you draw a line from the baseline into the treatment period. Place a ruler on the page that connects the two dots and draw a line through both the baseline and treatment periods. This will represent the slope in the target behavior. If this slope is rather steep in the favorable direction, you must consider whether it makes sense to treat the client for this behavior, or whether these data are amenable to data analysis.

Instructions on how to use Excel to draw this line are presented in Exhibit 20.1. This line is more statistically precise than the one drawn by hand as illustrated. A measurement that falls right on the line should be considered to fall on the unfavorable side of the line.

Once you have charted these recordings of target behavior, you could develop a table like Table 20.1.

TABLE 20.1   *Comparison of Baseline and Treatment Data When There Is a Slope*

	Baseline	*Treatment*
Number or recordings on the favorable side of slope	4 (50%)	8 (80%)
Number of recordings on the unfavorable side of slope	4 (50%)	2 (20%)
Total	8 (100%)	10 (100%)

EXHIBIT 20.4 • *Using the Excel File with the AB Design and Dichotomous Data*

1. Load the Excel software into your computer's memory.
2. Load the Excel file named AB, dichotomous, binomial. You will see the Excel spreadsheet on the screen with a file label at the top and instructions for what to do.
3. You are instructed on where to enter the number of favorable treatment recordings, the total number of treatment recordings, and the proportion of favorable baseline recordings.
4. You will instructions on where to find the value of *p*.
5. Print your statistical output.
6. Close the file without saving the results so that you can use this file again without encumbering it with the present data.

You could report these results as follows:

Of the six recordings of target behavior during the baseline period, only one was favorable. This represented a 17 percent rate of favorable behavior. Of the five treatment recordings, four were favorable, a rate of 80 percent. Thus, the client's behavior improved. The statistical question is whether this difference between baseline and treatment behavior can easily be explained by chance. These data were subjected to statistical analysis with the binomial test, which resulted in a *p* value of 0.003. Thus, statistical significance was achieved and the hypothesis was supported.

The caveat regarding the employment of statistics for single-system data is appropriate here because the binomial test is designed for data taken from independent samples.

The Standard Deviation Approach

In situations where you have interval baseline data sufficient to detect a trend (four or more recordings) in the client's target behavior, but the baseline pattern does not reveal a slope, you can employ the standard deviation in the examination of chance as an alternative hypothesis. Scores that are two standard deviations from the mean occur 5 times in 100; thus, this figure represents the 0.05 level of statistical significance.

The standard deviation measures the amount of variability in an array of data. If you have a mean treatment score that is at least two standard deviations better than the baseline mean, you have statistical significance at the 0.05 level. The procedures for employing this technique are:

1. Compute the mean of the baseline recordings.
2. Compute the standard deviation of the baseline recordings
3. Multiply the standard deviation of baseline recordings by 2 and add (or subtract) this value to the value of the mean of the baseline recordings. This is the figure the treatment mean has to beat in order to achieve statistical significance. (You add the two standard deviations when better target behavior is represented by higher scores; you subtract this figure if better behavior is represented by lower scores.)
4. Compute the mean of the treatment recordings and compare this value to the value achieved in step 3 in order to see if the treatment mean is better. If so, you have statistical significance at the 0.05 level.

EXHIBIT 20.5 • *Using Excel for the Standard Deviation Approach*

(When you have a full baseline without a slope)

1. Load the Excel software into active memory.
2. Load the file AB without slope (Std).
3. Enter your baseline scores in the cells according to the directions. (You cannot have more than 20 scores when you use this file.)
4. Enter your first treatment scores in the cells as instructed. (You cannot have more than 20 scores with this file.)
5. The directions will tell you where to find the mean for your baseline recordings, the mean for your treatment recordings, and the standard deviation of your baseline recordings.

6. See the directions for finding the cell that tells you the score your treatment mean must be in order for your treatment recordings to be significantly (p < .05) *higher* than the baseline mean. Use this figure if higher target scores mean improvement.
7. See the directions for finding the cell that tells you the score your treatment mean must be in order for your treatment recordings to be significantly (p < .05) *lower* than your baseline mean. Use this figure if lower target scores means improvement.

You can employ an Excel spreadsheet for computing this. Instructions are given in Exhibit 20.5. Before employing this file you will need to have baseline scores and treatment scores for your client. You will also need to be cognizant of whether improvement means higher scores or lower scores on your scale.

An Illustration   Let's suppose you have administered the Generalized Contentment Scale, which has scores that can range from a low of 0 to a high of 100, with higher scores representing more problems with contentment; thus, lower scores are better. You have administered this scale to your client with the following baseline scores: 65, 62, 61, 66, and 64. You have administered this scale during the treatment period with the following results: 43, 56, 45, 61, 44, and 41. Are your treatment scores significantly better than the baseline scores?

After you have employed the Excel file for this purpose, you should find the following:

Baseline mean = 63.6
Treatment mean = 48.33
Standard deviation of baseline = 2.07
Score to beat = 59.45

Thus, you achieved statistical significance because your treatment mean was lower than 59.45.

You could report your results as follows:

The client's baseline mean was 63.6, while the treatment mean was 48.33. This indicated improvement in life contentment because lower scores represent greater contentment. The statistical question is whether this difference can easily be explained by chance. The standard deviation approach was employed in the statistical analysis of these data. The standard deviation of baseline scores was 2.07. When the treatment mean is two standard deviations better than the baseline mean, statistical significance is achieved at the 0.05 level. The treatment mean that would represent a two standard deviation improvement was 59.45 or lower. The treatment mean for this client was 48.33; thus statistical significance was achieved. The hypothesis was supported.

The standard deviation is designed for data drawn from independent samples; thus, the caveat about the employment of statistical analysis of single-system data would be appropriate here.

Using the One-Sample t Test with a Single Score to Represent the Baseline

The one-sample *t* test should be used when you do not have enough baseline data to estimate the client's general condition prior to the treatment period. A good example would be when you have only one baseline recording. Another example would be when you have only two or three baseline recordings and have calculated a mean of these recordings as your single baseline score. In this case, you do not know the direction or variability of the client's condition as measured by your instrument. You only know the client's status at pretest. We have referred to this as the **limited AB design**.

If you have four or more baseline recordings, you normally have enough data to examine any possible trends in the client's target condition prior to treatment. In that case, I am suggesting that you employ the standard deviation approach.

If you have two or three baseline scores, you normally should compute the mean of these scores and use this figure to represent the baseline in the application of the one-sample *t* test. An exception to this rule of thumb is when you have three scores that suggest a clear slope in the client's baseline recordings. Normally, two or three scores is not enough to detect a clear trend. But if your data meet the qualifications of this exception, I suggest you employ the proportion approach.

When you employ the one-sample *t* test, you compare the mean of a number of treatment recordings to a single score that represents the client's condition prior to treatment.

My approach requires that you have the following conditions:

1. You have target behavior scores that can be treated as interval level measurement.
2. You have at least one score taken prior to the beginning of treatment, or the phase of treatment that is being tested. (*Note:* You could also use this approach if you have a threshold score to use in the comparison of the treatment scores, even if that score is not taken from your client.)
3. Your baseline data are not sufficient to detect a trend. This normally means you have three or fewer baseline recordings.

If any of these conditions are not present in your situation, you cannot use my simple approach to statistical analysis that employs the one-sample *t* test. It is advisable that there be four or more scores from the treatment period. The more scores, the more likely you will achieve statistical significance.

The one-sample *t* test examines the array of data from the treatment period and determines the likelihood that this array of data is significantly different from the single score representing

EXHIBIT 20.6 • *Using the one-sample t test with the AB design*

(When you have one score to represent the baseline)

1. Load the Excel software into active memory.
2. Open the file AB with single baseline score.
3. Enter the treatment scores in the cells as instructed. You cannot enter more than 20 scores for this spreadsheet.
4. Enter the single score that represents the baseline in the appropriate cell.

5. See the appropriate cell for the value of t for your data. If this is at least 2.35 and you have 4 or more treatment recordings, you will have statistical significance at the 0.05 level. With 10 or more recordings, you will have statistical significance with a t value of 1.83.
6. Print your output.
7. Close the file without saving the data, so new applications will not be encumbered with your old data.

the baseline. The greater the difference between the treatment scores and the single baseline score, the more likely you will achieve statistical significance. The less the variance in the treatment scores, the more likely you will achieve statistical significance.

An Illustration   Let's suppose you have a client who indicated during the intake session that she wanted to overcome her social anxiety through therapy. You gave her a social anxiety scale with higher scores representing higher anxiety. Her initial score at the intake session was 32. You began her therapy for this target behavior the next week and recorded her social anxiety on the same scale each week with the following results for the six weeks of the treatment period:

Week 1 = 33; Week 2 = 29; Week 3 = 31; Week 4 = 25; Week 5 = 29; Week 6 = 25

You will note a t value of 2.79 (ignore the negative sign). Your instructions reveal that a t value of 2.35 or higher is significant at the .05 level with four or more recordings. You have six recordings; therefore, you have achieved statistical significance.

You might report these results as follows:

This client's baseline score on social anxiety, taken at intake, was 32. The treatment scores were subjected to statistical analysis to determine if they were significantly lower than 32. Statistical significance was achieved ($t = 2.79$; $p < .05$); therefore, the hypothesis was supported.

Like the other statistical tests for single-system data, the employment of the one-sample t test is designed for data from independent samples; thus, the statistical caveat would be in order.

Summary

By now, you should be equipped to analyze data for the vast majority of single-system evaluations you are likely to undertake as a student or a human service professional. This analysis should be simple, in that you were only called upon to enter your data in an Excel file in the proper cells and seek your statistical answer in a designated cell. You did not have to learn how to use a statistical software package like SPSS or SAS. You also did not have to learn how to enter formulas into an Excel file. The procedures in this text should take very little time once you have read the instructions in the book. Hopefully, you will find these procedures sufficiently user-friendly that you will use them as a volunteer, not just when you are required to do so by your research course or agency manager.

Because this is a chapter that provides practical guidelines with specific examples, there is no knowledge quiz at the end.

Reference

Bloom, M., Fischer, J., & Orme, J. G. (2003). *Evaluating practice*. Boston: Allyn & Bacon.

21

Elementary Data Analysis with Group Designs

When you use group research designs, you are examining data from groups of clients who have been measured on the same scale. In this chapter, you will review instructions on how to determine the approach to take with group data, and you will go through procedures to execute a statistical analysis of data using the Excel files that accompany this text.

At the completion of this chapter, you will be able to:

1. Select an approach to statistical analysis for one group when you have posttest data and a threshold score for comparison.

2. Execute a statistical analysis with posttest data and a threshold score using the appropriate Excel file that accompanies this text.

3. Select an approach to statistical analysis when you have both pretest and posttest scores for one group, and execute the statistical analysis of these data using the appropriate Excel spreadsheet that accompanies this text.

4. Select an approach to statistical analysis when you have both pretest and posttest scores for two groups, and execute the statistical analysis of these data using the appropriate Excel spreadsheet that accompanies this text.

Overview

The most common group design for the human service practitioner is the **one-group pretest–posttest design**. With this design, you measure target behavior for a group of clients before treatment begins and again at the completion of treatment, using the same measurement device. The second most common design is the **comparison group design**, whereby you compare a treated group with a nontreated group. This normally takes the form of both pretest and posttest measurements of target behavior for both groups. The gain between pretest and posttest is compared between the two groups. The **alternative treatment design** is another common group design. In this case, you compare a group with one form of treatment with a group using another form of treatment in order to determine which is most effective. The analysis of data for the alternative treatment design is the same as the comparison group design because in both cases you are comparing two groups. You simply consider Treatment Model B to be the comparison group and Treatment Model A to be the treated group. Another design that you may find helpful is the **one-group posttest-only design**, in which you compare posttest scores for a group of clients to a threshold score that normally represents the client's pretreatment condition. Each of these designs will be included in this chapter.

Because we are employing group data in most of the analyzes presented here, we can say the data are drawn from independent samples. Thus, we can employ common statistical tests without the limitations inherent in the analysis of single-system data. (The single exception is the use of chi square for the pretest–posttest design with dichotomous data.)

The reason the term "elementary" is used here is related to the fact that more complicated, and technically more precise, methods of statistical analysis are available that will not be included. Instead, tests will be included that are appropriate from a statistical standpoint, but are more practical for the average human service practitioner than more technically complicated statistical tests.

A limitation of this elementary approach is that it applies only to situations in which target behavior can be treated as being measured at the interval level, or has been measured as a dichotomy. The other limitation mentioned above is that it applies to a limited number of research designs.

Figure 21.1 provides a decision tree to guide your selection of a method of data analysis. Terminal points in that chart direct you to Note A through Note F. This information follows the chart.

The guides which follow refer to terminal points from Figure 21.1. In the decision tree for this figure, you were given a reference to a particular note, or told you cannot use this guide. Specific instructions for your particular situation follow.

Note A: Comparing Posttest Scores with a Threshold Score

When you have posttest scores on a group of clients but no pretest scores, you can analyze these scores statistically if you have a threshold score for comparison. A threshold score is a single score that represents a given standard by which you are comparing your clients. You might use the mean score for your scale that was computed on untreated persons who are similar to your clients. For example, the Caregiver Burden Scale was tested on a sample of persons who were caring for a relative with dementia. This might be used as the threshold by which you would compare your clients. This means you would assume your clients were similar to this sample at the pretest time and you would compare your posttest scores to this mean score that represented your threshold. Even better than this would be a mean score you had computed on previous clients at intake. Another option might be to use as a threshold the score that represents "clinically depressed" as enumerated in the material on a given depression scale. This would be appropriate if you feel safe to assume that all your clients were clinically depressed at intake and your objective is to move them to a level of functioning that is better than this threshold.

It would be much better, of course, if you could measure your clients both before treatment and after treatment. It that case, you would refer to Note B or Note C, depending on your level of measurement. It is advised that you use Note A only when you can be confident that you can estimate the client's pretreatment condition.

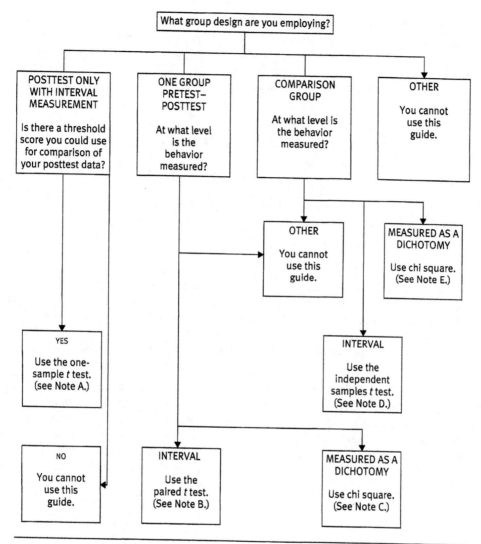

FIGURE 21.1 *A Guide for Data Analysis with Group Designs*

In order to employ the Excel spreadsheet for this task, you will need a threshold score and the posttest score for each person in your client group. The behavior must be measured at the interval level.

For example, suppose you were using the Parent Development Program as an intervention with persons identified with severe problems in parenting who have been confirmed for child abuse. The Index of Parental Attitudes measures the extent, severity, or magnitude of problems that family members have in their relationships with one another. Scores can range from 0 to 100, with higher scores representing more problems with parental attitudes. A clinical cutting score of 70 or higher is considered to represent a severe problem, indicating a high risk for violence. You did not have the opportunity to administer this test prior to treatment but you did so at the end of a six-month intervention period. You will assume the average score for this group would have been 70 or higher, so you will use 70 as the threshold score by which you will compare your posttest scores for your group of parents.

Your hypothetical posttest scores for the Index of Parental Attitudes were as follows:

Client Number	Score
1	54
2	72
3	65
4	45
5	51
6	37
7	55

The mean of the posttest scores is 54.1, clearly better than a score of 70. The statistical question is whether it is significantly better than 70. The one-sample t test can help with this question. It compares an array of scores from different people to a standard score to determine if the difference between this array of scores and the standard can be explained by chance.

Exhibit 21.1 gives instructions for employing this test for the analysis of data in this situation.

An Illustration   Let's apply the data from the example of scores on the Index of Parental Attitudes. You will enter these seven scores for the seven clients in your group and the standard score of 70 for comparison. Move down on the screen until you see the value of t and the mean. You will note the mean score is 54.14286 and the value of t is −3.86486. When you report these figures, you should round off to the nearest two decimal places. Don't be confused by the negative sign in front of the value of t (It simply indicates the mean was lower than the standard rather than higher, as you have hypothesized).

EXHIBIT 21.1 • *Using the Excel Spreadsheet for the Posttest-Only Design with a Threshold Score*

1. Load the Excel software into active memory.
2. Load the file Posttest-only with threshold score.
3. Enter the threshold score in the appropriate cell as instructed.
4. Enter the first group member's posttest score in the first cell for client data as instructed. Enter the second member's posttest score in the next cell, and so forth, until you have recorded each member's score in the assigned column.
5. The instructions will indicate where to find the mean for the posttest scores and the value of t. If you have at least 4 persons in your group, a t value of 2.35 is significant at the 0.05 level, while a t of 2.13 is significant with 5 or more persons, and a t of 1.83 or higher is significant with a group of 10 or more.

You could report these results as follows:

The cutoff score of 70 indicates a severe problem with parenting. This score was used as the standard by which the posttest scores of our clients were compared. The mean posttest score was 54.14, which is lower than 70 as hypothesized. The one-sample t test was applied to these data. This analysis revealed that the mean posttest score was significantly lower than the score of 70 ($t = -3.86$; $p < .05$). Thus, the hypothesis was supported.

The one-sample t test is designed to be employed with data drawn from independent samples. In your case, you have data drawn from independent samples; thus, you have no need to employ the caveat regarding autocorrelation, as you do with single-system designs.

Note B: Comparing Pretest and Posttest Scores for One Group with Interval Data

When you employ the one-group pretest–posttest design and your target behavior is measured at the interval level, you will have a pretest score and a posttest score for each client. For example, consider the scores on a depression scale for a group of clients given in Table 21.1.

The statistical question is whether the mean posttest score is significantly different from the mean pretest score. In the case of the hypothetical depression scores in Table 21.1 you are hoping for lower posttest scores because higher scores on this particular scale represent greater depression.

You can employ the **paired t test** in the statistical examination of these data, and you can do so without any special concern, because this test is designed to be used for these kinds of data. There is an Excel spreadsheet file that can be used. Before using this spreadsheet file, you will need to compute the following for each client: pretest score, posttest score, and gain score. The gain score is the amount the posttest score is superior to the pretest score. These scores must be considered appropriate for the interval level of measurement.

In order that higher gain scores represent higher gain, you must compute the gain score by subtracting the pretest score from the posttest score in cases where higher scores represent

TABLE 21.1 *Data Illustrating Pretest and Posttest Scores for One Group*

Client Number	Pretest Score	Posttest Score
1	32	26
2	36	25
3	25	24
4	29	29
5	31	18
6	29	17
7	26	28
8	38	26

EXHIBIT 21.2 • *Comparing Pretest and Posttest Scores for One Group Using the Paired t Test*

1. Load the Excel software into active memory.
2. Load the file One-group prepost, interval data into your computer's memory.
3. Enter the pretest score for your first client in the appropriate cell in the first column as instructed, and this client's posttest score in the appropriate cell in the next column as instructed. Enter each client's scores in the appropriate cells as instructed.
4. Review the instructions and find the cell with the mean pretest score and the mean posttest score. Your first question is whether the mean posttest score is better than the mean pretest score. If it is not, you should not examine the issue of statistical significance. Your hypothesis clearly is not supported.
5. Look in appropriate cell to find the value of *t* (the words "VALUE of *t*" are next to it). Then examine the notes about statistical significance.

improvement. If *lower* scores represent improvement, you must subtract posttest scores from pretest scores. You may have some clients with a negative gain, meaning they experienced a loss in functioning from pretest to posttest. If Michael Jones went from a self-esteem score of 20 at pretest to a score of 15 at posttest, assuming higher scores mean higher self-esteem, he would have experienced a loss of 5 points. This should be recorded as −5 in the gain column for this client. Be sure to enter the minus sign before the score.

An Illustration   Let's employ the paired *t* test in the examination of the data given with regard to pretest and posttest depression scores for eight clients. You must enter each pretest score, each posttest score, and each gain score. Because the Index of Parental Attitudes gives lower scores for better functioning, you will subtract the posttest score from the pretest score. In one of your cases, the posttest score was higher than the pretest. In this case, you have a negative gain score, which should be entered with the minus sign before the number.

After you have entered each of these scores for each of your clients, you will examine the spreadsheet to find the mean pretest score, the mean posttest score, the value of *p*, and the value of *t*. In our example, you will find the mean pretest score to be 30.75, the mean posttest score to be 24.125, the value of *p* to be 0.009569, and the value of *t* to be 3.238246.

You could report these results as follows:

The mean pretest score on the Index of Parental Attitudes was 30.75, while the mean posttest score was 24.13. Thus scores went down as hypothesized. The statistical question is whether this reduction in score (or improvement in attitudes) can be explained by chance. The paired *t* test was employed in the examination of the study hypothesis. The results indicated that posttest scores were significantly lower than pretest scores ($t = 3.24$; $p < .01$), which means the hypothesis was supported.

The results of your analysis of pretest and posttest scores using the paired *t* test is *not* hampered by the caveat about autocorrelation as you witnessed with regard to single-system data analysis. The paired *t* test is supposed to be used with the examples presented here regarding pretest and posttest scores measured at the interval level.

Note C: Comparing Pretest and Posttest Data When Behavior is Measured as a Dichotomy

A dichotomy is something with only two categories. If you have measured target behavior in terms of *Yes* versus *No*, you have a dichotomous variable. This could be illustrated by such comparisons as "attended school" vs. "did not attend school" or "complied with the treatment plan" vs. "did not comply with the treatment plan."

The approach to analysis used here employs the McNear test for the significance of changes. This is a special way to calculate chi square in situations like we are examining. For the one-group pretest–posttest design, the table will have *Pretest* and *Posttest* in the columns and *Yes* and *No* in the rows.

When you employ the pretest–posttest design with dichotomous data, place your data in a table like the data in Table 21.2, which uses a school social work example. In this example, the positive behavior is that the parent signed the child's homework card each day during the week that data were collected. Negative behavior would be exhibited by a parent failing to sign the homework card each day data were collected. Data were collected for one week prior to the initiation of the Special Homework Project (pretest period). Data were collected again during the week following the completion of the Special Homework Project (posttest period).

From Table 21.2, you can see that 14 parents who had not regularly signed the card in the pretest week had done so in the posttest week, while 4 parents who had regularly signed the card in the pretest week had not signed it in the posttest week. This represents the change from pretest to posttest. Another way to examine these data from a practical standpoint is to compare the number of parents engaged in positive behavior in the pretest period ($n = 7$) to the number of parents engaging in this behavior in the posttest period ($n = 17$). This is more than a doubling of parents engaging in the desired behavior.

A statistical test that can be used with these data is the McNear test for the significance of changes. It computes the value of chi square by comparing the 14 positive changes with the 4 negative changes to determine if this difference can easily be explained by chance. Before using the Excel spreadsheet for this purpose, you will need to compose a two-by-two table like this one. This means you will have the number of persons who were positive at pretest but negative at posttest, the number who were negative at pretest but positive at posttest, the number who were positive at both times, and the number who were negative at both times.

TABLE 21.2   *Dichotomous Data with the One-Group Pretest–posttest Design*

Pretest Period	Posttest Period		
	Yes (Did sign card)	No (Did not sign card)	Total
No (Did not sign card)	14	4	18
Yes (Did sign card)	3	4	7
Total	17	8	25

EXHIBIT 21.3 • *Comparing Pretest and Posttest Behavior for One Group When Behavior is Measured as a Dichotomy*

1. Load the Excel software into active memory.
2. Load the file One group prepost with dichotomous data.
3. Enter your data as instructed:
   a. The number of persons with negative pretest behavior but positive posttest behavior should be entered in the appropriate cell.
   b. The number of persons with positive behavior in both periods should be entered in the appropriate cell.
   c. The number of persons with negative behavior in both periods should be entered in the appropriate cell.
   d. The number of persons with positive pretest but negative posttest behavior should be entered in the appropriate cell.

4. Review the appropriate cell for the value of chi square. If this is at least 3.84, you have statistical significance at the 0.05 level, while a chi square value of at least 2.71 is significant at the 0.10 level.
5. In the appropriate cell, you will find the expected frequency for this configuration of data. If this is less than 5, you are not supposed to employ the chi square test. The binomial test would be more appropriate.
6. Print your output.
7. Exit this file without saving the data, so you can use the file again without encumbering the effort with the previous data.

Instructions for using the McNear test are given in Exhibit 21.3. Unlike the statistical problem with single-system data analysis, this test is appropriate for the data utilized because the persons in each cell are different persons. In other words, we do not need to employ the caveat about data drawn from related samples.

An Illustration   Let's apply the McNear test with the data in the example given regarding parental signatures on homework cards. After you enter these figures, you can refer to the appropriate cell for the value of chi square. In this case, chi square is 4.5, which is significant at the 0.05 level. You will also note that the expected frequency for these data is 9. Because this is higher than 5, we do not have a problem with the use of chi square.

Note D: Comparing Gain Scores between Groups with Interval Data

If you are employing the comparison group design, you can use an Excel spreadsheet to compare the gain scores of the two groups using the independent samples *t* test. This is appropriate if you are comparing two groups and have a measurement of target behavior that can be treated as interval.

You must first compute the gain scores for each person in each of the two groups. If higher scores represent improvement, you would subtract each person's posttest score from this person's pretest score in order to determine the gain score for that person. If lower scores represent improvement, you would subtract the pretest score from the posttest score.

The statistical question is whether the difference in gain scores between the two groups is easily explained by chance. If you employ the Excel spreadsheet for this task, you would enter

EXHIBIT 21.4 • *Using Excel to Compare Gain Scores for Two Groups*

You can employ the special Excel file for administering the independent samples *t* test when you are comparing the gain scores of two groups of persons. The following procedures apply to this application:

1. Load the Excel software into active memory of your computer.
2. Load the file labeled Comparison group, interval data.
3. Enter the gain score for the first person in the treatment group in the appropriate cell. Enter the gain score for the second person in the treatment group in the appropriate cell in the same column, and continue this process until you have entered the gain scores for each person in your treatment group in this column.
4. Enter the gain score for the first person in the comparison group in the second column as instructed. Enter the gain score for the second person in the comparison group in the appropriate cell in the same column, and continue this procedure until you have entered the gain scores for each member of your comparison group.
5. Review the instructions to find your *p* value and the value of *t*.
6. Print your output.
7. Exit the file without saving the results so you will not encumber your file with your previous data.

the gain score for each person in each group and examine the results. If the person had a loss, this would be treated as a negative gain score and would be entered with the minus sign before the score that represented the difference between the pretest and posttest scores.

Before using the Excel spreadsheet, you will need to have a pretest score for each client, a posttest score for each client, and a gain score for each client. You will also need to have the same for the comparison group members. The comparison group could be an untreated group or a group with a different treatment from your target group. Be sure to enter a negative sign for a person with a negative gain (a loss in functioning).

Note E: Comparing Groups When Behavior is Measured as a Dichotomy

When you compare groups with target behavior measured as a dichotomy, you can employ chi square and phi coefficient with data presented in a two-by-two table as illustrated in Table 21.3

The first thing to recognize in Table 21.3 is that 80 percent of the treatment group improved from pretest to posttest, while only 40 percent of the comparison group did so. This means that the success rate was double for the treatment group. Also, you can see the 40 percent improvement rate for the comparison group as an estimate of the effect of maturation on the target behavior, and conclude that these data suggest that the treatment made a difference for approximately 40 percent of the persons who received the service. (*Note*: 40 percent would likely have gotten better without treatment, but 80 percent improved, so the difference is 40 percent.) This means that treatment made a difference for 10 persons (40 percent of 25). If you convert this percentage to its fractional equivalent, you will have the figure of 0.40 (40/100 = 0.40), which is normally a good estimate of the value of phi coefficient, a measure of the degree

TABLE 21.3 *Comparing Dichotomous Data for Two Groups*

Was the patient found to be more likely to have taken medications at posttest than at pretest?	Treatment group (high-risk patients receiving medical social work services)	Comparison group. (high-risk patients on the waiting list for social work services)	Total
Yes	20 (80%)	20 (40%)	40
No	5 (20%)	30 (60%)	35
Total	25 (100%)	50 (100%)	75

of association between two variables. The actual value of phi coefficient is presented in the Excel file as reported later.

These data can be subjected to chi square and phi coefficient because these data are drawn from independent samples. This is true because each cell has persons who are different from the persons in the other cells. It is also true that the table has no cells with small frequencies, so there are no cells with expected frequencies less than 5. When you have frequencies less than 5, you often have expected frequencies less than 5. When you have expected frequencies less than 5, chi square is not supposed to be employed for statistical analysis.

In Exhibit 21.5, you will see instructions on how to use Excel to calculate chi square for your data. Before you access this file, you need to develop a table with your data showing the number of persons in the treatment group with positive results, and without positive results, and the number of persons in the comparison group with positive results and without positive results. In other words, you should compose a table like the one illustrated.

An Illustration   Let's apply the Excel file to the data presented regarding compliance with medication. You will enter the numbers 20 (Yes) and 5 (No) for the treatment group and 20 (Yes) and 30 (No) for the comparison group. You will find the value of chi square is 10.71429. The value of phi coefficient is 0.377964. Because chi square is greater than 3.84, you have achieved

EXHIBIT 21.5 • *Using the Excel File to Compare Two Groups When Behavior Is Measured as a Dichotomy*

You can use the special Excel file to employ chi square in the determination of statistical significance when you are comparing two groups with dichotomous data (where behavior is measured as either Yes or No). Employ the following steps:

1. Load the Excel software into active memory.
2. Open the file Comparison group, dichotomous data.
3. Enter your data for the treatment group in the appropriate cells.
4. Enter your data for the comparison group in the appropriate cells.

5. Review the appropriate cell for the value of chi square. If this value is 6.64 or higher, you have achieved statistical significance at the 0.01 level. If it is 3.84 or higher, you have achieved statistical significance at the 0.05 level. If your chi square value is 2.7 or higher, you have statistical significance at the 0.10 level.
6. Print your output.
7. Exit the file without saving it, so you can use this file again in the future without encumbering it with your present data.

statistical significance at the normal standard of 0.05. In fact, your chi square value is high enough to meet an even higher standard of 0.01.

You could report these findings as follows:

The data comparing the clients of the High-Risk Program of the Medical Social Work Department are presented in Table 21.3. These data reveal that 80 percent of the clients were compliant with medication at the posttest time, as compared with only 40 percent of those on the waiting list for service. This difference was subjected to statistical analysis with chi square and phi coefficient. The results of this analysis revealed a statistically significant difference between the two groups (chi square = 10.71; phi coefficient = 0.38; $p < .01$). The hypothesis was supported.

Summary

In this chapter, you have reviewed specific instructions on how to use a set of Excel spreadsheets to analyze data when selected group research designs were employed. This presentation was not exhaustive. There are several group designs that were not included in this presentation, and there are statistical tests not reported that could be useful when you have data that are different from the two situations presented (interval level data or dichotomous data). Furthermore, there are statistical tests available for practitioners which are more sophisticated than the ones presented here. Nevertheless, it is the assumption of the author that the situations presented will cover the majority of situations that will be encountered by the day-to-day practitioner in human services, and that more sophisticated tests are not essential.

Glossary

ABAB single-subject research design A research design in which a single subject is measured repeatedly during a baseline period (period A), is given a specific treatment and repeatedly measured during the treatment period (period B), is measured repeatedly during a second baseline period (the second A period), and a second treatment period when the same treatment is administered (the second period B).

AB single-subject research design A research design in which a single subject (client, group, organization, community) is measured on the dependent variable several times during a baseline period before treatment begins and is repeatedly measured on the dependent variable during the treatment period.

ABA single-subject research design A research design in which a single subject is measured on the dependent variable several times before treatment, followed by several measurements during the treatment period, followed by several measurements in the period that follows the completion of treatment.

ABC single-subject research design A research design in which a single subject is measured repeatedly during a baseline period (period A), is given a certain treatment and is repeatedly measured during this treatment period (period B); then the treatment is changed, with the client continually measured on the dependent variable during this second treatment period (period C).

Alternative treatment research design A research design in which different treatments are administered to two or more groups of clients and the progress of the groups is compared.

Analytic comparison The application of the method of agreement and the method of difference in logical inquiry.

Analytic induction A method of qualitative inquiry that is designed to test, or refine, a hypothesis. The process begins with a tentative hypothesis and cases are studied in light of that hypothesis, with each case either confirming the hypothesis or suggesting a modification of it.

Bracketing. The listing of one's own opinions on a subject in the content analysis of qualitative data so as to draw attention to a potential source of bias.

B single-system research design. A research design in which the target behavior for a single case (either client, group, organization, community, etc.) is repeatedly collected during the treatment period, but no data are collected prior to treatment.

Baseline period A period of time during which the client is not receiving treatment.

Basic experimental research design The assignment of people to two groups on a random basis, one group being given the intervention (the experimental group) and the other group being excluded from treatment (the control group). Both groups of people are measured on the dependent variable before treatment and again after treatment has been completed. The gain in functioning for the two groups is compared to see if the experimental group had a significantly greater gain than the control group.

BC single-subject research design A research design in which a single subject is measured repeatedly on the dependent variable during a treatment period (period B) and the treatment is changed and the subject is measured repeatedly during the second treatment period (period C).

Best practice Interventions that are believed by the experts to have the most promise of being effective. Often this term is employed to describe interventions that are evidence based, but the latter term is used somewhat differently in this book.

Case study A model of evaluation for a single case, which can be a person or something larger such as an organization or a community, in which data are collected on a wide variety of information about that single case and conclusions are drawn from the systematic analysis of this information.

Case study protocol A careful description of the investigative procedures and the rules that govern the inquiry in a case study.

Causation   The explanation of the reasons that events occur. In research, the concept of causation is treated cautiously because events typically have multiple causes and the pinpointing of causation is difficult. There are three conditions for the comprehensive treatment of the issue of causation: (1) an empirical relationship between the causal variable (independent variable) and the variable that it causes (dependent variable), (2) a logical time order in changes between the independent and dependent variables, and (3) the ruling out of other causes of the dependent variable.

Clinical evaluation research study   An evaluation study that is done to determine how well a specific intervention is working and to get ideas on how it could be improved. It is less broad in scope than a program evaluation and is more systematic than a simple clinical evaluation that might be undertaken for a given client among a set of practitioners working as a team.

Code   In content analysis, an abbreviation or symbol applied to a segment of words—most often a sentence or paragraph of transcribed field notes—in order to classify the words. There are levels of coding, with higher levels representing more broad themes.

Comparison group design   A research design in which a group of treated clients is measured before and after the intervention and gains in functioning are compared to the before and after measurements of a group that did not receive treatment. This design is also known as the nonequivalent control group design.

Content analysis   A method of qualitative data analysis whereby researchers examine artifacts of social communication in order to make inferences about the messages inherent in that information, e.g., the analysis of answers to open-ended questions on a questionnaire.

Content validity   The extent that a given method of measurement covers the total content of the concept being measured.

Convenience sample   A sample that is selected because of its convenience to the researcher, such as, for example, your present clients.

Credibility assessment   Testing the reliability of one observer's content analysis with that of another observer through the calculation of the degree of agreement.

Critical thinking   A method of shining a light upon various aspects of our arguments or positions, including the assumptions behind each part of an argument.

Deductive   A process of inquiry that begins with theory and moves to observation for the purpose of testing theory.

Dependent variable   The variable that is believed to depend upon or is caused by another variable, the other variable being known as the independent variable.

Descriptive research   Research that describes something with precision but does not attempt to explain it.

Dichotomous data   Data from a variable that is measured in only two categories, such as Yes and No.

Effect size   A method of standardizing the level of client gain between studies using different instruments by computing the number of standard deviations of gain.

Efficiency   The ratio of input to output, for example, the cost per counseling session.

Enumeration   The counting of comments on a given theme in content analysis of qualitative data.

Ethnography   The study of cultures in their natural settings through qualitative research methods.

Evaluative research   Research that is used to evaluate whether an intervention achieved its objectives.

Evidence-based practice   The explicit use of the best available evidence in making decisions about the care of individuals.

Explanatory research   Research that is designed to explain something, usually by examining the relationships among a set of variables to see if one offers an explanation of another.

Exploratory research   Research that is designed to develop knowledge about a relatively unknown phenomenon so that new theory can be developed or new insight can be acquired on its nature.

Face validity   A measurement device has face validity if it appears to knowledgeable people to be an accurate means of measuring the particular concept it is supposed to measure. This is the least objective of the various methods of assessing validity, but is often the only reasonable alternative for self-developed instruments.

Falsifiable   For an assertion to be falsifiable, there must be a way to observe phenomena that would fail to support the assertion.

Focus group   A method of gathering qualitative data that entails a group interview where semistructured questions are posed and the results are systematically analyzed.

Generalization   The application of knowledge about one group of study subjects to another group of persons.

Group research designs   A research design in which data are collecting on the same variable for a group of clients receiving the same service.

Grounded theory A qualitative research methodology designed to develop theory through a highly inductive, but systematic, process of discovery. A major focus is the observation of similarities and differences in social behavior across social situations.

History (as a threat to internal validity) When a client improves during the treatment period, it may be because of the treatment, or it may be because of a change in the client's environment, such as obtaining a job or getting a promotion. History as a threat to internal validity refers to changes in the client's environment that may be the cause of improvement.

Hypothesis A statement of the expected results of a research study on a given topic based on theory or explanations derived from existing knowledge. For example, one might hypothesize that clients will have higher self-esteem scores after treatment than before.

Independent variable The variable which is believed to cause the dependent variable to be the way it is.

Individualized scale A scale that has been tailored to the particular client.

Inductive A process of inquiry that begins with observations from which theory or generalizations are derived.

Input Energy that comes into a system, such as a client coming to the agency with a need that should be addressed by agency services.

Institutional Review Boards (IRB) An organizational entity that examines the proposals of researchers who plan to use human subjects in research.

Instrumentation The means used in a study to measure variables.

Internal consistency The tendency of items forming a common scale to operate the same way. For example, a self-esteem scale would have internal consistency to the extent that the items on the scale, when treated as separate variables, would correlate with one another when given to a sample of study subjects. Thus, if John has a higher score than Tom on item 1 on this scale, he would probably have a higher score than Tom on item 2 on this scale as well. If this were *not* the general pattern for items on this scale, then it would *not* be considered to have internal consistency. This situation would suggest that the items on this scale are not measuring the same thing.

Interval A level of measurement in which subjects are given scores on a scale in which the interval between each level is equal to the interval between each of the other levels. For example, the temperature of 32 is 1 degree lower than the temperature of 33 which is 1 degree lower than the temperature of 34. This scale is measured in reference to degrees on the scale, with each single degree being equal to each of the other degrees.

Levels of measurement The hierarchy of measurement for study variables, each level of which provides a different level of sophistication in measurement, and is suitable for different statistical tests. The levels are nominal, ordinal, interval, and ratio, in that order, from lowest to highest. A variable measured at a higher level can be treated as though it is measured at a lower level for statistical analysis purposes, if necessary. For example, a variable measured at the interval level can be treated as though it is measured at the ordinal level. However, researchers lose information when they do this, so it is not optimal.

Limited AB single-system research design A research design, not widely recognized in the literature, whereby a client is measured on target behavior prior to treatment and during the treatment period, but the pretreatment (baseline) recordings are not considered sufficient to detect a trend in behavior. The limited baseline recordings are treated as a single score that is compared to the treatment recordings of target behavior.

Logic Whether something makes sense when subjected to careful analysis through the principles of good reasoning.

Maturation The tendency of people to overcome their problems on their own through time and the normal process of growth, rather than through the activities of the intervention or program.

Methodology The phase of the research process in which the study is designed in a manner that adequately addresses the research question.

Model of the intervention The model of the intervention identifies the conceptual link between the structure of the intervention and the problem analysis and serves as a logical justification of the intervention design.

Negative relationship A relationship between study variables in which *high* values on one variable tend to be associated with *low* values on the other variables (with high values on one being associated with low values on the other). For example, a researcher would expect to find a negative relationship between self-esteem and depression, meaning that persons with higher self-esteem scores would tend to have lower scores for depression. Thus, if Paul has a higher score for self-esteem than Jim, he is likely to have a lower score on depression than Jim.

Nominal The lowest level of measurement. At the nominal level, the attributes of a variable are in categories that have no particular order (such as low, medium, and high). Examples include gender, political party affiliation, and favorite color.

Null hypothesis A statement that suggests there is no relationship between study variables or no gain in functioning for clients. It is a statement that is true if the study results can be explained by chance. In evaluation research, this stands in opposition to the research hypothesis, the latter being a statement of the results you expect to find from your data.

Objective The expected results or purpose of an endeavor. In evaluation research, the outcome objective is a measured amount of progress toward the achievement of the treatment goal, which is focused on the target behavior, whereas a process objective refers to the activities that will be used to achieve the intended outcomes.

Observation The measurement of something.

One-group pretest–posttest research design A research design in which a group of clients is tested on the dependent variable before treatment and again after treatment has been completed. The gain in functioning evidenced by these two tests serves as a measure of the effects of treatment.

One-group posttest-only research design A research design whereby target behavior is measured after treatment but not before treatment.

Ordinal The next level of measurement beyond nominal. Ordinal variables place subjects into categories that are ordered from low to high or most to least, and so forth. The response categories of "agree," "undecided," and "disagree" place respondents into categories of agreement that are ordered from most to least.

Outcome The intended result of the service process in regard to target behavior.

Output The product that comes from the process of a system. In evaluation terms, an output is a concrete way to quantify the service that was provided.

p The letter *p* is used to designate the estimate of the probability that a set of research data would occur by chance, represented by a fraction. The designation $p < .05$ means that these particular data would occur by chance less than 5 times in 100. The designation $p < .01$ indicates that this likelihood is less than 1 time in 100.

Personnel of the intervention A description of the types of practitioners who will deliver the services to the clients.

Program An organized set of activities designed to achieve a particular goal or a set of objectives for a major service or set of service activities of the agency.

A program normally is defined in broader terms than an intervention, which can be any attempt to improve client conditions.

Program evaluation An effort to apply the principles of scientific inquiry to program decision making.

Proposition A theoretical guess about the phenomenon under study.

Pseudoscience Any body of knowledge or methods that are erroneously regarded as scientific. It is distinguished from revelations or theology in that these claims do not pretend to offer scientific explanation, whereas the claims of pseudoscience do. In other words, pseudoscience is something that is parading as science.

Population The larger group from which a sample was selected.

Posttest A measurement of study subjects on the dependent variable after treatment has been completed.

Practical significance The extent to which a given set of study findings is noteworthy from a practical or clinical standpoint.

Pretest A measurement of study subjects on the dependent variable before treatment begins.

Probability The likelihood of the occurrence of something that is not a certainty. Statistical tests are used to estimate probability which is designated by the letter *p*.

Probability sample A sample drawn at random from the specified study population.

Problem formulation The first major phase of the research process, in which the research question is developed and the research problem is analyzed.

Process The activities of the agency's services that are designed to achieve the outcomes.

Purposive sample. A sample that is drawn from persons known to have special characteristics that are important to the research study.

Qualitative A means of observation (or measurement) whereby the data is in the form of words.

Quantitative A means of observation (or measurement) that is fixed, such as posing a question that places people in discrete categories (e.g., male or female) or gives them a number as a value for the response to the question (e.g., age).

Random sample A sample in which each person in the study population had an equal chance of being selected for the sample.

Ratio The highest level of measurement. Variables measured at the ratio level have all the characteristics of variables measured at the interval level, with the addition that all scores on the scale are based on a fixed zero point. A practical way to remember this characteristic is to realize that variables measured at the ratio level cannot have negative values, because 0 is the lowest possible value. For example, a person cannot have negative weight, or height, or age.

Reliability   The consistency of a means of measurement. If a scale is reliable, persons will respond to it in a consistent fashion at different points in time. If it has internal consistency, its parts should measure the same thing.

Research design   The protocol in evaluative research whereby study subjects are measured on the dependent variable and interventions are administered.

Sample   A portion of a larger entity. In a research study, it designates the study subjects from whom data were collected.

Sampling element   The unit of analysis for the evaluation study. For typical evaluation research studies, the sampling element (or unit of analysis) will be individual clients.

Sampling frame   The list of persons (or records or families) from which the sample will be selected.

Sampling interval   The number of sampling elements that will be skipped between selected elements when systematic random sampling is employed.

Saturation   The achievement of commonality on a given theme among segments of qualitative data in content analysis.

Science   A method of acquiring knowledge through the logical analysis of observations guided by theory.

Science-based intervention   A term often used to justify a program design on the basis that it is a logical solution to a given problem, given our understanding of the dynamics of that problem from scientific studies. This is different from evidence-based interventions, a label given for interventions that have been validated by specific studies of the effectiveness of the intervention in the treatment of a specific target behavior.

Scientific inquiry   A systematic process of inquiry that is designed to reduce the bias inherent in human observation through the application of both logic and objective measurement of social phenomena.

Single-subject research design (also known as single-system design)   A research design in which the study subject is a single subject and data are collected on the dependent variable repeatedly for this one subject. While the single-subject design is typically used with a single client, it can also be employed with a

single organization or community or group, providing that each is treated as a single unit for data analysis.

Snowball sampling   A method of selecting study subjects. Identify the small number of persons known to be members of the study population and ask them to identify other persons from this population, repeating this procedure with each new group until there is a sufficient sample size.

Standard deviation   A measure of variance for a distribution. It tells researchers to what extent the subjects in a particular sample are similar to or different from one another.

Standard deviation method of statistical analysis (for single-subject research)   A means of statistical analysis of single-subject research data when the trend during the baseline period is relatively level. Statistical significance is achieved if the mean for treatment recordings of the dependent variable is two standard deviations better than the mean for the baseline recordings.

Standardized scale   A scale that has been designed for use with any number of individuals who share a common condition such as depression, anxiety, and so forth.

Statistical significance   The likelihood that a given set of study findings would be expected to occur by chance.

Structure of the intervention   A description of the form and intensity of the services to be provided, including the definition of the unit of service and the number of units of service that are typically provided.

Testing (as a threat to internal validity)   As a threat to internal validity, testing refers to the effect of being tested. One may develop a sensitivity to the administration of a pretest, which may affect the posttest score. This is of special concern if the pretest and posttest deal with knowledge, because a subject may remember items on the pretest when taking the posttest and may have been especially sensitive to this specific piece of information. Thus, it may be this sensitivity rather than the intervention that mostly affected the gain measured by the posttest.

Test-retest reliability   To assess reliability using this method, a group of subjects is measured on the scale at two points in time, and the two scores for this same group of people is correlated. High positive correlations indicate reliability or consistency.

Theory   In the simplest terms, a theory is an attempt to explain something. Theories can be more or less formal and explicit or more or less sophisticated, but any attempt to explain is a theory, whether or not it is supported by scientific evidence.

Threats to internal validity In evaluative research, a threat to internal validity is something that may be the reason for the client's change in behavior other than the intervention. For example, a change in the client's work situation may be the reason that he is no longer depressed; thus, the treatment may not have caused the improvement in functioning. There is a variety of threats to internal validity, also known as alternative explanations. Among these threats are maturation, history, and testing, which are defined in this glossary. Some research designs do a better job of dealing with certain threats to internal validity than do others. In general, experimental designs which use random assignment of subjects to treatment and control (comparison) groups do a superior job of addressing the various threats to internal validity.

Threshold score A single score that represents a given standard by which you are comparing the data from your study subjects.

Transparency The tendency for measurement methods to be clear.

Treatment period A period during which the client is subjected to the intervention.

Triangulation The use of multiple sources of data in the pursuit of a research question.

t **test** A means of determining the statistical significance of data measured at the interval level for either two groups of subjects (*t* test for independent samples) or a single group of subjects measured at two points in time (*t* test for paired data). The formula for these two situations is not the same. When testing a directional hypothesis, a *t* value of 2.0 or greater is significant at the .05 ($p < .05$) level if the sample size is greater than five. Slightly lower *t* values are significant (at the .05 level) with larger samples. Consult a statistical text with a table of *t* values for further information.

Unit of analysis The entity on which you will collect data, such as an individual, a group, an organization, or a community.

Utilization-focused evaluation A model of evaluation whereby the researcher selects a group of people who have a research need and helps carry them through a research process, with the researcher as facilitator rather than leader or expert.

Validity The extent to which a **measurement** device truly measures the thing it is supposed to measure; the accuracy of a means of measurement.

Variable Something that varies in a study; an entity that takes on more than one value. For example, the variable of gender would be divided into the categories of male and female. A concept is not a variable in a given study unless it is measured in that study, and there is some variance in responses. The concept of gender could not be a variable in a study that included only females.

Index